M000236335

A Selection of QuarkXPress 4 Palettes

The Measurements palette

The Measurements palette comes in four flavors (text, picture, line, and Bézier controls), depending on what item is active. See the back of this card for more palettes.

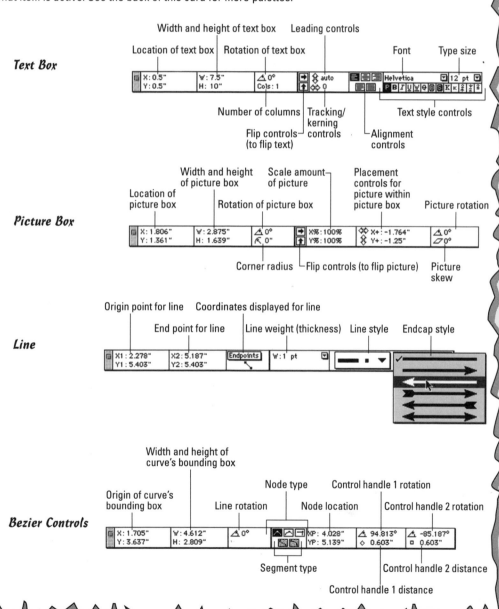

Text Box

- Location of text box — X: 0.5" / Y: 0.5"
- Width and height of text box — W: 7.5" / H: 10"
- Rotation of text box
- Number of columns — Cols: 1
- Flip controls (to flip text)
- Tracking/kerning controls
- Leading controls — auto / 0
- Alignment controls
- Font — Helvetica
- Type size — 12 pt
- Text style controls

Picture Box

- Location of picture box — X: 1.806" / Y: 1.361"
- Width and height of picture box — W: 2.875" / H: 1.639"
- Rotation of picture box — 0°
- Corner radius — 0"
- Flip controls (to flip picture)
- Scale amount of picture — X%: 100% / Y%: 100%
- Placement controls for picture within picture box — X+: -1.764" / Y+: -1.25"
- Picture rotation — 0°
- Picture skew — 0°

Line

- Origin point for line — X1: 2.278" / Y1: 5.403"
- End point for line — X2: 5.187" / Y2: 5.403"
- Coordinates displayed for line — Endpoints
- Line weight (thickness) — W: 1 pt
- Line style
- Endcap style

Bezier Controls

- Origin of curve's bounding box — X: 1.705" / Y: 3.637"
- Width and height of curve's bounding box — W: 4.612" / H: 2.809"
- Line rotation — 0°
- Node type
- Segment type
- Node location — XP: 4.028" / YP: 5.139"
- Control handle 1 rotation — 94.813°
- Control handle 1 distance — 0.603"
- Control handle 2 rotation — -85.187°
- Control handle 2 distance — 0.603"

QuarkXPress® 4 For Dummies®

Tool palette

Click on a tool to select it. The tool that you select determines what you can do with the keyboard and the mouse, as well as which menu entries are available.

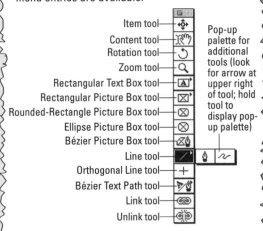

Item tool
Content tool
Rotation tool
Zoom tool
Rectangular Text Box tool
Rectangular Picture Box tool
Rounded-Rectangle Picture Box tool
Ellipse Picture Box tool
Bézier Picture Box tool
Line tool
Orthogonal Line tool
Bézier Text Path tool
Link tool
Unlink tool

Pop-up palette for additional tools (look for arrow at upper right of tool; hold tool to display pop-up palette)

Colors palette

Use this palette to control the color of items.

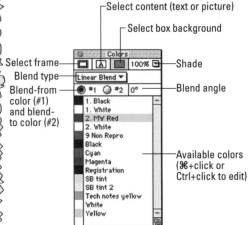

Select content (text or picture)
Select box background
Select frame
Blend type
Blend-from color (#1) and blend-to color (#2)
Shade
Blend angle
Available colors (⌘+click or Ctrl+click to edit)

Colors
100%
Linear Blend ▾
#1   #2   0°
1. Black
1. White
2. MW Red
2. White
9 Non Repro Black
Cyan
Magenta
Registration
SB tint
SB tint 2
Tech notes yellow
White
Yellow

Style Sheet palette

This palette lists the paragraph and character style sheets defined for the document.

Paragraph style names

Character style names

Keyboard equivalents for styles

Style Sheets
¶ No Style
¶ Byline   ⌘⌥F4
¶ Caption   ⌥F5
¶ Headline   ⌥F4
¶ Normal
A No Style
A Caption
A Headline
A Normal

Document Layout palette

Use this palette to create, delete, duplicate, and apply master pages and to rearrange document pages.

Single page
Facing page
Copy master page

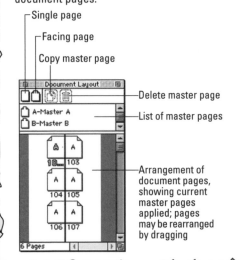

Delete master page
List of master pages

Document Layout
A-Master A
B-Master B

Arrangement of document pages, showing current master pages applied; pages may be rearranged by dragging

102 103
104 105
106 107

6 Pages

...For Dummies: #1 Computer Book Series for Beginners

 ®

References for the Rest of Us! ®

COMPUTER BOOK SERIES FROM IDG

Are you intimidated and confused by computers? Do you find that traditional manuals are overloaded with technical details you'll never use? Do your friends and family always call you to fix simple problems on their PCs? Then the ...*For Dummies*® computer book series from IDG Books Worldwide is for you.

...*For Dummies* books are written for those frustrated computer users who know they aren't really dumb but find that PC hardware, software, and indeed the unique vocabulary of computing make them feel helpless. ...*For Dummies* books use a lighthearted approach, a down-to-earth style, and even cartoons and humorous icons to diffuse computer novices' fears and build their confidence. Lighthearted but not lightweight, these books are a perfect survival guide for anyone forced to use a computer.

> *"I like my copy so much I told friends; now they bought copies."*
>
> **Irene C., Orwell, Ohio**

> *"Quick, concise, nontechnical, and humorous."*
>
> **Jay A., Elburn, Illinois**

> *"Thanks, I needed this book. Now I can sleep at night."*
>
> **Robin F., British Columbia, Canada**

Already, millions of satisfied readers agree. They have made ...*For Dummies* books the #1 introductory level computer book series and have written asking for more. So, if you're looking for the most fun and easy way to learn about computers, look to ...*For Dummies* books to give you a helping hand.

QUARKXPRESS® 4
FOR
DUMMIES®

by Barbara Assadi and Galen Gruman
with John Cruise

IDG Books Worldwide, Inc.
An International Data Group Company

Foster City, CA ♦ Chicago, IL ♦ Indianapolis, IN ♦ New York, NY

QuarkXPress® 4 For Dummies®

Published by
IDG Books Worldwide, Inc.
An International Data Group Company
919 E. Hillsdale Blvd.
Suite 400
Foster City, CA 94404
www.idgbooks.com (IDG Books Worldwide Web site)
www.dummies.com (Dummies Press Web site)

Library of Congress Catalog Card No.: 97-81227

ISBN: 0-7645-0242-5

Printed in the United States of America

10 9 8 7 6 5 4 3 2

1O/QV/QV/ZY/IN

Distributed in the United States by IDG Books Worldwide, Inc.

Distributed by Macmillan Canada for Canada; by Transworld Publishers Limited in the United Kingdom; by IDG Norge Books for Norway; by IDG Sweden Books for Sweden; by Woodslane Pty. Ltd. for Australia; by Woodslane Enterprises Ltd. for New Zealand; by Longman Singapore Publishers Ltd. for Singapore, Malaysia, Thailand, and Indonesia; by Simron Pty. Ltd. for South Africa; by Toppan Company Ltd. for Japan; by Distribuidora Cuspide for Argentina; by Livraria Cultura for Brazil; by Ediciencia S.A. for Ecuador; by Addison-Wesley Publishing Company for Korea; by Ediciones ZETA S.C.R. Ltda. for Peru; by WS Computer Publishing Corporation, Inc., for the Philippines; by Unalis Corporation for Taiwan; by Contemporanea de Ediciones for Venezuela; by Computer Book & Magazine Store for Puerto Rico; by Express Computer Distributors for the Caribbean and West Indies. Authorized Sales Agent: Anthony Rudkin Associates for the Middle East and North Africa.

For general information on IDG Books Worldwide's books in the U.S., please call our Consumer Customer Service department at 800-762-2974. For reseller information, including discounts and premium sales, please call our Reseller Customer Service department at 800-434-3422.

For information on where to purchase IDG Books Worldwide's books outside the U.S., please contact our International Sales department at 650-655-3200 or fax 650-655-3295.

For information on foreign language translations, please contact our Foreign & Subsidiary Rights department at 650-655-3021 or fax 650-655-3281.

For sales inquiries and special prices for bulk quantities, please contact our Sales department at 650-655-3200 or write to the address above.

For information on using IDG Books Worldwide's books in the classroom or for ordering examination copies, please contact our Educational Sales department at 800-434-2086 or fax 817-251-8174.

For press review copies, author interviews, or other publicity information, please contact our Public Relations department at 650-655-3000 or fax 650-655-3299.

For authorization to photocopy items for corporate, personal, or educational use, please contact Copyright Clearance Center, 222 Rosewood Drive, Danvers, MA 01923, or fax 978-750-4470.

is a trademark under exclusive license to IDG Books Worldwide, Inc., from International Data Group, Inc.

About the Authors

Barbara Assadi is Editor-in-Chief of Web content for Oracle Corporation in Redwood Shores, California. She served as editorial producer for *Macworld* magazine, responsible for developing content for the Web. Barbara managed Quark, Inc.'s Editorial Services department from 1993 to 1996, overseeing the creation of documentation, training materials, and marketing collateral. She is a frequent contributor to *Macworld* and *InfoWorld* magazines, and has co-authored five other books on desktop publishing, including the *Macworld QuarkXPress 4.0 Bible* (IDG Books Worldwide, Inc.).

Galen Gruman is executive editor at *Macworld* magazine in charge of news and features, as well as a frequent reviewer of desktop publishing software for *Macworld* and *InfoWorld*. A pioneer user of desktop publishing in profes-sional magazine production, Galen adopted the technology in 1986 for a national engineering magazine, *IEEE Software*. Galen's honors include the finals of the Computer Press Awards for best computer-oriented news story in a general-interest publication (1986) and winning best in-depth technical feature in the American Society of Business Press Editors Awards (1993), which he shared with Lon Poole and Arne Hurty of Macworld. He was president of the Computer Press Association from 1992 to 1995. Galen is co-author with Deke McClelland of *PageMaker 6 For Windows For Dummies, PageMaker 5 For Windows For Dummies, PageMaker 6 For Macs For Dummies*, and *PageMaker 5 For Macs For Dummies*. With Barbara Assadi, he co-authored the critically praised *QuarkXPress 3.1 For Windows Designer Handbook, Macworld QuarkXPress 3.2/3.3 Bible*, and *QuarkXPress 3.3 For Dummies*, all from IDG Books Worldwide, Inc.

John Cruise is a Denver-based freelance writer and publishing consultant. From 1988 until 1993, he worked for Quark, Inc., as a member of the QuarkXPress and Quark Publishing System development teams. As Quark's manager of technical communications, he wrote and edited software docu-mentation, end user training, and marketing materials. From 1995 until 1997, he was managing editor of *X-RAYMagazine*, a publication for users of QuarkXPress and other Quark software, and he was a contributing writer for the *Macworld QuarkXPress 4.0 Bible* (IDG Books).

Dedication

Barbara Assadi: To Lorene and Big Joe, with love.

John Cruise: To Ryan Bing Cruise, my delightful daughter.

Authors' Acknowledgments

The authors wish to thank Kathy Cox, Kathy Simpson, Andrea Boucher, Ted Cains, Kim Darosett, and Wendy Hatch of IDG Books for editing the book and Sherry Gomoll and her IDG Production and Proofreading team for getting this book into print; and Paul Kuzmic for his invaluable help in making sure the files arrived readable and intact.

We also thank Kelly Kordes Anton for her technical review of the content. Special thanks to the following people from Quark, Inc.: Fred Ebrahimi, Don Lohse, Elizabeth Jones, Amy Snetzler, and Bob Monzel.

Publisher's Acknowledgments

We're proud of this book; please register your comments through our IDG Books Worldwide Online Registration Form located at http://my2cents.dummies.com.

Some of the people who helped bring this book to market include the following:

Acquisitions, Development, and Editorial

Project Editors: Kathleen M. Cox, Kathy Simpson

Acquisitions Editor: Ellen Camm

Copy Editors: Andrea C. Boucher, Ted Cains, Kim Darosett, Wendy Hatch

Technical Editor: Kelly Anton

Editorial Manager: Colleen Rainsberger

Editorial Assistant: Paul E. Kuzmic

Production

Project Coordinator: Sherry Gomoll

Layout and Graphics: Cameron Booker, Lou Boudreau, Linda M. Boyer, J. Tyler Connor, Maridee V. Ennis, Angela F. Hunckler, Jane E. Martin, Heather Pearson, Brent Savage, Kate Snell

Proofreaders: Nancy Reinhardt, Christine Berman, Kelli Botta, Michelle Croninger, Rachel Garvey, Nancy Price, Rebecca Senninger, Janet M. Withers

Indexer: Sherry Massey

Special Help

Kelly Ewing, Project Editor; Darren Meiss, Editorial Assistant

---

General and Administrative

IDG Books Worldwide, Inc.: John Kilcullen, CEO; Steven Berkowitz, President and Publisher

IDG Books Technology Publishing: Brenda McLaughlin, Senior Vice President and Group Publisher

Dummies Technology Press and Dummies Editorial: Diane Graves Steele, Vice President and Associate Publisher; Mary Bednarek, Director of Acquisitions and Product Development; Kristin A. Cocks, Editorial Director

Dummies Trade Press: Kathleen A. Welton, Vice President and Publisher; Kevin Thornton, Acquisitions Manager

IDG Books Production for Dummies Press: Beth Jenkins Roberts, Production Director; Cindy L. Phipps, Manager of Project Coordination, Production Proofreading, and Indexing; Kathie S. Schutte, Supervisor of Page Layout; Shelley Lea, Supervisor of Graphics and Design; Debbie J. Gates, Production Systems Specialist; Robert Springer, Supervisor of Proofreading; Debbie Stailey, Special Projects Coordinator; Tony Augsburger, Supervisor of Reprints and Bluelines; Leslie Popplewell, Media Archive Coordinator

Dummies Packaging and Book Design: Patti Crane, Packaging Specialist; Kavish + Kavish, Cover Design

♦

The publisher would like to give special thanks to Patrick J. McGovern, without whom this book would not have been possible.

♦

Contents at a Glance

Cartoons at a Glance

By Rich Tennant

"YES, I'M NORMALLY LARGER AND MORE AWE-INSPIRING, BUT THIS IS ONLY A 4MB SYSTEM!"

page 89

"Your Elvis should appear bald and slightly hunched-nice Big Foot, Brad-Keep your two-headed animals in the shadows and your alien spacecrafts crisp and defined."

page 193

"It's a ten step word processing program. It comes with a spell-checker, grammar-checker, cliche-checker, whine-checker, passive/aggressive-checker, politically correct-checker, hissy-fit-checker, pretentious pontificating-checker, boring anecdote-checker and a Freudian reference-checker."

page 7

"WELL, SHOOT! THIS EGGPLANT CHART IS JUST AS CONFUSING AS THE BUTTERNUT SQUASH CHART AND THE GOURD CHART. CAN'T YOU JUST MAKE A PIE CHART LIKE EVERYONE ELSE?"

page 281

page 305

"It says,' Seth-Please see us about your idea to wrap newsletter text around company logo. Production!"

page 341

Fax: 978-546-7747 • E-mail: the5wave@tiac.net

Table of Contents

Introduction

· ·

*T*here's a story you may have already heard. A man is walking down the street when he comes upon a construction site where a group of three brick masons are busily at work. He stops to talk to the first brick mason and asks, "What are you doing?" The brick mason answers, "I'm putting bricks on top of other bricks."

The man continues down the sidewalk until he comes to the second brick mason. Again he asks the same question, "What are you doing?" The second brick mason answers, "I'm putting some bricks together to make a wall."

The man then walks on until he comes face-to-face with the third brick mason. The man poses the same question to the third brick mason: "What are you doing?" The third brick mason answers, "I'm building a beautiful cathedral."

Is QuarkXPress Too High-End for Me?

Right now, you may be wondering why on earth we are telling this story as part of the introduction to a book on QuarkXPress. Good question. But, when you think about it, the people who use QuarkXPress are a lot like those brick masons, and QuarkXPress is a lot like the mortar and bricks used by those brick masons to do their work.

What we are saying is this: There are all kinds of users of QuarkXPress. Some do very simple, one-color documents. Some do moderately challenging documents, which include photos, illustrations, and complex charts. Still others — like the third brick mason who was building a cathedral — use QuarkXPress to create high-end, highly designed and illustrated works of art.

QuarkXPress — like the mortar and bricks used by the brick masons in our story— is a *tool*. Nothing more, nothing less. It works for the world's most-celebrated designers. It also works for people who create simpler documents, such as school newsletters.

The point is, QuarkXPress can never be too high-end for you, or for anyone else, because you pick and choose which parts of this tool you need to use. Also, keep in mind that if you create *any* type of document, you can benefit from the program's features. Sure, it's true that if your documents are simple, you won't need to use all the sophisticated features in QuarkXPress. But, when you think about it, isn't it nice to know that these features are available when and if you ever need them? And that you won't outgrow the program as you become more proficient with document design? We think so.

How to Use This Book

Although this book has information that any level of desktop publisher needs to know to use QuarkXPress, this book is also for those of you who are fairly new to the field, or who are just becoming familiar with the program. What we try to do is to take the mystery out of QuarkXPress and give you some guidance on how to create a bunch of different types of documents. Here are some conventions used in this book:

- **Menu commands** are listed like this: Style⇨Type Style⇨Bold.

  If we describe a situation in which you need to select one menu and then choose a command from a secondary menu or list box, we use, for example: File⇨Get Picture (⌘+E on Mac, Ctrl+E in Windows). After the first mention, we drop the platform reference. This shorthand method of indicating a sequence of commands is often followed by the keyboard shortcut, as shown in this example.

- **⌘:** This is the Macintosh's Command key — the most-used shortcut key. Its Windows equivalent is **Ctrl.**

- **Key combinations:** If you're supposed to press several keys together, we indicate that by placing plus signs (+) between them. Thus Shift+⌘+A means press and hold the Shift and ⌘ keys, and then press A. After you've pressed the A key, let go of the other keys. (The last letter in the sequence does not need to be held down.) We also use the plus sign to join keys to mouse movements. For example, Option+drag means to hold the Option key (Alt on Windows) when dragging the mouse.

- **Panes:** QuarkXPress 4 has added an interface feature proving to be popular, called tabbed panes. This is a method of stuffing several dialog boxes into one dialog box. You see tabs, like those in file folders, and by clicking a tab, the options for that tab come to the front of the dialog box in what is called a *pane*.

- **Pointer:** The small graphic icon that moves on the screen as you move your mouse is a pointer (also called a cursor). The pointer takes on different shapes depending on the tool you select, the current location of the mouse, and the function you are performing.

✔ **Click:** This means to quickly press and release the mouse button once. On most Mac mice, there is only one button, but on some there are two or more. All PC mice have at least two buttons. If you have a multi-button mouse, click the leftmost button when we say to click the mouse.

✔ **Double-click:** This tells you to quickly press and release the mouse button twice. On some multi-button mice, one of the buttons can function as a double-click. (You click it once, the mouse clicks twice.) If your mouse has this feature, use it; it saves strain on your hand.

✔ **Right-click:** A Windows 95 feature, this means to click the right-hand mouse button. On a Mac's one-button mouse, hold the Control key when clicking the mouse button to do the equivalent of right-clicking in progams that support it. On multi-button Mac mice, assign one of the buttons to the Control+click combination. (Note that in Mac OS 8, the Control+click combination —called a context menu —is now a standard part of the Mac, so expect to see it used in a lot of programs, and don't be surprised if multi-button mice become standard, or at least common, on the Mac.)

✔ **Dragging:** Dragging is used for moving and sizing items in a QuarkXPress document. To drag an item, position the mouse pointer on on the item, press *and hold* down the mouse button, and then slide the mouse across a flat surface.

One last thing: If you need help setting up your computer, getting acquainted with its operating system, managing files, and doing other, so-called basics, you may want to take a look at *Macs For Dummies* and *Macintosh System 8 For Dummies* if you're a Mac user, or *PCs For Dummies,* and *Windows 3.1 For Dummies* or *Windows 95 For Dummies* if you're a Windows user. All of these references are published by IDG Books Worldwide, Inc.

How This Book Is Organized

We've divided *QuarkXPress 4 For Dummies* into six parts, not counting this introduction. Each part has anywhere from two to five chapters, so you don't have to wade through too much explanation to get to the information you need. Note that the book covers QuarkXPress on both Macintosh and Windows platforms. Because the application is almost identical on all three, we only point out platform-specific information when we need to, or when we remember to, or both.

We have also included some bonus content on the Dummies Web site (www.dummies.com): installing Quark; setting up your printer; recognizing good design; and a brief glossary.

Part I: Getting Started

Designing a document is a combination of science and art. The science is in setting up the structure of the page: How many places will hold text, and how many will hold graphics? How wide will the margins be? Where will the page numbers appear? And so on. The art is in coming up with creative ways of filling the structure to please your eyes and the eyes of the people who will be looking at your document.

In this part, we tell you how to navigate your way around QuarkXPress using the program's menus, dialog boxes, and tabbed panes. We also show you how to set up the basic structure of a document and then how to begin filling the structure with words and pictures. We also tell you how to bring in text and graphics created in separate word processing and graphics applications.

Part II: Adding Style and Substance

Good publishing technique is about more than just getting the words down on paper. It's also about tweaking the letters and lines — and the space between them — to make your pages shine. This part shows you how to do all that and a lot more, including tips on using XTensions to get more out of QuarkXPress and how to get your document out of your computer and onto some other medium, such as film or paper. We give you some solid suggestions on printing and working with all those other people in the world who know how to help you get the job done.

Part III: The Picasso Factor

Let's be honest. Pablo Picasso didn't become famous for realistically portraying people. His claim to fame is based on how he took facial features and then skewed, slanted, stretched, and shrunk them into new forms. Some folks loved his work; others found it hard to figure. But you had to admire the fact that it was unique.

We named this part of the book after the famous artist because it tells not only how to use QuarkXPress as an illustration tool, but how to take normal-looking text and graphics and distort them. Why would you want to do this? Good question. The answer could be that, like Picasso, you want to present ideas in a visually interesting way. Either that, or you want to see how your relatives might look with their faces rearranged. QuarkXPress enables you to manipulate text and art in interesting ways, and we show you how.

Part IV: Going Long and Linking

It wasn't so very long ago that you really couldn't create a book using QuarkXPress. Sure, you could make a newsletter or a flyer, but if your document had more than a dozen or so pages, you'd find yourself feeling antsy as you tried to keep track of figure numbers, table numbers, index entries — well, you get the idea. But now, with version 4, crafting long documents is a piece of cake. In this section, we show you how to handle long documents of all flavors, including those that link together several smaller documents into a whole.

Part V: Guru in Training

After you master the basics, why not pick up some of the tricks the pros use? In this part we show you how to customize QuarkXPress so that it fits you like a comfortable easy chair. We also explain how QuarkXPress works on PCs that use Windows and on Macs.

Part VI: The Part of Tens

This part of the book is like the chips in the chocolate chip cookies; you could eat the cookies without them, but you'd be missing a really good part. It's a part of extremes, of bests and worsts. It's like a mystery novel that's hard to put down until you read the very last word. In fact, you might even be tempted to start reading here and then go back to Chapter 1, but don't. The concepts in this book will make more sense to you if you read the other six parts of the book first.

Icons Used in This Book

So that you can pick out parts that you really need to pay attention to (or, depending on your taste, to avoid), we've used some symbols, or *icons* in this book.

When you see this icon, it means we are pointing out a feature that's new to version 4 of QuarkXPress.

This icon points out features that behave a bit differently on Windows machines and Macs.

If you see this icon, it means that we're mentioning some really nifty point or idea that you may want to keep in mind as you use the program.

If you skip all the other icons, pay attention to this one. Why? Because ignoring it could cause something really, really bad or embarrassing to happen, like when you were sitting in your second-grade classroom waiting for the teacher to call on you to answer a question, and you noticed that you still had your pajama shirt on — backwards. We don't want that to happen to you!

Sometimes things work a certain way for no apparent reason. When you see this icon, it means you are about to read about some QuarkXPress mystery. But don't worry: We tell you how to solve it.

Once in awhile, we give you some step-by-step instructions to follow. We don't do it all the time, though, because we don't want you to confuse this book with the documentation that came with your package of QuarkXPress. And just to make the difference between the two books really clear, you should notice a couple of things:

- ✔ The cover of this book is a bright, happy yellow, unlike the cover of your QuarkXPress documentation.

- ✔ We take a light approach in explaining things to you in this book (in fact, we even attempt some jokes now and then); your QuarkXPress documentation is serious, boring, grown-up stuff.

This icon tells you that we are about to pontificate on some remote technical bit of information that might help explain a feature in QuarkXPress. The technical info will definitely make you sound impressive if you memorize it and recite it to your friends.

Where to Go from Here

QuarkXPress is an extremely versatile desktop publishing tool. The time you take to become familiar with Quark's many capabilities will be amply repaid in your ability to create the types of documents you want and need, from the most basic to the most bizarre. QuarkXPress can take you anywhere you want to go in desktop publishing. So get going!

Part I
Getting Started

The 5th Wave

By Rich Tennant

"It's a ten-step word processing program. It comes with a spell-checker, grammar-checker, cliche-checker, whine-checker, passive/aggressive-checker, politically correct-checker, hissy-fit-checker, pretentious pontificating-checker, boring anecdote-checker and a Freudian reference-checker."

In this part . . .

We take you from blank screen to a text-filled document, helping you navigate your way around QuarkXPress using the program's menus, dialog boxes, views, and tabbed panes. And we explain the basics about how to get QuarkXPress to do what you want it to: First you build a box and then you start to fill it with text or graphics. All this just to get you started.

Chapter 1

Introducing QuarkXPress

- -

In This Chapter

▶ Getting familiar with menus, dialog boxes, and keyboard shortcuts

▶ Exploring the Tool and Measurements palettes

▶ Moving along with mouse pointers

- -

*W*hen the first personal computer shipped in the early 1980s, a quiet revolution began. The turning point in that revolution was the introduction of desktop publishing in the mid-1980s, which let anyone anywhere become a publisher. Soon, anyone with a message could get it out to the world. And that revolutionized much of business and society. You too are a revolutionary — by buying QuarkXPress and this book, you have taken up the cause.

You've chosen well. Over the years, QuarkXPress has become the best desktop publishing tool. Professionals know that, which is why they have made it the standard for magazine, newspaper, and catalog publishing. But QuarkXPress's strengths as a business-publishing tool have been lost in that high-end focus. Fortunately, business publishers — those doing employee communications, newsletters, proposals, documentation, and so forth, as well as advertisements, magazines, catalogs, and newspapers — have begun to discover the power of QuarkXPress, and the folks at Quark have rewarded that discovery by making the latest version of QuarkXPress, version 4, friendly to business publishing. For example, it adds the ability to index documents, create tables of contents, and create multi-chapter books. (We cover those later in this book.)

Although you've chosen your tool well, you may feel a little daunted. After all, QuarkXPress is a powerful program, and its interface — the menus, dialog boxes, and other on-screen instruments that let you apply its features — is necessarily complex. To help you become comfortable with QuarkXPress, so that you can unleash its power, read on. This chapter introduces you to QuarkXPress's interface, so that you can learn to work with it effectively. It's just like working with a new person — once you get to know each other, you can do great things together. It's time to get to know QuarkXPress.

If you're like most of us, the first time you tried to record a program on your VCR, you fumbled with the buttons and switches, and maybe — after an hour or so — resorted to reading the instructions. (Okay, admit it: You maybe even mumbled an expletive or two.) See, when you use *anything* for the first time, it's bothersome. Figuring out the way things work takes time, because you have to get to know the *user interface* (the technical term for arrangement of dialog boxes, menus, windows, and other on-screen elements a program provides for you to tell it what to do, and for it to tell you what it's done).

A Familiar Interface

What lessens the new-user pain with QuarkXPress is the user interface's strong similarity to the features used by other Macintosh and Windows programs. If you use other programs, you already know how to use such QuarkXPress interface components as file folders, document icons, and the set of menus at the top of the document window.

When you open a document in QuarkXPress, the program displays a document window similar to the ones shown in Figures 1-1a and 1-1b.

Remember that this book is for both Macintosh and Windows users. We use both Mac and Windows screen shots throughout the book, sticking with one platform within a chapter for consistency's sake — unless the two platforms' versions of QuarkXPress have significant differences, in which case we show screens from both.

✔ The *ruler origin box* lets you reset and reposition the ruler origin, which is the point at which the side and top rulers are 0 (zero).

✔ The name of the open document appears on the *title bar,* located below the menu bar on the Mac and above the menu bar in Windows. You can move the document window around in the screen display area by clicking and dragging the title bar.

✔ If you have reduced or enlarged a document, clicking the *zoom box* on the Mac or the *restore box* in Windows, at the top right corner of the document window, returns it to its previous size.

✔ You can make a document all but disappear by minimizing it (in Windows) or turning it into a WindowShade (on the Mac). To minimize a document, click the *minimize box* in the document's title bar. To make a document into a WindowShade, double-click its title bar or click its *WindowShade box* on the Mac.

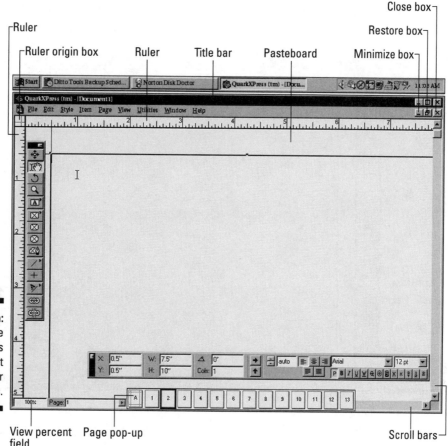

Figure 1-1a:
The
QuarkXPress
document
window for
Windows.

View percent   Page pop-up
field

Scroll bars

✔ The *vertical* and *horizontal rulers* on the left and top of the window reflect the measurement system currently in use.

✔ The *pasteboard* is a work area around the document page. You can temporarily store text boxes, picture boxes, or lines on the pasteboard. Items on the pasteboard do not print.

✔ QuarkXPress displays a shadow effect around the document page. The shadow indicates the edges of the document.

✔ If you select Automatic Text Box in the New dialog box (which you access by selecting New⇨Document from the File menu), a text box appears on the first page of the new document.

✔ Clicking and dragging the *size box* on the Mac resizes the document window as you move the mouse. In Windows, you can drag any side of the window to resize it.

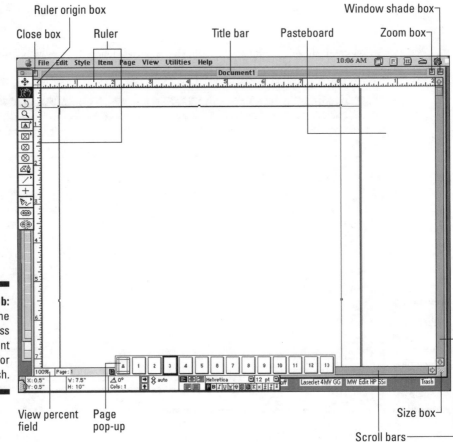

Figure 1-1b:
The
QuarkXPress
document
window for
Macintosh.

Ruler origin box

Close box   Ruler   Title bar   Pasteboard

Window shade box

Zoom box

View percent field   Page pop-up

Size box

Scroll bars

- ✔ The *View Percent* field shows the magnification level of the page that's currently displayed. To change the magnification level, enter a value between 10 and 800 percent in the field; then press the Return key or click elsewhere on the screen. Use the shortcut Control+V on the Mac or Ctrl+Alt+V in Windows to highlight the View Percent field.

- ✔ Switch pages using the *page pop-up.*

- ✔ Use the *scroll bars, boxes,* and *arrows* to shift the document page around within the document window. If you hold down the Option or Alt key while you drag the scroll box, the view of the document is refreshed as it "moves."

- ✔ Close a document by clicking its *close box.* On the Mac, you can also use the shortcut ⌘+W; in Windows, use Alt+F4.

Menus

The menu bar appears across the top of the document window. To display a menu using a Mac, click the menu title and, if you have a Mac older then OS8, hold down the mouse button. (In Windows, just click the menu title; there's no need to hold down the mouse button.)

From the menu, you can select any of the active menu commands. QuarkXPress displays inactive menu commands with dimmed (grayed-out) letters. When commands are dimmed, it means that these commands are not currently available to you — they're inactive.

To select one of the active menu commands, hold down the mouse button as you slide through the menu selections. (As you get more used to the program, you can avoid using menus by using the keyboard equivalents for menu selections instead. Keyboard equivalents are displayed to the right of the command names in the menu.)

If an arrow appears to the right of a menu command, QuarkXPress displays a second, associated menu when you choose that command. Sometimes this secondary menu appears automatically when you highlight the first menu command; other times, you must continue to hold down the mouse and slide it to the submenu name in order to activate the menu. (Again, in Windows, there's no need to hold down the mouse button; just click the arrow to make the submenu appear.) Figure 1-2 shows the Style menu and the secondary menu that appears when you select the Font menu command.

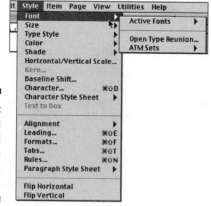

Figure 1-2:
Selecting
menu and
submenu
items in
QuarkXPress.

Dialog boxes

Some menu commands are followed by a series of dots called an ellipsis (. . .). If you choose a menu command whose name is followed by an ellipsis, a *dialog box* appears. Figure 1-3 shows an example of a dialog box. Dialog boxes give you a great deal of control over how QuarkXPress applies specific features or functions to your document.

Some dialog boxes also contain *submenus.* If a menu has a submenu associated with it, an arrowhead appears to the right of the menu entry. In addition to submenus, QuarkXPress includes several *pop-up menus,* which appear when you make certain selections in a dialog box. Figure 1-3 shows a pop-up menu for text justification.

Figure 1-3:
The
Paragraph
Attributes
dialog box,
showing the
Alignment
pop-up
menu in the
Formats
pane.

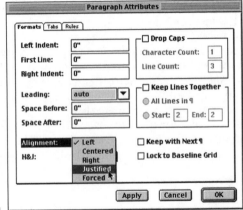

QuarkXPress uses a new kind of dialog box, called a tabbed pane, that merges several dialog boxes into one. You often see several tabs — similar to what you see on a file folder in an office cabinet — in a dialog box. Click the tab, and its pane comes to the forefront, showing you the options for that pane. You simply work with each pane you want within the dialog box. You can see three tabs (Formats, Tabs, and Rules) in Figure 1-3.

Keyboard shortcuts

You can select some QuarkXPress functions through pull-down menus, some through palettes, some through keyboard shortcuts, and some through all three options. Most new users begin by using menus because menus are so readily available. But as you become more comfortable with using the program, you'll want to save time by using keyboard shortcuts.

Working with contextual menus

Windows 95, Windows NT 4, and Mac OS 8 all use a technique called contextual menus to save you time. By right-clicking an item in Windows, or Control+clicking on the Mac, you get a menu of options just for that item. This saves you time going through menus, dialog boxes, and palettes. QuarkXPress 4.0, unfortunately, really skimps when it comes to contextual menus. The feature isn't supported at all in the Mac version, and the Windows version supports just three contextual menus:

✔ When you right-click on a page, or an item on a page, you get the contextual menu shown in the following figure. Some options will be grayed-out based on what is selected. For example, if you right-click on a page, you get just the top set of options — those that control the view. If you select a text box, you get all the options.

✔ When you right-click on a style in the Styles palette, you get the following contextual menu, which lets you add and delete styles quickly. We're surprised that Quark didn't offer similar contextual menus for all the palettes, although we won't be surprised to see such menus added in a future revision.

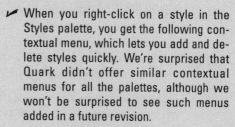

✔ Finally, if you click on a document window's title bar, you get a menu that lets you close or move the window.

Suppose that you want to move from page one of a document to page three. You can change pages by choosing Go To from the Page menu, or you can use the keyboard shortcut: Press and hold the Command key (⌘) or Ctrl key while you press the J key. In this book, we write this key combination as follows: ⌘+J (Macintosh shortcut) or Ctrl+J (Windows shortcut).The Macintosh shortcut will appear first, followed by the Windows shortcut. If the two platforms use the same shortcut, we list the shortcut just once.

In most cases, the Mac's ⌘ key and the Windows Ctrl key are the same, as are the Mac's Option key and the Windows Alt key. Shift is the same on both, while Control is a key found only on the Mac and that key's function has no Windows equivalent. On both platforms, the Return key is the same as the Enter key (some keyboards use one word, while some keyboards use the other); in neither case do we mean the Enter key that appears on the keyboard's numeric keypad at the far right of the keyboard. (To avoid confusion, we say "Return" for the key that inserts a new paragraph or activates a command, and we say "keypad Enter" when we mean the key on the numeric keypad.)

Palettes: A Cool New Wrinkle

One of the coolest features of the QuarkXPress interface is its *palettes,* which let you perform a wide range of functions on an open document without having to access pull-down menus. Palettes are the biggest time-saving feature of the QuarkXPress interface, and undoubtedly you will find yourself using a couple of the palettes — the Tool palette and the Measurements palette — all the time.

The Tool palette

The Tool palette, shown in Figure 1-4, is the one you use any time you fiddle with a document in QuarkXPress. When you first open the program, the Tool palette appears along the left edge of your computer's monitor; if it's not there, you can get it to appear by selecting Show Tools from the View menu (or pressing F8). This palette contains tools you use to create, change, link, view, and rotate text boxes, picture boxes, and lines.

Figure 1-4:
The
QuarkXPress
Tool palette
(on the left
side of the
screen).

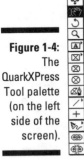

To use a tool on the palette, you first need to activate the tool. To activate a tool, use the mouse to place the cursor on the tool icon you want to use and then click the mouse button. Depending on which tool you select, the cursor takes on a different look to reflect the function the tool performs (see "A Myriad of Mouse Pointers" later in this chapter). When you click the Linking tool, for example, the cursor looks like links in a chain.

In the chapters that follow, we explain in greater detail many of the functions you can perform with the Tool palette. But, for now, here are brief descriptions of each tool.

Item tool

 These tools all should be at the same level, below the Tool palette level, which should be at the same level of all the palettes, below the Palettes level. The Item tool takes care of the *external* aspects of an item on a page. The Item tool controls the size and positioning of items. When you want to change the shape, location, or presence of a text box, picture box, or line, use the Item tool. The Item tool lets you select, move, group, ungroup, cut, copy, and paste text boxes, picture boxes, lines, and groups. When you click the Item tool on a box, the box becomes *active,* which means that you can change or move the box. Sizing handles appear on the sides of the active box; you can click and drag these handles to make the box a different size.

Content tool

 The Content tool controls the *internal* aspects of items on a page. Functions that you can perform with the Content tool include importing (putting text into a text box or putting a picture into a picture box), cutting, copying, pasting, and editing text.

To edit text in a text box, first select the Content tool. Then select the areas of text you want to edit by clicking and dragging the Content tool to highlight the text or by using different numbers of mouse button clicks, as follows:

- ✔ **To position the cursor:** Use the mouse to move the I-beam pointer (it looks like a large capital *I*) to the desired location and click the mouse button once.

- ✔ **To select a single word:** Use the mouse to move the pointer within the word and click the mouse button twice.

- ✔ **To select a line of text:** Use the mouse to move the pointer within the line and click the mouse button three times.

- ✔ **To select an entire paragraph:** Use the mouse to move the pointer within the paragraph and click the mouse button four times.

- ✔ **To select the entire document:** Use the mouse to move the cursor anywhere within the document and click the mouse button five times.

In a picture box, the Content tool cursor changes to a hand shape. You can use this tool to move the contents of the picture box. You also can use it when manipulating the picture's contents, such as applying shades, colors, or printing effects.

Rotation tool

 Use the Rotation tool to rotate items on a page. Using the Rotation tool, you can click a text box, picture box, or line and rotate it by dragging it to the angle you want. You also can rotate items on a page in other ways, which include using the Measurements palette and the Modify command in the Item menu.

Zoom tool

You may want to change the magnification of a page on-screen. For example, you may be making copy edits on text that is set in 8-point type; increasing the displayed size of the text makes it easier to see what you are doing as you edit. The Zoom tool lets you reduce or enlarge the view you see in the document window. When you select the Zoom tool, the cursor looks like a small magnifying glass; when you hold the cursor over the document window and click the mouse button, QuarkXPress increases or decreases the magnification of that section of the screen in increments of 25 percent. (To increase magnification, click anywhere with the Zoom tool active. To decrease magnification, hold the Option or Alt key while clicking with the Zoom tool active.)

Another way to change the magnification of the page is to enter a percentage value in the bottom-left corner of the document window; when a page is displayed at actual size, the percentage is 100. QuarkXPress lets you select any viewing percentage, including those in fractions of a percent (such as 49.5 percent), as long as you stay within the range of 10 to 800 percent.

Text Box tools

QuarkXPress needs to have a text box on the page before it can let you import text from a word processor file or before it will let you enter text directly onto a document page using the word processing features built into QuarkXPress. You can instruct QuarkXPress to create text boxes on each page of the document automatically. Or you can create a text box manually — which you do using the Text Box tools. We discuss Text Box tools in more detail in Chapter 3. (Note that right below the Text Box tools is a set of similar-looking tools used to create boxes that hold graphics, called Picture Box tools.)

To create a text box, select the desired Text Box tool and place the cursor at the approximate location where you want the box to appear. Click the mouse button and hold it down as you drag the box to size.

 Notice the arrow to the right of the Text Box tool's icon: This arrow indicates that if you hold down on the icon, a pop-up menu appears to show alternative Text Box tools. Select any of those alternative tools, and it becomes the default tool shown in the Tool palette. The seven Text Box tools produce different shapes (see Figure 1-5), and they function as follows:

✔ **Rectangle Text Box tool:** This produces the standard rectangles in which most text is placed. The Rectangle Text Box tool should be the default tool for most users. Hold down the Shift key while drawing the box to get a perfect square.

✔ **Rounded-Rectangle Text Box tool:** This tool produces rounded corners. You can adjust the degree of rounding, called the *corner radius*. Hold down the Shift key while drawing to get a perfect square.

✔ **Oval Text Box tool:** This tool produces an ellipse. Hold down the Shift key while drawing to get a perfect circle.

✔ **Concave-Corner Text Box tool:** This tool produces boxes that have the corners notched out. You can adjust the degree of notching, called the *corner radius*. Hold down the Shift key while drawing to get a perfect square.

✔ **Beveled-Corner Text Box tool:** This tool produces boxes that have their corners beveled (cut off by diagonal lines). You can adjust the degree of cut-off, called the *corner radius*. Hold down the Shift key while drawing to get a perfect square.

✔ **Bézier Text Box tool:** This produces polygons (shapes composed of a series of flat sides) and polycurves (shapes composed of a series of curves) as well as shapes that combine both sides and curves. This tool works differently than the other Text Box tools: Rather than holding down the mouse, you click and release at each corner (or *node*, in graphics-speak). When you want to complete the box, click back on the origin point. (Notice how the pointer changes to a circle from the normal cross.) If you click and drag for a little bit at each desired node, you see the Bézier control handles appear that let you create a curve. You can have both straight and curved sides based on how you use the mouse at each node — experiment to get the hang of it. (And if you want to convert a straight side to a curve, you can do so, as we describe in Chapter 4. Chapter 11 explains how to use the Bézier tools to draw curved shapes.)

✔ **Freehand Text Box tool:** This tool produces curved shapes — shapes composed of a series of curves. The box takes shape as you move the mouse, as if your mouse were a pen tracking on paper. To complete the box, you usually bring the mouse back to the origin point and then release the mouse button. (Notice how the pointer changes to a circle from the normal cross.) If you release the mouse button before you return to the origin point, however, QuarkXPress draws a straight line from where you released the mouse to the origin point.

The Concave-Corner, Beveled-Corner, Bézier, and Freehand Text Box tools are new to QuarkXPress 4.0. The Bézier tool lets you draw the kinds of shapes that the previous version's Polygon tool did, as well as new kinds of curved shapes.

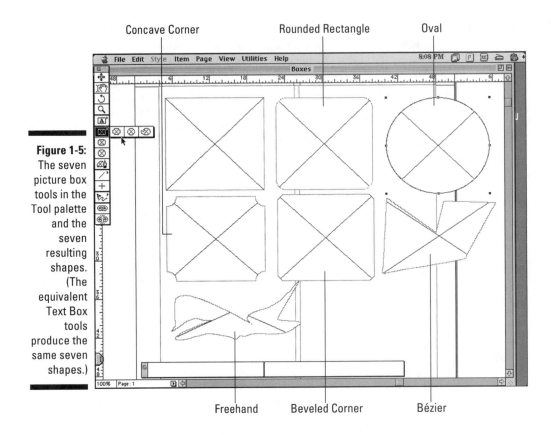

Concave Corner   Rounded Rectangle   Oval

Figure 1-5:
The seven picture box tools in the Tool palette and the seven resulting shapes. (The equivalent Text Box tools produce the same seven shapes.)

Freehand   Beveled Corner   Bézier

Picture Box tools

Picture boxes hold graphics that you import from graphics programs. QuarkXPress offers four Picture Box tools. When you refer to Figure 1-4, notice how the Tool palette has fixed locations for three Picture Box tools: the Rounded-Rectangle, Oval, and Bézier tools. There is a fourth location for a Picture Box tool — by default, this location is set to display the Rectangle Picture Box tool, as shown in Figure 1-4 — that has a pop-up menu that lets you replace the default tool with one of the other three tools: Concave-Corner, Beveled-Corner, and Freehand picture boxes. (See the "Changing the Tool palette's line-up" sidebar later in this chapter for more information on changing the arrangement of the Tool palette to suit your style.) The following list describes the Picture Box tools in detail:

⊠   ✔ **Rectangle Picture Box tool:** This tool produces the standard rectangles that most pictures are placed in. This should be the default tool for most users. Hold down the Shift key while drawing the box to get a perfect square.

Curving the French way

Bézier curves are named for Pierre Bézier, the French engineer and mathematician who created the curves in the early 1970s as a way of controlling mechanical cutting devices, commonly known as numerical control. (*Bézier* is pronounced bez-ee-AY or BAY-zyay, depending on whether you prefer the English or French pronunciation.)

Drawing lines on a computer is not tough, but manipulating them — changing their shape,

curve, and dimensions — can be. But remember: When you work with pen and paper, you can't alter your lines once they're drawn. So while the process of working with Bézier curves on a computer can at first be a little intimidating, you get the payoff of being able to change any shape at will. Chapters 3 and 11 explain how use Bézier tools in more detail.

- ✔ **Rounded-Rectangle Picture Box tool:** This tool produces rounded corners. You can adjust the degree of rounding, called the *corner radius*. Hold down the Shift key while drawing to get a perfect square.

- ✔ **Oval Picture Box tool:** This tool produces an ellipse. Hold down the Shift key while drawing to get a perfect circle.

- ✔ **Concave-Corner Picture Box tool:** This tool produces boxes that have their corners notched out. You can adjust the degree of notching, called the *corner radius*. Hold down the Shift key while drawing to get a perfect square.

- ✔ **Beveled-Corner Picture Box tool:** This tool produces boxes that have their corners beveled (cut off by a diagonal line). You can adjust the degree of cut-off, called the *corner radius*. Hold down the Shift key while drawing to get a perfect square.

- ✔ **Bézier Picture Box tool:** This produces Bézier shapes, which are composed of a series of flat sides and/or curves. This tool works differently than the other picture box tools: Rather than holding down the mouse, you click and release at each corner (or *node,* in graphics-speak). When you want to complete the box, click back on the origin point — or, to make it simpler, just double-click anywhere and QuarkXPress will add the last segment for you automatically. (Notice how the pointer changes to a circle from the normal cross.) If you click at each desired node, you get a series of straight sides. If you click and drag for a little bit at each desired node, you see the Bézier control handles appear that let you create a curve. You can have both straight and curved sides based on how you use the mouse at each node. Experiment to get the hang of it. (If you want to convert a straight side to a curve, you can do so, as we describe in Chapter 4.)

✔ **Freehand Picture Box tool:** This produces curved shapes — shapes composed of a series of curves. The box takes shape as you move the mouse, as if your mouse were a pen tracking on paper. To complete the box, you usually bring the mouse back to the origin point and then release the mouse button. (Notice how the pointer changes to a circle from the normal cross.) However, if you release the mouse button before you return to the origin point, QuarkXPress draws a straight line from where you released the mouse to the origin point.

The Concave-Corner, Beveled-Corner, Bézier, and Freehand Picture Box tools are new to QuarkXPress 4.0. The Bézier tool lets you draw the kinds of shapes that the previous version's Polygon tool did, as well as shapes based on curves, which you could not do with the previous version. Figure 1-5 shows the shapes you can create with these tools.

Line tools

The four Line tools let you draw lines, or *rules*. After you draw a line, you can change its thickness (*weight*) or style (dotted line, double line, and so on). The standard Line tools are:

✔ **Orthogonal Line tool:** This tool produces straight lines that are completely horizontal or vertical.

✔ **Diagonal Line tool:** This tool produces straight lines at any desired angle. If you hold down the Shift key while drawing, the lines are constrained to be perfectly horizontal, perfectly vertical, or at a perfect 45-degree angle. (Note that the QuarkXPress manual simply calls this the Line tool, but we use the name Diagonal Line tool so that you don't mix it up with the other three Line tools.)

The Diagonal Line tool has a pop-up palette that lets you replace it with two new Line tools:

• **Bézier Line tool:** This tool produces curved lines, with a curve segment between each location you click.

• **Freehand Line tool:** This tool produces curved lines that follow the motion of your mouse — similar to drawing with a pen on paper.

As with the Text Box and Picture Box pop-up palettes, you can change the arrangement of the Tool palette's Line tools to suit your style.

To use any of the Line tools, click the tool to select it and position the cursor at the point where you want the line to begin.

✔ For the Diagonal Line, Orthogonal, and Freehand Line tools, click and hold down the mouse button as you draw the line. When the line is approximately the length you want, release the mouse button.

✔ For the Bézier Line tool, click at each point, as described for the Bézier Picture Box and Text Box tools. If you click and drag for a little bit at each desired node, you see the Bézier control handles appear that let you create a curve. You can have both straight and curved sides based on how you use the mouse at each node — experiment to get the hang of it. After you draw a line, use the Measurements palette to select the line weight and line style.

Text Path tools

You can now draw four kinds of text paths — lines that text will follow — to create text that flows in any direction rather than being confined within a text box. The four Text Path tools work like the Line tools; they are:

✔ **Freehand Text Path tool:** This tool produces curved text paths that follow the motion of your mouse — similar to drawing with a pen on paper.

The Freehand Text Path tool has a pop-up palette for the three other Text Path tools.

✔ **Orthogonal Text Path tool:** This tool produces straight text paths that are completely horizontal or vertical.

✔ **Bézier Text Path tool:** This tool produces curved text paths, with a curved segment between each location you click.

✔ **Line (or Diagonal) Text Path tool:** This tool produces straight text paths at any desired angle. If you hold down the Shift key while drawing, the paths are constrained to be perfectly horizontal, perfectly vertical, or at a perfect 45-degree angle. (Note that the QuarkXPress manual calls this simply the Text Path tool, but we use the name Line (or Diagonal) Text Path tool so that you don't mix it up with the other three Text Path tools.)

As with the Text Box and Picture Box pop-up palettes, you can change the arrangement of the Tool palette's Text Path tools to suit your style.

Linking and Unlinking tools

The bottom tools in the Tool palette are the Linking tool (top) and the Unlinking tool (bottom). The Linking tool lets you link text boxes together so that overflow text flows from one text box into another. Use the Unlinking tool to break the link between text boxes. Linking is particularly useful when you want to *jump* text — for example, when a story starts on page one and jumps to (continues on) page four.

Changing the Tool palette's line-up

By default, the main Tool palette shows the Rectangle Picture Box tool, with its pop-up palette, followed by the Rounded-Rectangle, Oval, and Bézier Picture Box tools. Frankly, we were a bit mystified about why the Rectangle Picture Box tool can be replaced on the Tool palette (via its pop-up palette, as explained in the following instructions) when three less-used picture box tools are fixed. Rectangular boxes are by far the most common, so we thought it made more sense to have the Rect-angle tool fixed and let some other tool be replaceable.

The designers of QuarkXPress, however, are a step ahead of us. You can actually change what the Tool palette displays to make it match your preferences. The following scenarios show you why the QuarkXPress designers chose to make the most-used Picture Box tool (the Rectangle) the one with the pop-up palette:

✔ Suppose, for example, that you want the Beveled-Corner Picture Box tool on the Tool palette. Hold down the Control or Ctrl key, and then hold the mouse button on the Rectangle Picture Box tool to activate the Picture Box pop-up palette. Still hold-ing down the Control or Ctrl key and the mouse button, move the mouse cursor to the Beveled-Corner Picture Box tool and release the mouse button. Presto! The Beveled-Corner Picture Box tool is now on the Tool palette.

✔ Now suppose that you don't want the Oval Picture Box tool on the Tool palette. In-stead, you want it on the Picture Box pop-up palette. Control+click or Ctrl+click the Oval Picture Box and, presto again, it dis-appears from the Tool palette and is now part of the Picture Box pop-up palette.

You can use the same technique to change the arrangement of four types of tools: Text Box, Picture Box, Line, and Text Path. You can iden-tify these groups of tools by looking for a tool with the arrow that indicates a pop-up menu. That tool and the ones that follow until the next such tool (or until the Link tool) are all part of the same group and can be collapsed or expanded.

The Measurements palette

The Measurements palette was first developed by Quark and is now being widely imitated by other software developers. This palette is one of the most significant innovations to take place in the evolution of desktop publishing, and (honest!) you will use it all the time. The Measurements palette gives you precise information about the position and attributes of any selected page element, and it lets you enter values to change those specifications. If you want to see the Measurements palette, you need to have a document open as you choose View⇨Show Measurements, or press F9.

The information displayed in the Measurements palette depends on the element currently selected. When you select a text box, the Measurements palette displays the text box position coordinates (X: and Y:), size (W: and H:), amount of rotation, and number of columns (Cols:), as shown in Figure 1-6. Using the up- and down-pointing arrows on the palette, you can modify the leading of the text box (or you can simply type a value in the space next to the arrows); use the right- and left-pointing arrows to adjust kerning or tracking for selected text. (If you're unfamiliar with these typographic terms, check out Chapter 5.)

Figure 1-6:
The
Measure-
ments
palette
when a text
box is
selected.

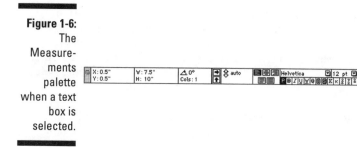

Specify text alignment — left, center, right, or justified — by using the alignment icons. In the type section of the palette, you can control the font, size, and type style of selected text.

For a picture box, the Measurements palette displays a different set of information: Here, the Measurements palette shows the position of the box (X: and Y:), its size (W: and H:), the amount it is rotated, its corner radius, its reduction or enlargement percentage (X%: and Y%:), its repositioning coordinates (X+: and Y+:), the amount of picture rotation within the box, and the amount of slant. Figure 1-7 shows the Measurements palette for a picture box.

Figure 1-7:
The
Measure-
ments
palette
when a
picture box
is selected.

Figure 1-8:
The
Measure-
ments
palette for a
straight line
or text path.

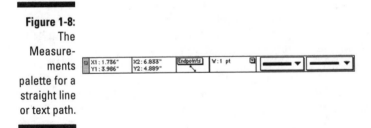

For a line or text path, the Measurements palette displays the location coordinates (X: and Y:), line width, line style, and endcap (line ending) style. The line style pop-up menu lets you select the style for the line. Figure 1-8 shows the Measurements palette for a line. Note that if you select a freehand or Bézier line, the Endpoints section of the Measurements palette will be replaced with an icon that controls the line's rotation.

If you select a Bézier or freehand element's node or curve, you get controls for the nodes, as shown in the Measurements palette in Figure 1-9. Chapter 11 explains what the controls do.

Figure 1-9:
The
Measure-
ments
palette for a
node or
curve
segment.

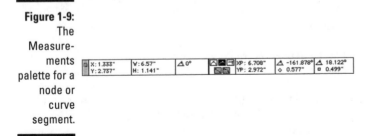

The Document Layout palette

With the Document Layout palette, shown in Figure 1-10, you can create, name, delete, move, and apply master pages, which hold page elements such as graphics and margins that QuarkXPress can apply automatically to new pages, much as a style sheet works to apply standardized formatting to text. You also can add, delete, and move document pages. To display the Document Layout palette, choose Show Document Layout from the View menu, or press F10. Take a look at Chapter 17 for more information on master pages.

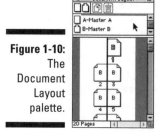

Figure 1-10:
The
Document
Layout
palette.

The Colors palette

Figure 1-11 shows the Colors palette. The Colors palette lets you designate the color and shade (percentage of color) you want to apply to text, pictures, and backgrounds of text and picture boxes. You also can produce color blends, using one or two colors, to apply to box backgrounds. To display the Colors palette, choose Show Colors from the View menu, or press F12. Color is covered in more detail in Chapter 15.

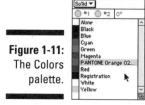

Figure 1-11:
The Colors
palette.

The Style Sheets palette

The Style Sheets palette lists the names of the style tags attached to selected paragraphs and also lets you apply style sheets to paragraphs. To display the Style Sheets palette, choose Show Style Sheets from the View menu, or press F11. Style sheets are covered in depth in Chapter 6.

The Trap Information palette

One of the features that has made QuarkXPress the program of choice among professional publishers is one that you'll likely never have to worry about: *Trapping* refers to the technique of extending one color so that it slightly overlaps an adjoining color, preventing the gaps between two abutting colors that sometime result from misalignment of plates on a printing press. In the Trap Information palette, you can set or change trapping specifications for selected items. To display the palette, use Show Trap Information from the View menu or press Option+F12 or Alt+F12. Check out Chapter 15 for more on color.

A word of warning: Don't use the Trap Information palette unless you know what you're doing. This palette is considered an expert feature, and using it inexpertly can produce uneven results when you print your document.

The Profile Information palette

Another expert feature is the Profile Information palette, used to set or change color profiles for selected items. Color profiles make slight adjustments to an object's colors to compensate for differences among color input and output devices. Most users don't have to worry about this feature, and if they do, their service bureau will let them know when to worry about it. To display this palette, use Show Profile Information from the View menu. Color is covered in more detail in Chapter 15.

A word of warning: Don't use the Profile Information palette unless you know what you're doing. The Profile Information palette is another expert feature of QuarkXPress, and using it without knowing precisely what you need to use it for can produce uneven results when you print your document.

The Lists palette

QuarkXPress now lets you create lists based on paragraph styles that you can use to build tables of contents, tables of figures, and so on. In the Lists palette, shown in Figure 1-12, you can set or change list settings, as described in Chapter 16. To display the palette, use Show Lists from the View menu or press Option+F11 or Alt+F11. Chapter 18 covers list creation in detail.

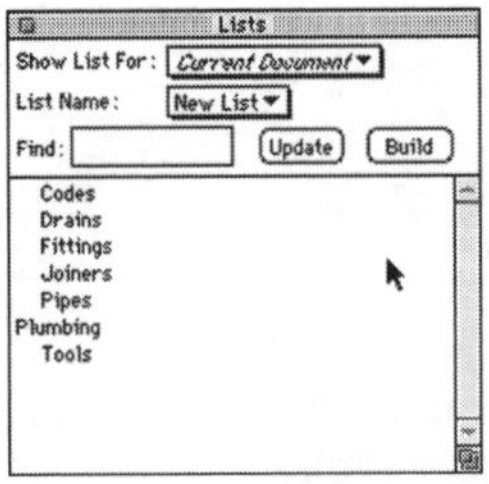

Figure 1-12: The Lists palette.

The Index palette

QuarkXPress now lets you create indexes based on words that you specify in this palette, shown in Figure 1-13 and described in more depth in Chapter 18. To display the palette, use Show Index from the View menu.

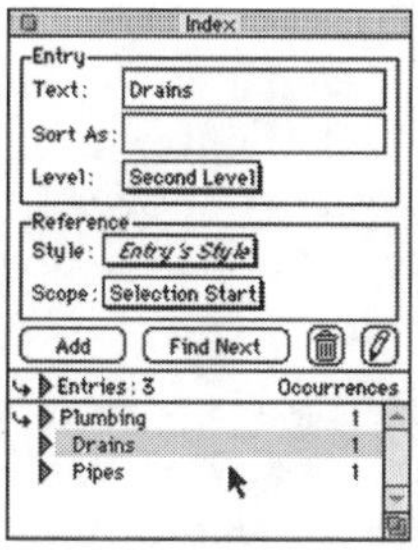

Figure 1-13:
The Index
palette.

Library palettes

QuarkXPress lets you store layout elements (text or picture boxes, lines, or groups) in one or more library palettes. To use this feature, select the element that you want to store from the document or the pasteboard, and drag it into an open library palette. Because you can have several library palettes, you can group items into specific libraries, such as one for each project or, say, one for logos and one for employee photos. You then can use items stored in the library in other documents. To create a library palette, choose File⇨New⇨Library. Chapter 18 covers libraries in detail.

A Myriad of Mouse Pointers

When you use the Macintosh or Windows, you use the mouse. You also use the mouse with QuarkXPress. What you notice after awhile is that the program gives you a visual hint about what tool you are currently using by changing the mouse pointer (also called *cursor*) so that it looks different. Here are the various renditions of the mouse pointer you can expect to see in QuarkXPress:

✔ **Standard pointer:** Appears as you move through dialog boxes, menus, and windows, and as you move over nonselected elements. The standard pointer is the most common pointer.

✔ **Creation pointer:** Appears if you have selected a box or line tool. Use this pointer to draw boxes and lines.

✔ **Sizing pointer:** Appears if you select one of the handles on a text or picture box (with either the Item or Content tool selected) or on a line. You can resize the item by holding down the mouse button and dragging the handle.

 ✔ **Item pointer:** Appears if the Item tool is selected and you have selected a box or line. You can move the selected item by holding down the mouse button and dragging the item.

 ✔ **Lock pointer:** Appears if the Item tool is selected and you have selected a locked text box, picture box, or line. The lock pointer indicates that the box will not move if you try to drag it (you can move it, however, by changing the coordinates in the Measurements palette or via Item⇨Modify).

 ✔ **I-beam (text) pointer:** Appears if the Content tool is selected and you select a text box. If the cursor is blinking, any text you type inserts where the cursor appears. If the cursor is not blinking, you must click at the location in the text box where you want to edit text.

 ✔ **Grabber pointer (also known as the page-grabber hand):** Appears if the Content tool is selected and you have selected a picture box containing a graphic. You can move the graphic within the box by holding down the mouse button and dragging the item.

 ✔ **Zoom-in pointer:** Appears if you select the Zoom tool and click the mouse button (clicking the mouse button zooms in on the image by the predefined amount, which by default is 25 percent). You can also select an area to zoom into by clicking one corner of the area of interest, holding down the mouse button, dragging the mouse to the opposite corner, and then releasing the button.

 ✔ **Zoom-out pointer:** Appears if you select the Zoom tool and hold down the Option or Alt key while clicking the mouse button (clicking the mouse button zooms out by a predefined amount, which by default is 25 percent).

 ✔ **Link pointer:** Appears if you select the Link tool. Click the pointer on the first text box and then on the second text box in the chain of boxes through which you want text to flow. If there are more boxes, repeat the process (for example, link box two to box three, then box three to box four, and so on). You can switch pages while this tool is active to flow text from one box to another across pages.

 ✔ **Unlink pointer:** Appears if you select the Unlink tool. Click the pointer on the first text box, then on the second text box in the chain of boxes that have the link that you want to break. If there are more boxes to unlink, repeat this process for each pair of boxes to be unlinked. You can switch pages while this tool is active to unlink text flow across pages.

Chapter 2

Viewing It Your Way

. . . .

In This Chapter

▶ Understanding the View menu

▶ Controlling how a document displays onscreen

. . . .

Do you ever wonder how sitting in front of a computer all those hours is affecting your eyesight? Do you find yourself hunched over, nose to screen, trying to read the really small print? Well, you're not alone. And those nice people who brought you QuarkXPress are doing their part to save your eyes by providing some nifty ways for you to change how documents appear onscreen such as by zooming in to make things larger or by creating thumbnail pages so you can see how well your page layouts work together.

This chapter helps you get up close and personal with Quark by giving you tips on taking control using the View menu.

To change the way you see a document in Quark, simply, choose one or more preset options from the View menu. You can change views, or zoom in and out on the document, by a variable amount (between 10 percent and 800 percent) at any time. To do so, enter a percentage value in the box in the corner of the open document window (bottom-left side, next to the page number).

The ability to expand the view to 800 percent is new to QuarkXPress 4. In previous versions of the program, the maximum amount by which you could expand the view was 400 percent. The added magnification comes in handy when checking fine details.

The View Menu

The View menu (see Figure 2-1) lets you control the display of items onscreen.

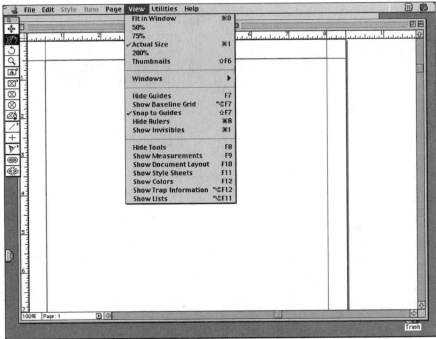

Figure 2-1:
The View
menu.

The menu has four sections that break down as follows:

🖛 The first portion of the menu holds the view option commands (covered later in this section under "Using the preset options").

🖛 The second segment lets you control how multiple documents are displayed and lets you switch among several open documents. (This section is actually a whole different menu — the Window menu — in the Windows version of QuarkXPress.)

• The Tile Documents option is particularly useful if you are lucky enough to have multiple monitors, which give you enough room to see several documents at the same time. (In Windows, you can choose Tile Horizontally or Tile Vertically.)

• The Stack Documents option simply keeps the windows offset slightly so that all the document names are visible.

In QuarkXPress for Windows, the tile and stack options are in the separate Window menu, which also has a handy option that closes all open windows.

🖛 The third part of the menu provides commands that control the display of positioning aids: guides, baseline grid, rulers, and invisibles (tabs, returns, and so on). You can toggle features on and off; if a command is active, a check appears next to its name.

✔ The final part of the View menu contains commands that display or hide QuarkXPress palettes. You can toggle features on and off; if a palette is open, its option changes from Show to Hide. We explain palettes in Chapter 1.

The preset view options in QuarkXPress are menu commands that scale the document view to a set of sizes preset by Quark. The preset view options in the View menu are:

✔ **Fit in Window (⌘+0 [zero] on the Macintosh, Ctrl+0 [zero] in Windows):** Fits the page into the area of the document window.

✔ **50%:** Displays the document page at half its actual size.

✔ **75%:** Displays the document page at three-fourths of its actual size.

✔ **Actual Size (⌘+1 or Ctrl+1):** Displays the document page at actual size, which may mean that you can see only part of the page onscreen.

✔ **200%:** Displays the document page at twice its actual size.

✔ **Thumbnails (Shift+F6):** Displays miniature versions of the document pages. Figure 2-2 shows a thumbnail view with page 2 selected (highlighted).

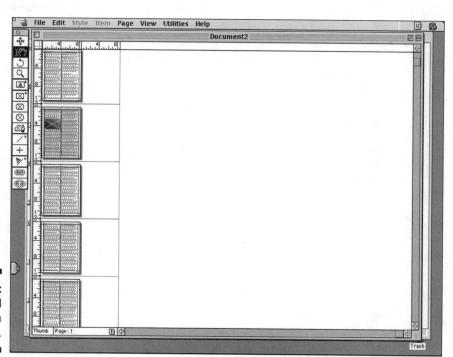

Figure 2-2: A thumbnail view of a document.

View-Changing Tips and Tricks

In addition to the present view commands mentioned in the previous section, QuarkXPress offers some alternative ways of changing views. We find the following methods to be particularly useful:

✔ To increase the page view in 25-percent increments, select the Zoom tool. (It looks like a magnifying glass.) When you place the mouse pointer in the document with the Zoom tool selected, the pointer changes to a magnifying glass. Each time you click the mouse button, the view increases in 25-percent increments, up to a maximum of 800 percent. To decrease the page view in 25-percent increments, hold down the Option or Alt key as you click the mouse button.

✔ To increase the view by 25 percent, an even easier method is to hold down the Control key and click the mouse. This works only on the Mac.

✔ To zoom in on a specific area, click the Zoom tool, select a corner of the area you want to zoom in on, hold down the mouse button, drag to the opposite corner of the specified area, and release the mouse button.

✔ For all these Zoom-tool options, you can change the increment from its default of 25 percent to any other amount by making changes in the Tool pane of the Document Preferences dialog box (choose Edit⇨ Preferences⇨Document or ⌘+Y or Ctrl+Y).

✔ Another easy way to change your view is to use the keyboard shortcut (Control+V or Ctrl+Alt+V), which highlights the view percentage in the bottom-left corner of your QuarkXPress window. Just enter the new percentage (you don't need to enter the % symbol) and then press Enter or Return. If you want to go to the thumbnail view, enter **T** instead of a percentage.

See Chapter 19 for information about changing default document and application preferences, to get still more control over the way QuarkXPress handles your documents.

Chapter 3

All about Boxes

In This Chapter

▶ Building text boxes and picture boxes

▶ Linking text boxes

▶ Creating special effects with boxes

L et's face it — when you think of a flat piece of paper with words and pictures on it, you don't intuitively know that those words and pictures are held in boxes, right? Not if you're like most people we know. And the boxes that we're talking about now are not your typical supermarket boxes. In fact, they are unlike any three-dimensional boxes that you may be familiar with. About the only way in which QuarkXPress boxes are similar to those you know is that they also hold stuff — but the stuff is two-dimensional text and pictures.

Surprised? You're not alone. It never fails to amaze brand-new QuarkXPress users that just about everything on a page produced in this program must be placed into a box. QuarkXPress boxes may not be able to hold a great deal of memorabilia, but they are pretty powerful just the same; they serve as the placeholders for the text and pictures that you use to build a page. These boxes not only define the layout of a page by controlling the size and placement of pictures; they also delineate the white space between an illustration and its caption, and they identify the portion of a page's real estate that is covered with words.

Yes, these boxes do a lot. And if you spend any time at all working with QuarkXPress, you'll get comfortable with its text boxes and picture boxes in no time flat.

Getting Basic with Boxes

Composing a page in QuarkXPress involves arranging and rearranging the program's basic building blocks, which include *text boxes* (which hold text) and *picture boxes* (which hold graphics). After you create text and picture boxes, you can fill them with appropriate contents. (Don't worry too much about getting the two types of boxes mixed up; QuarkXPress won't allow you to put text inside a picture box or a picture inside a text box.) You also can perform an amazing number of changes on the boxes, such as moving them, changing their size, adding color, and rotating them.

Tools to use

In Chapter 1, we show you the QuarkXPress Tool palette. The fact that the Tool palette contains 14 tools for creating boxes — seven for text boxes and seven for picture boxes — reflects how important boxes are to page design in QuarkXPress.

You use the Text Box tools in the Tool palette to draw text boxes. You also can have QuarkXPress automatically create a single text box on each page, which we tell you how to do later in this chapter in the section "Making It Automatic." When you have a text box, you can enter text directly into it by typing on your computer's keyboard, or you can import text from a word processor file.

Below the Text Box tools in the Tool palette, you find tools for creating picture boxes, lines, and text paths (lines or shapes along which you can place text). Unfortunately, you can't ask QuarkXPress to draw picture boxes for you automatically because the program isn't designed to work that way. So if you want to have a picture on a page, you need to pick one of the picture box tools shown in Figure 3-1 — Rectangle, Rounded Corner, Beveled Corner, Concave Corner, Oval, Bézier, or Freehand — to draw it.

You can change a picture box to a text box (and vice versa) by choosing Item⇨Content and then choosing Text from the Content submenu. You can also choose None to change a picture box or a text box to a box that does not contain anything. Boxes with no content are handy for creating illustrations because you can still use the box as a shape, modifying it by adding a frame, a background color, a blend, and so on.

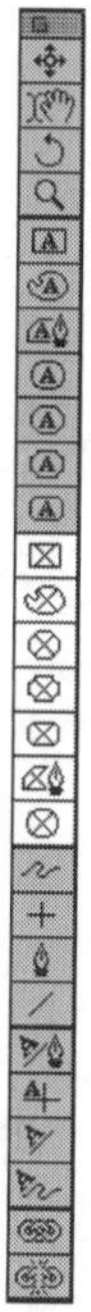

Figure 3-1:
QuarkXPress
offers
seven tools
for creating
picture
boxes.

Building Text Boxes

To position text on a page with QuarkXPress, use a text box. You can create a text box by drawing a manual text box using the mouse or by having the program make a text box for you — automatically.

Manual text boxes are nice when you want to draw a box of any size, watch the box develop on-screen as you draw it, and place it in any spot on the page. Later, you can change things about the box, such as its number of columns and the width of its margins.

In Chapter 5, we show you how to go about filling a text box with text. But before you get to that point, you need to know how to create a simple, rectangular text box manually. It's easy. Just follow these steps:

1. **Create a new document by choosing File⇨New⇨Document and clicking OK in the New Document dialog box.**

   You can use the default settings in the New Document dialog box.

2. **Select the Rectangle Text Box tool from the Tool palette.**

   (In case you've forgotten, the Rectangle Text Box tool looks like a little rectangle with a capital *A* in its center.)

Notice that when you move the mouse pointer into the document page, the mouse pointer changes to look like a crosshair.

3. **Holding down the mouse button, drag the mouse to draw a text box of the size that you want.**

If you want the text box to be a perfect square, hold down the Shift key while you draw the box. To create a perfect circle, use the Oval Text Box tool and hold down the Shift key when dragging.

4. **Release the mouse button.**

Now step back and admire your work. Is the box the size and location you want it? If not, the easiest way to adjust the box is to use the Measurements palette to change values. (If you're looking at your screen right now and can't find the Measurements palette, display it by choosing View⇨Show Measurements or pressing F9.)

The X and Y numbers in the Measurements palette show you where the box is on the page. The W and H numbers in the palette show you the width and height of the box. You can change any of these numbers by highlighting the value that you want to change in the Measurements palette and typing a new number. Simple as that.

Active and inactive boxes

Suppose that you've already drawn a text box or a picture box. And after looking at the box, you decide that it's too small, and it's also too high on the page. What to do? Do you scrap the box and start over, hoping for better luck the next time you create it?

No, you know that deleting the box and drawing it again will take too long, plus (to be honest about it) it would mean that you're chickening out. Be brave! You can fix that box, and we show you how in the section "Taming the wild text box" later in this chapter. But before you can do the first thing to the box, you have to *activate* it.

As we tell you in Chapter 1, *selecting* an item, using the Content tool or the Item tool, is the same as activating it. Before you can make changes in a text box or picture box — or any item, for that matter — in QuarkXPress, you must select it, or activate it, so that the program can access it to make the changes that you want.

Figure 3-2 shows two boxes. The box on the left is inactive, or unselected. The box on the right is active, or selected. Activating the box enables you to modify it in many ways. As you can see, telling when a box is active is easy because little black boxes, called *sizing handles,* appear on its sides and corners.

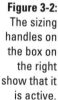

Figure 3-2:
The sizing handles on the box on the right show that it is active.

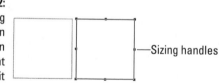

Sizing handles

Taming the wild text box

You probably know at least one person who can be called a control freak. You know — the friend who goes berserk when he finds that a piece of paper on his desk is rotated at an angle, instead of being perfectly aligned with the pencil box; the hostess who follows you around her house, carrying a towel to wipe everything you've touched; or the boss who insists on reading every word you write and knowing where you are each minute of the day.

Hey, being a control freak is not usually considered something to be proud of. But when you get into desktop publishing, taking control is necessary and highly valued. The capability to try and make things perfect soon takes over even non-control freaks, and you find yourself spending hours tweaking every element on the page.

So relax. When you're building a page, being a control freak is perfectly okay. Honestly, half the fun of using QuarkXPress is the unbelievable amount of control it gives you over everything in a page layout.

Text boxes are among the things over which you have complete control when you use QuarkXPress. Once you create a text box, you can exercise that control using the Modify dialog box.

Here's how you make this dialog box appear:

1. **Make sure that the text box is active (look for the sizing handles around it).**

   You can activate it with either the Content tool or the Item tool.

2. **Choose Item⇨Modify to display the Modify dialog box for text boxes, shown in Figure 3-3, or press ⌘+M (on the Macintosh) or Ctrl+M (in Windows) as a shortcut.**

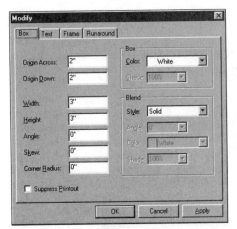
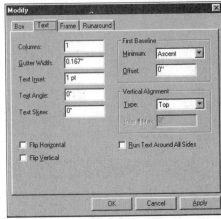
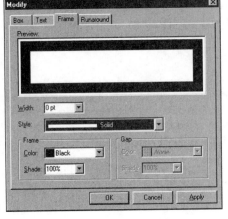
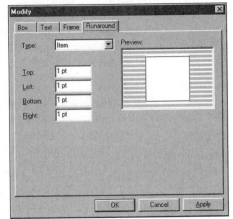

Figure 3-3:
The four
panes of
the Modify
dialog box
for text
boxes: Box,
Text, Frame,
and
Runaround.

As you can see by looking at Figure 3-3, the four panes of the Modify dialog box enable you to tweak a text box to your heart's content. By entering values, choosing items from pop-up menus, checking or unchecking boxes, and so on, you can modify the appearance of the box and set other box properties.

The Box pane lets you adjust the position and appearance of a text box, including the following:

✔ The box's size and position on the page

✔ The angle of the box's rotation

✔ The *skew angle* (or slant) of the box and the text within

✔ The amount of roundness applied to the box's corners

✔ The color — or colors, in the case of a two-color blend — and shade applied to the box's background

The Text pane lets you adjust the placement and appearance of the text in the box, including the following:

- ✔ The number of columns and the space between columns
- ✔ The distance between the edge of the box and the text within
- ✔ The angle of the lines of text within the box
- ✔ The skew angle of the text
- ✔ The placement of the first line of text relative to the top of the box
- ✔ The vertical alignment of the text
- ✔ How text flows within the box when an item is placed in front of the box
- ✔ The option to flip the text within a box along a vertical and/or horizontal axis

The Frame pane (explained in detail in Chapter 13) lets you apply a frame around a text box and to specify the style, width, color, and shade of the frame, as well as the color and shade applied to the gap between dotted, dashed, and multiple-line frames.

The Runaround pane (covered in the section, "Running Around," later in this chapter) lets you control the flow of text that's in a box behind the active box.

Several of the text-box characteristics that you control via the Modify dialog box — position, height and width, number of columns, and angle — you can also set by entering new values in the Measurements palette. In fact, users with a bit of practice under their belts almost always prefer the convenience of the palette method.

The best way to make yourself comfortable with settings for text boxes is to experiment on your own. Take a few minutes to create some simple, rectangular text boxes, fill them with text, and then fiddle with them. Be adventuresome: Try to use both the Modify dialog box and the Measurements palette, and see which one you like best.

Creating irregular text boxes

In addition to the four Text Box tools that allow you to create text boxes based on rectangles, QuarkXPress offers two tools — the Bézier Text Box tool and the Freehand Text Box tool — for creating irregular boxes that have straight or curved edges. You also have the option to convert any box shape into any other shape (explained in Chapter 11). Be careful, though — If you create a document full of irregularly shaped text boxes, the visual effect can at best be described as hodgepodge. In other words, don't make your document ugly just because you can, okay?

Figure 3-4 shows two text boxes created with the Bézier Text Box tool: A straight-edged box and a curved-edge box.

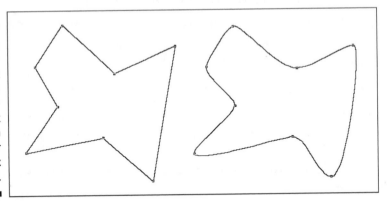

Figure 3-4:
A straight-edged box and a curved-edge box created with the Bézier Text Box tool.

Here's how to create a straight-edged (polygon) Bézier text box with the Bézier Text Box tool:

1. **Select the Bézier Text Box tool.**

2. **Click and release the mouse button to establish the first point of your box.**

3. **Move the mouse to where you want to establish the next point; then click and release the mouse button.**

4. **Continue to establish the points of your box by moving the mouse and then clicking and releasing the mouse button.**

5. **To close the box, click on the first point that you created. You can also close a box by double-clicking anywhere to create a final point.**

   When you double-click, a final point is created, and a final segment is automatically drawn back to the first point.

Here's how to create a curved-edged Bézier text box with the Bézier Text Box tool:

1. **Select the Bézier Text Box tool.**

2. **Hold down the mouse button as you drag the mouse in the direction of the next point; then release the mouse button.**

   You don't have to drag the mouse all the way to the next point; you can release the mouse button after you drag the mouse a short distance in the general direction. The first point, along with two control handles that indicate the curve slope, is established.

3. **Move the mouse to where you want to establish the next point, drag a short distance in the direction of the following point, and then release the mouse button.**

4. **Continue to establish the points of your box by moving the mouse and then clicking, dragging, and releasing the mouse button.**

5. **To close the box, click the first point that you created or double-click anywhere.**

   If you double-click, a final point is created, and a final segment is automatically drawn back to the first point.

Here's how to create a curved-edged Bézier text box with the Freehand Text Box tool:

1. **Select the Freehand Text Box tool.**

2. **Hold down the mouse button and then drag the mouse, using it like a pencil to create any shape you want.**

3. **To close the box, drag the crosshair mouse pointer back to the first point and release the mouse button.**

   You can also release the mouse button at any time to have QuarkXPress create the final segment by drawing a line from the current position of the crosshair mouse pointer to the point of origin.

Don't worry about getting your shape exactly right as you create it; you can always tweak it afterward. Also, you can create shapes that contain straight edges and curved edges by combining the techniques for creating straight-edged and curved Bézier boxes.

After you create a Bézier box, you can adjust it by clicking and dragging points and edges. Before you try to adjust a Bézier box, make sure that a check mark appears before the Edit⇨Shape command in the Item menu. (An easier shortcut is to use Shift+F4 on the Mac or F10 in Windows to switch between editing the box's shape and changing its dimensions or position.) If Edit⇨Shape is not checked, you can adjust the height and width of a Bézier box, but you can't move its points or edges. Here are a few things to keep in mind when you change the shape of a Bézier box:

✔ If Edit⇨Shape is checked when you click anywhere on or within a Bézier box, the entire box becomes active, and all points are displayed. You can then drag the point or segment that you want to move.

✔ To move multiple points at the same time, hold down the Shift key and click the points; then drag any of the selected points.

✔ If you pause a moment before dragging a point or segment, QuarkXPress redraws the contents of the box as you drag.

> ✔ To add new points, hold down the Option or Alt key and click a segment at the place where you want the point to appear.
>
> ✔ To delete a point, hold down the Option or Alt key and click on the point.

Bézier boxes can contain three kinds of points (corner points, smooth points, and symmetrical points) and two kinds of segments (curved and straight). You can change any kind of point or segment into any other kind. Chapter 11 explains how to change the shape of Bézier boxes by changing points and segments.

Making a box automatically

Howie is a desktop publisher. He likes to tinker with page layout to see exactly how everything works. He has no problem spending hours in front of the computer, getting all his layout ducks in a row, luxuriating in the depth and breadth of controls offered by QuarkXPress.

Pamela, on the other hand, is always rushed. In her job, she's responsible for producing two newsletters every week. She works at speed, collecting QuarkXPress shortcuts the way that some kids collect baseball cards.

Howie is perfectly comfortable with manually creating every text box that appears in his document. Pamela, who would be driven crazy by the very thought of such a time-consuming approach, has found a way to have QuarkXPress automatically and precisely create a text box for her on every page. She uses the program's Automatic Text Box feature each time she creates a new document.

Suppose that Pamela is going to create a two-page flyer, and she wants the text to appear on each page in two columns. She starts a new document (by choosing File⇨New⇨Document, or by pressing ⌘+N or Ctrl+N), which causes the New Document dialog box to appear (see Figure 3-5). In the Column Guides area, she specifies 2 columns. She also makes sure that the Automatic Text Box check box is checked.

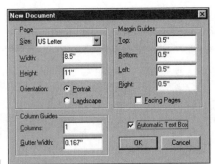

Figure 3-5:
The New
Document
dialog box.

That's all she has to do; QuarkXPress takes care o'
creating a two-column text box on each page of t'

When Automatic Text Box is checked, QuarkX'
new pages when text overflows an automatic te.
contains an automatic text box. (QuarkXPress does n
automatically if the Auto Page Insertion option in the Gene.
Default Document Preferences dialog box is set to None. To disp
dialog box, choose Edit⇨Preferences⇨Document, or press ⌘+Y or c.
you don't check Automatic Text Box, you need to draw text boxes and lin.
them manually with the Linking tool before you place text in them; to do so,
choose File⇨Get Text (or press ⌘+E or Ctrl+E). Manual linking is covered
later in this chapter in the section called "Linking and unlinking text boxes."

One nifty thing about choosing Automatic Text Box when you create a
document is that as text flows in from an external word processing program,
QuarkXPress automatically adds as many pages as necessary to accommodate the imported text. This feature is handy if you're creating long documents, such as catalogs and books.

Linking and unlinking text boxes

Automatic text boxes are great for creating multipage documents in which
text automatically flows from page to page. In other situations, however, text
must flow not from one page to the next page, but from one page to a
different, nonconsecutive page or from one box to another within a single
page. A newsletter layout, for example, may require a story that begins on
page 1 to finish on page 4. How do you make this *jump* (or "continued on"
instance) happen? You link the two boxes.

An easy way to remember linking in QuarkXPress is to think of text boxes as
being links in a chain, just like a metal chain that has links connected to
other links. The only difference is that in QuarkXPress, you are linking boxes
that hold text. Because you can't link a text box to another box that already
contains text, however, you need to do your linking before you fill the boxes
with text. Here's how you link empty text boxes:

1. **Open the document to the page that contains the first text box that
   you want to use in the linked chain of text boxes.**

2. **Click the Linking tool (the second tool from the bottom of the Tool
   palette; it looks like a piece of chain) to select it.**

3. **Position the mouse pointer anywhere inside the text box that will be
   the first box in the chain.**

   Notice that the mouse pointer changes to look like a chain link.

4. Click the mouse button.

Notice that the text box has a moving dashed line around it, which tells you that this box is the start of the link.

5. Go to the page that contains the text box that will be the next box in the chain.

To get to that page, choose Page⇨Go to (or press ⌘+J or Ctrl+J).

6. Position the mouse pointer in the next text box that you want to use in the chain; then click the mouse button.

The second text box is now linked to the first. If you enter or import into the first box more text than it can hold, the overflow text flows to the second box, even if the text boxes are separated by several pages. As text is entered/imported, it flows on to any other boxes in the text chain.

7. Repeat Steps 2 through 6 until all the text boxes that you want to use in the chain are linked.

How do you know whether two text boxes are linked? Simply activate either of the boxes; then select the Linking tool and look for the large gray arrow that indicates the flow of text from one text box to another. Figure 3-6 shows you what this linking arrow looks like.

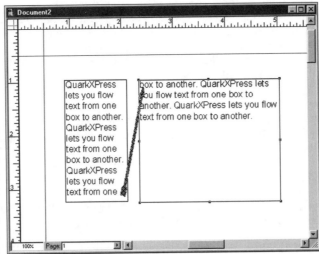

Figure 3-6:
The arrow shows that the two text boxes on the page are linked.

As nice as it is to link text boxes, being able to change your mind about how the text does or doesn't flow is also nice — meaning that you want to be able to unlink two or more linked text boxes. Here's how:

1. **Open the document to the page that contains the text box that you want to unlink from a chain.**

2. **Click the Unlinking tool (the bottommost tool in the Tool palette) to select it.**

3. **Position the mouse pointer in the text box, hold down the Shift key, and then click the mouse button.**

   This step unlinks the selected text box from the chain while retaining links between the preceding box in the chain and the following box in the chain. If you want to break the chain entirely, click the arrowhead on the top-left side of the box to break the link from the preceding box, or click the tailfeathers on the bottom-right corner of the box to break the link to the following box (in this case, don't hold down the Shift key).

4. **To unlink additional text boxes, repeat Steps 2 and 3.**

As you spend more time with QuarkXPress, you'll find that being able to link boxes and unlink boxes is very useful.

Building Boxes for Pictures, Too

If you know how to create text boxes, you've probably already made a thousand or two of them (or maybe just five or six). But when you look at a page with nothing but text boxes on it, you start to realize that it looks . . . well, kind of *boring*. What you need is a picture or two or ten.

Pictures, or graphics, do more than just add visual interest to a page. A well-designed graphic actually can convey more information than a block of text can convey. As the old saying goes, "A picture is worth a thousand words," and a photo, drawing, or chart truly can convey some very meaningful ideas.

Okay, you're convinced. It's time to start adding some pictures to the page, and you do this by creating picture boxes and filling them with pictures.

First, you need to select one of the seven picture-box tools in the Tool palette. The choices of picture-box tools are the same as those for text boxes: Rectangle, Rounded Corner, Beveled Corner, Concave Corner, Oval, Bézier, and Freehand.

Start with a simple, rectangular picture box by following these steps:

1. **Open the document to the page on which you want to draw the picture box.**

2. **Click the Rectangle Picture Box tool to select it.**

3. **Position the crosshair mouse pointer at the location where you want one of the corners of the picture box to appear.**

4. **Hold down the mouse button and drag the mouse to shape the picture box.**

5. **Release the mouse button to create the box.**

To draw a picture box that is perfectly square, hold down the Shift key as you draw the box. To create a perfect circle, use the Oval Picture Box tool and hold down the Shift key while dragging.

Setting picture-box specifications

Just as it does with text boxes, QuarkXPress allows you to be pretty darned picky about every part of a picture box. To establish a bunch of parameters for your picture box, use the five panes of the Modify dialog box for picture boxes. Figure 3-7 shows the Picture, Runaround, and Clipping panes (the Box and Frame panes, shown in Figure 3-3, are identical for text boxes and picture boxes). This dialog box enables you to size and position a picture box precisely, rotate it, scale it, skew (slant) it, and add color to its background. You also can use this dialog box to position or crop an image inside the picture box that holds it.

If you specify custom values in the Picture pane of the Modify dialog box before you import a graphic into it, the settings are applied to the imported graphic. But if, for some reason, you reimport the graphic (or any other) into the picture box, QuarkXPress ignores the custom settings and uses the default settings.

Changing the size and position of a picture box

After you draw a picture box, you can tweak it in many ways. The most common way is to use the Measurements palette, where you can change the size of the box by entering different W (width) and H (height) values, and you can change the position of the box by entering different X (vertical) and Y (horizontal) coordinates. You can make the same changes in a Bézier picture box, and when you activate an individual point (the "corners" connecting the sides of the Bézier bar) by clicking it, the Measurements palette lets you adjust the point and its control handles.

Actually, QuarkXPress gives you a rich selection of ways to change the size and position of a picture box:

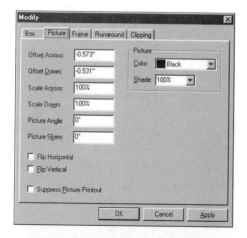

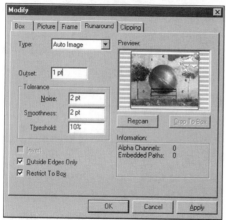

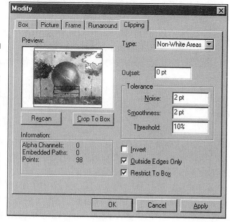

Figure 3-7:
The Modify
dialog box
for picture
boxes:
Picture,
Runaround,
and
Clipping
panes.

✔ **First way.** In the Box pane of the Modify dialog box (to display the dialog box, choose Item⇨Modify or press ⌘+M or Ctrl+M):

- Enter values in the Origin Across and Origin Down fields to control the position of the box.
- Enter values in the Width and Height fields to control the size of the picture box.
- Enter values in the Angle and Skew fields to rotate and slant the picture box, and so on.

To see the results of changed values, click the Apply button.

Although it works fine, we aren't enthusiastic about this method because the Modify dialog box takes up a great deal of space, which can make it difficult to see what's happening to the picture box as a result of the new values you're entering.

✔ **Second way.** In the Measurements palette

- Enter different values in the X and Y fields to position the picture box.
- Enter different values in the W and H fields to resize the box.
- Enter a different value in the Angle field to rotate the box.

Press Return or Enter to exit the palette and apply the new values.

This method is our favorite, because it lets you see the result of your work as it happens.

✔ **Third way.** Use the Item tool to drag the box into position. Use the same tool to grab the handles of the box to resize it.

Holding down ⌘+Option+ Shift or Ctrl+Alt+Shift as you resize a box causes both the box and the graphic to resize proportionately. Holding down just Option+ Shift or Alt+ Shift resizes the box proportionately without affecting the image. Holding down only the ⌘ or Ctrl key allows you to disproportionately resize both the box and the picture. If you hold down no modifier keys, you can disproportionately resize the box, but the picture's size is unaffected.

Creating odd shapes

On occasion, to add visual interest to a page, you may want to import a graphic into a nonrectangular picture box, such as an oval, a circle, a straight-edged polygon, or a curved shape. But as with irregular text boxes, we recommend that you keep the use of this trick to a minimum. More than that, we recommend that you *not* use irregular boxes unless you are using them for a well-reasoned and well-planned effect. Okay, okay, you've heard the lecture. Now exactly how *do* you create irregular picture boxes? Exactly the same way that you create irregular text boxes:

✔ The Rounded-Corner, Beveled-Corner, and Concave-Corner Picture Box tools provide alternatives to square-cornered boxes, and the Oval Picture Box tool allows you to create both ovals and a perfect circle (by holding down the Shift key as you drag).

✔ With the Bézier Picture Box tool, you can create straight-edged boxes, curved-edge boxes, and boxes that have both straight and curved edges.

✔ The Freehand Picture Box tool lets you create Bézier boxes by using the mouse as a freehand drawing tool.

Pouring in the picture

With an empty text box, you have the option to import text or to type it yourself. The only way to fill an empty picture box, however, is to import a picture. After you draw a picture box, you're ready to fill it with a picture. Here are the steps that you follow:

1. **Open the document to the page that holds the picture box that you want to fill with a picture; then click the picture box to activate it.**

2. **If it's not the selected tool, click the Content tool.**

3. **Choose File⇨Get Picture (or press ⌘+E or Ctrl+E).**

   You see the Get Picture dialog box.

4. **Locate the graphic file that you want to bring into the picture box.**

5. **Select the file and then double-click the file or click OK.**

   The graphic appears in the picture box.

When the picture box is filled with the imported graphic, chances are good that you'll want some changes made so that the graphic fits the picture box. Use the Content tool to move a picture within a box. Here are some pointers for moving or changing the size of a graphic:

✔ To center the graphic in the picture box, press Shift+⌘+F or Ctrl+Shift+M.

✔ To fit the graphic to the box's dimensions, press Shift+⌘+F or Ctrl+Shift+F. (Notice that this action distorts the graphic, if necessary, to fit it into the shape of the picture box.)

✔ To fit the graphic to the box while maintaining the proportion between the width and height of the graphic (or its *aspect ratio*), press Option+Shift+⌘+F or Ctrl+Shift+Alt+F. When you use this command, QuarkXPress fits the graphic as best it can but leaves white space in areas of the picture box that are not covered by the graphic.

In addition to importing pictures into picture boxes, you can copy a picture from one box and paste it into another. You can also copy a picture onto the Clipboard from an image-editing or illustration program, switch to QuarkXPress, and paste the picture into a picture box. You should avoid using this method, however, because the original image file is not used when the document is printed.

Using Tricky Layout Effects

No self-respecting desktop publisher would be caught without a bag of layout tricks. You could say that tricks are as necessary to a desktop publisher as flies to a frog, slop to a hog, or biscuits to a dog. What we are trying to say is that it's definitely worth your while to learn how to create some tricky effects with text and picture boxes.

Running around

One feature of QuarkXPress that distinguished it from its various competitors early on is its flexible runaround capability. A *runaround* is an area in a page's layout where you don't want text to flow. You may want text to run around the edges of a picture box or the edges of the picture within the box, for example, so that the text won't run through the box or picture. Text runaround enables text to flow around an item, wrapping the text around the item's contours.

A text runaround occurs when an item is placed in front of a text box that contains text. Therefore, depending on the order in which you created the items that you want to include in a text runaround, you may have to adjust the stacking order, or layering, of the items. (See Chapter 11 for more information about adjusting the stacking order of items.)

To specify how text runaround works, you use the Runaround pane of the Modify dialog box. To display this pane, select the box, line, or text path that you want text to run around; choose Item⇨Modify (or ⌘+M or Ctrl+M) to display the Modify dialog box; and then click the Runaround tab. Alternatively, choose Item⇨Runaround (or press ⌘+T or Ctrl+T). You see the Runaround pane of the Modify dialog box for text boxes and picture boxes in Figure 3-8.

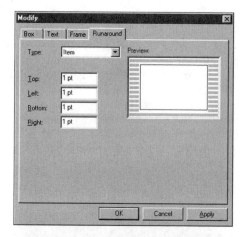

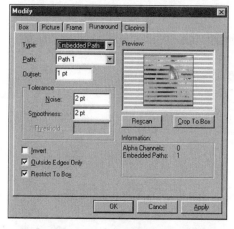

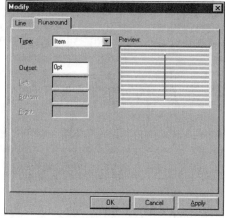

Figure 3-8:
The
Runaround
pane of the
Modify
dialog box
for text
boxes,
picture
boxes, and
lines.

QuarkXPress gives you two runaround options for text boxes, three options for lines and text paths, and several options for picture boxes. You choose an option by selecting it in the Type list in the Runaround pane of the Modify dialog box. When you choose an option, the Preview window indicates how the text will flow. Here are the choices for text boxes and boxes with no content:

✔ **None.** When you choose this option, QuarkXPress flows the text behind the active box as though no item appeared there. Figure 3-9 shows the overprinting of text that occurs when you choose None for a text box.

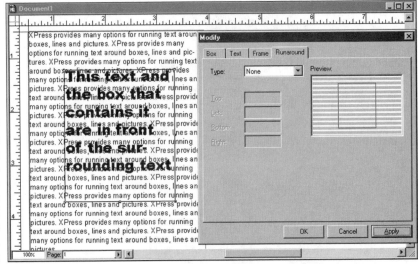

Figure 3-9:
Selecting None as the Type for a text-box runaround creates this overprint.

✔ **Item.** Figure 3-10 shows the effect of Item runaround. Notice that you can determine how far away from the box the text will flow by entering values in the Top, Left, Bottom, and Right fields of the Runaround pane. In the figure, we set this amount as 6 points.

Here are the choices for lines and text paths:

✔ **None.** Flows the text behind the active line or text path.

✔ **Item.** Flows text around the active line or text path. Note that if the active item is a text path, the runaround text behind is not affected by the text on the path — only by the path itself. As a result, the text on the path can overlap and obscure the text that's behind.

✔ **Manual.** Flows text around the image as it does when you choose Item. Enter a value in the Outset field to specify the distance between the line or text path and the runaround text.

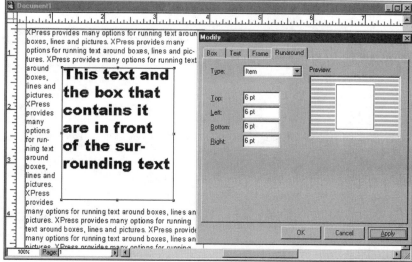

Figure 3-10:
An example
of Item
runaround
for a text
box.

If you choose Manual, QuarkXPress creates an editable shape, called a *runaround path*, around the active line or text path. If you activate the line or text path, you can edit the runaround by choosing Item⇨Edit⇨Runaround (or pressing Option+F4 or Ctrl+F10) and then dragging points, control handles, and segments.

Here are the choices for picture boxes:

- ✔ **None.** Flows the text behind the active picture box and picture.

- ✔ **Item.** Flows text around the active box.

- ✔ **Auto Image.** Creates a runaround path around the image within the box and flows text around the runaround path. Figure 3-11 shows an Auto Image runaround.

- ✔ **Embedded Path.** Creates a runaround path based on a picture-embedded path drawn in Adobe Photoshop and runs text around this path.

- ✔ **Alpha Channel.** Creates a runaround path based on an alpha channel built into a TIFF image by a photo-editing application and runs text around this path. (An *alpha channel* is an invisible grayscale picture used to edit the image to which it is attached.)

- ✔ **Non-White Areas.** Creates a runaround path based on the picture's contrast. If you choose Non-White Areas, the Outset and Tolerance controls allow you to customize the runaround path.

- ✔ **Same as Clipping.** Runs text around the clipping path specified in the Clipping pane of the Modify dialog box. (A clipping path is a shape created in an image-editing program that isolates a portion of a picture.)

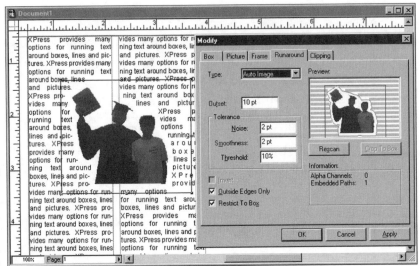

Figure 3-11:
An example
of Auto
Image
runaround.

✔ **Picture Bounds.** Creates a runaround path based on the rectangular shape of the imported graphic. The runaround area includes the white background of the original picture file.

The Outset, Tolerance, and Invert options require a knowledge of sophisticated image-editing techniques, so we don't cover them here. (If you use these options, watch how the preview window shows the effects of your settings.)

The Outside Edges Only option should normally be checked because it prevents text from getting inside a shape's interior gaps (for example, inside the hollow part of a doughnut shape).

Restrict to Box should also normally be checked; if unchecked, your text would wrap around any part of the image cropped by the box. (In other words, if your picture is larger than the picture box containing it, the part visible in the box is the cropped portion. The rest of the picture still exists but won't display or print. If Restrict to Box is not checked, QuarkXPress assumes you want the text to wrap around the entire picture, not just the part visible in the picture box. Although at times you may want such a "ghost wrap," those times are rare.)

If you run text around an item that's placed in front of a single column of text, by default QuarkXPress runs text on only one side of the item — whichever side can hold more text. If you want the text to run around both sides of an obstructing item, you must select the box that contains the runaround text, display the Text pane of the Modify dialog box (choose Item⇨Modify, or press ⌘+M or Ctrl+M), and check the Run Text Around All Sides check box.

Rotating boxes

You can rotate both text boxes and picture boxes in QuarkXPress. If used well, rotated boxes can add additional spark to the appearance of a page. Again, as with the other tricks in your layout bag, use rotation sparingly for best results.

Figure 3-12 contains a text box that was duplicated twice. One of the copies was rotated 45 degrees; the other, 90 degrees.

You can control the rotation of text boxes, picture boxes, or no-content boxes in three ways:

✔ **Option 1.** Select the box and choose Item➪Modify (or press ⌘+M or Ctrl+M) to display the Modify dialog box. If necessary, click the Box tab; then enter a rotation amount between 360 (degrees) and –360 in the Angle field.

To rotate the box clockwise, use a negative value in the Angle field; to rotate the box counterclockwise, use a positive value in the Angle field.

✔ **Option 2.** Select the box and then click the Rotation tool in the Tool palette to select it. Position the mouse pointer at the point around which you want to rotate the box (click the center of the box if you want to rotate it around its center, for example); then hold down the mouse button and move the mouse pointer away from the point where you clicked. Continue to hold down the mouse button as you drag in a circular direction — clockwise or counterclockwise.

✔ **Option 3.** Enter a rotation value in the Angle box of the Measurements palette.

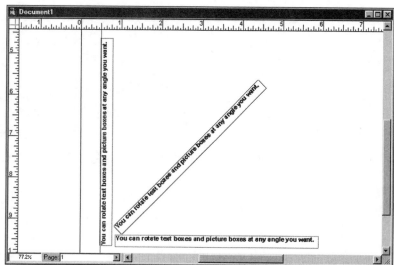

Figure 3-12:
Rotated text boxes are useful for such things as photo and illustration credit lines, product packaging, and coupons.

There's no single, correct way to rotate boxes. Experiment with all three options to see which method is most comfortable for you.

To rotate boxes, do the following steps:

1. **Open the document to the page that holds the text box or picture box that you want to slant.**

2. **Click the box to make it active.**

3. **Choose Item⇨Modify (or press ⌘+M or Ctrl+M) to display the Modify dialog box.**

4. **If not already selected, click the Box tab to select it.**

5. **In the Skew field, enter a value between 75 and –75.**

   A positive number slants the box to the right; a negative number slants the box to the left.

If you apply a skew value to a box, any text or picture within the box is also slanted. You can also specify a skew value for the contents of the box — text or picture — by displaying the Text or Picture pane of the Modify dialog box and entering a value between 75 and –75 in the Text Skew or Picture Skew field. Figure 3-13 shows a slanted text box.

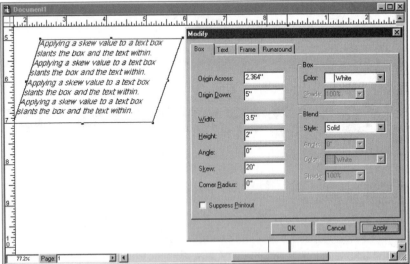

Figure 3-13:
The slanted text box in this example was achieved by entering a value of 20 in the Skew field in the Box pane of the Modify dialog box.

Anchoring boxes within text

In the old days of publishing — maybe ten years ago — graphic designers used wax or spray mount and a rubber roller to adhere galleys of text and halftones to paste-up boards. QuarkXPress not only frees you from such manual drudgery, but also allows you to do something that wasn't possible before the advent of electronic publishing. You have the option to anchor picture boxes and text boxes, as well as lines and text paths, within text so that the boxes move with the text if editing causes the text to reflow. This feature is great if, for example, you create catalogs that contain product pictures. You can paste a picture box within each product description. If the text is subsequently edited, you don't have to worry about having to reposition all the pictures, because the pictures have been anchored within the text.

Anchoring an item within text isn't difficult, but it requires a sequence of actions — including switching tools — that's a little bit tricky. Here's how you anchor a box:

1. **If it's not already selected, click the Item tool.**

2. **Click the box that you want to anchor within text.**

3. **Choose Edit⇨Copy (or press ⌘+C or Ctrl+C).**

   You can also choose Edit⇨Cut (or press ⌘+X or Ctrl+X). You won't need the original box after you anchor it, so in the long run, cutting it probably is easier.

4. **Click the Content tool to select text.**

5. **Click within a text box at the point in the text where you want to paste the copied/cut box.**

6. **Choose Edit⇨Paste (or press ⌘+V or Ctrl+V).**

You can anchor any box, including Bézier boxes and boxes that have been rotated or skewed. After you anchor a box within text, you can modify the contents of the box the same way that you modify the contents of an unanchored box. One thing that you can't do, however, is move an anchored box with the Item tool, because QuarkXPress treats an anchored box much the same as it treats a character within text. To delete an anchored box, click to its right with the Content tool to place the cursor next to it; then press Backspace or Delete. You can also delete an anchored box by highlighting it as you would a text character and then pressing Backspace or Delete.

If you click an anchored box, a pair of small icons appears on the left edge of the Measurements palette. If you click the top button (Align with Text Ascent), the top of an anchored box aligns with the top of the characters on the line that contains it; if you click the bottom button (Align with Text Baseline), the bottom of an anchored box aligns with the baseline of the line that contains it. The Box pane of the Measurements palette also allows you to specify the alignment of an anchored box, and it offers an Offset box that allows you to adjust the position of baseline-aligned anchored boxes.

A few pitfalls are involved with anchoring boxes within text. Here are some things to look out for:

- ✔ If the item that you're anchoring is wider than the column you're pasting it into, the item won't fit. When you paste, you create a text overflow. To avoid this problem, make sure that the item you're anchoring is narrower than the column that will contain it.

- ✔ If the item that you're anchoring is taller than the leading of the paragraph that you paste it into, the anchored item can cause uneven leading or obscure some of the surrounding text.

- ✔ If you want to anchor a box that's taller than the leading of the paragraph that will contain it, the safest practice is to anchor the box at the beginning of the paragraph (that is, make the anchored box the first character of the paragraph).

- ✔ You cannot anchor a group of items.

In Figure 3-14, the picture boxes in the left and right margins have been anchored in a two-column text box. The anchored box in the left column is a simple rectangle. The box was pasted at the beginning of the paragraph; the top of the box is aligned with the top of the first line. The anchored box on the right is aligned with the baseline of the first line of a paragraph. The box was rotated and slanted before it was anchored (although you can apply rotation and skew to a box after you anchor it, too).

QuarkXPress now allows you to anchor lines into text; anchoring lines work just like anchoring boxes.

Figure 3-14: Anchored boxes, like the pair of picture boxes in this example, flow with text. The anchored boxes were created from the originals in the margins.

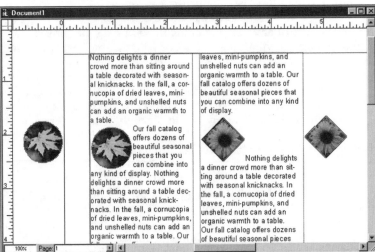

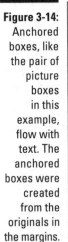

Chapter 4
A Picture Is Worth...

*O*kay, we admit it: Many documents don't need graphics. But any document that you would go to the trouble of laying out probably does. The graphic may be as simple as a logo or as complex as a series of annotated photos. When all is said and done, graphics are instrumental parts of publications, and you'll be using them in your layouts. How do you get those graphics ready for use in QuarkXPress, and how do you fine-tune them after you place them in your layout? That's what this chapter's all about.

A Tale of Two Graphic Formats: Vector and Raster

Graphics come in two basic formats: vector and raster, better known as drawing and bitmap. A *vector graphic* is made up of objects, such as lines and circles. A *raster graphic* is made up of a series of dots, as is a photo in a newspaper. Don't confuse the type of graphic format with the kind of program that created it. Adobe Photoshop, for example, saves graphic files as bitmaps, even though it has tools for adding lines and circles; Photoshop converts those lines and circles to a series of dots as soon as you draw them.

To keep *raster* and *vector* straight, just remember what you use each format for. Typically, you use raster graphics for photos, scanned images, and painted images, whereas vector graphics best serve you in drawn or illustrated images. Enlarging a raster image makes each dot bigger and the overall image coarser (as when you put a magnifying glass over a newspaper photo); enlarging a drawing, though, just makes the drawing bigger (without looking grainy or coarse). Why? The answer rests entirely in the physical makeup of rasters and vectors. Remember that a raster image is composed only of those dots — and that bunch of dots is *all* you have to work with. But a vector image is composed of instructions like "Okay, Doc, now draw a line so thick from here to there and make it red." When you enlarge that image, the instruction just changes things like the definitions of "here," "there," and "so thick."

Pick a Format, Any Format

Preparing graphics is not hard; in many cases, you can just load them directly into your QuarkXPress document. But sometimes you need to do some preparation work. QuarkXPress was designed to handle a slew of graphics types, including some that you may never have heard of. Go through the following laundry list:

- **BMP (Windows Bitmap).** The bitmap format introduced with Windows is popular for lower-end programs, such as Microsoft Publisher. On a PC, look for the extensions .BMP and .DIB.

- **CT (Continuous Tone).** A variant of TIFF, continuous tone is created by high-end photo-retouching systems, such as Scitex. On a PC, look for the extension .CT or .SCT.

- **DCS (Document Color Separation).** This variant of EPS includes color-separation files, so it's actually five files: one for each of the four publishing colors (cyan, magenta, yellow, and black — known as the CMYK color system), plus a file that contains a preview image and instructions on how to combine the four color files. On a PC, look for the extensions .EPS and .DCS. (DCS Version 2.0 can have more than the four standard publishing colors, so you could find more than five component files.)

- **EPS (Encapsulated PostScript).** EPS is the publishing standard for drawings created by programs such as Adobe Illustrator, Macromedia FreeHand, and CorelDRAW. Except for Illustrator, you need to export files to this format from the drawing program's native format (Illustrator's native format *is* EPS). On a PC, look for the extensions .EPS and .AI.

- ✔ **GIF (Graphics Interchange Format).** This bitmap format, developed for the CompuServe online service, can be imported only by the Windows version of QuarkXPress. Look for the extension .GIF.

- ✔ **JPEG (Joint Photographers Expert Group).** This bitmap format uses file compression to make large files of photos and other scanned images into files of reasonable size. The trade-off is that the compression can make the image lose some detail. If you want to import JPEG files, make sure that the JPEG Import filter is in your XTension folder. On a PC, look for the extension .JPG. See Chapter 9 for more about XTensions.

- ✔ **MacPaint.** This bitmap format supports only black and white, which means that it's pretty much a goner in today's color marketplace. QuarkXPress for Windows does not support this format.

- ✔ **PCX (PC Paintbrush).** This bitmap format is the reigning bitmap format on PCs; it even predates Windows. High-end users junked it for TIFF because only recently did PCX add support for high-color (16-bit and 24-bit) images. If you're using the Macintosh version of QuarkXPress, make sure that the PCX Import filter is in your XTension folder. On a PC, look for the .PCX extension.

- ✔ **Photo CD.** This format was developed by Eastman Kodak for its corporate attempt to move consumers from film to CD for picture processing. That gambit didn't work, but it did create a standard for photo libraries that is rapidly taking over the publishing industry as the medium for storing stock photos. If you want to import Photo CD files, make sure that the Photo CD Import filter is in your XTension folder. On a PC, look for the extension .PCD.

- ✔ **PICT (Picture).** This Mac format is actually two formats: a drawing format and a bitmap format. In both cases, QuarkXPress imports the format. On a PC, look for the extension .PCT.

- ✔ **RLE (Run-Length Encoded).** The bitmap format used by OS/2 is a variant of BMP. On a PC, look for the extension .RLE.

- ✔ **TIFF (Tagged Image File Format).** Probably the most popular bitmap format for designers on the Mac (and fairly popular on the PC, too), this format is the standard for many scanners and photo-editing programs, because it supports 24-bit images (with millions of colors). PC TIFF and Mac TIFF are slightly different, but QuarkXPress reads them both. On a PC, look for the extension .TIF. For Macintosh users, the LZW Import filter must be in your XTension folder if you want to import LZW-compressed TIFF graphics. For QuarkXPress for Windows, the lzwXT filter must be installed.

- ✔ **Windows Metafile.** This drawing format is similar to the Mac's PICT, in that it is the native format for the operating system. On a PC, look for the extension .WMF.

If you've tried to import any of the preceding formats, only to have QuarkXPress refuse do so, QuarkXPress probably thumbed its nose at you for one of two reasons. One possible explanation is embarrassingly obvious: The file may not be in the format that you think it's in (or it may be corrupt). The other explanation isn't so obvious: The right import filter may not be installed in your XTension folder for QuarkXPress to handle that file type. Filters for several popular file formats are installed automatically when you install QuarkXPress, but others are not.

If you're not accustomed to using any of these formats, don't sweat it. You can probably convert whatever formats you've been using to a format that QuarkXPress can handle. If you're doing your illustration work in Freehand or CorelDraw, for example, you'll find that these programs can save or export in one or more of the listed formats.

Even though QuarkXPress supports all these formats, we recommend that you stick to just two formats for your graphics — TIFF and EPS (including DCS) — because they offer the most flexibility and/or the best output. Runners-up are PCX, Photo CD, PICT, and Windows Metafile. As for the rest, use them if you have them, but ask your artists (or the person who buys your clip art and stock photos) to get the images in one of the formats that we recommend.

Why only these few formats? QuarkXPress offers a slew of controls for TIFF (see Chapter 12 for details) that it doesn't provide for other bitmap formats. EPS provides the best-quality output, allows you to embed fonts, and supports color separations better than any other drawing format. EPS's only down side is that it requires a PostScript printer, which many Windows users may not have (the PCL printer format is popular in Windows). PCX, PICT, and Windows Metafile are good second choices because they are so popular, but their formats don't offer the same capabilities for high-end output that TIFF and EPS do. Photo CD is fast becoming the standard format for stock photos — it's the photographic equivalent of clip art — so you'll likely have many images in this format to work with.

Get Those Files in Shape

The more complex the graphics format, the more choices you need to make when creating images in it. If many of these options seem to be way over your head, stifle your impulse to panic; creating graphic files isn't as complex as it seems to be at first. If our terms ring no bells for you, you probably just haven't yet created graphics using a program with features that give you all these choices. But do check out these options, and even if you don't know what they mean, try to implement them (or tell the artist who provides your graphics what we recommend).

The many shades of TIFF

TIFF comes in black and white, in grayscale, in indexed color, in RGB color, and in CMYK color. You can have LZW compression, Packbits compression, or no compression. You can save the alpha channel or ditch it. You can save in Mac byte order or PC byte order. Is that too many choices or what?

Don't worry if you don't understand these choices. We tell you what to do when you need to choose them. Here are some surefire tricks that you can use to simplify TIFF:

- ✔ **If your output will be color-separated, save in CMYK (cyan, magenta, yellow, and black; the colors used in process color printing) color.** If you import an RGB TIFF into QuarkXPress, you can separate it into CMYK colors when you print color separations — but only if you have activated Quark's color management software (make sure the Quark CMS XTension is installed, and make sure color management is turned on via Edit⇨Preferences⇨Color Management). If your output will be black and white, save in gray scale for photographic images and in black and white for images that have only black or white (no shades of gray).

- ✔ **Use LZW compression or no compression.** Sometimes, an image displays incorrectly in QuarkXPress if you save it with LZW compression. An incorrect display means that an error occurred in the TIFF file and that you need to regenerate the TIFF file. If regenerating the file still doesn't work, just save it uncompressed. Don't use other forms of compression that may be available in your image-editing software. Macintosh users: make sure that the LZW Import filter is in your XTension folder if you want to import LZW-compressed TIFFs; for Windows users, this filter is called lzwXT.

- ✔ **Save the alpha channel for 24-bit images.** In this case, an alpha channel helps guarantee accurate color reproduction for the finer colors. Many programs don't give you the option not to save the alpha channel.

- ✔ **Use the byte order for the system in which you're using the file,** even though QuarkXPress can handle both PC and Mac byte orders. The reason for you to pay attention is that other programs aren't as forgiving, so why create a possible problem? If a program can't handle the byte order of a different platform, the image looks like a photographic negative. If that situation ever occurs in QuarkXPress, you can use the Style⇨Negative command or Shift+⌘+- or Ctrl+Shift+- on the image to make it right again.

EPS options galore

Encapsulated PostScript files can be complex because so many things can go into them. To keep the EPS universe simple and manageable, follow these hints for every EPS file that you get:

✔ If the file is in color, make sure that all the colors in it were defined with the same color model (CMYK or RGB). In some cases, you have one of those two models plus a spot color: Pantone, Trumatch, or some other special color library. If you can, have the drawing program translate those spot colors to either CMYK or RGB; use CMYK if you will output to an imagesetter. Keep spot colors in their original format only if you plan to print those colors on their own plates. Also, if you're not using (or your drawing program doesn't support) CMYK colors, it's best to name your colors when you create them. That way, they appear in QuarkXPress's list of colors, from which you can apply them to other objects or decide whether to color-separate them. (For details on color, see Chapter 15.)

✔ If the file includes text, either have the program embed the fonts inside the drawing or convert the text to curves (if the program has an option to do so; programs such as FreeHand, Illustrator, and CorelDraw do). Either option ensures that the fonts print correctly on your printer. If you can't use either option, make sure that your computer has the same fonts that you'll print the QuarkXPress layouts from.

✔ If you have a choice for the EPS preview format, choose TIFF. The preview is what you see onscreen when you import the file into QuarkXPress; it's an electronic snapshot of what the instructions in the EPS file will create during printing. Windows and Mac programs usually use different preview formats, so you may get a gray rectangle on-screen in QuarkXPress when you import an EPS file created on one platform but used on the other. The image still prints. But if you can ensure that QuarkXPress will have the preview in a format that it definitely supports (such as TIFF), go ahead and do so.

✔ If you use the DCS version of EPS, make sure that all five files are in the same folder or directory as the master file (the file that you actually load into QuarkXPress). Typically, these files end in .C, .M, .Y, and .K (yes, that spells CMYK!) or a similar scheme that uses those letters to identify the color-separated components. (Some DCS files have more than five files if they use colors in addition to the CMYK basics.)

Photo CD enabled

The Photo CD format uses compression to keep its file a manageable size, which means that you need decompression software (in addition to the QuarkXPress Photo CD import filter) to read those files into QuarkXPress.

If you plan to use Photo CD images, you should be aware of the following platform-specific requirements:

✔ On a Mac, make sure that QuickTime and Apple Photo Access are installed in the Extensions folder inside the System Folder. Both come with the Mac OS in versions 7.5 and later.

✔ On a PC, make sure that PCDLIB.DLL or PCDLIB32.DLL is installed in either the WINDOWS\SYSTEM directory or the XPRESS\XTENSION directory. Windows 95 and NT 4 come with the necessary files, as do QuarkXPress for Windows and other programs, which is why you may find the Photo CD files in several places.

On a Mac, Photo CD files often come in several resolutions. Pick the resolution that you need — nothing finer. The finer the resolution (that is, the bigger the number), the bigger the file, the slower the print time, and the slower the screen-redraw time. You can usually select the 768-by-512 or 192-by-128 resolutions unless your photos will take more than a third of a page or so.

What to Look for in Acquiring Graphics

Treating graphics as an afterthought is easy to do because they're separate elements in your document that are often supplied by someone else. But you need to spend as much time selecting your graphics as you do on anything else. Good graphics are vital components of an excellent layout, and bad graphics — even only one — can make an otherwise nice design look, well, bad.

Keep in mind that taste is a personal issue, and you won't find any clear-cut standard of right or wrong that makes your graphics decisions for you. But, just as is true for layout design and typography, you have to follow some basic principles to ensure that you choose good graphics.

✔ **Professional art is well-composed.** The size, position, and perspective fit the image. An image should look off — such as having part of the image cropped off or being at an odd angle — only if the intent is to look different — jarring, weird, distorted, avant garde. In most cases, the subject should be the main element of attention (near the center and not dwarfed by other elements) and should be fully visible.

✔ **Professional art requires clean lines, sufficient white space (areas not filled with objects), and attention to detail.** Again, if the intent is to be jarring or highly stylized (as in a cartoon), an artist breaks these rules. But even in stylized art, you can tell something that's a mishmash (random stuff everywhere), that's crude (more like a kid's drawing that the parents wouldn't post on the refrigerator), or that's sloppy (pieces of elements obviously missing or awkwardly put together) from something that's energetic (many elements to look at) and well thought out.

✔ **Professional art fits the overall image of the publication it's in.** *Rolling Stone* magazine uses a range of adventuresome styles that wouldn't work in *Macworld* or *Architectural Digest*. *Macworld* uses a refined, stylized, and fun look that wouldn't work in *Rolling Stone* or *Architectural Digest*. *Architectural Digest* uses classic, clean, rich styles that wouldn't work in *Rolling Stone* or *Macworld*. You get the drift.

✔ **Professional art conveys its message clearly.** The more messages crammed into the art, the harder the art is to understand and the less the art will support the text that it is paired with. Think about driving down a commercial street and looking at storefronts. If 58 signs clutter up one store window, you lose track of what kind of store it is or what's on sale, and you keep looking for a store that clearly labels what's inside or what's on sale.

No matter what style you want your publication to have, make sure you think of art in concert with the typography, layout, and words in your publication. They all need to work together, reinforcing both your basic image and the basic content in the publication.

Good art can come from almost anywhere. If you have a staff or contract artist or photographer (or both), that's one source. But most people have to rely on supplied images, including clip art, photo houses (places that keep libraries of photographs and charge you a fee to republish them), and scanned-in images. We talk more about art in Part III.

When it's time to select art, you have to work with what's available, and the variety can be overwhelming. Styles can range from simple sketches to elaborate full-color renderings. To give you an idea of what you may find, Figure 4-1 shows 12 different clip art images from a variety of sources. As you can see, some of the images look very rough — the chicken at the upper-left corner is a good example — and these rougher images look like something you picked up from a clip art book. (That's *not* a compliment!) Such images can look cheap, and that impression of cheapness reflects on your publication. Other clip art images look polished, though — which also reflects on your publication.

No matter where you get your images, look for TIFF or Photo CD formats if you're printing to an imagesetter or commercial printer. Programs like QuarkXPress will reliably print color from images in these two formats.

Avoiding collection overkill

You can find disks and CDs full of clip art and stock photos from many sources. (A stock photo is not a picture of a barnyard animal — it's actually an image that a photo house has on stock for rental to publications; the photographic version of clip art.) Just look in the back of your favorite computer magazine (like *Macworld* or *PC World*) or at your favorite software dealer. Mail-order catalogs often include stock photos, and more and more art and publishing programs include sample images.

Figure 4-1:
A sampler
of clip art
shows the
variety of
styles and
subjects
available.

When you shop for clip art and photo collections, be careful. You don't have to worry about poor quality — the materials are usually fine. What you do have to worry about is buying materials you won't use. For example, Corel Corp. (613-728-3733) offers dozens of CDs with 100 photos on each in its Professional Photos series. The $50 CDs are organized thematically — such as Tigers, France, Paris, and Northern California. We've checked out a few of these CDs, and the images are nice-looking and of good quality. But who needs 100 pictures of tigers? For the collections of photos of countries or regions, just what are the chances that you'll find the picture you want of, say, Roman ruins in southern France from the France CD? Not great. Maybe there's one picture, but it doesn't quite have the look you want — that's typical. Getting 100 photos or pieces of clip art for $50 or $25 may seem to be a great deal, but chances are you won't use anywhere near the whole lot of them.

We don't mean to pick on Corel — this problem exists with almost every clip art and stock photo collection, including the ClickArt, 3G Graphics, Metro ImageBase, PicturePak, and other clip-art collections featured in many mail-order catalogs. However, if you use, say, just five images in a 100-image, $50 CD, that's only $10 each, which is still a good deal. Just realize that one of these CDs or disk collections with tons of images probably will just scratch the surface of your needs, and if you rely on clip art and stock photos, you can expect to pay hundreds of dollars to build a versatile collection from a variety of titles to suit your needs.

But we don't want you to think that no photo collection is worth having. One worthwhile collection is the Visual Symbols Sampler from CMCD, which uses renowned photographer Clement Mok's works. This CD is bundled free with Apple's PhotoFlash 2.0 image management and touch-up software. (This software is for Macs only, although the symbols CD can be used by both Macs and PCs. PhotoDisc sells CMCD's works plus their own; you can reach them at 206-441-9355 or http://www.photodisc.com.) Artville offers collections of cartoons and illustrations, as well as photos; you can reach them at 608-243-1215 or at http://www.artville.com.

What makes programs like the CMCD Symbols Sampler so useful? The photographed symbols are basic enough that you can use them as part of other artwork, which is the secret to widespread use: images that can be integrated with other art and thus appear fresh even when used in more than one place. As you can see in the sample images in Figure 4-2, the photos all have stark backgrounds that are easy to crop out in Adobe Photoshop or any other image-editing program (one that can handle the Photo CD format, of course).

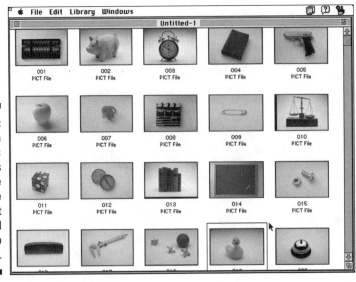

Figure 4-2:
A collection of basic symbols is more versatile than most clip art and stock photo collections.

In addition to CD and disk collections, you can get stock photos from stock photo houses, which are companies that keep huge inventories of photos, such as the Bettman Archives. Note that these companies charge for each use of an image: If you use an image three times, you pay for it three times. That holds true even if you alter the image or combine it with other images. Make sure that you know what the usage rules and costs are before you publish any images from a photo house. Also, see if the photo house offers the image in electronic format, such as TIFF, to save you the effort of scanning in the photo from a print.

Checking out online services

You also can find clip art and stock photos — both single images and collections — on online services and bulletin board services (BBSs). The quality of these photos varies widely, of course, based on the skills of their creators.

Some of the images are offered as shareware — if you like the images, you send in a fee; if you don't, you don't. Others are available as freeware — a gift from someone who needs to share their talents with the world. Whether you frequent CompuServe, America Online, or some other service, look in forums devoted to desktop publishing and art. Each service has an index of forums available.

The Desktop Publishing Forum on CompuServe (access it by typing GO DTPFORUM) is a great forum for all sorts of publishing utilities, fonts, and artwork. This forum is our favorite place to find Quark- and publishing-related files. America Online also has a publishing forum (GO DTP) that has a decent collection of fonts (in the Font Petting Zoo) and graphics (in the software library).

Scanning in photos and images

A treasure trove of images can be found in the photos you and your friends have taken. Vacation pictures, pictures of buildings or monuments, pictures of friends (perhaps at a picnic or at work), pictures of a job site — all may depict what you want to illustrate in your publication.

If you use a picture of a person for publication, though, make sure that you get permission first. Although you don't need to do so for pictures of crowds, you must extend this courtesy when a person (or several people) is the clear focus of the image. After all, how would you feel if you were perusing a magazine and unexpectedly saw a picture of yourself?

If you have a scanner, you can convert photos to TIFF files and import them into QuarkXPress. We describe how you can do this later in this chapter.

Unless you're producing mass-market magazines like *Macworld,* which need professional photographers and high-end scanners, you will find that a decent flat-bed scanner and a decent 4-inch by 6-inch color print can easily meet your needs. With a good flat-bed scanner starting at just $170, it's a must-have investment (check out Umax Technologies' scanners first, since they're usually very well rated).

Don't scan in images or drawings published elsewhere — that's theft of copyright. To steer clear of copyright infringements, the images you print need to fall into one of three categories:

- ✔ **Original.** Created by you or someone you employ. Note that a freelancer doesn't count as an employee; the "someone you employ" has to be someone on staff (on payroll), which legally makes the art a "work for hire" — legal-speak for "I pay your salary, so I own your work."

- ✔ **Publicly available.** Old enough that the copyright has expired (usually 75 years after it was created or 50 years after the creator has died), or created by an agency of the federal government (such as NASA's space photos — we paid for them, so we can use them).

- ✔ **Licensed (a.k.a. commissioned).** Sold to you either for one-time use (such as from a stock photo house or freelance artist) or for unlimited use (such as from a stock photo or clip art collection). If someone offers you free use, get it in writing in case there's a dispute later.

An advantage to scanning in images, whether photos or art, is that you then can edit or modify the scanned-in images with an image-editing tool like Adobe Photoshop, Fractal Design Painter, or (on Windows only) Corel PHOTO-PAINT. For example, you can take a color photograph or pencil sketch, convert it to gray scale, and then use color to highlight certain elements. Or you can make a collage from several images.

Bringing in Graphics

All *right* already! Enough background! It's time to get to the heart of the matter: placing graphics in your layout. In Chapter 3, you see how to create the boxes that contain text and graphics. Now you're ready put those boxes to use.

Here are the steps that you need to follow to successfully and easily bring graphics into your QuarkXPress layout:

1. Select the Content tool or the Item tool.

2. Select the box that you want to place the graphic in.

3. Choose File⇨Get Picture (or press ⌘+E or Ctrl+E).

   The Get Picture dialog box appears, as shown in Figures 4-3 (Mac) and 4-4 (Windows).

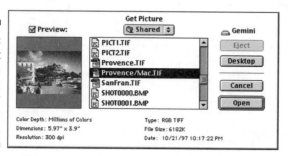

Figure 4-3:
The Get Picture dialog box for Macintosh QuarkXPress.

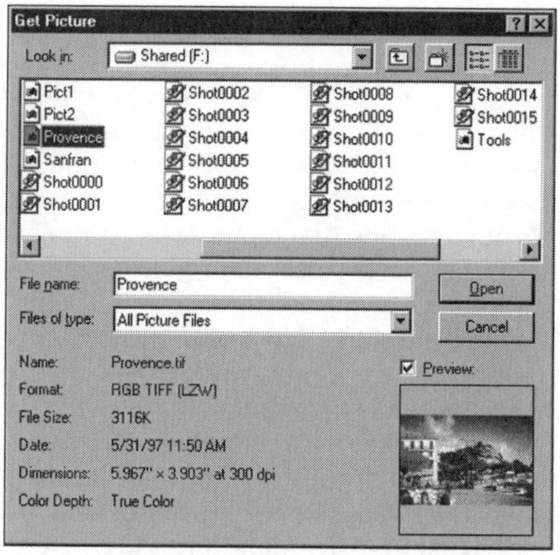

Figure 4-4:
The Get Picture dialog box for Windows QuarkXPress.

4. **Navigate the folders and drives until you find the image that you want to import.**

   If the Preview box is checked, QuarkXPress displays a thumbnail version of the image when you click the filename; this preview is meant to help you see whether it's the one you want. The preview may take a few moments to display after you select an image.

5. Click Open.

The picture appears in the box that you selected in Step 2. In some cases, QuarkXPress takes a few moments to load the file, particularly if it is more than 200K, has millions of colors, or is a compressed file (such as JPEG or Photo CD).

 QuarkXPress treats objects differently, depending on what tool is selected. If you select the Content tool, you can work with the contents of a box — the text or graphics.

 If you select the Item tool, you can work with the box itself. Thus, to move an image within its box, select the Content tool; to move the box and the image inside it, select the Item tool.

Making the Graphics Fit

Importing graphics isn't so hard, now is it?

But wait — the image doesn't fit the box! What's going on?

When QuarkXPress imports a graphic, it does so at the graphic's original size. If the original is 6 inches square, QuarkXPress makes the image 6 inches square, no matter what size the box that it's being placed in is. We think that QuarkXPress should have a preferences option to make imported graphics fit the boxes that they're being placed in — but it doesn't, so you have to do the dirty work yourself.

 In some cases, this lack of automatic fit can fool you into thinking that the graphic was never imported, because the picture box looks empty. What really happened is that the graphic has a margin (created in your graphics program), and all you're seeing is the margin, which of course looks like nothing. When QuarkXPress places a graphic in a picture box, it puts the top-left corner of the graphics file in the top-left corner of the picture box. When you see nothing, that means that the margin is wider and deeper than the picture box's size.

 Following are a few ways to get your graphic to fit:

✔ Just drag the handles to resize the picture box to fit the image.

✔ If you want the graphic to fit the box's current size, make sure the Content tool or the Item tool is selected; then press Ctrl+Shift+Option+⌘F or Ctrl+Shift+Alt+F. That finger-wrenching keyboard shortcut makes QuarkXPress resize the image so that it fits the box. Make sure that you press all four keys. If you miss the Option or Alt key and press just Shift+⌘+F or Ctrl+Shift+F, you get a distorted version of the image; it will be resized differently along the length than along the width. (No, we don't know why the more common option has the harder-to-use key combination.) The difference? The first shortcut keeps the image's original proportions, whereas the second makes the image fit the size of the box, distorting it if necessary. Figure 4-5 shows what happens when you use each option.

Another keyboard shortcut — Shift+⌘+M or Ctrl+Shift+M — centers a graphic within the box. This shortcut won't resize your image, so you'll still likely use Shift+Option+⌘+F or Ctrl+Alt+Shift+F to make your image fit in the box.

In addition to taking advantage of QuarkXPress's automatic controls, you can manually reposition, or crop, a graphic within a box. The easiest way to reposition a graphic manually is to start with the Content tool active. Then just click the graphic and move it. The pointer becomes a hand (called the grabber hand) when you position it over the graphic. Hold down the mouse button and move the mouse — and watch the graphic move within the box. Release the mouse button when you're done.

You also can specify how much you want the image to move within the box. QuarkXPress uses a floating palette — the Measurements palette — that allows you to control text attributes, graphics attributes, and box attributes. Figure 4-6 shows the Measurements palette with the settings for the picture box in the top-left corner.

The X% and Y% values show the amount of scaling (in the figure, 47.6 percent); you can change those values by typing new ones in the boxes and then pressing Enter or Return.

Figure 4-5:
The effects of fitting a graphic to a box: proportionally (top left) and nonproportionally (top right). The original image, unscaled and cropped, is at the bottom.

Figure 4-6:
The
Measure-
ments
palette
allows you
to resize
and
reposition
graphics
within a
picture box.

You also can change the position of the graphic by changing the X+ and Y+ values. A positive number moves the image to the right for X+ and down for Y+. Another method is to click the arrows to the right of the X+ and Y+ boxes. These arrows nudge the image up, down, left, or right, depending on which arrow you click. (Hold down the Option or Alt key to nudge an image in tiny steps: 0.001 unit of the current measurement, such as inches or picas.) You can, of course, use a combination of these techniques. Use the grabber hand to roughly position the graphic and then fine-tune the place-ment by using nudge arrows and/or changing the X+ and Y+ values manually. A harder way to change these settings is to choose Item⇨Modify (or press ⌘+M or Ctrl+M) to get to the Picture pane of the Modify dialog box, where you can change the Scale Down, Scale Across, Offset Down, and Offset Across values. That method is too much work, though.

When your graphics are in, sized, and positioned the way you like them, you can move on to using graphics as embellishments.

Managing Graphics

Getting pictures into your QuarkXPress documents is easy, but getting them in is only part of the job. You also have to keep track of your imported pictures throughout the production process to make sure that everything goes smoothly when it's time to output final pages.

You may not know it, but when you import a picture into QuarkXPress, you don't actually import the entire picture file. If QuarkXPress added imported picture files to documents when you imported a picture, the size of the documents would get out of hand. A few high-resolution scans could easily produce a QuarkXPress document that exceeds 10MB. So instead of importing entire graphic files, QuarkXPress imports only a low-resolution version of each image. This image is what you see when you rotate, crop, resize, or otherwise alter a picture. When you print the picture, the original file is sent to the printer.

Dealing with modified pictures

After you import a picture, you should be aware of several pitfalls. First, if somebody modifies a picture that you imported into a QuarkXPress document, you want to reimport the picture before you print it. If you don't update a picture that's been modified, QuarkXPress warns you when you print it and gives you a chance to update the graphic. If you do update the graphic, however, you won't get to see the modified graphic before it's printed, and you may be in for a surprise. You have two options for updating modified pictures:

✔ You can update individual pictures manually in the Pictures pane of the Usage dialog box. (To display this dialog box, choose Utilities➪Usage.) The scroll list displays information on an imported TIFF file that was modified after it was imported. If you click the More Information button, QuarkXPress displays additional information about the picture whose name is highlighted in the scroll list. To update a modified picture, click its name and then click Update. Hold down the ⌘ or Ctrl key when you click to update multiple pictures.

✔ You can have QuarkXPress update modified pictures for you automatically. The Auto Picture Import list in the General pane of the Document Preferences dialog box provides two choices — On and On (Verify) — that automatically update modified pictures when you open a document. (To display the Default Document Preferences dialog box, choose Edit➪Preferences➪Document, or press ⌘+Y or Ctrl+Y.) If you choose On (Verify), QuarkXPress displays a dialog box when it updates a modified picture.

Dealing with moved pictures

Sometimes, pictures get modified after you import them; other times, they get moved from their original locations. When you import a picture, QuarkXPress records its storage location so that it knows where the picture file is located when it's time to print. But if you move a picture file after you import it, QuarkXPress won't be able to find it. If this situation occurs, QuarkXPress warns you when you try to print the picture and provides you the option of reestablishing the link to the missing file.

You can also reestablish links to missing pictures via the Pictures pane of the Usage dialog box. (To display this dialog box, choose Utilities⇨Usage.) To update a missing picture, click it and then click Update. QuarkXPress displays a standard Open dialog box that allows you to locate and select the missing file. Sorry — you have to do this part yourself. QuarkXPress isn't smart enough to figure out the location of missing picture files.

Keeping track of picture files is particularly important if you use a service provider to produce final output. In addition to providing your QuarkXPress documents to your service bureau, you must provide all imported pictures. If you don't include picture files, your provider can still output your documents, but the low-resolution previews will be used instead of the original high-resolution picture files. Not very pretty.

Collecting pictures for output

In documents that contain many pictures, keeping track of all the pictures can be tricky, but collecting them all manually in preparation for output could challenge one's sanity. Fortunately, QuarkXPress does this job for you. Just choose File⇨Collect for Output. In addition to collecting picture files, QuarkXPress can generate a report that contains printing-related information about the document, including a list of fonts used, XTensions required for output, and the document's page size.

You must save a document before you can collect files with the File⇨Collect for Output command. QuarkXPress asks whether you want to save an unsaved document or save changes to a modified document.

Chapter 5

Bringing in the Text

. . . .

. . . .

Give some people a computer, a word-processing application, and some paper, and they think that they're full-fledged publishers, ready for the big leagues.

But you aren't so easily fooled. *You* know better. That's why you're reading this book, right? You know that you can't do serious, fancy, cool-looking professional publishing with the same application that kids typically use for typing school papers. You're ready for the big leagues, or at least you're dreaming of getting there. That's why you use QuarkXPress.

Hey, don't get us wrong. We have nothing against word processors; in fact, we use them all the time. It's just that we don't want you to be misled about what word processors can do — or do well.

The big advantage that QuarkXPress has over word processors is that QuarkXPress gives you tremendous control over the appearance of every item on a page, down to the tiniest unit of spacing between characters or lines of text. Word processors, on the other hand, are built to make filling page after page with text easy. These programs often give you some layout features and typographic features — multiple columns, bold and italic characters, and so on — but they lack the precision and depth of control that's available in QuarkXPress. And professional-looking publishing requires precision and depth of control — along with a great deal of creative flexibility.

But using word processors is not at all uncommon for people using QuarkXPress. Actually, you have a choice about how to get text onto a page: You can create text right within QuarkXPress text boxes (by using the built-in text editor), or you can create text in a separate word processor and then import the text into QuarkXPress.

Chances are good that you'll find yourself both importing text and entering text in QuarkXPress. But if you plan to use a separate word processor to create text, check out this chapter for some tips on how to make the process go smoothly.

Using Word-Processor Files with QuarkXPress

Whether you're deciding what's for lunch or what to wear, having a bunch of choices is always nice. And you have a bunch of word processors to choose among when looking for one that will import nicely into QuarkXPress.

The Macintosh version of QuarkXPress can import the following Mac word-processor formats: Microsoft Word 3.0 up to 6.0, WordPerfect Version 3, WriteNow 3.0, Microsoft Works 1.1 and 2.0, and Claris MacWrite Pro and MacWrite II. QuarkXPress for Windows can import the following Windows word-processor formats: Word versions 2.0, 6.0, 7.0 (95), and 8.0 (97), and WordPerfect versions 4.0 through 7.0.

Keep one important point in mind. Because word processors are updated according to their manufacturers' schedules — which do not necessarily coincide with Quark's — you have no guarantee that QuarkXPress will import files easily from a particular updated version of one of these packages. If your word processor is not in the preceding list, it's a good idea to test the "importability" of your text to see how everything works before you get into a production or deadline situation. If you run into problems, try saving the word-processor file to one of the text file formats that QuarkXPress supports — most word processors allow you to do this.

If your test shows you're stuck, don't despair. Some manufacturers of word processors offer import/export filters for QuarkXPress. Nisus, creator of Nisus Writer, for example, includes a filter that allows you to import and export Nisus Writer files with QuarkXPress. You can also check Quark's Web site at `ftp://ftp.quark.com/xpress/xtensions/` for new and updated filters.

Getting the Text Ready to Import

Suppose that you're already familiar with how to format text within the word processing program that you have on your computer — that is, you know how to create text, flow it into two columns, add a header and footer, and italicize and bold selected sections of text. Doing as much as possible within the word processing file and then importing the text into QuarkXPress may seem to be a good thing to do.

But is this a good thing to do? No way, José. Fact is that, unless you plan ahead, you risk losing some of the work that you did in the word processor after you import the text into QuarkXPress. Now why would you want to waste your valuable time?

Keep it simple: All you need is text

Here's a good guideline: When using a word processor to create a file that you intend to import into QuarkXPress, remember that you'll be importing only *text*, not a polished document. If you keep this simple thought in mind, you'll resist the temptation to do more formatting than necessary in the word processor. To make the most of your investment: use the power of QuarkXPress for your *document* formatting. Therefore, knowing that the text will be imported into QuarkXPress, what word-processing features should you go ahead and use?

If you tell QuarkXPress to keep them when you import text into a text box, style sheets from Microsoft Word and WordPerfect come across, along with their associated text. Figure 5-1 shows the Get Text dialog box that appears when you import text from a word processor. Be sure to check Include Style Sheets to make sure that style sheets get imported along with the text. We explain more about style sheets in Chapter 6.

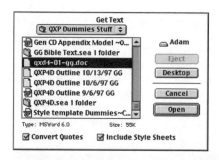

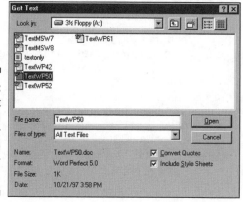

Figure 5-1:
The Get Text dialog box for Macs (top) and for Windows.

One key to successfully importing text into QuarkXPress is to avoid using the graphics and layout features of the word processor. Limit your word-processor text formatting to the kind that enhances the reader's understanding or that places emphasis, such as boldfacing, italicizing, and varying type style.

If you use Microsoft Word and Corel WordPerfect, by far the most popular word processors in use today, rest assured that these formats import into QuarkXPress:

- Boldfaced, outlined, italicized, and shadow characters
- Underlining (in Word, all underlining changes to a single underline)
- Color
- Font changes
- Varied point sizes
- Small caps
- Strikethrough characters
- Subscript
- Superscript
- Special characters

If you use a different word processor supported by QuarkXPress, these same features should import, but there's no guarantee — so do a test before using a format other than Word or WordPerfect. After QuarkXpress takes care of the characters in your text, you can deal with issues on a bigger scale — tables, headers and footers, and more that you may have included in your word-processor files. Can any of them be saved? The sections that follow let you know what to expect.

Tables: Don't bother

If you decide to create a table in a word-processor file and then import the file into QuarkXPress, be forewarned that the table will disappear. Ergo, take heed: If you like tables in your documents, wait until you are using QuarkXPress to format them.

On the other hand, if you format a table with tabs (whether or not you make the tabs line up properly using style sheets), you can import the table into QuarkXPress along with the rest of the text in the file and can then modify the styles in QuarkXPress as needed. Just be sure to check the Include Style Sheets check box in the Get Text dialog box. Basically, to create a table for import by QuarkXPress, simply separate each column with a tab and each row with a paragraph return. If your word processor uses style sheets, make sure the table text uses a unique style so you can set up the tabs in QuarkXPress just once (in that table text's style) and have all the table text use those tabs automatically. (Chapter 6 covers style sheets in depth.)

If you create a table in a spreadsheet or database program (such as Lotus 1-2-3, Microsoft Excel, or Claris FileMaker Pro), you can import the table into QuarkXPress, but not smoothly. You need to choose between saving the files as tab-delimited ASCII text or as graphics. If you save the files as tab-delimited ASCII text, you need to do some work inside the QuarkXPress document, setting tab stops to line everything up (just as you would with tabbed text imported from a word processor). If you save the files as graphics, you won't be able to change any of the data in QuarkXPress.

Bottom line: Use QuarkXPress to format your tables.

Headers and footers: They disappear

In case you don't know, *headers* are pieces of information, such as the name of the current chapter, that appear at the tops of pages in a document. *Footers* appear at the bottoms of pages and usually include information such as the current page number and the name of the document.

As a QuarkXPress user, you need to get into the habit of thinking about headers and footers as layout issues rather than text issues. Because these elements are layout issues, you should wait until you are working on your document in QuarkXPress before you worry about them. For one thing, your document no doubt will paginate differently in QuarkXPress; if it does, the page numbers in headers or footers will be useless, even if they did import into QuarkXPress (which they don't).

So headers and footers are features that are useless to you in QuarkXPress.

Footnotes: They dance to the end

Several word processors include a footnoting feature that allows you to do two things: (1) mark certain spots in text with a number and (2) have the number and some corresponding text appear at the bottom of the page containing the footnote.

If you import a word-processor file that contains footnotes into QuarkXPress, the footnotes no longer appear on the same page as the text that they reference. Instead, all the footnotes for the document appear at the end of the imported text. Also, the superscript or subscript footnote indicators in the body of the document may not import correctly.

In-line graphics: Worth a try

Most Macintosh and Windows word processors support *in-line graphics* —
pictures that you import into your word processor and associate with
certain sections of text. In most cases, QuarkXPress can import the in-line
graphics with your text. Importing this way works for Microsoft Word and
WordPerfect files; you may need to experiment a bit if you use another word
processor that allows in-line graphics.

One caveat: Graphics that you embedded in your word-processor document
by using the Mac's Publish and Subscribe feature or OLE (a Mac and
Windows Publish and Subscribe–like feature from Microsoft) do not import
into QuarkXPress.

In-line Graphics import into QuarkXPress in the form of their previews, not
as their original formats — when they import at all. Because of this quirk,
the versions of the in-line graphics that end up in your QuarkXPress document probably will have a lower resolution in your QuarkXPress layout than
they had in their original word-processor file.

Style sheets: Way to go!

QuarkXPress allows you to import styles created in Microsoft Word and
WordPerfect *if* you check the Include Style Sheets check box in the Get Text
dialog box before you import the text. (To display this dialog box, choose
File➪Get Text, or press ⌘+E or Ctrl+E.) Even if you don't always use style
sheets in your word processor, it's a good idea to always check the Include
Style Sheets box.

Tune in again when we tell you more about style sheets in Chapter 6.

XPress tags: Your secret code

Are you keen on secret codes? QuarkXPress has them in the form of a nifty
(although tough to learn) feature that allows you to insert tags into text that
you're preparing to import into QuarkXPress. These secret codes are
referred to as *XPress tags*; you can use them to give QuarkXPress instructions on how to format text that's being imported into a QuarkXPress
document. XPress tags are actually ASCII (text-only) text containing embedded codes that tell QuarkXPress which formatting to apply. XPress tags are
similar to macros, and you embed them in the text that you create in your
word processor.

Word-processing mistakes to avoid

After you figure out that QuarkXPress does a very good job of importing text from word processors, be careful not to fall victim to the temptation of using all the features of the word processor simply because they're there. Here are some pointers to keep in mind:

✔ **Don't spend too much time doing extensive formatting in your word processor.** A word processor's style sheets are always much less sophisticated, with fewer options than the effects you can achieve in QuarkXPress. Avoid using any layout-related features in the word processor, such as page numbers, headers and footers, and multiple columns — QuarkXPress simply ignores them.

✔ **Don't use the word processor as though it were a manual typewriter.** In other words, don't press the Return or Enter key at the end of each line of text — only at the end of a paragraph. If you forget to skip this old-standby task, you will have to spend considerable time in QuarkXPress removing all the unnecessary returns, which can clutter an otherwise tidy document. Also, don't use two spaces between sentences; professional typesetters never do that. (You can fix such mistakes within QuarkXPress by using its find-and-replace feature, but it's better not to make these mistakes in the first place.)

✔ **Don't try to use multiple word spaces or multiple paragraph returns to align words or lines of text on-screen.** You want to use QuarkXPress to tweak the spacing of words and characters because it's so easy and much more precise.

✔ **Notice the version number of your word processor.** If the program is a couple of versions older or newer than what your version of QuarkXPress supports, you could have trouble when you import a text

file from the word processor. If in doubt, create a test file of text, using all the features that you're likely to use, and import it into a text box in a test QuarkXPress document. You may find that you need to make adjustments to the list of word processing features that you can use with QuarkXPress.

✔ **Don't use the fast-save option on files that you plan to import into QuarkXPress.** That is, if your word processor *has* a fast-save option (an option that writes information about what's been changed in a text file at the end of the file, instead of rewriting the entire file each time you do a save). The fast-save option could cause problems with the imported text files. We suggest that you turn off fast save for files that you will be importing into QuarkXPress. With today's super-speedy hard drives, the time that you gain by using fast save is barely noticeable anyway. In the following figure, the fast-save option is disabled.

The point of all these points is this: If you want to use a separate word processor, use it. But you should limit what you do in that program to plain old text entry, saving the fancy stuff for when you import the text into QuarkXPress.

XPress tags, when used correctly, are fairly powerful, but they are not widely used because of some drawbacks. The most significant shortcoming is the fact that you can't use XPress tags with the formatting that's available in your word processor. If you create a file in Microsoft Word, for example, you cannot use XPress tags to apply a style to a paragraph while using Word's ability to boldface and italicize text. If you want to use XPress tags, you must use them for every formatting instruction in the file, and you must save the file as an ASCII (text-only) file.

If you want to experiment with XPress tags, refer to the QuarkXPress documentation. We'd be surprised, though, if you end up using these tags in place of the formatting features that are available in your word processor.

Filling the Text Box with Text

Here comes the part that you've been waiting for. You've created a QuarkXPress document, the document has text boxes, and you're ready to fill the boxes with some text.

You can fill text boxes in one of two ways: You can use the built-in QuarkXPress word processor to type text (you simply select the text box, select the Content tool, and start typing), or you can import text from a word processor into the text box. Follow these steps to import the text:

1. **With the QuarkXPress document open, select the Content tool.**

2. **Click the text box into which you want to import text.**

   If the text box is empty, the flashing I-beam pointer is displayed in the top-left corner.

   But what happens when you want to import some text into a text box that already has some text in it? No problem. Simply click where you want the imported text to begin; text is always imported wherever the I-beam pointer is flashing. Importing text does not remove the text that is already in the text box; it simply bumps the text that follows the I-beam pointer to the end of the inserted text. If you want to replace existing text with imported text, highlight the text that you want to replace before you choose FileÍGet Text.

3. **Choose File⇨Get Text (or press ⌘+E or Ctrl+E) to display the Get Text dialog box.**

4. **Select the text file that you want to place in the text box.**

5. **If you want QuarkXPress to automatically change typewriter-type double dashes, straight quotation marks, and apostrophes to their more sophisticated typographic equivalents, check the Convert Quotes check box.**

   If you want to include the style sheets used in the word processor, check the Include Style Sheets box.

6. **Click OK.**

   The text flows into the text box or the linked chain of text boxes.

Part II
Adding Style and Substance

The 5th Wave   By Rich Tennant

The GENIE in the MACHINE

"YES, I'M NORMALLY LARGER AND MORE AWE-INSPIRING, BUT THIS IS ONLY A 4MB SYSTEM!"

In this part . . .

Good publishing technique is about more than getting the words down on paper. It's also about tweaking the letters and lines — and the space between them — to make your pages shine. We also tell you how to use XTensions, plug-ins to the program that beef up its capabilities. This part shows you how to do all that and a lot more, including tips on how to get your document out of your computer and onto some other medium, such as film or paper. We also give you some solid suggestions on how to print and how to work with all those other people in the world who know how to help you get the job done.

Chapter 6

You've Got Real Style

Although you've heard about them, you've probably never really been into *style sheets*. Yet you know some people who use them on every single document. But something inside you says, "Style sheets? Document formatting? Whoa! Save it for the big-time publishers!" We think you should reconsider. Surely you must realize by now that half the fun of desktop publishing is being able to automate some of the tasks that used to take so long. QuarkXPress makes setting up styles for your documents easy. Best of all, using style sheets saves you tons of time and lets you guarantee formatting consistency.

Style sheets are just about the best invention since the snooze alarm. They define basic specifications for your text: typefaces, type sizes, justification settings, and tab settings. If you select a paragraph and apply a style sheet to it, the paragraph automatically formats itself to the font and size specified in the style sheet. Even better, with the addition of character styles to QuarkXPress 4, you can now apply styles to any text selection, not just whole paragraphs.

Just think of all the time this automatic styling saves you. Instead of applying each and every attribute individually to text, you can just tell QuarkXPress that you want particular swaths of text to take on all the formatting attributes established in a style tag. Then — with one click of the mouse — you send QuarkXPress on its merry way to format your document quicker than you can take a sip of coffee.

Like many features of publishing, style sheets come with their own jargon, which would be helpful for you to know:

✔ **Style sheet:** The group of formatting attributes (styles) in a document. It's called a *sheet* because, in times before electronic publishing, typesetters had typewritten sheets that listed the formatting attributes they had to apply to specific kinds of text, such as body copy and headlines. QuarkXPress treats style sheets as part of the document.

✔ **Style or style tag:** These two terms refer to a group of formatting attributes that you apply to one or more paragraphs or to selected text. You name the group, or style, so that you can apply all the attributes to the document at once. For example, in text styled body text, you may indicate the typeface, type size, leading, and so on as part of that body text style. The word *tag* is used because you "tag" selected paragraphs or selected text with the style you want to apply. Because the word *style* also sometimes refers to a character attribute, such as italics or underline, many people use *style tag* to refer to the group of attributes. This distinction helps you avoid confusing the two meanings. (Note that QuarkXPress uses the phrase *style sheet* for what we call a style or style tag; we decided it was better to use the industry-standard term to go with Quark's term.)

Styles work in two places: You can apply them to selected paragraphs or text in your QuarkXPress document or to paragraphs (but not selected text) in the word processing text you plan to import. Don't worry: We explain how to do it both ways in the sections that follow.

Paragraph versus Character Styles

In previous versions of QuarkXPress, you could use paragraph styles to save attributes for entire paragraphs only. If you needed to format individual words, you had to do that manually.

QuarkXPress 4 adds an amazing new feature: character styles, which let you save the attributes for selected characters, as well.

Paragraph and character styles are not an either/or proposition. You use both:

✔ The time-saving part about paragraph styles is that you apply them to whole paragraphs. For example, first-level heads might have a Header 1 style, captions a Caption style, bylines a Byline style, body text a Body Text style, and so on. Specifying a style for all paragraph types that you often use is a great idea. With a paragraph style, all the text in the paragraph receives the same settings: fonts, size, leading, alignment, hyphenation, and so on.

✔ The beauty of the new character styles feature is that you can ensure consistent typography throughout your document. A paragraph style does that for entire paragraphs, but documents often have pieces of text that always get the same formatting. For example, drop caps might always use a specific font and be compressed, or the first few words after a bullet might always appear bold and be in a different font. By creating a character style named Drop Cap with the settings for those specific characters, you can ensure that you always apply the correct settings. Think about it: Before character styles, you had to apply each setting yourself — font, size, perhaps even baseline shift — and hope that you both remembered the correct settings and used the same settings each and every time. With character styles, QuarkXPress remembers for you. And as with paragraph styles, if you change the style sheet's settings, all the text using the style automatically updates throughout your document. Cool!

To help you distinguish between paragraph and character styles, QuarkXPress precedes the names of styles with either a ¶ to indicate a paragraph style or an **A** to indicate a character style. You see these symbols in the Style Sheets dialog box (covered in the next section), in the Append dialog box (covered later in this chapter), and in the Style Sheets palette (also covered later in this chapter).

Styling Your Style Sheets

We promised you it would be easy, and you can see that we were right! You find the keys to creating, changing, and applying styles in one spot: the Style Sheets dialog box, which you access via Edit⇨Style Sheets or Shift+F11 (see Figure 6-1).

Figure 6-1:
You can do almost anything you want to style sheets from within the Style Sheets dialog box (Edit⇨Style Sheets or Shift+F11).

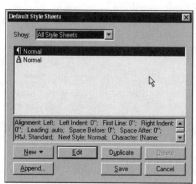

Learn it once, use it twice

You can always apply character and paragraph formatting to selected text in your QuarkXPress document, whether or not you use style sheets. The good news is that once you understand the dialog boxes used to set formatting for style sheets, you know the dialog boxes and menus needed to locally format text outside of style sheets. QuarkXPress uses the same system for both kinds of formatting:

✔ The Style menu's Font, Size, Type Style, Color, Shade, Horizontal/Vertical Scale, Track, and Baseline Shift menu options are the same as the formatting options in the Edit Character Style Sheet dialog box.

✔ The Character Attributes dialog box (Style⇨Character or Shift+⌘+C or Ctrl+Shift+C) is the same as the Edit Character Style dialog box.

✔ The Style menu's Alignment and Leading menu options are the same as the same-name options in the Formats pane of the Edit Paragraph Style Sheet dialog box.

✔ The Formats pane (Style⇨Formats, or Shift+⌘+F or Ctrl+Shift+F), Tabs pane (Style⇨Tabs, or Shift+⌘+T or Ctrl+Shift+T), and Rules pane (Style⇨Rules, or Shift+⌘+N or Ctrl+Shift+N) of the Paragraph Attributes dialog box are the same as those in the Edit Paragraph Style Sheet dialog box.

So you see, by knowing how to format text through style sheets, you can format any kind of text in QuarkXPress.

Oops! We almost forgot a couple of style-related functions that you set somewhere outside the Style Sheets dialog box. You set the hyphenation controls in the H&Js dialog box (Edit⇨H&Js, or Option+⌘+H or Ctrl+Shift+F11). You control character and space scaling by accessing the Character pane in the Document Preferences dialog box (Edit⇨Preferences Document, or ⌘+Y or Ctrl+Y). We get to these in Chapter 8. If you're new to this style sheet business, give yourself some time to experiment. After all, you can always delete any style sheet you dislike by simply highlighting the style in the Style Sheets dialog box and clicking the Delete button.

We *told* you it was easy!

What's inside the Style Sheets dialog box?

The Style Sheets dialog box, shown in Figure 6-1, gives you several choices for editing style sheets. Your choices are as follows:

✔ **New** lets you create a new style from scratch or create a new style based on an existing style. Note that the New button is a drop-down button — if you click it, it becomes a pop-up menu with two choices: ¶ Paragraph and **A** Character. You need to tell QuarkXPress whether you want to create a paragraph or character style.

Suppose that you just spent 15 minutes defining text settings through the Style menu or Measurements palette. Can you turn these settings into a style? Yes. All you need to do is position your text cursor anywhere on the text that has the desired settings. Then open the Style Sheets dialog box and choose New. All settings automatically appear in the new style you create. Alternatively, you can Control+click or right-click any style name in the Style Sheets palette (made visible via View⇨Show Style Sheets or F11) to get a pop-up menu that shows the New command.

✔ **Edit** lets you make changes to an existing style. Alternatively, you can Control+click or right-click any style name in the Style Sheets palette (made visible via View⇨Show Style Sheets or F11) to get a pop-up menu that shows the Edit command.

✔ **Duplicate** makes copies of all the attributes of an existing style and gives the duplicate style the name Copy of style. You then can change any attribute settings, including the style name.

✔ **Delete** lets you delete existing styles. A dialog box asks you to confirm the deletion if you applied the style to text in the current document. Any text using a deleted style retains the style's attributes, but the Style Sheets palette and style menu show these paragraphs as having No Style. Alternatively, you can Control+click or right-click any style name in the Style Sheets palette (made visible via View⇨Show Style Sheets or F11) to get a pop-up menu that has the Delete command in it. Note that if you delete a style sheet that you applied to text, QuarkXPress asks you which style sheet to apply instead. You can choose No Style, which leaves the text formatting untouched while removing the style sheet, or pick another style sheet and apply it to the text.

✔ **Append** lets you copy a style from another QuarkXPress document.

✔ **Save** saves all the style changes you make in the Style Sheets dialog box. If you forget to save styles when leaving the dialog box, the changes won't take effect, so try to remember to save, okay?

✔ **Cancel** makes the program ignore all style changes you made in the Style Sheets dialog box since you last saved changes.

Notice how QuarkXPress shows you the settings for the selected paragraph or character style in the Description area at the bottom of the Style Sheets dialog box. Reading this area is a great way to double-check your settings.

The Edit Character Style Sheet dialog box

The best place to start creating styles for a document is with character styles because paragraph styles use character styles to format their paragraphs' text. Even if a paragraph uses a particular character style, you can use that same character style for selected text. Doing this saves you effort when you're creating paragraph styles because you can create several similar paragraph styles that all use the same character style; you define the text formatting once in the character styles and just change the paragraph formatting (such as indentation or space above) in the various paragraph styles based on it. We talk about editing paragraph styles in the next section.

The default setting for Normal is left-aligned, 12-point Helvetica with automatic leading. To change any attributes of Normal, close all open documents, access the Style Sheets dialog box by selecting Edit➪Style Sheets or pressing Shift+F11, and edit the Normal style in the usual way, described in the next two sections. These settings become the new defaults for all future new documents. Any style tag created without a document open becomes part of the default style sheet for all new documents.

Figure 6-2 shows the Edit Character Style Sheet dialog box, where much of the action of setting up styles happens.

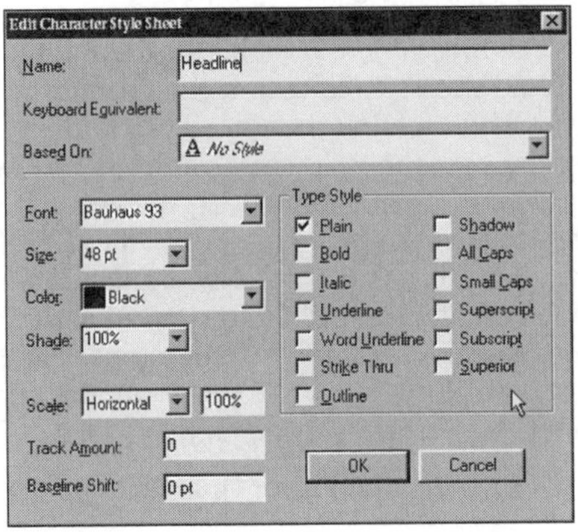

Figure 6-2:
The Edit
Character
Style Sheet
dialog box.

Following are explanations of the fields in the Edit Character Style Sheet dialog box:

- **Name** shows the name of an existing style you're editing; the field is empty if you're working on a new style.

- **Keyboard Equivalent** lets you set up key shortcuts that make it easier to quickly apply styles to text. To enter keyboard equivalents, press the actual function key (F1 through F15) you want to use, including any combinations with Shift, Option, ⌘, Alt, or Ctrl.

QuarkXPress includes a keyboard template that lists function-key equivalents for often-accessed commands. You can override the original commands by assigning function keys to style sheets, but, if you do, you lose the ability to access the commands assigned to those keys.

✔ **Based On** allows you build a group of styles by basing the group on another style. Then, if you decide to change the group, you only need to change the original base style and those changes automatically apply to the rest of the group. For instance, if you had five body text styles created using the "Based on" option and using the same font, instead of altering all five style sheets to change your body text font, you merely edit the base style, and the remaining styles in the group reflect the font change.

✔ **Font** is where you choose the typeface. The pop-up list shows all the fonts installed in your system, as shown in Figure 6-3. If you type the first few letters of a font's name, the menu automatically scrolls to the first font whose name begins with those letters.

Figure 6-3:
The Font
pop-up
menu in
the Edit
Character
Style Sheet
dialog box.

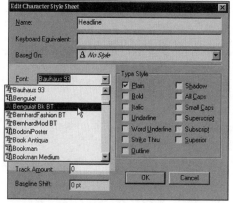

QuarkXPress for Windows adds a code before each font name — T1 or TT — to indicate whether a font is a Type 1 PostScript font (best when using service bureaus) or a TrueType font (fine for laser printers).

✔ **Size** allows you to pick the type size in points (the standard measurement for text size, of which there are 72 to an inch). You can pick from the pop-up list's sizes or simply type in any size you want in the field. (You can specify type size to three decimal places, such as 12.123 points. If you enter more decimal places than that, QuarkXPress ignores them.)

✔ **Color** lets you choose the color for text. Any color defined in the document (see Chapter 15) appears in this list.

✔ **Shade** lets you determine how dark the selected color (including black) appears. You can pick from the pop-up list's percentages or enter your own figure (to three decimal places).

✔ **Scale** allows you scrunch the type either horizontally (width) or vertically (height); pick which you want from the pop-up menu. Then enter a percentage value for how much you want to expand (widen) or condense (compress) the size — values less than 100% condense the type; values greater than 100% expand the type.

✔ **Track Amount** adjusts the spacing between all characters, moving them closer together (a negative number) or farther apart (a positive number). See Chapter 5 for more on tracking and its cousin, kerning.

✔ **Baseline Shift** lets you move text up or down relative to other text on the line (the baseline is the imaginary line that type rests on). A negative number moves the text down; a positive number moves it up.

✔ **Type Style** is where you set the typeface settings. Check all the appropriate boxes. Note that some settings disallow others: Underline and Word Underline override each other, as do All Caps and Small Caps, and Subscript and Superscript. Selecting Plain deselects everything else.

QuarkXPress dialog boxes often include pop-up menus to help you make selections faster. For example, in the Edit Character Style Sheets dialog box, Font, Size, Color, and Shade all offer pop-up menus. You also can enter the value you want directly into the box.

When you finish selecting the character formatting for your new or edited character style sheet, click OK. You return to the Style Sheets dialog box shown back in Figure 6-1.

The Edit Paragraph Style Sheet dialog box

After you deal with character styles, you can create or edit the paragraph style sheet. Use New to create a new one, or click an existing paragraph style and click Edit to change it. You get the Edit Paragraph Style Sheet dialog box shown in Figure 6-4. You see four panes, which we go through in sequence. You can use these Edit Paragraph Style Sheet features in any order and ignore the ones that don't apply to the current style.

The General pane

The default pane is the General pane, as shown in Figure 6-4.

The first two options are the same as their counterparts in the Edit Character Style Sheet dialog box:

✔ **Keyboard Equivalent** allows you assign a shortcut key to a paragraph style.

✔ **Based On** lets you make the paragraph style use a previously created style sheet's settings (and to update the current style sheet if the style sheet it's based on is changed in the future).

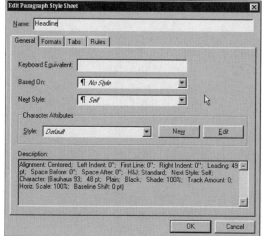

Figure 6-4:
The General
Pane of
the Edit
Paragraph
Style Sheet
dialog box.

The other settings are unique to the Edit Paragraph Style Sheet dialog box:

✔ **Next Style** lets you establish linked styles. For example, suppose you specify that a headline style always be followed by a byline style, which will always be followed by a body text style. If you choose Next Style, here's what happens after you enter a headline: As you type text into the QuarkXPress page, every time you enter a paragraph return after typing a byline, the style automatically changes to the body text style. If your style is used on paragraphs typically followed by other paragraphs using the same style, such as body text, leave Next Style set to Self.

✔ **Style** tells QuarkXPress which character style to use in this paragraph style (this is why we suggest you create the character styles first). If you want to create a new character style, you can do so by clicking the New button. You can also edit an existing character style by picking it from the Style pop-up menu and then clicking the Edit button.

The Formats pane

You do most of your work in creating a paragraph style in the Formats pane. Figure 6-5 shows this pane.

Here are the options:

✔ **Left Indent** indents the entire paragraph's left margin by the amount you specify.

✔ **First Line** indents the first line of a paragraph — a common thing to do with body text. A typical setting makes the indent the same as the text's point size (equal to an em space).

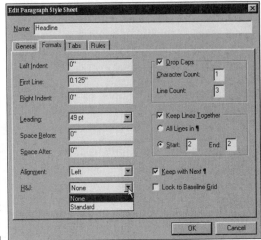

Figure 6-5:
The
Formats
pane of
the Edit
Paragraph
Style Sheet
dialog box.

✔ **Right Indent** indents the entire paragraph's right margin by the amount you specify.

You don't have to use the same measurement system in this — or any — dialog box. The Left Indent and Right Indent could appear in inches while the First Line appears in picas and points. For example, if we want the first line to be an em space, which is the same as the point size, we can enter 0p9, which means 0 picas and 9 points, instead of figuring out how many inches that was. We could as easily enter 9 pt to indicate 9 points.

✔ **Leading** sets the space between lines. Enter the leading you want, type auto to apply the Auto settings specified in the Document Preferences dialog box's Paragraph pane (Edit⇨Preferences⇨Document or ⌘+Y or Ctrl+Y), or use the pop-up menu to select Auto.

✔ **Space Before** lets you insert a fixed amount of space before the paragraph. Note that this space is not inserted if the paragraph happens to start at the top of a page, column, or text box. An example of when to use this setting is for headlines within a story. You typically want some space between the text and the headline. Add it here.

✔ **Space After** is like Space Before, except it adds space after a paragraph. It's pretty rare that you use both on the same paragraph.

✔ **Alignment** tells QuarkXPress whether to align the text to the left margin, to align the text to the right margin, to center the text, or to align the text against both margins (justified). Note that Force Justify makes the last line of a paragraph align against both margins (rarely used), while the regular Justify option leaves the last line aligned only to the left.

- **H&J** is where you pick the hyphenation and tracking settings for the paragraph. You create such H&J sets via Edit⇨H&Js or Option+⌘+H or Ctrl+Shift+F11. Chapter 8 covers this in detail.

  We recommend that you always create an H&J set called None that has hyphenation disabled. For several kinds of text, such as headlines and bylines, you won't want the text to be hyphenated, so you need such an H&J set.

- **Drop Caps** lets you make the first character(s) in a paragraph large and dropped down into the text, as shown in Figure 6-6. This is a popular technique for introductions and conclusions. Use the Character Count box to indicate how many characters are to be oversized and dropped down (1 is typical); use Line Count to determine how deep the drop is (2, 3, and 4 are typical). We think drop caps are more effective if you boldface the dropped character(s) or change the font, as we did in the last two examples in Figure 6-6. If you have a huge drop cap, as we do in the bottom of the figure, you may not need a bold drop cap — it's a question of judgment and taste.

- **Keep Lines Together** ensures that a paragraph's lines are kept together, rather than split at a column break or page break. You can set this field so that all lines are kept together by selecting the All Lines in ¶ radio button, or you can specify how many lines in the beginning and end of a paragraph must be kept together by entering the desired values in the Start and End boxes and clicking the radio button next to the Start box.

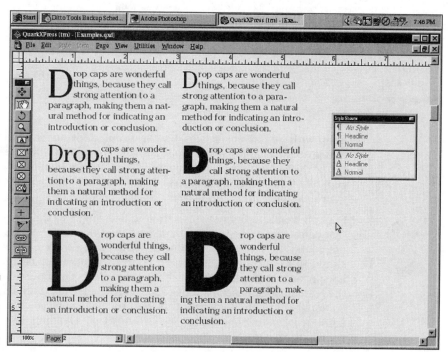

Figure 6-6:
Examples of
drop caps.

Many typographers hate orphans and widows — not people who are orphaned or widowed, but text that is isolated from the rest of its paragraph. An *orphan* is the first line of text in a paragraph that is at the bottom of a column or page, isolated from the rest of its paragraph (on the next column or page); a *widow* is the last line of a paragraph that is by itself at the top of a page or column (see Figure 6-7). To prevent such typographic horrors, the typographically correct set the Start and End fields to 2 to force QuarkXPress to avoid such lonely lines. However, doing so means that the bottoms of your columns may not align, because QuarkXPress may have to move text from the bottom of a column to prevent a widow or an orphan. We agree that widows are a bad thing when it comes to printing, but we think orphans are just fine, so we recommend that you leave Start at 1 and set End to 2. To avoid the uneven column bottoms that result when QuarkXPress moves widowed text, add a few words to each of your document's shorter columns — QuarkXPress puts back a line of text at the bottom of each column so that all of your text aligns properly.

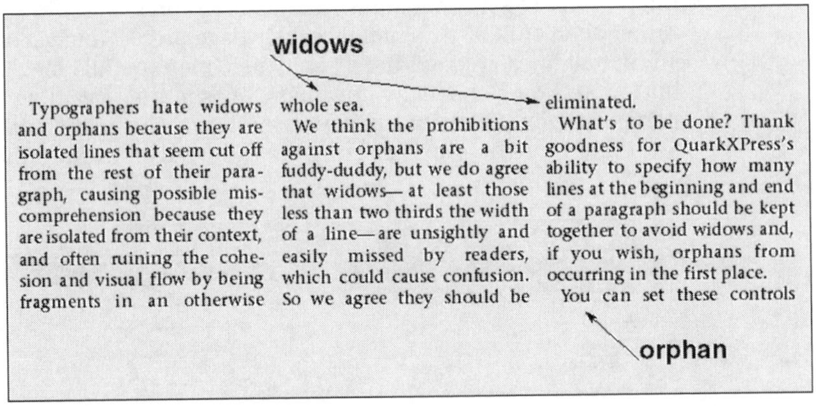

widows

Typographers hate widows and orphans because they are isolated lines that seem cut off from the rest of their paragraph, causing possible miscomprehension because they are isolated from their context, and often ruining the cohesion and visual flow by being fragments in an otherwise whole sea.

We think the prohibitions against orphans are a bit fuddy-duddy, but we do agree that widows— at least those less than two thirds the width of a line—are unsightly and easily missed by readers, which could cause confusion. So we agree they should be eliminated.

What's to be done? Thank goodness for QuarkXPress's ability to specify how many lines at the beginning and end of a paragraph should be kept together to avoid widows and, if you wish, orphans from occurring in the first place.

You can set these controls

orphan

Figure 6-7: Examples of widows and orphans.

✔ **Keep with Next ¶** ensures that a paragraph does not separate from the paragraph that follows. For example, you wouldn't want a headline at the bottom of a column or page; to make sure the headline does not separate from the body text that follows, check Keep with Next ¶ in your headline paragraph style.

✔ **Lock to Baseline Grid** ensures that all text aligns to the baseline grid that you set up in the Paragraph pane of the Document Preferences dialog box (Edit⇨Preferences⇨Document, or ⌘+Y or Ctrl+Y). Figure 6-8 shows this pane and highlights the part that sets the baseline grid. Locking a paragraph to the baseline grid means QuarkXPress ignores the leading specifications if needed to ensure that text aligns from column to column. If you use this feature, make sure you set the Increment amount the same as your body text's leading, so you don't get awkward gaps between paragraphs.

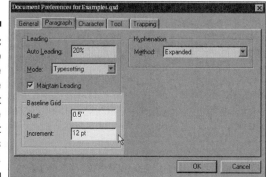

Figure 6-8:
Where to
set the
baseline
grid amount
in the
Document
Preferences
dialog box.

The Tabs pane

The Tabs pane lets you set up tabs in your paragraphs — handy for creating tables and aligning bullets and the text that follows them. Figure 6-9 shows the Tabs pane.

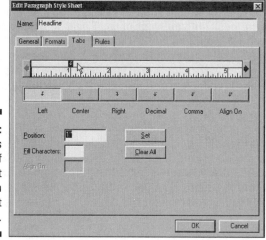

Figure 6-9:
The Tabs
pane of
the Edit
Paragraph
Style Sheet
dialog box.

In the Tabs pane, you can't help but see a ruler that you use to set your tabs. Under the ruler you see buttons for each kind of tab: left-aligned, center-aligned, right-aligned, decimal-aligned, comma-aligned, and character-aligned (Align On). (If you choose Align On, enter the character you want the tab to align to in the Align On field.) The text aligns to the tab's location based on the type of alignment chosen. Figure 6-10 shows examples of all six types of alignments.

Figure 6-10:
Examples of
the six tab
alignments
plus a tab
leader.
Note
the tab
indicator at
the 2-inch
position.

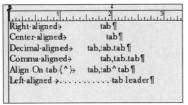

Click the button for the alignment you want; then click the ruler where you want that tab to appear. If you miss the exact spot you want, just click the tab location and, holding down the mouse button, move the mouse to the left or right as needed until you get to the desired location. Notice how the Position box shows the current location.

If you prefer to be exact, you can just click the button for the alignment you want and then enter the position you want in the Position box. Enter a new number to change its position if you got it wrong the first time. When the new tab is where you want, click the Set button to tell Quark you're done and ready to enter a new position for a new tab. You can alter a tab's position by clicking it in the ruler and entering a new value in the Position box.

Either way you set the position, you can change the alignment by selecting the tab and clicking a new alignment button.

If you create several tabs and want to get rid of them all, just click the Clear All button. To delete an individual tab, select it with the mouse, hold down the mouse button, and drag the tab outside of the ruler. Release the mouse button, and the tab disappears. Or select the tab and press the Backspace key or the Delete or Del key.

When creating a tab, you may want a *leader* or *fill* character. For example, to get a series of dots between text in a table of contents and its page number, you'd have a tab between the text and the number. By giving that tab a fill character of a period (.), you get your row of dots. You can enter two fill characters in QuarkXPress; the tab alternates the two characters. For example, entering += as the fill characters results in a leader like +=+=+=+=+=+=+=. More commonly, you would have a period and a space as your two leader characters, so the periods are not packed too tightly together.

The Rules pane

Using the Rules pane, you can insert ruling lines above and/or below your paragraphs (see Figure 6-11). This feature is handy especially for underlining kickers, headlines, and other such elements. Sure, you can use the underline settings in the Edit Character Style Sheet dialog box, but that gives you no control over the type of underline, its position, color, or pattern. In the Rules pane, you set the rules for these rules.

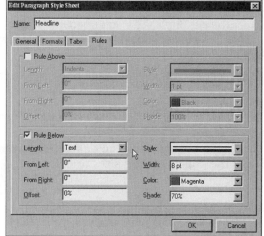

Figure 6-11:
The Rules pane of the Edit Paragraph Style Sheet dialog box.

First, decide whether you want the rules above and/or below your paragraph. Check the Rule Above and Rule Below box as appropriate. You can set the two rules independently, which is why you see the exact same specifications twice, once for each rule. You're not seeing double — QuarkXPress is simply giving you identical controls for each rule. Here's what you have control over:

- ✔ **Length** lets you choose between Text, which makes the rule the same width as the text (the top or bottom line of the paragraph, depending on whether the rule is above or below, if the paragraph has multiple lines), or Indents, which makes the rule a specific length.

- ✔ **From Left** tells QuarkXPress how far from the column's left margin to start the rule, if you selected Index in the Length pop-up menu.

- ✔ **From Right** tells QuarkXPress how far from the column's right margin to end the rule, if you selected Index in the Length pop-up menu.

- ✔ **Offset** is tricky. You can enter a percentage from 0% to 100% to move the rule away from the text, but the difference between 0% and 100% is just a point or two. Or you can enter a value like 1.0" or –9 pt to position the rule relative to the text. Larger positive numbers move the rule above the text's baseline; a value of 0 puts the rule at the baseline, while a negative number moves the rule below the baseline. (The maximum and minimum values depend on the point size and leading; QuarkXPress tells you when you exceed the specific text's limits.) You simply have to experiment with these settings until you get what you want.

- ✔ **Style** lets you select the rule style. The pop-up menu displays any rules defined in the Dashes & Stripes dialog box (Edit⇨Dashes & Stripes); Chapter 12 covers this in detail.

- ✔ **Width** is the rule's thickness. Choose from the pop-up menu's sizes or enter your own in the field.

- ✔ **Color** lets you select a color for the rule. Any color defined in the document (see Chapter 15) appears in this list.

- ✔ **Shade** lets you set the percentage of the color selected (including black). Choose from the pop-up menu's sizes or enter your own in the field.

The QuarkXPress Style Sheets dialog box has a nifty new feature that makes style management simpler. In the Show pop-up menu, you can choose which style sheets you want to display: All Style Sheets, Paragraph Style Sheets, Character Style Sheets, Style Sheets in Use, and Style Sheets Not Used. Those last two come in really handy.

Making styles happen

When you count them up, you really have three possible ways to apply a style. You can see two of the ways (Options 1 and 2) in Figure 6-12:

- ✔ **Option 1:** Use the Style⇨Paragraph Style Sheet and Style⇨Character Style Sheet menu options.

- ✔ **Option 2:** Use the Style Sheets palette, shown on the right side of the figure (View⇨Show Style Sheets, or F11). This option is our favorite way to apply styles in most cases.

- ✔ **Option 3:** Use the keyboard shortcut, if you defined one in the Style Sheets dialog box. (In Figure 6-12, we did not invoke a shortcut key.) Although this option is the fastest method, use it only for very commonly used styles because you need to remember the keyboard shortcuts that you assign.

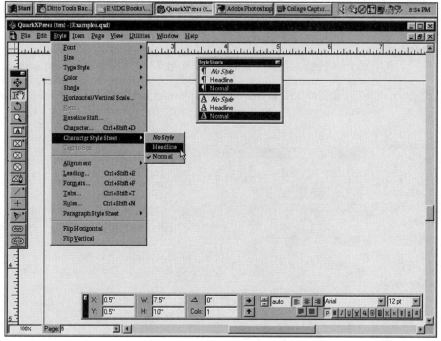

Figure 6-12:
QuarkXPress
offers three
ways to
apply style,
including
menus and
a palette.

If you aren't convinced that style sheets can save you a great deal of time, we suggest you take a few minutes and give them a try, and then compare formatting a document with them to formatting a document without them. Most desktop publishers find style sheets to be terrific time-savers, and we think you will, too.

Altering Styles

Decisions, decisions. Just when you think you've created a great style, you think again and decide to make some little changes to it so that it can be even better — you know, add half a point to the size of your headline, make your byline italic, change the leading on your body copy — those kinds of changes.

Again, you can easily make changes to a style: Simply open the Style Sheets dialog box, select the style sheet you want to change, and click Edit. You then can change attributes as you want. You also can use this approach to create new styles based on current ones or to create duplicate styles and modify them to make new ones.

If you want to compare two styles, QuarkXPress has a great new feature that makes it easy to do so. Select the two styles in the Style Sheets dialog box (⌘+click or Ctrl+click the second style so that the first style remains selected as well). Then hold down the Option or Alt key and see the Append button become the Compare button. Click Compare, and you get a dialog box like the one shown in Figure 6-13. With this new feature, you can now tell quickly how styles differ, making it easier for you to identify the styles that you need to alter to ensure typographic consistency in your document.

Figure 6-13:
The new
Compare
option
shows the
differences
between
two styles.

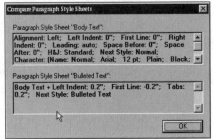

Based-on styles

When you create styles for a document, you probably want several similar styles, perhaps with some styles even being variations of others. For example, you may want both a body text style *and* a style for bulleted lists that's based on the body text style.

No problem: QuarkXPress uses a technique called *based-on formatting* in its styles. By selecting the Based On option in the Edit Character Style dialog box, you can tell QuarkXPress to base the Bulleted Text character style on the Body Text character style (in which you defined typeface, point size, leading, justification, hyphenation, indentation, tabs, and other attributes). You then modify the Bulleted Text character style to accommodate bullets — by changing the indentation, for example. The great thing about based-on formatting is that, later, if you decide to change the typeface in Body Text, the typeface automatically changes in Bulleted Text and in all other character styles that you created or edited based on Body Text — saving you a great deal of work in maintaining consistent styles.

Duplicating styles

Another nifty way to change an existing style or create a new one is to duplicate an existing style and then edit the attributes in that duplicate.

Duplicating a style is similar to creating a based-on style, except that the new style does not automatically update if you modify the style it is duplicated from — unless you base the style that you duplicated or edited on another style.

Replacing styles

With QuarkXPress 4, you can now replace style sheets in your document as easily as you can change text. In fact, you use the same method: the Find/ Change feature (Edit⇨Find/Change, or ⌘+F or Ctrl+F). When you use this feature, you may wonder how you can replace style sheets because you see no obvious option to do so. The trick is to uncheck the Ignore Attributes check box; doing so enlarges the dialog box to make room for new options (see Figure 6-14).

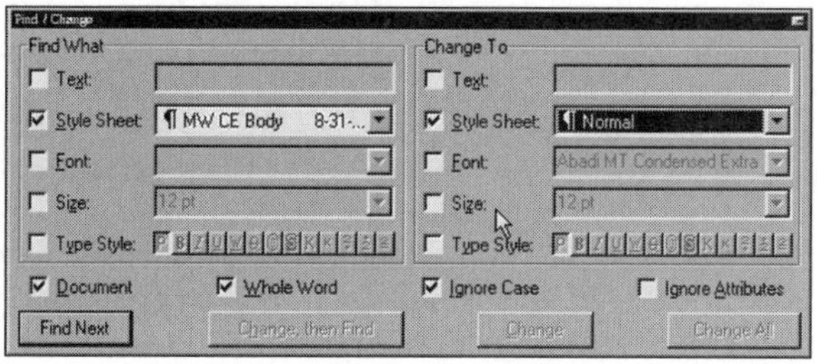

Figure 6-14:
The Find/
Change
dialog box
with the
new Style
Sheet
options
checked.

To replace one style sheet with another, check the Style Sheet check boxes in the Find What and Change To sections of the Find/Change dialog box and then use the pop-up menus to specify which style sheet should replace another. When you do this, make sure you're at the beginning of your document or story — QuarkXPress only searches from the text cursor's location, ignoring text before it. (A *story* is the QuarkXPress term for text in the current text box and any text boxes linked to it.) (To replace the style throughout the document, make sure that the Document check box is selected; to replace the style only in the current story, make sure the Document check box is unchecked.)

Click the Find Next button to find the first occurrence of the style you want to replace. Then click Change All to have QuarkXPress replace all occurrences of that style from that point on, or click Change Then Find to replace the found text's style and look for the next occurrence, or click Change to change the found text's style, but not look for the next occurrence.

Note that replacing a style sheet does not get rid of that style sheet — it simply retags all the text that uses the original style sheet with the new style sheet.

Importing Styles

Sometimes you find yourself in a situation where you already have style sheets in one QuarkXPress document that are *just right* for what you need in another one. Have no fear — you don't need to start the process all over again. Just copy styles from one document to another.

Copying styles between documents

You copy styles between documents by selecting the Append button in the Style Sheets dialog box to open the Append Style Sheets dialog box (see Figure 6-15). This dialog box is similar to the dialog box for opening a QuarkXPress document. You can change drives and directories as needed to select the QuarkXPress document that has the style sheet you want. You can also append style sheets through the Append dialog box (File➪Append), which also lets you append other settings, such as color definitions.

In previous versions of QuarkXPress, when you selected a document from the Append Style Sheets dialog box and clicked OK, QuarkXPress copied all of that document's styles — except those with the same name as styles in your current document. You couldn't pick and choose individual styles to import. But QuarkXPress 4 changes all that. Now you can select the individual styles you want to copy. And if a style you select to append has the same name as one already in the current document, you get to choose whether to override the current style with the one you want to copy, cancel the appending of that style, or append the style anyhow but give it a new name.

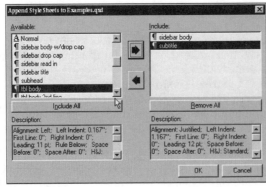

Figure 6-15:
The Append Style Sheets dialog box.

Importing styles from a word processor

Some people create text right inside the text boxes of a QuarkXPress document (using the QuarkXPress built-in text editor). Others prefer to use a separate word processing program for drafting the text and import that text later into QuarkXPress. Either way works fine, and both methods let you take advantage of style sheets.

QuarkXPress lets you import paragraph styles created in Microsoft Word and Corel WordPerfect. To make the process of importing text files that include style sheets work smoothly, we suggest that you first make sure there's a check in the Include Style Sheets box — at the bottom of the Get Text box — as shown in Figure 6-16.

Figure 6-16:
Check the
Include
Style
Sheets
option
when you
import a
word-
processor
document
that has
style sheets
associated
with it.

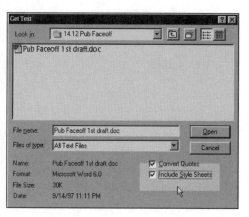

You also use the Include Style Sheets option if you want to import text saved in the XPress Tags format (described in an appendix of the QuarkXPress documentation). Although the purpose of the XPress Tags format is to embed style tags and other formatting information in your text, you still must remind QuarkXPress to read those tags during import. Otherwise, QuarkXPress imports your text as an ASCII file and treats all the embedded tags as regular text without acting upon them.

If you check the Include Style Sheets check box for word-processor formats that have no style sheets, QuarkXPress ignores the setting. Thus, if you typically import style sheets with your text, get into the habit of always checking this box; checking the box does not cause any problems when importing other text formats.

If the imported style sheet has a style tag that uses a name already in use by the QuarkXPress document, QuarkXPress gives you the option of renaming the imported style tag or ignoring it and using the existing QuarkXPress style tag in its place. It's nice to be able to resolve style conflicts so easily, and this capability is just one more reason to use style sheets. (In previous versions of QuarkXPress, the program would add an asterisk [*] to the end of the word-processor style's name if a QuarkXPress style by the same name existed. You then had to delete that imported style and tell QuarkXPress to substitute the existing QuarkXPress style. Much easier now, eh?)

As you can tell, we are style-sheet fans to the core. Style sheets are a cool invention. They save you time. And saving time saves you money. And we all know that saving money is a good thing.

Chapter 7

Working with Special Characters

*B*efore desktop publishing, you could always distinguish homegrown publications from the professionally produced kind by the difference in typography. Homegrown publications were typewritten and either dittoed, mimeographed, or photocopied; professional publications were typeset. Anyone could spot the difference: In a homegrown publication, you saw two hyphens (- -) as a dash, while in a professional publication, you saw the (—) character; an apostrophe or single quote was (') in a homegrown publication, while in a professional publication it was (') or ('). And, of course, a homegrown publication used (") as the double quote character, while a professional publication used (") or ("). Not to mention the fact that professionally produced publications also had accents on letters (at least sometimes), different styles of characters, a whole slew of symbols (at least sometimes), and even characters of different sizes.

Then came desktop publishing. Soon anyone with a Mac or PC had access to the same typeset characters. The only problem was that most people didn't know how to use these characters. All sorts of keyboard commands could be used to get these characters, but who could remember them all? So you kept seeing (- -) and (') and (") in documents that looked professional; you could tell that the documents had come off of someone's laser printer because of those telltale typewriter characters.

But working with special characters soon became simpler with QuarkXPress. Quark would automatically convert the typewriter dashes and quotes into typographic dashes and quotes — but only when you imported text. Not until version 3.3 came out in 1994 did Quark add the ability to generate those quotation characters as you typed text. Unfortunately, you still have to type in dashes the hard way — by using special keyboard commands — even with the 1997 version 4. Still, automating the quotes goes a long way toward helping your publications look professionally produced. Today, it's nearly impossible to tell by the characters alone whether a publication is professional or homegrown.

Typographic Characters

Your otherwise-humble authors are typographic snobs, so we think everyone should use the curly quotes and the long-line dash instead of the typewriter symbols. Why? Because professional typographers always use them, and they've become synonymous with professionalism. And besides, they're so easy to use now that you have no excuse not to use them.

Quotes and dashes

One of the first things you should do in QuarkXPress is to set it up to automatically type in the professional characters for you.

Go to the Interactive pane in the Applications Preferences dialog box (Edit⇨Preferences⇨Application, or Option+Shift+⌘+Y or Ctrl+Alt+Shift+Y), as shown in Figure 7-1. You can ignore most of the dialog box for now; only the options highlighted in the middle affect typography. Make sure that the Smart Quotes option is checked: Smart Quotes converts quotes as you type (sorry, it won't do dashes).

If you're not publishing in English, you can select a different set of quote characters through the Format pop-up menu also shown in Figure 7-1.

For many preferences, to make them affect all QuarkXPress documents, you have to make sure that no document is open before you change the preferences. Otherwise, the changed preferences will apply only to that document. But any preferences set via the Application Preferences dialog box affect all documents, whether or not a document was open when you set those preferences. Here's a case where you can lower your guard.

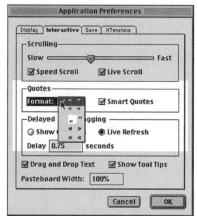

The
Interactive
pane lets
you set up
automatic
conversion
of keyboard
quotes
into their
typographic
equivalents.

In text files that you import, you can ensure that QuarkXPress converts the quotes and, yes, even the dashes, by checking the Convert Quotes box when you import (File⇨Get Text, or ⌘+E or Ctrl+E). So you don't forget to check that box each time you import, QuarkXPress leaves the box checked for all future imports until, of course, you uncheck it. Figure 7-2 shows how the dialog box should look when you take the precaution of keeping the Convert Quotes box checked.

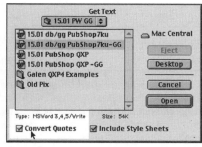

Figure 7-2:
When
importing
text, check
the Convert
Quotes
box to
automatically
convert
keyboard
dashes and
quotes.

The Mac has many built-in shortcuts for special characters and symbols, and QuarkXPress adds some of its own. Windows also supports many symbols, although it uses special codes for most, rather than keyboard shortcuts. So, when you refer to the shortcut tables throughout this chapter (starting with Table 7-1), keep the following three conditions in mind:

✔ Not all keyboard shortcuts are available in all programs. This is truer in Windows than on the Mac, because Windows programs generally have less consistency among themselves than Mac programs.

✔ Not all symbols are supported in all fonts; for symbols listed as *not supported,* you may be able to find a symbol or pi font that includes the symbol (as used here, *not supported* means that the symbol is not available in standard fonts).

✔ To use the Windows codes, hold the Alt key and enter the four-digit numeral code from the numeric keypad, not from the numbers on the keyboard (above the letters). The Mac does not use an equivalent numeric system; instead, all characters are accessible through some shortcut combination.

Table 7-1	Shortcuts for Quotes and Dashes	
Character	*Mac Shortcut*	*Windows Shortcut*
Open double quote (")*	Option+Shift+[	Shift+Alt+[*or* Alt+0147
Close double quote (")*	Option+Shift+]	Shift+Alt+] *or* Alt+0148
Open French double quote («)*	Option+\	Ctrl+Alt+[*or* Alt+0171
Close French double quote (»)*	Option+Shift+\	Ctrl+Alt+] *or* Alt+0187
Open single quote (')*	Option+[	Alt+[
Close single quote (')*	Option+]	Alt+]
Breaking em dash (—)**	Option+Shift+- (hyphen)	Ctrl+Shift+= *or* Alt+0151
Nonbreaking en dash (–)	Option+- (hyphen)	Ctrl+= *or* Alt+0150
Nonbreaking em dash (—)	Option+⌘+=	Ctrl+Shift+Alt+=

* All of these quotes are automatically generated when you type if the Smart Quotes option is selected in the Interactive pane of the Application Preferences dialog box (Edit⇨Preferences⇨ Application). Typing an apostrophe creates an open or closed single quote as appropriate, and typing a keyboard quote (") creates an open or closed double quote as appropriate. For double quotes, you can choose the quotation style to match those used in several European languages; you set the quotation style in the Application Preferences dialog box. These quotes are also automatically generated when you have the Convert Quotes check box selected when importing text files via Edit⇨Get Text.

** The breaking em dash is automatically generated when you have the Convert Quotes check box checked when importing text files via Edit⇨Get Text.

Ligatures (only for Macs)

After you set up your Application Preferences dialog box to enable smart quotes, if you use a Mac, the very next thing to do is go to the Character pane in the Document Preferences dialog box (Edit⇨Preferences⇨ Document or ⌘+Y). Here, you set up the treatment of ligatures, which are special forms of characters that are linked together. Figure 7-3 shows the appropriate pane, with the ligature section highlighted.

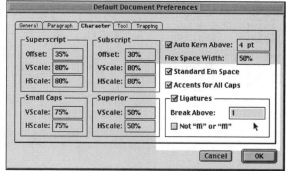

Figure 7-3: Check the Ligatures box in the Character pane to enable ligatures (available on the Mac only).

The Character pane is different in Windows than on the Mac because Windows does not support ligatures. To say that another way: You see no ligature options in the Windows QuarkXPress dialog box (Edit⇨ Preferences⇨Document or Ctrl+Y). When you bring a Mac file that has ligatures into Windows QuarkXPress, QuarkXPress translates the ligatures back to regular characters. If you move the file back to the Mac, the ligatures reappear. There's a slight chance that such translation could affect the line length in your document, so double check to make sure you didn't gain or lose a line or two.

To reiterate, *ligatures* are linked-together characters seen in many books, where you find the combination of *f* and *i* typeset not as *fi* but as *fi*. Such a combination avoids having the dot on the *i* get in the way of the top curve or the bar of the *f*. There's also an *fl* ligature, an *ffi* ligature, and an *ffl* ligature.

Figure 7-4 shows some ligatures up close. Other ligatures than these occur in some fonts, but QuarkXPress automatically handles only these four; for others (assuming that the font supports other ligatures), you have to enter the ligature code manually (a process we describe later in this chapter).

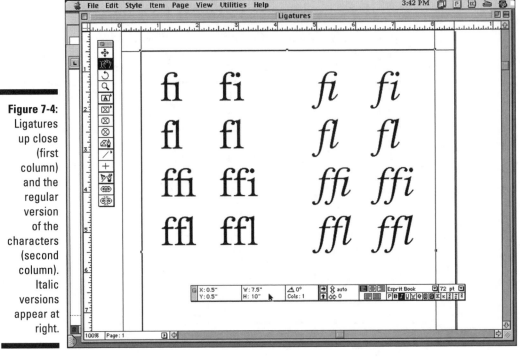

Figure 7-4:
Ligatures
up close
(first
column)
and the
regular
version
of the
characters
(second
column).
Italic
versions
appear at
right.

Now you see them, now you don't

If you use ligatures, you may find that sometimes the combined characters appear as a ligature and sometimes they don't. Ligatures vary because of the spacing computations used by QuarkXPress.

Ligatures make sense when characters are close together, because that's when pieces of the characters may overlap (which is the problem that ligatures were designed to solve). But when text is spaced more widely, the characters won't overprint; in such a case, you have no reason to combine them. In fact, if you did combine them, you'd have a weird appearance (well, actually, your document would have a weird appearance) because most letters would have space between them *except for* the ligatures.

QuarkXPress automatically figures out when the characters should be combined into ligatures and when they should not, so don't worry about it. In fact, QuarkXPress is so smart that if you did a search for the word *first* and the *fi* was a ligature in your test, QuarkXPress would find the ligature even though you entered *fi* in the Find dialog box.

If you use the codes to insert the actual ligature character *fi* or *fl* (see Table 7-2), you won't be able to search for words using those ligatures unless you also use the ligature code in your search text.

Table 7-2	Shortcuts for Ligatures*	
Character	*Mac Shortcut*	*Windows Shortcut*
fi	Option+Shift+5	*not supported*
fl	Option+Shift+6	*not supported*
ffi	*no shortcut*	*not supported*
ffl	*no shortcut*	*not supported*

* Automatically generated if you check the Ligatures box in the Character pane of the Document Preferences dialog box (Edit⇨Preferences⇨Document).

When you use the codes in Table 7-2, you actually put in the ligature character; when QuarkXPress generates the ligatures for you, it keeps the actual letters in your document but substitutes for them both onscreen and when printing the ligature characters. Note that these coded ligature characters may appear in your Find dialog box as a square. That's okay: QuarkXPress still searches for the actual character. Also note that using codes to generate ligatures, rather than using the QuarkXPress automatic ligature feature, also causes the spelling checker to flag words with the coded-in ligatures as suspect words. The lesson: Don't code-in ligatures. It's not worth the hassle.

Accented and Foreign Characters

You don't have to use accents for words like *café* that came to English from another language. *Cafe* is quite acceptable. But adding the accent to the *e* gives the word a bit more sophistication (plus it helps people pronounce it *ka-fay* rather than *kayfe!*). Of course, if your publication is international, you want to use the international characters and accents.

First, decide how you want to treat accents on capital letters. If you use accents, you always use them on lowercase letters, but you have an option for uppercase letters — so long as you are consistent and either always use the accents on capitalized letters or never use them within the same publication. QuarkXPress lets you make consistent decisions on accents with ease.

In the Character pane of the Document Preferences dialog box (Edit⇨Preferences⇨Document, or ⌘+Y or Ctrl+Y) shown back in Figure 7-3, you have an option called Accents for All Caps. If you check that option, all accented letters keep their accents when capitalized. If you don't check that option, the accent is removed when the letters are capitalized and reinstated when the letters are lowercased. With this option, you can always add the accents as you type and then have QuarkXPress take care of handling the uppercase letters.

So how do you get the accents in the first place? Table 7-3 shows the various codes. Note that the Mac and Windows platforms handle accents and foreign characters differently, as we explain in the next two sections.

Table 7-3	Shortcuts for Accents and Foreign Characters	
Character	*Mac Shortcut*	*Windows Shortcut*
acute (´)*	Option+E *letter*	' *letter*
cedilla (ç)*	*see Ç and ç*	' *letter*
circumflex (^)*	Option+I *letter*	^ *letter*
grave (`)*	Option+' *letter*	` *letter*
tilde (~)*	Option+N *letter*	~ *letter*
trema (¨)*	Option+U *letter*	" *letter*
umlaut (¨)*	Option+U *letter*	" *letter*
Á	Option+E A	' A *or* Alt+0193
á	Option+E a	' a *or* Alt+0225
À	Option+' A	` A *or* Alt+0192
à	Option+' a	` a *or* Alt+0224
Ä	Option+U A	" A *or* Alt+0196
ä	Option+U a	" a *or* Alt+0228
Ã	Option+N A	~ A *or* Alt+0195
ã	Option+N a	~ a *or* Alt+0227
Â	Option+I A	^ A *or* Alt+0194
â	Option+I a	^ a *or* Alt+0226
Å	Option+Shift+A	Alt+0197
å	Option+A	Alt+0229
Æ	Option+Shift+ `	Alt+0198
æ	Option+ `	Alt+0230 *or* Ctrl+Alt+Z
Ç	Option+Shift+C	` C *or* Alt+0199

Character	Mac Shortcut	Windows Shortcut
ç	Option+C	` c *or* Alt+0231 *or* Ctrl+Alt+,
Đ	*not supported*	Alt+0208
ð	*not supported*	Alt+0240
É	Option+E E	` E *or* Alt+0201
é	Option+E e	' e *or* Alt+0233
È	Option+` E	` E *or* Alt+0200
è	Option+` e	` e *or* Alt+0232
Ë	Option+U E	" E *or* Alt+0203
ë	Option+U e	" e *or* Alt+0235
Ê	Option+I E	^ E *or* Alt+0202
ê	Option+I e	^ e *or* Alt+0234
Í	Option+E I	' I *or* Alt+-205
í	Option+E i	` i *or* Alt+0237
Ì	Option+` I	` I *or* Alt+0204
ì	Option+` i	` i *or* Alt+0236
Ï	Option+U I	" I *or* Alt+0207
ï	Option+U i	" I *or* Alt+0239
Î	Option+I I	^ I *or* Alt+0206
î	Option+I i	^ I *or* Alt+0238
Ñ	Option+N N	~ N *or* Alt+0209
ñ	Option+N n	~ n *or* Alt+0241
Ó	Option+E O	' O *or* Alt+0211
ó	Option+E o	' o *or* Alt+0243 *or* Ctrl+Alt+O
Ò	Option+` O	` O *or* Alt+0210
ò	Option+` o	` o *or* Alt+0242
Ö	Option+U O	" O *or* Alt+0214
ö	Option+U o	" o *or* Alt+0246
Õ	Option+N O	~ O *or* Alt+0213
õ	Option+N o	~ o *or* Alt+0245
Ô	Option+I O	^ O *or* Alt+0212
ô	Option+I o	^ o *or* Alt+0244
Ø	Option+Shift+O	Alt+0216

(continued)

Table 7-3 *(continued)*

Character	*Mac Shortcut*	*Windows Shortcut*
ø	Option+O	Alt+0248 *or* Ctrl+Alt+L
Œ	Option+Shift+Q	Alt+0140
œ	Option+Q	Alt+0156
Þ	*not supported*	Alt+0222
þ	*not supported*	Alt+0254
Š	*not supported*	Alt+0138
š	*not supported*	Alt+0154
Ú	Option+E U	' U or Alt+0218
ú	Option+E u	' u or Alt+0250 *or* Ctrl+Alt+U
Ù	Option+` U	` U or Alt+0217
ù	Option+` u	` u or Alt+0249
Ü	Option+U U	" U or Alt+0220
ü	Option+U u	" u or Alt+0252
Û	Option+I U	^ U or Alt+0219
û	Option+I u	^ u or Alt+0251
Ý	*not supported*	` Y or Alt+0221
ý	*not supported*	` y or Alt+0253
Ÿ	Option+U Y	" Y *or* Alt+0159
ÿ	Option+U y	" y *or* Alt+0255
Spanish open exclamation (¡)	Option+1	Ctrl+Alt+1 *or* Alt+-0161
Spanish open question (¿)	Option+Shift+/	Ctrl+Alt+/ *or* Alt+0191
French open double quote («)**	Option+\	Ctrl+Alt+[*or* Alt+0171
French close double quote (»)**	Option+Shift+\	Ctrl+Alt+] *or* Alt+0187

* On the Mac, enter the shortcut for the accent and then type the letter to be accented. For example, to get *é*, type Option+E and then the letter *e*. In Windows, if the keyboard layout is set to United States-International — via the Keyboard icon in the Windows Control Panel — you can enter the accent signifier and then type the letter (for example, type ' and then the letter *e* to get *è*).

** Automatically generated if the Smart Quotes option is selected in the Application Preferences dialog box (Edit⇨Preferences⇨Application) and the French quotes are selected in the Quote pop-up list, also in the Application Preferences dialog box.

Pretty daunting, you say? Relax. It's not as bad as it looks. Just follow the advice in the following two sections to reduce the effort needed to produce the most commonly accented letters.

Because the process for using accents and foreign characters on Windows differs significantly from the Mac, we cover the procedures for the two platforms separately.

Foreign characters on the Mac

For the five most common accent marks — the *grave* (`), the *acute* (´), the *circumflex* (ˆ), the *tilde* (˜), and the *umlaut* or *trema* (¨) — you can have the Mac automatically generate the accented character by first entering the code for the accent you want and then the letter you want it applied to. You see those codes back in Table 7-3: Option+' for grave, Option+E for acute, Option+I for circumflex, Option+N for tilde, and Option+U for umlaut (or trema). Thus, Option+E followed by an *o* results in ó. If you type a combination and get two characters (rather than an accented character), you've just discovered that the font you're using doesn't support that particular accented letter.

For some characters, you have to enter a specific code. For example, no accent code exists to generate the *cedilla* in ç, so you have to enter the code Option+C to get it. Table 7-3 shows these characters as well.

A few specific visual options help you as well. You can use the Key Caps software that comes with the Mac, shown in Figure 7-5. (You can find the KeyCaps software under the Apple menu or, if you removed the software or never installed it, on the Tidbits disk of your system disks, in the Apple Items folder; in System 7.5, System 7.6, and Mac OS 8, look for it in the Custom install option list.)

You can also use the $39 shareware control panel PopChar Pro, shown in Figure 7-6, available on popular online services, as well as on the *Macworld* Web site (www.macworld.com/software/).

Both the Key Caps and PopChar Pro utilities show you keyboard layouts and let you select the characters you want; they also display the shortcuts for the characters. We prefer PopChar Pro, because you can set it to pop up when you click an upper corner of your screen and because it shows all available characters on one screen, letting you double-click them for immediate insertion into your document. Key Caps makes you hold the Option, ⌘, and other keys to see what's available for keyboard combinations using them.

Figure 7-5:
The Key
Caps utility
lets you
select
special
characters,
including
accents.

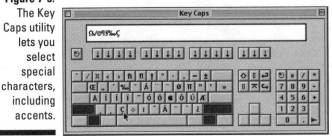

Figure 7-6:
The
PopChar
Pro utility
displays all
available
characters
at once.

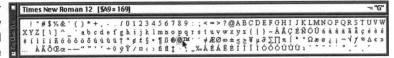

When you create your text, you can also use the special symbol features that come with your favorite word processor. Microsoft Word 6.0 or 5.x (via Insert⇨Symbol) and WordPerfect 3.x (via Insert⇨Symbols) both have an option to insert special characters from a PopChar Pro-like list. Figure 7-7 shows the two dialog boxes. Also, Word 6.0 lets you assign your own shortcuts for symbols and foreign characters (for use within Word only).

QuarkXPress 4 cannot read the latest versions of Word (Word 97 on Windows and Word 98 on the Mac) or WordPerfect for Windows 8. If you use those programs, you need to save your files in a previous format: Windows Word 95 (7.0) or 6.0; Mac Word 6.0, 5.x, 4.0, or 3.0; Windows WordPerfect 6.x; and Mac WordPerfect 3.5, 3.1, or 2.1.

Finally, if the foreign character you want simply is not available in your font, you may need to buy a version of the font that has the characters you want. Generally, you find Cyrillic, Greek, and other character sets for popular fonts like Times and Helvetica; in a pinch, you can use one of these characters with a similar font like Palatino or Univers. But if you use decorative or other less-universal fonts, you may not be able to get a version with the special characters you need. And keep in mind that the Symbol font that comes with the Mac includes most Greek letters.

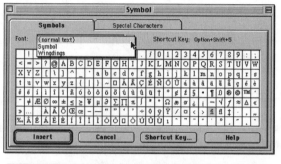

Figure 7-7:
The
special-
character
dialog
boxes in
Word 6.0
(top) and
WordPerfect
3.5 (bottom).

Foreign characters in Windows

For the six most common accent marks — the grave (`), the acute (´), the circumflex (^), the tilde (˜), the cedilla (˒), and the umlaut or trema (¨) — you can have Windows automatically generate the accented character by first entering a character that invokes the accent you want and then the letter you want it applied to. Table 7-3 at the beginning of this section shows those characters: ' for grave, ' for acute and cedilla, ^ for circumflex, ~ for tilde, and " for umlaut (or trema). Thus, ' followed by an *o* results in *ó*. If you type a combination and get two characters, rather than an accented character, it means that font doesn't support that particular accented letter.

For Windows to generate these accented characters, you need to set it to use the US-International keyboard layout. Figure 7-8 shows the sequence.

First, you go to the Windows Control Panel, in which you click the Keyboard icon. (The Control Panel usually resides in the Start button's main menu, so you can usually access it via Start⇨Settings⇨Control Panel, unless it was moved elsewhere.) That opens up the Keyboard dialog box also shown in the figure. Go to the Language pane, where you click the Properties button to change the Keyboard Layout option from United States to United States-International.

Sometimes when you set Windows to use the United States-International keyboard layout, you get frustrated. You type along, minding your own business, and all of a sudden you get an accented character instead of the quoted text you wanted. For example, you type `A man` but get ` man` instead. What to do? Get into the habit of typing a space after the `` ` ``, ", and ' characters. Allowing for that extra measly space prevents unintended, spontaneous accents. Why? Because typing a space after those specific characters — or, for that matter, after the ^ and ~, too — tells Windows to type those characters rather than prepare for the possibility of adding an accent if the next character is accentable.

For some foreign characters, you have to enter a specific code. For example, no accent code exists to generate the *hacek* in š, so you have to enter the code Alt+0154 (using the numerals on the numeric keypad, not the numerals above the letter keys) to get hacek. In some cases, you use keyboard shortcuts to get these foreign characters, such as Ctrl+Alt+Z to get the diphthong (æ) character. Table 7-3 shows these codes and shortcuts. You also can use these shortcuts if you don't use the United States-International keyboard layout. Note that some programs may use the shortcuts for something else, in which case you can't use them to generate the foreign character.

What do you do in those cases? Read on.

A few visual options can help you as well. You can use the Character Map software that comes with Windows. (It should be in the Accessories group — accessed via Start⇨Programs⇨Accessories — unless someone moved it; if you removed it or never installed it, run the Windows setup and select it for installation.) We move Character Map to our Startup group so that we always have it available in the Start menu as a minimized icon. Figure 7-9 shows Character Map.

Notice how the Character Map magnifies the character that your pointer is currently on? It also displays the code for the selected character and lets you select and copy characters to the Windows Clipboard so that you can paste them into your text. You can even change fonts if the character you want is available in a different font than your text uses. (A choice of fonts comes in very handy when inserting foreign characters, like Greek or Cyrillic, not available in standard fonts.) We change fonts all the time and suspect that you may, too.

If you close Character Map, you have to relaunch it from the Accessories or Startup group (or whatever group you put it in). Unfortunately, you can't easily prevent this, so try to get in the habit of minimizing.

When you create your text, you can also use the special symbol features that come with your favorite word processor. Whether you use Microsoft Word 6, 95, or 97 (via Insert⇨Symbol) or WordPerfect 6, 7, or 8 (via Insert⇨Character, or Shift+F11), you have an option to insert special

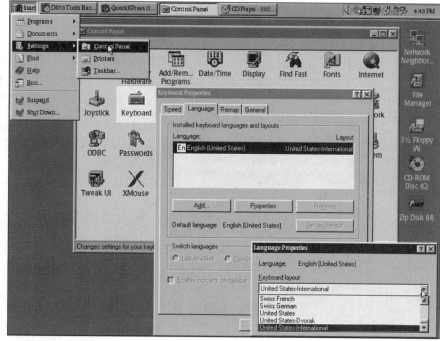

Figure 7-8:
By changing your keyboard layout to United States-International, you can have Windows automatically create accented characters.

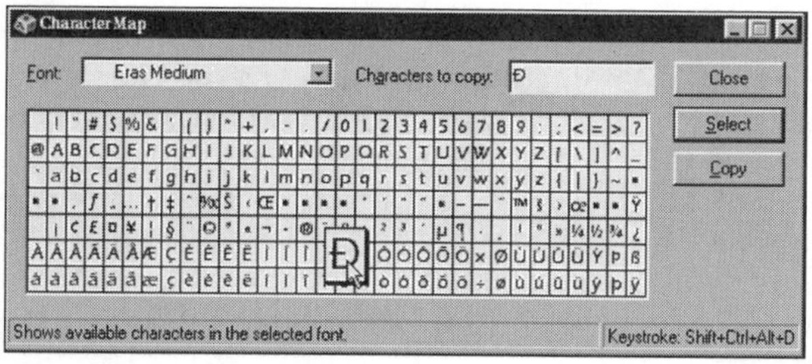

Figure 7-9:
The Character Map utility lets you select special characters, for use in your document.

characters from a Character Map-like list. Figure 7-10 shows the two dialog boxes. Word lets you assign your own shortcuts for symbols and foreign characters (for use within Word only); WordPerfect ships with TrueType fonts in several character sets (including Greek, Cyrillic, Japanese, Hebrew, Arabic, mathematical, and phonetic).

QuarkXPress 4 cannot read the latest versions of Word (Word 97 on Windows and Word 98 on the Mac) or WordPerfect for Windows 8. If you use those programs, you need to save your files in a previous format: Windows

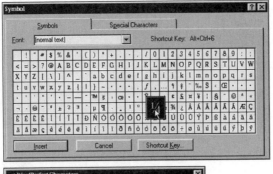

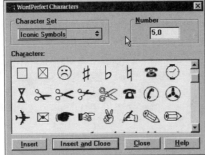

Figure 7-10:
The Special
Character
dialog
boxes in
Word 95
(top) and
WordPerfect
6.1 (bottom).
Later
versions of
the two
programs
have the
same dialog
boxes.

Word 95 (7.0) or 6.0; Mac Word 6.0, 5.x, 4.0, or 3.0; Windows WordPerfect 6.x; and Mac WordPerfect 3.5, 3.1, or 2.1.

Finally, if the foreign character you want simply is not available in your font, you may need to buy a version of the font that has the characters you want. Generally, you can find Cyrillic, Greek, and other character sets for popular fonts like Times and Helvetica; in a pinch, you can use one of these characters with a similar font like Palatino or Univers. But if you use decorative or other less-universal fonts, you may not be able to get a version with the special characters you need. And keep in mind that the Symbol font that comes with Windows includes most Greek letters.

Special Punctuation

"What's the deal with punctuation?" you may ask. "That's what grammar books are for." True enough, but you can use some tricks to access special punctuation in addition to the typographic versions of quotes and dashes we talk about earlier in this chapter. You can't automate the other punctuation you may need — QuarkXPress won't substitute, for example, an ellipsis (...) when you type three periods (. . .). Besides, you may not even know how to access these characters because they're not on your computer. The sections that follow show you how to get those characters. Table 7-4 shows the shortcuts to get them into your document.

Table 7-4	Shortcuts for Other Punctuation	
Character	*Mac Shortcut*	*Windows Shortcut*
Ellipsis (...)	Option+; (semicolon)	Ctrl+Alt+. (period) *or* Alt+0133
En bullet (•)	Option+8	Shift+Alt8 *or* Alt+0149
Nonbreaking hyphen (-)	⌘+=	Ctrl+Shift+hyphen
Discretionary (soft) hyphen (-)	⌘+- (hyphen)	Ctrl+- (hyphen)
Nonbreaking en dash (–)	Option+- (hyphen)	Ctrl+= *or* Alt+0150
Nonbreaking space	⌘+spacebar	Ctrl+spacebar
Breaking en space	Option+spacebar	Ctrl+Shift+6
Nonbreaking en space	Option+⌘+spacebar	Ctrl+Shift+Alt+6
Breaking punctuation space	Shift+spacebar	Shift+spacebar
Nonbreaking punctuation space	Shift+⌘+spacebar	Ctrl+Shift+spacebar
Breaking flexible space	Option+Shift+spacebar	Ctrl+Shift+5
Nonbreaking flexible space	Option+⌘+spacebar	Ctrl+Shift+Alt+5

The many bullets (all nonlethal)

A *bullet* is a form of punctuation that starts an element in a list. On a typewriter, you use an asterisk (*) to indicate a bullet. But in desktop publishing (and in modern word processing), you have the real thing: the character that typographers call an *en bullet* (•).

You can find *many* more bullets than the en bullet that we all know and love. First off, bullets don't even have to be round. They can take any shape — squares, stars, arrows, or triangles. They can be hollow or solid. They can be a small version of a corporate logo. They could be some other symbol — anything that clearly demarcates the start of a new item. Take a look at the symbol characters in Table 7-5 and also look at what symbols come with the Symbol and Zapf Dingbats fonts on most computers. While you're at it, check out the Wingdings fonts that ships with Windows and with the Mac version of Microsoft's Word 6.0 and Office 4.2 software. Figure 7-11 shows some example bullets.

You can use tons of symbols as bullets. For now, though, just make sure that you don't use an asterisk when you can use a bullet — it would be too tacky for words.

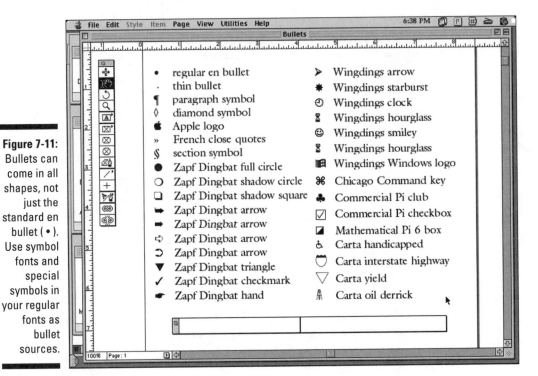

Figure 7-11:
Bullets can
come in all
shapes, not
just the
standard en
bullet (•).
Use symbol
fonts and
special
symbols in
your regular
fonts as
bullet
sources.

Ellipses

On a typewriter, you use three periods — some people put spaces around them, others don't — to indicate an *ellipsis,* the character (...) that indicates missing text, particularly in quoted material. You can also use it to indicate that a speaker trailed off when talking.

The nice thing about using the actual ellipsis character is this: As text moves within a column, some of the periods won't appear at the end of one line with the rest at the beginning of the next line. Of course, you can get around that design *faux pas* by typing the three periods with no spaces, which would make QuarkXPress see them as a single "word." But, if you do that, then the spacing within the ellipsis could be too tight or too loose, because it would be stretched or compressed like the other words on the line by the QuarkXPress justification feature. If you use the ellipsis character, the space between its constituent dots can't change, so the ellipsis always looks like, well, an ellipsis.

If you just don't like the look of three consecutive periods *or* a font's ellipses character, you have a third option: Use nonbreaking spaces between the periods. Spaces are covered later in this chapter.

Hyphens

Normally, a hyphen's a hyphen, right? Not always. If you want to hyphenate two words to a third, such as in "*Star Trek*–like," the proper typographic style, according to the World Typography Police, is to use an en dash instead of a hyphen (compare "*Star Trek*–like" to "*Star Trek*-like"). But using a regular hyphen is still no crime. You can also use variants of the hyphen, which Chapter 8 describes in more detail. These variants control the positioning of the hyphen; to a reader, a hyphen looks like a hyphen and an en dash looks like an en dash.

Spaces

A space is one of those characters you take for granted. So many people who get into desktop publishing wonder what all the fuss is about concerning different kinds of spaces. As with hyphens, the basic reasons for the different kinds of spaces is to affect positioning. What you need to know here is that you can use several fixed-size spaces that come in really handy when trying to align numbers in a table. An *en space* is the width of most numerals, and a *punctuation space* (also called a *thin space*) is the width of a comma or period. (In some popular fonts, like New Century Schoolbook, use an en space for punctuation as well as for numerals. And in a few decorative fonts, the numerals and punctuation don't correspond to any of the fixed spaces' widths.) So, if you try to decimal-align *10,000* and *50.12* against the left margin, you'd put three en spaces and a punctuation space in front of *50.12*. Figure 7-12 shows the results.

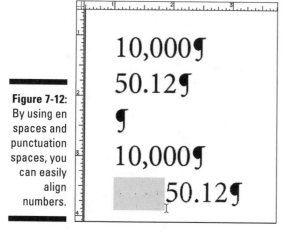

Figure 7-12: By using en spaces and punctuation spaces, you can easily align numbers.

Another type of fixed space is called the *flexible space*, or *flex space* for short. The user defines this space (via the Flex Space Width field in the Character pane of the Document Preferences dialog box, which you access via Edit⇨Preferences⇨Document, or ⌘+Y or Ctrl+Y). You enter its value in terms of the percentage of an en space. To get a punctuation (thin) space, you'd enter 50%; to get an em space, you'd enter 200%. Or you can create your own type of space and enter another value from 1% to 400%.

Unfortunately, you can't use these fixed spaces when right-aligning text. Say that you want to decimal-align *10,000* and *50.12* against the right margin. Based on the preceding example, you'd expect to put a punctuation space and two en spaces after the *10,000* before right-justifying the two numbers. But that won't work. QuarkXPress ignores spaces at the end of a line when it right-aligns (it does see them when centering, though). To get Quark to space correctly (rather than just space out) when you right-align, you have to use the tab feature in QuarkXPress instead, as we explain in Chapter 6.

Working with Symbols

We're amazed at how many special characters there are. You get more than 100 with each regular font, and scores if not hundreds of fonts (called symbol or pi fonts) contain nothing but symbols. Some people use symbols all the time; others rarely. Your own use of symbols depends on the kind of text you work with. Table 7-5 shows the shortcuts for the symbols that most Mac and Windows fonts offer. For symbol and pi fonts, you have to use the documentation that came with the font or a keyboard-character program (like the Mac's Key Caps utility, the PopChar Pro shareware program for Macs, or the Windows Character Map utility) to see what's available. The section "Accented and Foreign Characters" earlier in this chapter covers these programs in more detail.

Table 7-5	Shortcuts for Symbols	
Character	*Mac Shortcut*	*Windows Shortcut*
Legal		
Copyright (©)	Option+G	Shift+Alt+C *or* Ctrl+Alt+C *or* Alt+0169
Registered trademark (®)	Option+R	Shift+Alt+R *or* Alt+0174
Trademark (™)	Option+2	Shift+Alt+2 *or* Alt+0153
Paragraph (¶)	Option+7	Shift+Alt+7 *or* Ctrl+Alt+; *or* Alt+0182
Section (§)	Option+6	Shift+Alt+6 *or* Alt+0167

Character	Mac Shortcut	Windows Shortcut
Dagger (†)	Option+T	Shift+Alt+T *or* Alt+0134
Double dagger (‡)	Option+Shift+T	Alt+0135
Currency		
Cent (¢)	Option+4	Alt+0162
Pound sterling (£)	Option+3	Alt+0163
Yen (¥)	Option+Y	Ctrl+Alt+- (hyphen) *or* Alt+0165
Measurement		
Foot (')	*not supported**	Ctrl+'
Inch (")	*not supported**	Ctrl+Alt+"
Mathematics		
One-half fraction (½)	*not supported*	Ctrl+Alt+6 *or* Alt+0189
One-quarter fraction (¼)	*not supported*	Ctrl+Alt+7 *or* Alt+0188
Three-quarters fraction (¾)	*not supported*	Ctrl+Alt+8 *or* Alt+0190
Infinity (∞)	Option+5	*not supported*
Multiplication (×)	*not supported*	Ctrl+Alt+= *or* Alt+0215
Division (÷)	Option+/	Alt+0247
Root (√)	Option+V	*not supported*
Greater than or equal (≥)	Option+>	*not supported*
Less than or equal (≤)	Option+<	*not supported*
Inequality (≠)	Option+=	*not supported*
Rough equivalence (≈)	Option+X-	*not supported*
Plus or minus (±)	Option+Shift+=	Alt+0177
Logical not (¬)	Option+L	Ctrl+Alt+\ *or* Alt+0172
Per mil (‰)	Option+Shift+R	Alt+0137
Degree (°)	Option+Shift+8	Alt+0176
Function (f)	Option+F	Alt+0131
Integral (∫)	Option+B	*not supported*
Variation (∂)	Option+D	*not supported*
Greek beta (ß)	Option+S	Ctrl+Alt+S *or* Alt+0223

(continued)

Table 7-5 *(continued)*

Character	*Mac Shortcut*	*Windows Shortcut*
Greek mu (μ)	Option+M	Alt+0181
Greek Pi (Π)	Option+Shift+P	*not supported*
Greek pi (π)	Option+P	*not supported*
Greek Sigma (Σ)	Option+W	*not supported*
Greek Omega (Ω)	Option+Z	*not supported*
Miscellaneous		
Apple logo ( )	Option+Shift+K	*not supported*
En bullet (•)	Option+8	Shift+Alt+8 *or* Alt+0149
Light (◻)	Option+Shift+2	Ctrl+Alt+4 *or* Alt+0164
Open diamond (◊)	Option+Shift+V	*not supported*

* To get these characters, turn off the Smart Quotes feature in the Interactive pane of the Document Preferences Dialog box (Edit⇨Preferences⇨Document). However, note that the next time you open the document in QuarkXPress, you may find these characters have been translated into their typographic-quote equivalents.

Why dingbats are smart

When you hear "dingbat," you may think of Edith Bunker, of Archie Bunker, Meathead, and *All in the Family* fame. But, in publishing, a dingbat is no dummy. A dingbat is a symbol used to end a story or serve as a graphical embellishment for a certain type of text. It's sort of like a bullet, one that you can use at the beginning of each byline, for example, at the beginning of a continued line, or at the end of the text so that you know a story is over. A dingbat is a visual marker. And, as with bullets, you have a whole host of choices available to you. Take a look at the symbols in Figure 7-12 and in Table 7-5 of the regular text for some dingbat ideas. Many people use a square (hollow or solid), but you can be more creative than that. Maybe you can use a version of your company or publication logo. Or you even could use a stylized letter: *Macworld*, for example, uses a stylized *M*.

When you use dingbats, remember that you have choices in how you use them. For dingbats that end a story, you usually have the dingbat follow the last text, with an en space or em space separating them (see Table 7-4). If your text is justified against both margins, it's common to have the dingbat flush right in the last line of the story. To make it flush right, you set up a tab stop equal to the width of your column. So if your column is 2½ inches wide, you would set up a right-aligned tab at 2½ inches. (Chapter 6 covers how to set up tabs.) A shortcut is to use Option+tab or Shift+tab, which sets up a right-aligned tab at the right edge of the column.

You would use the same techniques to place, say, a square before the text *Continued on page 14* or to place, say, a hollow square before a byline.

Chapter 8
Devil in the Details

*P*robably everyone's least favorite part of publishing is the proofreading and attention to small text details, whether setting tabs so they align on a decimal or remembering to use italics whenever appropriate. Details get missed. In practically every magazine you read, there's a typo. No matter how many people look at a story, errors amazingly get through.

Although there's no magic cure for these errors, you can substantially reduce them. Old-fashioned proofreading by a fresh pair of eyes — not the author's, not the editor's, and not the layout artist's — is the first and best line of defense so that all concerned have a chance to find and replace incorrect text, fix spelling errors, and fit copy. A close second is setting exacting typographic controls over hyphenation and justification; these settings often catch errors of both grammar and ease of reading. And, although technically not a mistake, poor spacing and justification can lead the reader to misread text — and a "reado" is as bad as a typo because it causes a problem for the reader.

But buck up. It's not all doom and gloom. Follow the advice in this chapter, and you'll minimize — and maybe on a good week even eliminate — imprecision and errors.

Replacing and Correcting Text

One of the most-used text editing features is correcting text by replacing a word or a chunk of text with another word or chunk of text. Sometimes you want to replace just one instance of a word or phrase; other times, you want to replace a word or phrase every time it occurs in the document.

For example, imagine that you are working on the brochure for courses that teach people about traveling to Indonesia. You decide that you need to change each instance of the word "Bali" to "Indonesia." What's the best way to do this?

Actually, you have a couple of choices:

✔ You can go back to your original word processor document, make the changes there, and then reimport the text into your QuarkXPress document. (We don't like this method simply because it involves too many steps!)

✔ Or you can use QuarkXPress's built-in replace function, which you access through the Find/Change dialog box, shown in Figure 8-1.

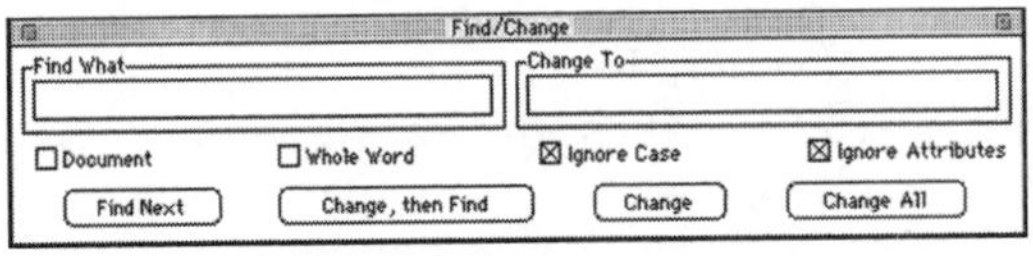

Figure 8-1:
The Find/
Change
dialog box.

To replace text throughout the current *story,* which is defined as the text in the currently selected text box and all the text boxes linked to it, use the Find/Change dialog box, which you access via Edit⇨Find/Change (⌘+F on Macintosh, Ctrl+F in Windows). You also can replace text throughout the entire current document.

As you can see, the QuarkXPress replace function works like the standard search and replace tool found in most word processing programs. You can search for whole words or for words whose capitalization matches the words or characters you type in the Find What field.

The Find/Change dialog box lets you choose whether QuarkXPress should look for a whole word. (If the Whole Word box is unchecked, the program finds the string of characters wherever it appears.) You can also have the program search and replace a word — regardless of its capitalization — by selecting Ignore Case. If the Document box is checked, the replace affects all stories and text in your document. The other buttons, such as Find Next, work as they do in word processing programs.

Changing text attributes

The Find/Change dialog box has another function that is incredibly cool. You can find and replace text attributes, typefaces, and sizes.

You can also find and replace text that is set according to a specific paragraph or character style.

These Find/Change capabilities can be useful if, for example, you want to change all instances of 12-point Helvetica in a document to 11.5-point Bookman.

To access these options, uncheck Ignore Attributes in the Find/Change dialog box. When Ignore Attributes is deselected, the dialog box expands and offers you attribute-replacement options, as Figure 8-2 shows.

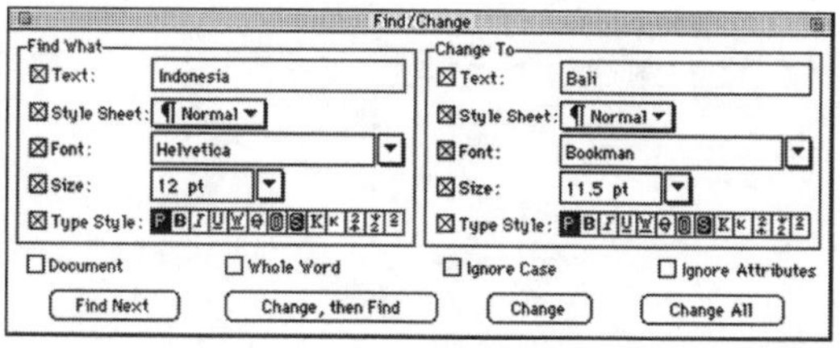

Figure 8-2:
The expanded Find/ Change dialog box lets you search for specific text attributes.

In the example shown in Figure 8-2, any text set in 12-point Helvetica is being replaced with 11.5-point Bookman text.

You can select specific text, typeface, and styles for both the search and replace functions by checking the Text, Style Sheet, Font, Size, and Type Style check boxes in the Find what and Change to columns of the dialog box.

If you want to use an attribute, check an attribute box in the Type Style field of the dialog box. Remove the check mark if you don't want to use an attribute (such as bold) in your search and replace. Clicking a box once unchecks it if it is checked and checks it if it is unchecked.

If you leave Text unchecked in the Find What column, you replace attributes
only. You may do this to change all underlined text to word-underlined text,
all bold text to small cap text, all News Gothic bold text to News Gothic bold
italic, or all 8-point text to 8.5-point text.

Removing carriage returns

It's not uncommon for QuarkXPress users to receive text files for typesetting
that have several extra carriage returns entered between paragraphs. The
Find/Change feature in QuarkXPress gives you an easy way to remove these
unwanted carriage returns.

You can use Find/Change to find and delete extra carriage returns, but you
can't do it by simply typing in a carriage return in the Find/Change dialog
box field because pressing the Return key activates the Find button. Instead,
you need to use the symbol for a new paragraph, \p.

Enter two consecutive return symbols, \p\p, in the Find what field and then
enter one return symbol, \p, in the Change to field. Figure 8-3 shows what the
Find/Change dialog box should look like when you are about to begin removing unwanted carriage returns, which are also referred to as *hard returns*.

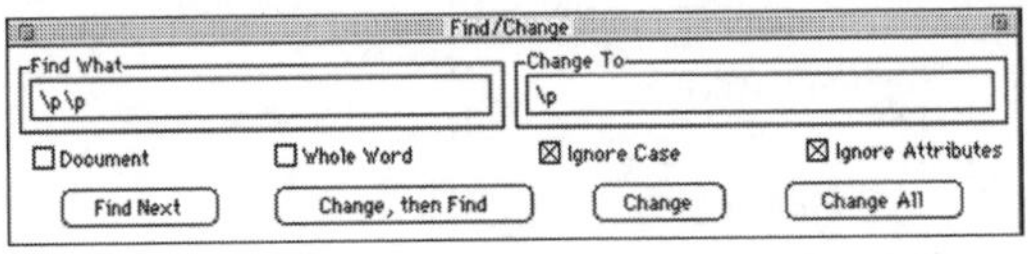

Figure 8-3:
Removing
extra
carriage
returns.

Find/Change	
Find What	Change To
\p\p	\p

☐ Document　☐ Whole Word　☒ Ignore Case　☒ Ignore Attributes

[Find Next]　[Change, then Find]　[Change]　[Change All]

If the text you are working with has multiple carriage returns between
paragraphs, you may need to repeat this Find/Change procedure a number
of times.

What do you do if there's a hard return at the end of each line of text, in
addition to the extra hard returns between paragraphs? If you simply delete
all the hard returns by using a Find/Change procedure similar to the one
shown in Figure 8-3 (where you would search for \p and replace it with
nothing), you would lose all paragraph breaks. So you need to follow a two-
step procedure:

✔ First, search for paragraph breaks that are marked by two hard returns,
\p\p, and replace the paragraph breaks with another character that is
not used in the document, such as # (the pound sign).

✔ Then search for all the hard returns and replace them with nothing
(enter \p in the Find what field and leave the Change to field blank).

After you have deleted the hard returns, you need to reinsert the paragraph breaks. To do this, enter the character you used to replace the paragraph breaks (# in our example) in the Find what field, and enter \p in the Change to field and perform Find/Change again. See Chapter 21 for a list of codes that you can use to find non-character items, such as new lines and tabs.

Setting Tabs

Use tabs when you want to line up text into columns to create lists, tables, and other columnar data. QuarkXPress provides six paragraph tab options: Left, Center, Right, Decimal, Comma, and Align on. Tabs can be tricky, and it takes some practice to know how to use them effectively.

If you've ever used a typewriter, you are familiar with typewriter tabs, which are left-aligned only: You press the tab key, and that moves the carriage to a new left margin. But QuarkXPress offers a wide variety of tabs, which are available through the Paragraph Attributes pane, which you access via Style⇨Tabs (⌘+Shift+T or Ctrl+Shift+T). Each type of tab has its own mark on the tab ruler, which appears when you are setting tabs. Figure 8-4 shows the Paragraph Attributes pane.

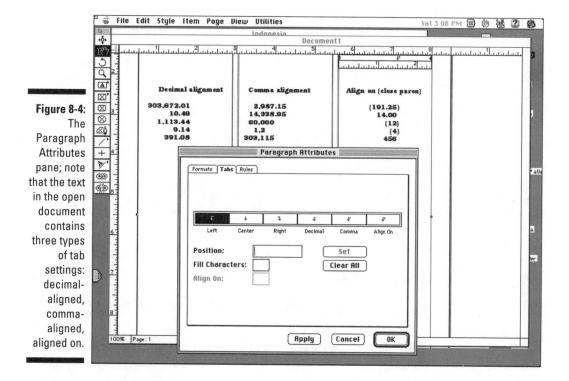

Figure 8-4: The Paragraph Attributes pane; note that the text in the open document contains three types of tab settings: decimal-aligned, comma-aligned, aligned on.

In Figure 8-4, the columns of copy in the open document have been set with three different tab settings:

- ✔ **Decimal** (shown in the left column). Numbers with a decimal (.) that are typed in after the tab will align on the period, or decimal. This tab setting is useful if you have columns of numbers that include decimal places.

- ✔ **Comma** (shown in the center column). Numbers with a comma (,) that are typed in after the tab will align on the comma. This tab setting is handy if you have some dates with decimal places, such as 31.001, and some without, such as 2,339.

- ✔ **Align on** (shown in the right column). With this option, you select which character you want the text to align on. In the example in Figure 8-4, we aligned a column of numbers with the closing parenthesis.

Three additional tab settings, which are not shown in the open document in Figure 8-4, include:

- ✔ **Left.** Text typed after the tab will align to the tab as if the tab were a left margin. This is, by far, the most popular tab setting.

- ✔ **Center.** Text typed in will be centered, with the tab stop serving as the center of the text.

- ✔ **Right.** Text types in after the tab; it aligns to the tab as if the tab were a right margin. The right tab setting is often used with tables of numbers because the numbers align with all of their rightmost digits in a row.

The default for tabs is one left tab every half inch. If you want to apply different tab settings that you can use throughout the document, choose Edit⇨Style Sheets (Shift+F11), and then select the Tabs pane. If you are working on a specific paragraph or want to override a style for one paragraph, choose Style⇨Tabs (⌘+Shift+T or Ctrl+Shift+T) to access the Paragraph Attributes pane.

You can place thousands of tabs in a paragraph (in earlier versions of QuarkXPress, you were limited to 20 tabs), and you can use any printing character to fill the space between tabs.

Specifying your own tabs

After you have accessed the Paragraph Attributes pane, here's how you set your own tabs:

1. **Select the Alignment you want (Left, Center, Right, Decimal, Comma, Align On).**

2. **Either type in the numeric position for the tab in the Position box or move your mouse to the Tab ruler and click to set the position of the tab.**

You can also specify tabs for a selected paragraph or range of paragraphs by choosing Style⇨Formats (⌘+Shift+F or Ctrl+Shift+F) and selecting the Tabs pane, and then clicking on the ruler displayed above the box or column.

As we mention earlier, setting tabs in QuarkXPress is simple, but the process can be tricky if you've never done it before. For example, it takes time to learn how using tabs with the various Alignment options mentioned above affects your document. We recommend that you take a few minutes to practice setting some tabs so that you will be comfortable with the process.

Using leader characters in tabs

A leader character, also known as a *tab leader,* is a series of characters that runs from text to text within tabular material. An example of a tab leader is the series of dots (periods) that you sometimes see between a Table-of-Contents entry and its corresponding page number. A tab leader's purpose is to guide the reader's eye, especially across a wide distance on a page.

QuarkXPress calls a tab leader a *fill character.* To define a leader, enter up to two characters in the Fill Character box in the Paragraph Attributes pane. If you enter two characters, they alternate to fill the space between the defined tab stop and the place where you pressed the tab key. In Figure 8-5, we use a space and a period as the two fill characters.

Note that, in Figure 8-5, we've left the Paragraph Attributes pane open so that you can see the entries we made. The resulting tab leaders can be seen at the left side of the open document, above the Paragraph Attributes pane.

Getting Copy to Fit

Copy fitting is just what it sounds like: The process of fitting text into the layout. Sometimes you feel as though you're trying to squeeze 20 pounds of lemons into a five-pound bag. If your original, unmodified text fits the layout the first time through, consider it a stroke of luck because that's not what usually happens.

Copy fitting, when done well, can make your document look very professional. It can also save you money. For example, imagine that you have the budget to produce an eight-page document. You flow your text in and find

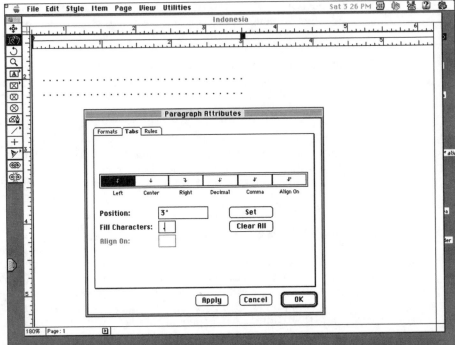

Figure 8-5:
You can use
one or two
characters
to fill a tab
space.

that you have eight-and-a-quarter pages to deal with. By doing a good job of copy fitting, you can make the text fit into eight pages and save yourself the expense and hassle of adding an additional signature to your booklet. A *signature* is a printed sheet, after it has been folded. Signatures, which consist of four pages (or multiples of four with modern printing presses), got their name because originally the person doing the folding had to initial his or her work.

You have a number of ways to make copy fit onto a page or within a column. Sometimes you can use just one method; sometimes you have to use a combination of methods to make text fit in the available space.

Having more text than space is most common. Therefore, the following tips assume that the goal is to shorten text. But you can use the same procedures in reverse to expand text. *Note:* We give these tips in order of preference; use the last two tips only if you can't make text fit using the first few:

✔ **Edit text** to remove extra lines. Watch for lines at the end of a paragraph that have only a few characters. Getting rid of a few characters somewhere else in the paragraph may eliminate these short lines, reducing the amount of page space needed while keeping the amount of text removed to a minimum.

- ✔ **Adjust the tracking of the text** so that the text occupies less space and, especially, so that short lines are eliminated.

- ✔ **Tighten the leading** by a half or quarter point. Because this is such a small change, the average reader won't notice it; it may even save you a few lines per column, which can add up quickly.

- ✔ **Reduce the point size** by a half point. This action saves more space than is first apparent, because it allows you to place a few more lines on the page and put a bit more text in each line. You can change point size in the style sheet or select text and use the type-size controls in the Measurements palette.

- ✔ **Reduce the horizontal scale** of text to a slightly smaller percentage (perhaps 85 percent) to squeeze more text in each line by entering a percent value in the Horizontal Scale field (with the text selected, choose Modify from the Item menu).

- ✔ **Vary the size of columns** by setting slightly narrower column gutters or slightly wider margins.

Try applying these copy-fitting techniques globally to avoid a patchwork appearance. You can, however, change the tracking on individual lines; if you limit tracking changes to no more than 20 units, the changes won't be very noticeable.

Winning the Spelling Bee

Many people dread spelling; that's why word processors and publishing programs come with spelling checkers. But there's a catch: Spelling checkers work by being based on lists of words. Sure, spelling dictionaries sometimes contain 500,000-odd words (QuarkXPress's has a "mere" 120,000), but industry-specific terms like *PowerPC* or people's names rarely show up in these dictionaries. So you can't completely automate spell-checking. Sorry, but you need to have another dictionary somewhere around for referral.

The two best dictionaries are Merriam-Webster's *Third International,* the publishing standard, and Houghton Mifflin's *American Heritage,* which specializes in explaining word origins and usage notes. Webster's *Ninth Collegiate* is a smaller version of the *Third International* and is a fine reference for editors' and writers' desks; usually, your proofreader has the *Third International.*

Although you can't automate spell-checking, you can make it a part of your routine. You should spell-check your text in the word processor before laying it out in QuarkXPress. You also should spell-check it again in QuarkXPress after you finish your layout but before you print it. You'll be surprised how much text gets added or changed in layout, after the stories are officially "done."

QuarkXPress provides an internal spelling checker, accessed via the Utilities menu, shown in Figure 8-6. The menu option is Check Spelling, which has three submenus: Word, Story, and Document. You can jump directly to these options via ⌘+L or Ctrl+W for Word, Option+⌘+L or Ctrl+Alt+W for Story, and Option+Shift+⌘+L or Ctrl+Alt+Shift+W for Document. Chances are that you'll use the Story and Document options the most — the ones with the hardest-to-remember shortcuts. (A story is all text in the current text box and in all text boxes linked to that text box. A story is usually the contents of an imported text file.)

To access the Story or Word options, you have to have the Content tool active and the text pointer on a piece of text. You don't have to select a word to spell-check a word; just have the text pointer somewhere on the word. If you have multiple words selected and you use the Word spell-checking option, QuarkXPress will spell-check only the first word in the series. You can't spell-check a highlighted range of words.

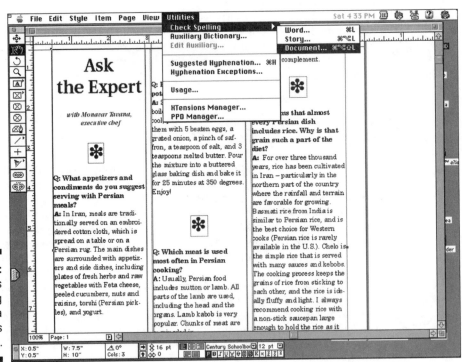

Figure 8-6:
You access the spelling checker via the Utilities menu.

Running the spelling checker

If you are spell-checking the entire document or the current story, you get the dialog box shown in Figure 8-7. You click OK to continue, which displays the dialog box shown in Figure 8-8. If you are spell-checking just a word, you go directly to the dialog box in Figure 8-9, which is a more compact version of the dialog box in Figure 8-8.

Figure 8-7:
QuarkXPress first reports how many words it checked and how many it didn't recognize.

Figure 8-8:
QuarkXPress shows you each suspect word in turn.

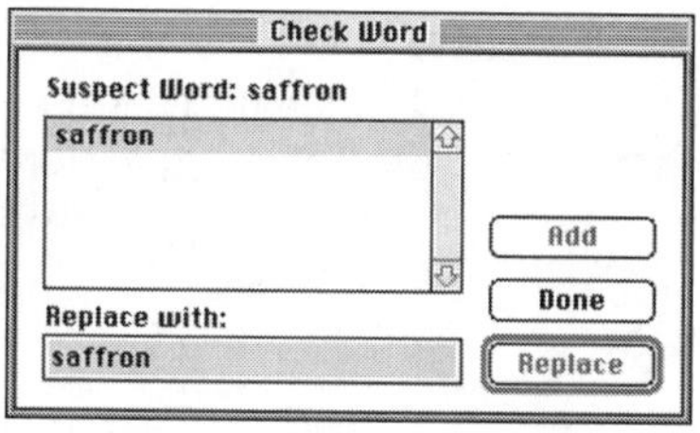

Figure 8-9:
When you spell-check a single word, you go directly into this limited version of the dialog box in Figure 8-8.

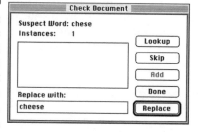

The dialog boxes in Figures 8-8 and 8-9 differ in several ways:

✔ The Check Word dialog box has no capability to move on (via the Skip button) to the next suspect word (an option that doesn't make sense for one-word spell-checking), as the Check Story or Check Document dialog boxes do.

✔ The Check Word dialog box automatically looks for possible correct words to replace the suspect word with; the other dialog boxes require that you click the Lookup button to get a list of possible replacements. If one of those words is the correct one, just click it and then click Replace, or just double-click the word in the list.

✔ The Check Word dialog box has no Add button, which lets you add words to your personal dictionary (explained a little later in this section).

What you can do in all three dialog boxes is select a new word and click the Replace button to have QuarkXPress make the replacement. If the word appears several times, QuarkXPress tells you how many times the word is used and replaces all instances when you click Replace.

You may notice that the spelling-checker has no OK button or close box. To leave the spelling-checker, you must click Cancel or go through all the suspect words. If you click Cancel, will any changes made up to that point, either words you replaced or words you added to your spelling exception dictionary, be retained? Yes. That's counterintuitive to what the Cancel button usually does, but here it's really an OK button. Go figure.

Setting up your personal dictionaries

If you've experimented with QuarkXPress's spelling checker, you probably noticed that the Add button stays gray. So what's it there for? For the Add button to become active, you need to set up an auxiliary dictionary, a personal dictionary of words that QuarkXPress's own dictionary (the file XPress Dictionary on the Mac and the file XPress Dictionary.DCT in Windows) doesn't know about.

To set up an auxiliary dictionary, use Utilities➪Auxiliary Dictionary, which displays the dialog box shown in Figure 8-10. Any existing dictionaries in the current folder will be displayed. You can select one of them, move to a different directory to select a different dictionary, or click the New button to create a new auxiliary dictionary.

Figure 8-10:
You create
or switch to
a different
auxiliary
spelling
dictionary
via the
Auxiliary
Dictionary
dialog box.

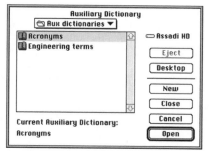

In the case of Figure 8-10, we had set up an auxiliary dictionary for the current document previously, so the name of that dictionary is displayed in the Current Auxiliary Dictionary field.

As is true for other global preferences, QuarkXPress works differently if no document is open than if one is. If you create or change auxiliary dictionaries when no document is open, QuarkXPress uses that auxiliary dictionary for all future documents (until you change the dictionary again). If a document is open, the auxiliary dictionary is created or changed specifically for that document.

The Windows QuarkXPress Auxiliary Dictionary dialog box looks a little different than its Mac counterpart because it follows the Windows conventions for an Open or Save dialog box. But it has all the same features and buttons. You should know one other thing about the auxiliary dictionaries in Windows QuarkXPress: Although the main dictionary (XPress Dictionary.DCT) uses the extension .DCT, the auxiliary dictionaries use the extension .QDT (such as Computer.QDT).

After you create the auxiliary dictionary, you have to add words to it. Actually, you don't have to add them right then — you just add words as you find them in the spelling checker by clicking the Add button when you come across a word like *PowerPC* that is correct but unknown to QuarkXPress. Or, if you know some of the words you want to add already, you can use Utilities⇨Edit Auxiliary to invoke the dialog box shown in Figure 8-11. You also can use this dialog box to remove incorrect words (maybe someone was too fast on the trigger and clicked Add by accident).

Figure 8-11:
The Edit
Auxiliary
Dictionary
dialog box
does what
its title
says.

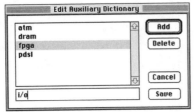

Edit Auxiliary Dictionary

atm
dram
fpga
pdsl

Add
Delete
Cancel
Save

i/d

Be sure to click the Save button after making changes to your auxiliary dictionary. Otherwise, the changes won't be saved.

Notice as you add words that case does not matter. If you enter *PowerPC*, it will display as *powerpc*. The use of only lowercase ensures that the word won't be flagged as incorrect if it were typed in all caps. Or, for a word like *uninstall*, which is not in QuarkXPress's own dictionary file, this use of only lowercase ensures that the word isn't flagged if the first letter is capitalized at, for example, the beginning of a sentence or in a title — *uninstall*, *Uninstall*, and *UNINSTALL* are all considered to be the same by QuarkXPress's spelling checker, which just keeps the form *uninstall* in its dictionary file.

But this lowercase-only approach means that you can't set QuarkXPress to flag incorrectly capitalized words (for example, some people refer to Quark Xtensions, when the correct capitalization is *XTensions*). Your word processor probably has case-sensitive (which means it looks at the capitalization of words, not just at the sequence of letters in them) spell-checking, but QuarkXPress does not. That's another reason to do a spell-check in your word processor before importing the text into QuarkXPress.

Because auxiliary dictionaries are just files, you can share them over a network, which is a great way to maintain spelling consistency among several users. You also can have different dictionaries for different projects (if your work involved very different types of audiences). But one thing you can't do is share dictionaries between Windows and Macintosh users. The two dictionary formats are not compatible, and there is no way to translate either dictionary into the other's format.

By maintaining an up-to-date spelling dictionary and spell-checking at key points in the editing and layout process, you can greatly reduce typographical mistakes. Some typos (for example, words that are spelled correctly but are actually the wrong word) won't be caught this way, however, so you still need a person to proofread. But at least the obvious mistakes will have been caught by the time a proofreader sees your text.

Hyphenating the Right Way

Hyphenation is even harder for many people than spelling. Where do you break a word? Between two consonants? After a syllable? There really are rules you can follow, but the English language is so full of exceptions that you may think that it's hardly worth learning the rules unless you are a copy editor.

As it does for spell-checking, QuarkXPress offers automatic hyphenation. In fact, the hyphenation is so good that you'll rarely need to add words to its exception dictionary — although you can if you want. Before you do that, though, you need to know how to specify hyphenation, which we cover in the next section.

Creating hyphenation sets

Any ink-stained newspaperman (or woman) can tell you what an H&J set is. But in case you don't have an ink-stained newsperson nearby, we clue you in: An H&J set is newspaper lingo for a hyphenation and justification set — the specifications for how words are divided across lines and how the text in each line is spaced. We cover some of the spacing features later in this chapter.

To set up hyphenation settings, you use Edit⇨H&Js (⌘+Option+H or Option+Shift+F11 on Mac, Ctrl+Shift+F11 in Windows) to bring up the H&Js dialog box, shown in Figure 8-12. When you first open this dialog box, you see just one listing in the H&J list: Standard. Edit this listing first so you can establish the hyphenation settings you want as the default for your text styles. Once you've edited Standard to your liking, you can create additional H&J sets for other needs. For example, you may want an H&J set called No Hyphen for text (like headlines and bylines) that should have no hyphenation.

Figure 8-12:
The H&Js dialog box is your gateway to hyphenation control.

As is true for other global preferences, QuarkXPress works differently if no document is open than if one is. If you create or change H&J sets when no document is open, QuarkXPress uses that H&J set for all future documents (until you change the dictionary again). If a document is open, the H&J set is created or changed just for that document. You can tell whether the H&Js are being edited globally for all new documents or locally for the currently opened one: If the dialog box says Default H&Js (as shown in Figure 8-12), you're changing the global settings; if it says H&Js for *document name*, you're changing the settings locally for whatever *document name*'s real name is (the real name will display in the title, not *document name*).

To edit an existing H&J set, select its name from the list and double-click it. To create an H&J set, click the New button. Either way, you get the Edit Hyphenation & Justification dialog box shown in Figure 8-13. The fields at the left are the ones that affect hyphenation.

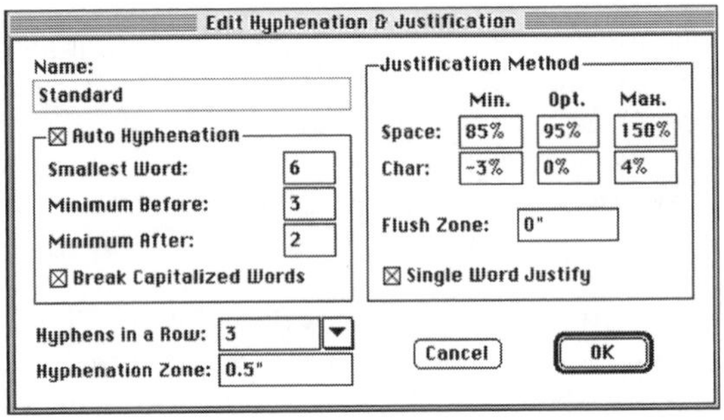

Figure 8-13:
The Edit
Hyphenation
&
Justification
dialog box
contains
hyphenation
controls at
its left side.

Edit Hyphenation & Justification				
Name:		**Justification Method**		
Standard			Min.	Opt.	Max.
⊠ Auto Hyphenation		Space:	85%	95%	150%
Smallest Word:	6	Char:	-3%	0%	4%
Minimum Before:	3				
Minimum After:	2	Flush Zone:	0"		
⊠ Break Capitalized Words		⊠ Single Word Justify			
Hyphens in a Row:	3 ▼	Cancel	OK		
Hyphenation Zone:	0.5"				

Take a close look at the values in Figure 8-13; compare them to the values in your copy of QuarkXPress. Our values differ from yours because we've edited the Standard settings in our copy of QuarkXPress to work best in multicolumn layouts like newsletters, newspapers, and magazines. Here's how each setting works:

- **Name.** If you clicked New, enter the name for the H&J set here. (H&J sets are named, just as style sheets are.) If you clicked Edit to edit the Standard H&J set, you won't be able to edit the name.

- **Auto Hyphenation.** If this box is checked, hyphenation is turned on for any style sheet that uses this H&J set. If the box is unchecked, hyphenation is turned off for any style sheet that uses this H&J set.

- **Smallest Word.** This field tells QuarkXPress to ignore words with fewer characters than that field's value. The default is 6, so any word of five or fewer characters won't be hyphenated. The default value of 6 is a good one because few words of 6 or fewer letters are unable to fit on a line with other text or will look good if they are split across two lines, so there's little reason to change this default value. (One possible reason for changing it: a case where you have wide columns — say, 6 inches or more — in which case there's plenty of room for words so a value of 8 would be fine.)

✔ **Minimum Before.** This field tells QuarkXPress how many characters in the word must precede a hyphen. Thus, if you leave the value set to the default of 3, QuarkXPress will not hyphenate the word *Rolodex* as *Ro-lodex,* even though that's a legal hyphenation for the word. The first place that QuarkXPress will hyphenate would be after the *l*, but that's an incorrect hyphenation point, so QuarkXPress would insert the hyphen after *Rolo.*

✔ **Minimum After.** This field is like Minimum Before, except that it tells QuarkXPress the minimum number of characters in a word that must follow the hyphen. The default is 2, although many people change that to 3 so QuarkXPress won't hyphenate verbs before the *-ed*, as in *edit-ed.* Many publishers think that looks tacky. It's a personal choice.

✔ **Hyphens in a Row.** The default is Unlimited, which means that theoretically every line could end in a hyphen. Having too many end-of-line hyphens in a row makes the text hard to read because it's hard to keep track of what line to move onto next. We suggest 3 as a good setting, although 2 and 4 are fine, too. The smaller the number, the greater the chance that QuarkXPress will have trouble spacing text in a line; a line that could really use a hyphen would be prohibited from having one just because it happened to come after that maximum number of consecutive hyphenated lines. (For example: If you set Hyphens in a Row to 2 and a particular paragraph turns out to have two hyphens in a row somewhere, even though the third line could really use a hyphen to avoid awkard spacing, QuarkXPress won't be able to hyphenate that line.)

When you confront this spacing situation, don't despair — and don't change the settings in your H&J set. Just type a regular hyphen followed by a space. (If you try to use the soft hyphen — ⌘-hyphen or Ctrl+hyphen — to create a break on that third line, QuarkXPress won't add the hyphen because soft hyphens respect the Hyphens in a Row setting.) But add a regular hyphen and space only when everything else in the layout is finished — if your text were to reflow, you might find a hyphen and space in the middle of a word in the middle of a line. Oops! This cheat lets you get around the H&J limitations without changing a standard that works most of the time. And, if you're unsure where to hyphenate a word (and no dictionary's handy), just click on the word and use Utilities⇨Suggested Hyphenation (⌘+H or Ctrl+H) to have QuarkXPress show you where hyphens may be added.

✔ **Break Capitalized Words.** This box does just what it says. Some typographers frown on hyphenating proper names, like *Macworld* or *Alexander*. We think it's a silly prohibition, so make sure this box is checked. Better a broken name than awkward spacing around it.

✔ **Hyphenation Zone.** For text that is left-aligned, right-aligned, or centered, this box tells QuarkXPress how far from the outside margin to look for opportunities to hyphenate. Hyphenation Zone helps you prevent awkward gaps — something that looks like a kid's smile with no front top teeth — because a word happened to hyphenate halfway into the line. Set the zone to at least 10 percent of the column width (15 percent is better), but to no less than 0.2 inches. Thus, for a 1.5-inch-wide line, a good setting would be 0.225 inch (though you can round that to 0.2 or 0.25); that's 1.5 (inches) × 0.15 (percent). For justified or force-justified text, this setting has no effect, though, because all the text is aligned to both the left and right margins, which means that the text has no possible gaps for you to worry about.

When you click the New button, the new H&J set takes the attributes of the Standard H&J set, so it's best to edit Standard to your liking before creating new sets. That way, attributes that you'll have in several sets (such as having Auto Hyphenation and Break Capitalized Words checked) are automatically copied into the new sets. If you want to duplicate an H&J set and then make slight modifications to it (perhaps two sets are identical except for the Hyphenation Zone settings), select one of the sets in the H&J dialog box and click the Duplicate button; then modify (and rename) that duplicate set.

Figure 8-14 shows the effects of different hyphenation settings. We've used really skinny columns because thin columns emphasize the differences between hyphenation settings. The wider the columns, the less noticeable the differences because QuarkXPress has more text to play around in while adjusting spacing.

Click OK when you're done creating or modifying an H&J set (or click Cancel if you want to abort those settings). That puts you back in the H&Js dialog box, from which you can create or edit other sets. When you're done, be sure to click Save to save all the work you've done — if you click Cancel, your work's toast.

If you created H&J sets in another document, you can import those sets into the current QuarkXPress document by using this mini-procedure: Click the Append button (it really should be named Import — Append makes it sound like it will copy the current H&J set to another set, not *from* it) and then navigate the dialog box to find the document you're importing from. But remember that *all* H&J sets in that document will be imported into your current document with one exception: If both documents have H&J sets with the same name, importing sets into the current document will not affect its

H&J set. For example, suppose that the current document has the H&J sets Standard and No Hyphen, while the other document has the H&J sets Standard and Masthead. When you import H&J sets from the other document, Masthead will be copied into the current document but Standard won't be copied, and the current document's Standard H&J set will remain unaffected.

If you want to copy H&J sets from another document and make them the default for all future documents, make sure that no document is open in your copy of QuarkXPress before you import H&J sets from that other document. This is a great way to copy standards from a client's system to your system, or from a master document to a new employee's copy of QuarkXPress.

After you set up your H&J sets — many documents will have just two: Standard and No Hyphen — edit your style sheets so that each style uses the appropriate H&J set. Headlines, bylines, and other categories of display type usually are not hyphenated, while body text, bios, captions, and sidebars usually *are* hyphenated. You also can apply an H&J set to a selected paragraph (or several selected paragraphs) by using the Paragraph Attributes pane — Style⇨Formats (⌘+Shift+F or Ctrl+Shift+F) — and changing the H&J value to the H&J set you want to apply.

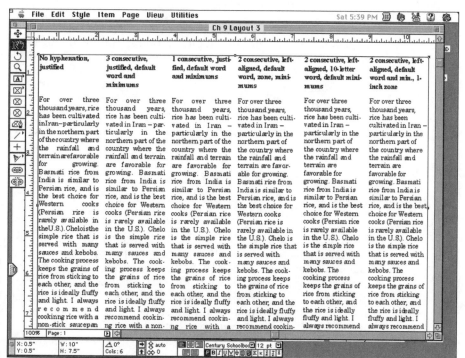

Figure 8-14:
The effects
of different
hyphenation
settings.

Personalizing your hyphenation

As you can do for the spelling dictionaries, you can create your own personal hyphenation dictionaries, in which you tell QuarkXPress how to hyphenate words it doesn't know about. You also can use personalized hyphenation to change the default hyphenation for words that are hyphenated differently based on their pronunciation (such as the verb *pro-ject* and the noun *proj-ect*) or sometimes on what dictionary they appear in (such as *service*, which can be hyphenated as *ser-vice* or *serv-ice*, depending on which dictionary you consult).

To add your own hyphenation, use Utilities⇨Hyphenation Exceptions. You get the dialog box shown in Figure 8-15. (Looks a lot like the dialog box for spelling exceptions, doesn't it?)

Figure 8-15:
The
Hyphenation
Exceptions
dialog box.

Just enter the word into the Hyphenation Exceptions dialog box whose hyphenation you want to personalize, include hyphens where it's okay for QuarkXPress to hyphenate the word, and click Add. (If you want to prevent a word from being hyphenated, enter it with no hyphens.) To delete a word, select it from the list and click Delete.

When you're all done, click Save. Clicking Cancel wipes out any changes you made.

Preventing "Reados"

The other half of the H&J set — the J, or justification — controls the spacing of text. It's easy to overlook this aspect of typography and just go with the defaults. But you don't want to do that. How you set your spacing has a subtle but important effect on readability. QuarkXPress assumes that you're doing single-column-wide documents, which is fine for reports and price lists. But, for multicolumn documents, the default settings can result in spacing that leaves awkward gaps between words and can make the space between characters in words open enough that you might not be sure whether the characters make one word or two.

Default spacing

Take a look at Figure 8-16. It's the Edit Hyphenation & Justification dialog box described in the preceding section (Edit⇨H&Js⇨Edit). As in the previous section, we've changed the QuarkXPress defaults to what we believe are better settings. The results are that the characters in a word are closer together and no unsightly gaps remain between words. You can experiment with the values, but, before you do that, read on to find out what those values mean.

All settings for justification are in the section of the dialog box labeled Justification Method. At the top are six fields that determine how your text is spaced between characters and words; the spacing of text between characters and words is called letter spacing and word spacing, respectively. The first row determines the space between words; the second row controls the space between characters within a word. Generally, you want tighter space within a word than between words so that words look unified and the space between them is easily discernible. The three columns determine the rules by which QuarkXPress spaces characters and words.

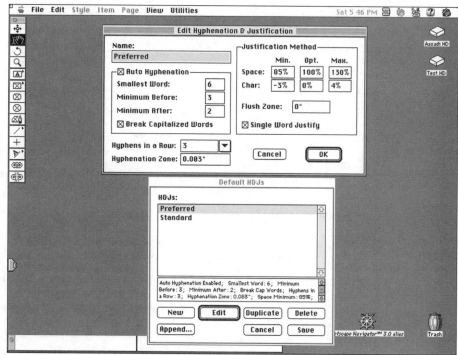

Figure 8-16:
The justification half of the Edit Hyphenation & Justification dialog box contains the authors' preferred settings.

The spacing columns may not make sense at first because they behave differently depending on how the text is aligned. If text is left-aligned, right-aligned, or centered, QuarkXPress always uses the Opt. (optimum, or target) values. If the text is justified or force-justified, QuarkXPress tries to meet the Opt. values; if it can't meet those values, though, it will use a value in the range between the Min. (minimum) and Max. (maximum) values. And if that doesn't work, then it will use a value greater than the Max. value. QuarkXPress *never* uses less than the Min. Settings.

Because of how QuarkXPress applies spacing, setting the Opt. values to 100% for words and 0% for characters works best. Those particular Opt. values tell QuarkXPress to use the defaults from the font's internal spacing specifications. (Presumably, the font's designers picked those specs for a good reason.)

For the Min. settings, we prefer 85% for words and –3% for characters. That prevents words and letters from getting too close, but it also helps balance any spaced-out text with slightly cramped text, keeping the overall average closer to the Opt. values. For Max., we allow a greater difference from Opt. than we do from Min., because the human eye can handle extra space better than it can too little space.

Local space controls: Tracking and kerning

But wait, there's more! You can override the spacing settings for selected text or even with a style sheet. But, pray, why would you do this? Consider these scenarios:

- Perhaps some text is too spacey, or you know that if some text were just a little closer together, you'd get the text to rewrap and take one line less. Here's where you would use QuarkXPress's tracking feature to tighten (or loosen) the space among characters in a selected block of text.

- Or maybe your Standard H&J set's justification settings work fine for your body text but not for your headlines. Rather than create a new H&J set for headlines, you just adjust the tracking settings in your Headlines style sheet to compensate for the difference.

- Or maybe only a few characters don't quite mesh. Here and there, a couple of letters in a word seem to be too close or too far apart. Just use the QuarkXPress kerning feature to adjust the space between those two characters.

Tracking and kerning are pretty much the same thing — ways to adjust the spacing between characters. So what's the difference? The scope of the adjustments they make. *Kerning* adjusts spacing between just two characters, while *tracking* adjusts spacing between all characters selected. QuarkXPress uses the same menus for these two features because they really are just variations of the same feature. Thus, you see Style⇨Kern if your text pointer happens to be between two characters, but you see Style⇨Track if you select several characters. Similarly, the horizontal arrows on the Measurements palette adjust kerning if the pointer is between two characters, and they adjust tracking when several characters are selected.

Figure 8-17 shows the Character Attributes pane, which appears when you select Style⇨Kern or Style⇨Track. Figure 8-18 shows how you can use the Measurements palette to modify kerning or tracking.

Using the keyboard shortcuts or the Measurements palette to adjust tracking and kerning is best because you can see the effects of your changes as you make them.(Otherwise, you need to make the longer effort of opening a dialog box, entering a value, closing the dialog box, seeing the result, reopening the dialog box to further adjust the spacing, and so on.) Use ⌘+Shift+}or Ctrl+Shift+}, to increase spacing in $1/20$th em increments and ⌘+Shift+Option+} or Ctrl+Alt+Shift+} to increase spacing in $1/200$th em increments. To decrease spacing, use ⌘+Shift+{ and Option+Shift+⌘+{ on the Mac and Ctrl+Shift+{ and Ctrl+Shift+{ and Ctrl+Alt+Shift+{ in Windows.

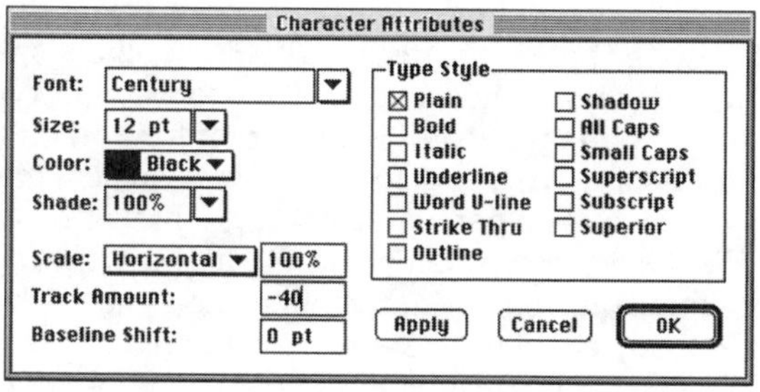

Figure 8-17: Access kerning and tracking via the Style menu to get the Character Attributes dialog box.

Character Attributes	
Font: Century	Type Style
Size: 12 pt	☒ Plain ☐ Shadow
Color: Black	☐ Bold ☐ All Caps
Shade: 100%	☐ Italic ☐ Small Caps
	☐ Underline ☐ Superscript
Scale: Horizontal 100%	☐ Word U-line ☐ Subscript
Track Amount: -40	☐ Strike Thru ☐ Superior
Baseline Shift: 0 pt	☐ Outline
	Apply Cancel OK

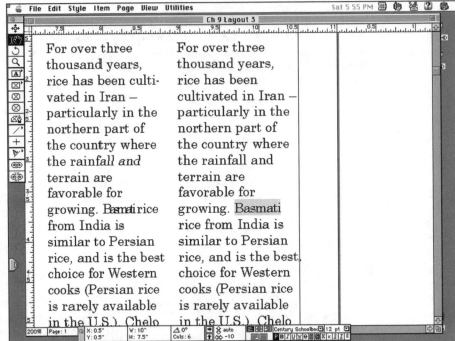

Ch 9 Layout 3

For over three thousand years, rice has been cultivated in Iran — particularly in the northern part of the country where the rainfall and terrain are favorable for growing. Basmati rice from India is similar to Persian rice, and is the best choice for Western cooks (Persian rice is rarely available in the U.S.) Chelo

For over three thousand years, rice has been cultivated in Iran — particularly in the northern part of the country where the rainfall and terrain are favorable for growing. Basmati rice from India is similar to Persian rice, and is the best choice for Western cooks (Persian rice is rarely available in the U.S.) Chelo

Figure 8-18:
You also can set kerning and tracking via the Measurements palette.

The values QuarkXPress uses for tracking and kerning are not percentages, as they are for the H&J sets' spacing options. Instead, for tracking and kerning QuarkXPress uses a unit of measurement called (of all things) a *unit* — a handy little length that measures all of $^1/_{200\text{ths}}$ of an em space. An em space is as wide as a font is high; thus, an em space for 9-point type is 9 points wide. That means that a unit is $^9/_{200\text{ths}}$ of a point for 9-point type, $^8/_{200\text{ths}}$ (or $^1/_{50\text{th}}$) of a point for 8-point type, and so on. As you can see, then, a unit really is another way to express a percentage: 0.05% (that's the decimal way to represent $^1/_{200\text{th}}$). That's a pretty small value. So, in the Measurements palette, QuarkXPress jumps in 10-unit increments when you click the left and right arrows to adjust tracking or kerning. You of course can select your own precise values by entering in a number. A positive number adds space; a negative number removes it.

Chapter 9
The Hows and Whys of XTensions

*N*ow we're going to ask you to put your creative mind to use. Imagine that QuarkXPress, instead of being a page-layout program, is a prefabricated, one-room house. Your copy of the house sits on a street with a dozen other houses just like it. You breathe a sigh of relief when you find out that your next-door neighbor, a wild saxophone player who keeps you up at night with his playing, has decided to build a music room onto his house. A few weeks later, your other next-door neighbor gives birth to triplets and begins to build a second story to house all the little darlings. You, on the other hand, have a better idea for how to personalize your home: You decide to add a greenhouse room in front of the house so that you can keep your orchid collection healthy and growing in any season.

The point of this homely analogy is that, like the neighbors described above, QuarkXPress users all have different likes and needs. Just as the people in our imaginary neighborhood were not satisfied with simply living in their identical little prefab houses, publishers and designers also would not be satisfied if they were forced to use only one flavor of QuarkXPress. It's obvious (when you think about it) that someone using the program to produce a two-color school newspaper has different needs than a designer using QuarkXPress to create process color ads for magazines.

Probably the wisest thing the people who created QuarkXPress ever did was to realize that every user of this program is unique. By maintaining a continuing dialog with their customers, Quark's developers came to understand that it would be impossible to create a single application that would meet the needs of every user. So, instead of trying to make the program all things to all people, adding a truckload of features that would inhibit the overall performance of the program, the developers created an ingenious architecture that allows QuarkXPress to be customized to suit the needs of each individual user.

Quark's architecture meets these needs by allowing *XTensions* to be developed. XTensions are add-on programs that target specific needs not otherwise addressed by QuarkXPress. XTensions, which are available both for QuarkXPress for Macintosh and QuarkXPress for Windows, are developed both by Quark and by hundreds of third-party XTension developers.

Why would you need an XTension? Suppose that you produce documents that are full of complicated tables. Rather than try to use QuarkXPress to format tables, you can simply buy an XTension that automates most of the formatting, saving you hours and hours of production time. Maybe you need to turn your QuarkXPress pages into HTML pages for use on a Web site. You can buy an XTension to do the job. In other words, XTensions let you add to the power of QuarkXPress in a way that is customized to exactly the kind of publishing you do.

How X'Tensions Happen

When you install an XTension, it "merges" with QuarkXPress. After an XTension is installed, you access it directly from within QuarkXPress by simply clicking on a menu or menu item that appears for each XTension.

We show you in a minute how this works. But first, you need to know a few things about how XTensions work. Think of these things as the rules of the game.

Understanding the rules

XTensions are easy to install and easy to use, as long as you keep a few general rules in mind:

- XTensions must be installed in the XTension folder that comes with QuarkXPress.

- XTensions take up system memory, so keep unused or infrequently used XTensions in a different folder or subdirectory. Users can use the XTension Disabled folder that is created automatically when you install new XTensions. In QuarkXpress 4.0, both platforms have an XTension Disabled folder that the XTension Manager shuttles XTensions between.

✓ An installed XTension adds itself to one or more of the regular QuarkXPress menus, or it adds its own menu(s) and/or palette(s), or a combination of these.

Installing XTensions

Installing XTensions is a matter of placing the XTension in the XTension folder. XTensions, in the XTension folder, are enabled in the XTensions Manager dialog box automatically. You install most XTensions by dragging the XTension's icon onto the XTension folder, using the following steps:

1. **Insert the CD or floppy that holds the XTension into the CD or floppy drive.**

2. **Open the QuarkXPress folder and locate the XTension folder.**

3. **Open the XTension CD or floppy icon by double-clicking it.**

4. **If the XTension CD or floppy contains an installer, double-click the installer icon and follow the directions on the screen; if the XTension does not come with an installer, drag the XTension icon onto the XTension folder.**

After the XTension is installed, you can use it as soon as you relaunch QuarkXPress. You don't need to restart the computer.

Using the XTensions Manager

After you have a collection of XTensions in your XTension and XTension Disabled folders, you can use the XTensions Manager utility to activate and deactivate them. However, because XTensions load when QuarkXPress is starting up, you have to relaunch QuarkXPress to have the changes take effect. Figure 9-1 shows the XTensions Manager, which you access by choosing Utilities⇨XTensions Manager.

XTensions show up as new menu items, palettes, or dialog boxes. In the example shown in Figure 9-2, the added XTensions created new menu items (Show Document Content, Show Shared Elements, Show Attributes Inspector) at the bottom of the View menu. Notice that we also added an XTension that created a new menu, QX-Effects, in the menu bar.

Some Sample XTensions

Hundreds of XTensions are available. We won't list them all for you here; it would be a futile effort, anyway, because new XTensions enter the market every day. If you want a complete list of XTensions, the best way to get one

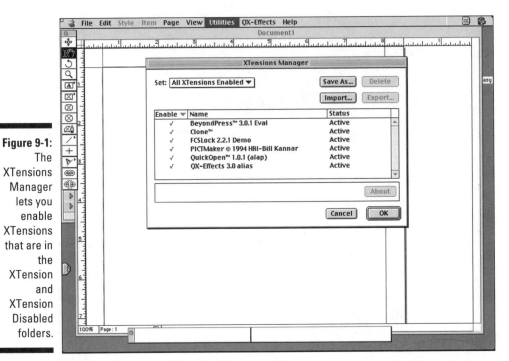

Figure 9-1:
The XTensions Manager lets you enable XTensions that are in the XTension and XTension Disabled folders.

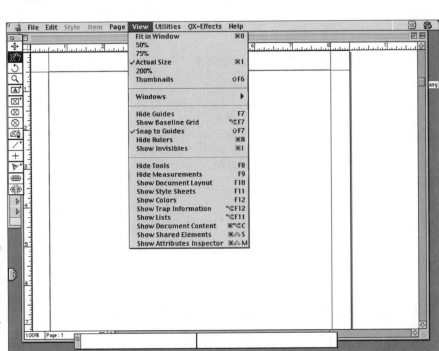

Figure 9-2:
XTensions appear as new menus or as new menu items.

is to call one of the independent companies who market XTensions and who serve as a clearinghouse between QuarkXPress users and XTension developers. XChange (www.xchangeus.com) is one of these companies; XT-Now (www.xt-now.com) is another.

Online services, such as America Online or CompuServe, that have desktop publishing forums are another source of XTensions or demo versions. Quark posts free XTensions on these online services as well, and you often find other free or shareware XTensions that may offer the features you need at a price lower than what you would pay for a more complete commercial product.

Still another source is Quark, Inc.'s electronic mailing service called XTNEWS. This is a free e-mail service that offers information about XTensions. To subscribe, send a message to xtnews@xtensions.quark.com. Use the word "subscribe" as the subject of your message.

And now, a word (actually, quite a few words) about some XTensions that we think are particularly cool. You'll find them on the Web sites listed earlier, as well as in the CD that accompanies our MacWorld QuarkXPress 4 Bible, also published by IDG Books Worldwide, Inc.

QuickOpen, from A Lowly Apprentice Production

Quark meant well when it created the Nonmatching Preferences dialog box that automatically appears when you open a document whose preference settings differ from the QuarkXPress defaults. The problem is that, in almost every case, you want to keep the document preferences; so this dialog box becomes an annoyance. But there's now a way to turn off this dialog box in QuarkXPress. If you install QuickOpen from A Lowly Apprentice Production (free, Mac only), this dialog box is turned off, and QuarkXPress automatically uses the document preferences. Windows users get a poor man's version of QuickOpen, native in 4.0; because Keep Document Settings is now linked to the Enter key, it's easier to bypass the annoying dialog box.

BeyondPress from Astrobyte

BeyondPress is an XTension that is a particularly powerful design tool. If you decide to use it, you may not need a dedicated HTML layout program to fine-tune Web pages. Using QuarkXPress and BeyondPress in tandem, you can

Figure 9-3:
BeyondPress's
Application
Preferences
dialog box
lets you
specify how
items are
added to
the export
list in the
Document
Content
palette.
Another
option lets
you specify
a browser
for viewing
the Web
pages you
create.

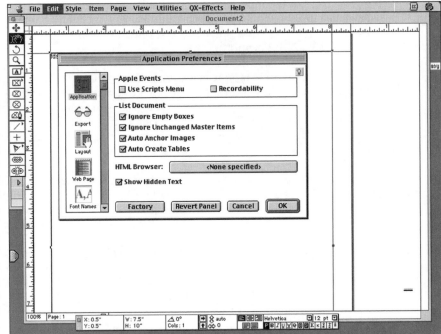

✔ Export text and pictures from existing QuarkXPress documents in HTML format while optionally adding additional images, headers, footers, sound, video, and Java applets (see Figure 9-3).

✔ Create Web pages from scratch from within QuarkXPress.

✔ Repurpose the content of existing print documents within new Web-optimized HTML documents created within QuarkXPress.

✔ Simultaneously create separate print and Web versions of publications within QuarkXPress. If you need to create Web pages, you'll find BeyondPress to be so nifty, you'll wonder how you ever managed without it.

FlowMaster from Tobias Boskamp

Tobias Boskamp is a one-person XTension developer. His FlowMaster XTension ($149, Mac and Windows) is designed for QuarkXPress users who go to great lengths to get their text to flow just right.

In some cases, even the slightest change in the flow of text can be disastrous. But the reality is that — for a variety of reasons — text sometimes reflows. Perhaps your service bureau is using a different version of QuarkXPress than you, or maybe some of their fonts are newer than yours.

Or perhaps you're a Mac user who has received a QuarkXPress document from a Windows user, and you don't have all the required fonts. If you want to avoid reflow problems, check out FlowMaster from Tobias Boskamp.

QX-Effects from Extensis

Extensis is well respected as the leading purveyor of add-ons and plug-ins for desktop publishing and graphics software. The company's QX-Tools ($99, Mac only) is the most popular collection of XTensions, and QX-Effects is a nice addition to a well stocked publisher's tool kit.

Before QX-Effects, designers who needed to create drop shadows, bevels, or embosses had to build them in an image-editing application and then import the image into QuarkXPress. QX-Effects (see Figure 9-4) lets you create these effects inside QuarkXPress. By converting them to TIFF files, you can apply shadow, bevel, glow, and embossing effects to text and picture boxes.

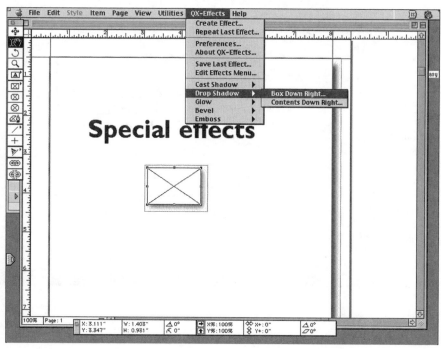

Figure 9-4: QX-Effects lets you apply shadows, such as the shadow around the picture box, and the document page itself, shown here.

HX PowerUnderline from HanMac

HanMac is a small XTension developer that offers a couple of add-ons targeted to a specific need or two. HX PowerUnderline ($71, Mac only) is one such offering.

If you need to add underlines to text, QuarkXPress offers two type-style options: underline and word underline. But that's about it. You have no control over the appearance and placement of underlines, and the color of underlines is the same as the color applied to the text. But with HX PowerUnderline (see Figure 9-5), you can create custom underlines beneath highlighted text, and you also have the option to create framed boxes around highlighted text.

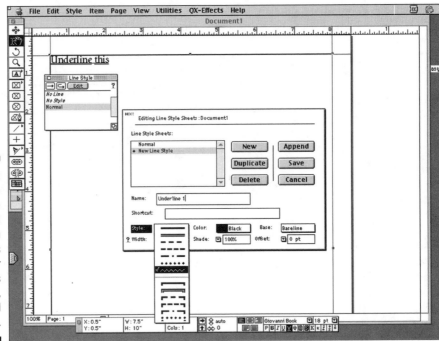

Figure 9-5: HX Power-Underline lets you add custom underlines beneath, or boxes around, highlighted text.

Clone from Second Glance

Second Glance's Clone XTension ($99, Mac only) was designed for QuarkXPress users who want to create multi-up labels without the hassle of duplicating a single original and manually positioning all of the copies. Essentially, Clone is a simple but powerful step-and-repeat utility for creating labels of any kind. The commercial product includes more than 100 templates for Avery labels, including name tags, VCR labels, and return addresses.

If you don't find what you need among the bundled templates, you have the option to create your own. To create a multi-up label, open the appropriate template, use the QuarkXPress typographic and page layout tools to design the label, and then choose Clone from the Utilities menu (see Figure 9-6).

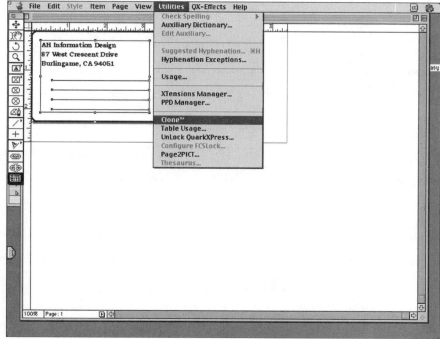

Figure 9-6: After you set up the label, choose Clone from the Utilities menu. The results of the clone operation are shown in Figure 9-7.

A new document is created with multiple copies of the label designed (see Figure 9-7).

Put some label paper in your printer and you're ready to print labels.

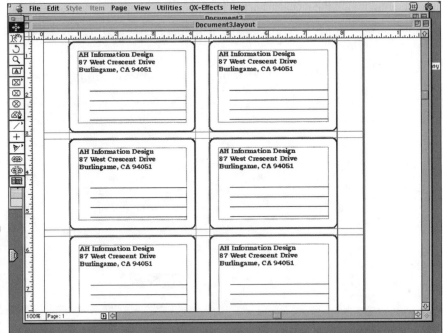

Figure 9-7:
A multi-up label page set up with the Clone XTension.

If You Have a Need . . .

We show you these sample XTensions to give you an idea of the types of things that they can do. If you have a particular need that isn't addressed by QuarkXPress, we encourage you to see if you can find an XTension that will take care of it.

Chapter 10

Printing to Pages

● ●

● ●

*A*fter your document is designed and laid out, you may actually want to see a printed copy. Go for it! This chapter covers printing with QuarkXPress. For basic printing, you can choose File⇨Print (or press ⌘+P or Ctrl+P). Why stick with the basics, though, when you can have control of some of the details?

Getting Ready to Print

When you are ready to print a QuarkXPress document, first make sure that the Document Setup dialog box and Setup pane in the Print dialog box are set up the way you want them to be. These dialog boxes allow you to change the size of the document and control the way that it prints; they also allow you to specify paper size, the orientation of images on the page, and the page image size. To display the Document Setup dialog box, choose File⇨Document Setup (or press Option+Shift+⌘+P or Ctrl+Alt+Shift+P). To display the Setup pane of the Print dialog box, choose File⇨Page Setup (or press Option+⌘+P or Ctrl+Alt+P). Figure 10-1 shows the dialog boxes.

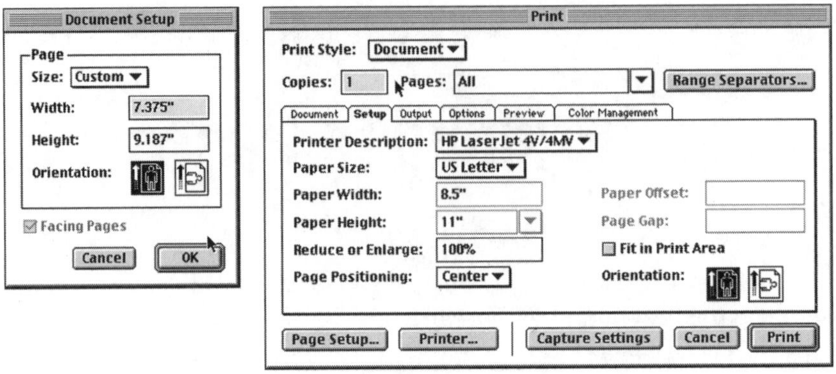

Figure 10-1:
The
Document
Setup
dialog box
and the
Print dialog
box's Setup
pane.

How to set up your document

The Document Setup dialog box is where you set the size of your printed page. The dimensions set in this dialog box determine where the crop marks appear, if you print registration and crop marks (as described in "The Document Pane" later in this chapter). Options that you can set in the Setup pane include the following:

- ✔ **Printer Description.** This pop-up menu contains the printers for which a PostScript printer description file (PPD) is available. On the Mac, these files are installed in the Printer Descriptions folder (in the Extensions folder, which is inside the System Folder), although QuarkXPress also finds them if they are in a folder named PPD within the QuarkXPress folder. In Windows 95, these files are typically installed in the WINDOWS\SYSTEM folder. Printers should come with a disk that contains these files and installs them in the appropriate Mac or Windows location. QuarkXPress has printer descriptions that are appropriate for common printers and imagesetters.

- ✔ **Paper Size, Paper Width, and Paper Height.** For the Paper Size option, choose the size of the paper that will be used in the printer. The size of the paper that you will be using does not always correspond directly to the trim size of your final document. Notice that if you select a printer that can print on nonstandard pages (such as an imagesetter), the Paper Width and Paper Height options become active so that you can specify the size of the paper.

- ✔ **Paper Offset and Page Gap.** The Paper Offset and Page Gap controls apply to imagesetters; don't change these settings unless your service bureau directs you to do so. But do ask what the service bureau prefers the first time that you work with a service bureau.

If you have elements that bleed off the page and you are printing on a commercial printing press, make sure that the paper size is larger than the document size by at least $^1/_4$ inch wide and $^1/_4$ inch tall ($^1/_8$ inch on each side).

✔ **Reduce or Enlarge.** You can scale a page before you print it by entering a value between 25% and 400%. Printing at reduced scale is particularly useful if your document's page size is large and if you can get by with a reduced version of the document for proofing purposes.

✔ **Page Positioning.** This pop-up menu allows you to align the page within the paper that it is being printed on. Your choices are Left Edge (the default), Center (centers both horizontally and vertically), Center Horizontal, and Center Vertical.

✔ **Fit in Print Area.** This option calculates the percentage of reduction or enlargement necessary to ensure that the document page fits fully within the paper size. Almost every printer has a gap along at least one edge where the printer grasps the paper (usually with rollers) to move it through the printing assembly. The printer can't print in this gap, so a document that is as large as the paper size usually has part of it cut off along one or more edges of the paper. Checking this option ensures that nothing is cut off.

✔ **Orientation.** Click the icon that looks like a portrait to get *portrait,* or vertical, orientation of the document (taller than wide). The horizontal icon produces pages with a *landscape,* or horizontal, orientation (wider than tall).

Mac-specific options

Some setup options are specific to the Mac, as shown in Figure 10-2. In Mac QuarkXPress, you get one set of these options by clicking the Page Setup button in the Print dialog box and then clicking the Options button; you get a second set of these options by clicking the Printer button and then clicking the Options button. (In Mac OS 8, you may not see these buttons; instead, you may have a pop-up menu in the Page Setup and Print dialog boxes that includes a menu called Options, Print Options, or PostScript Options.)

The controls vary from printer to printer, but here are the basic options:

✔ Check the Substitute Fonts box to substitute Times for New York, Helvetica for Geneva, and Courier for Monaco. Leaving this box un- checked means that the printer will print bitmap versions of these system fonts instead (unless the appropriate TrueType or PostScript Type 1 versions are installed).

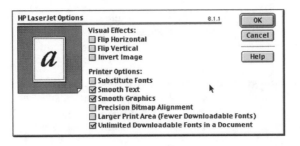

Figure 10-2:
The Mac's
platform-
specific
print-setup
dialog
boxes.

✔ To smooth the printing of bitmap fonts for which no PostScript or TrueType font is installed, check Smooth Text. You usually should leave this option unchecked, because you probably have the PostScript or TrueType versions of most of the bitmap fonts that you use.

✔ To smooth printed bitmap images, check Smooth Graphics. You may want to avoid using this option if you are printing screen shots, because it may make text in dialog boxes look strange or hard to read.

✔ If you use many fonts, check Unlimited Downloadable Fonts in a Document. This option may make printing take a bit longer, but it ensures that all your text prints in the correct font (especially text in imported EPS pictures).

✔ Check Precision Bitmap Alignment or Larger Print Area (Fewer Downloadable Fonts) only if your service bureau or printing expert asks you to do so.

Avoid setting anything in these global dialog boxes that you can also set in QuarkXPress. It's better to set up local printer settings within your QuarkXPress documents than to use these global settings.

Windows-specific options

Figure 10-3 shows the options that are specific to Windows. You get these options by clicking the Properties button in the QuarkXPress Print dialog box.

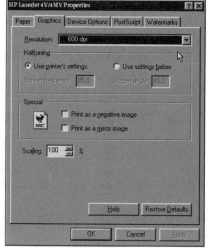

Figure 10-3:
Windows-
specific
options for
printer
setup.

The key options are found in the following panes:

- ✔ **Graphics pane:** Be sure to set the resolution to the highest value that your printer supports.

- ✔ **Device Options pane:** These options are specific to each type of printer, so look at the options for your printer and make sure that the settings match your printer's capabilities.

- ✔ **PostScript pane:** The options you may need to adjust are those in the PostScript Output Format pop-up menu, but leave these untouched — the default is "PostScript (optimize for speed)" — unless your service bureau asks for a change.

Avoid setting anything in these global platform dialog boxes that you can also set in QuarkXPress. It's better to set up local printer settings within your QuarkXPress documents than to use these global settings.

Understanding the Anatomy of a Print Dialog Box

When the page is set up for printing and the printer is set up for printing, you are ready to actually print the document. To print a document, choose File➪Print (or press ⌘+P or Ctrl+P) to open the Print dialog box. This dialog box has five panes (or six, if you have the Quark CMS XTension installed and active), as well as several options that are common to all the panes. (One of those panes is the Setup pane, covered in the preceding section "How to Set Up Your Document.") Change any options and choose OK, and QuarkXPress sends your document to the printer (or file, if you are printing to a PostScript file).

The Print dialog box has undergone a major transformation in QuarkXPress 4.0. The pane design is new, and you also find altered controls throughout.

Some common options

No matter what pane is open, the following options are always available:

- **Print Style.** You choose the print style — a saved set of printer settings — from this list. Print styles are covered in the section "Creating Print Styles" later in this chapter.

- **Copies.** Enter how many copies of the document you want to print.

- **Pages.** Specify which pages you want to print. You can enter a range (such as **3-7**), a single page (such as **4**), a set of unrelated pages (such as **3, 7, 15, 28**), or a combination (such as **3-7, 15, 28-64, 82-85**). (If you prefer to use something other than a hyphen to indicate a range and a comma to indicate separate pages, click the Range Separators button and substitute your preferred symbols.) Choose All from the pop-up menu to print all pages, or type **All.**

The capability to specify noncontiguous page ranges is new in QuarkXPress 4.0, unless you're used to using the QuarkPrint XTension.

- **Capture Settings.** This new button remembers the current Print dialog-box settings and returns you to your document. This option allows you to make a change and return to the Print dialog box later without having to reestablish your settings.

- **Print.** This button prints the document.

- **Cancel.** This button closes the Print dialog box without printing.

- **Page Setup.** This button opens the Mac's Page Setup dialog box, covered in the "How to Set Up Your Document" section in this chapter.

- **Printer.** This button opens the Mac's Print Options dialog box, covered earlier in the "Mac-Specific Options" section in this chapter.

Windows QuarkXPress does not have the Page Setup or Printer buttons. But this program does have the Properties button, which displays the properties for the current printer, and the Printer pop-up menu, from which you choose the printer that you want to use. (On the Mac, you use the Chooser or, if you're using the desktop printing feature, the Finder's Printing menu to select the printer.)

How to use the section-numbering feature

If you use the QuarkXPress section-numbering feature to create multiple sections in your document, you must enter the page numbers exactly as they are labeled in the document. (The label for the current page appears in the bottom-left corner of your document screen.) Include any prefix used, and enter the labels in the same format (letters, roman numerals, or regular numerals) used in the section whose pages you want to print.

Alternatively, you can indicate the absolute page numbers by preceding the number with a plus sign (+). Suppose that you have an eight-page document with two sections of four pages each. You label pages 1 through 4 as AN-1 through AN-4 and label pages 5 through 8 as BN-1 through BN-4. If you enter **BN-1 - BN-4** in the Pages field of the Print dialog box, QuarkXPress prints the first four pages of the section that uses the BN- prefix. If you enter **+5 - +8**, QuarkXPress prints document pages 5 through 8 — which again includes BN-1 through BN-4.

The Document pane

In the Document pane, shown in Figure 10-4, you set up the basic page attributes. (Notice that QuarkXPress 4.0 drops the old Cover Page option, which allowed you to specify whether a cover page prints.)

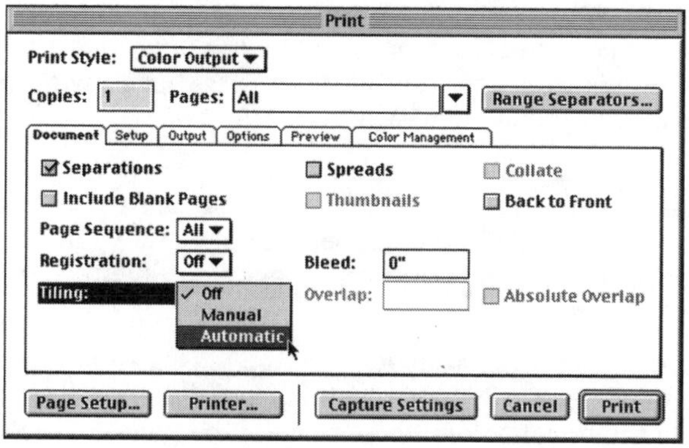

Figure 10-4:
The
Document
pane.

The following items describe the options in the current version of QuarkXPress and how to use them:

> ✔ **Separations.** This option prints color separations, putting each color on its own sheet (or negative) for use in producing color plates.

✔ **Include Blank Pages.** Sometimes, you want blank pages to print, such as when you are outputting pages to be photocopied and want to use the blank pages as separators between sections of your document. Check this option to output blank pages; uncheck it to print only pages that contain text or graphics.

✔ **Spreads.** If your printer can print facing pages on one sheet of paper (such as if you have an 11-inch by 17-inch printer and your pages are $8^{1}/_{2}$ by 11 inches or smaller), and you want them printed that way, check this option.

You may not want to use the Spreads option for outputting to an imagesetter if you have bleeds, because no extra space is available for the bleed between the spreads. If you use traditional perfect-binding (square spines) or saddle-stitching (stapled spines) printing methods, in which facing pages are not printed contiguously, do not use this option.

✔ **Thumbnails.** To get a miniature version of your document printed several pages to a sheet, choose this option.

✔ **Collate.** This option remains grayed out unless you are printing more than one copy. If checked, this option prints a full copy of the document and then repeats as many times as copies are specified. If unchecked, this option prints the number of copies of each page before going on to the next page (such as 10 copies of page 1, followed by 10 copies of page 2, and so on). Collating takes longer for a printer than not collating does, but it may save *you* time.

✔ **Back to Front.** If checked, this option reverses the printing order, so that the last page comes first, followed by the next-to-last page, and so on. This option is handy for output devices that print with the pages facing up, rather than facing down.

✔ **Page Sequence.** You can choose All, Odd, or Even to print the specified type of pages from whatever range you choose in the Pages drop-down list. Thus, if you choose Odd and specify a page range of 2-6, pages 3 and 5 print. Notice that this option is grayed out if you checked the Spreads option.

✔ **Registration.** This option adds registration marks and crop marks, which you need if your document is being professionally printed. A printer uses the registration marks to align the page correctly on the printing press. Registration crop marks define the edge of the page (handy if you are printing to paper or negatives larger than your final page size). If you print color separations, enabling registration marks also prints the name of each color on its negative and includes a color bar in the output, so that the printing-press operator can make sure that the right colors are used with the right plates. You can choose to have registration centered, off-center, or turned off. If you check Registration, you have the added option of choosing Centered or Off Center registration marks. Centered is the default.

Use the Off Center registration option when your page is square or nearly square. Choosing Off Center makes it easy for the press operator to tell which sides of the page are the left and right sides and which are the top and bottom sides, thus reducing the chances that your page will be rotated accidentally.

✔ **Tiling.** For documents that are larger than the paper you're printing them on, choose Manual or Automatic to have QuarkXPress break your page into smaller chunks that fit on the page; then you can stitch those pages together. QuarkXPress prints marks on your pages to help you line up the tiles. Here's how the options work:

  • If you choose Auto, QuarkXPress determines where each tile breaks. You can specify the amount of tile overlap by entering a value (between 0 and 6 inches) in the Overlap field.

  • If you enter a value in the Overlap field, QuarkXPress prints that overlapped area on both adjacent tiles, giving you duplicate material with which you can overlap the tiles to help in alignment.

  • If you check the Absolute Overlap option, QuarkXPress makes sure that the overlap is always exactly the value specified in the Overlap field. If this option is unchecked, QuarkXPress centers the tiled image on the assembled pages, increasing the overlap if necessary.

  • If you choose Manual, you decide where the tiles break by repositioning the ruler origin in your document. For all pages selected, QuarkXPress prints the tiled area whose top-left corner matches the ruler's origin. Repeat this step for each tiled area. Choose the Manual tile option if certain areas of your document make more logical break points than others do.

✔ **Bleed.** This field is where you tell QuarkXPress how much room to leave around the document edges for elements that bleed off. This option is useful when you are printing to a file or to an imagesetter to ensure that the bleed is not inadvertently removed or shortened. A value of $^1/_8$ inch (0.125 inch) suffices for most work.

The Output pane

The Output pane, shown in Figure 10-5, is where you set many attributes for printing to an imagesetter, whether you're producing black-and-white documents or color-separated documents. You also use this pane for printing to a standard printer and to set resolution and color modes. The following two sections explain the options for both types of printers.

QuarkXPress offers several advanced printing options that are designed for professional publishing. Options that are not available for non-PostScript printers (such as color options) are grayed out in the Print dialog box.

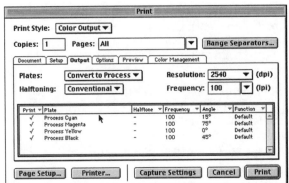

Figure 10-5:
The Output
pane.

Here's how the standard settings work in the Output pane of the Print dialog box:

- ✔ **Print Colors.** This pop-up menu (available only if the Separations option is not checked in the Document pane) allows you to select Black & White, Grayscale, and (for a color printer) Composite Color. The Grayscale option is handy for printing proof copies on noncolor printers; it is also helpful if you have a color image that you cannot otherwise convert to grayscale for use in a black-and-white document. If the Black & White option is checked, colors may appear as solid whites or blacks if they are printed on a noncolor printer. The Composite Color option prints color images in color.

- ✔ **Plates.** Appearing where the Print Colors pop-up menu does if the Separations option is checked in the Document pane, you use this menu to determine whether all spot and process (CMYK) colors are output to their own individual plates (Spot & Process) or whether all the spot colors (such as Pantone) are converted to the four process plates (Convert to Process). The answer depends on the capabilities of your printing press and the depth of your budget; typically, you choose Convert to Process.

- ✔ **Halftoning.** Use this pop-up menu to choose the halftone settings specified in QuarkXPress (the Conventional Option) or to use the defaults in your printer. For black-and-white and composite-color printing, you typically choose Printer, unless you chose halftoning effects from the QuarkXPress Style menu (you'd then want to choose Conventional). For color separations, only Conventional is available, because QuarkXPress has to do the halftoning calculations itself so that it can also figure out the color trapping.

✔ **Resolution.** Choose the *dpi* (dots per inch) at which the imagesetter prints the document. The minimum resolution for most imagesetters is 1270 dpi. Notice that setting the resolution within QuarkXPress does not override the actual settings of the imagesetter. But if you choose a lower setting in QuarkXPress than the printer is set for, all images are halftoned at the lower resolution.

✔ **Frequency.** Specify the *lpi* (lines per inch) for your target printer. QuarkXPress chooses an initial setting based on the Resolution setting, but you can choose other popular frequencies from this pop-up menu.

The Options pane

The Options pane is almost exclusively designed for people who use an imagesetter to create film negatives. Typically, your service bureau adjusts these settings or tells you how it wants you to set them. Figure 10-6 shows the Options pane.

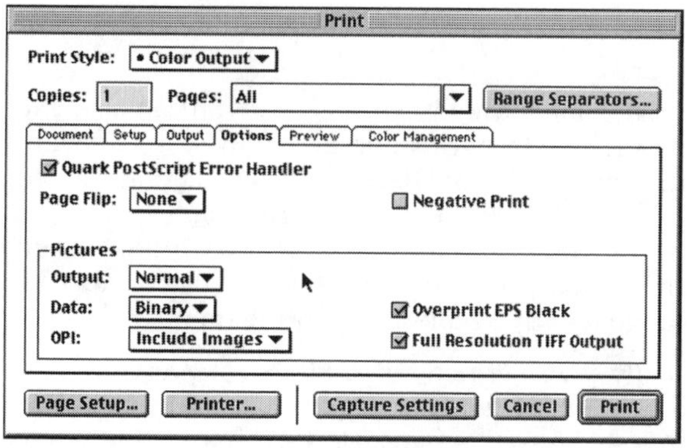

Figure 10-6:
The Options pane.

> Print
>
> Print Style: [• Color Output ▼]
>
> Copies: [1] Pages: [All] [▼] [Range Separators...]
>
> [Document] [Setup] [Output] [**Options**] [Preview] [Color Management]
>
> ☑ Quark PostScript Error Handler
> Page Flip: [None ▼]   ☐ Negative Print
>
> ┌ Pictures ─────────────────────────────┐
> │ Output: [Normal ▼]   ⬉   │
> │ Data: [Binary ▼]   ☑ Overprint EPS Black │
> │ OPI: [Include Images ▼] ☑ Full Resolution TIFF Output │
> └──────────────────────────────────────┘
>
> [Page Setup...] [Printer...] │ [Capture Settings] [Cancel] [Print]

The Page Flip and Negative Print options determine how the film negatives (or positives) are actually produced. The Output, Data, OPI, Overprint EPS Black, and Full Resolution TIFF Output options have to do with how pictures are printed. The following list describes how each option works:

✔ **Quark PostScript Error Handler.** This check box enables a neat utility that helps you diagnose output problems on a PostScript printer. PostScript is a language, and programs sometimes use it incorrectly — or at least differently than the printer expects, which leads to incorrect output and often to no output at all. If this option is checked, QuarkXPress prints a report when it encounters a PostScript error and even prints the problem page to the point where the error occurred, to help you narrow down the problem (which may be in an imported image, for example).

✔ **Page Flip.** This pop-up menu allows you to mirror your page; your options are Horizontal, Vertical, and Horizontal & Vertical. You use this feature if your service bureau requests that the page be flipped; otherwise, leave this option at the default setting (None). Reasons to flip a page have to do with reading and emulsion. *Reading* is the direction in which the page prints on a negative (to the left or to the right), and *emulsion* is the stuff on the negative that holds the image. Different printing presses expect the reading to be different ways and the emulsion to be on a specific side of the negative. The Page Flip settings allow your service bureau to adjust how the pages print in anticipation of these needs.

✔ **Negative Print.** This option prints an inverse image of your pages, exchanging black for white and dark colors for light ones. Your service bureau uses this option if it has imagesetters that can print both positives and negatives (so that the service bureau can have the correct output based on what it's printing on). Have your service bureau tell you when to use this option.

When Negative Print is checked and a page is flipped either horizontally or vertically, the page is printed right-reading, emulsion side down, which is the typical setting in the United States for printing presses.

✔ **Output.** The default setting is Normal, but you can also choose Low Resolution or Rough from this pop-up menu. Normal means that the pictures print normally; Low Resolution means that the pictures prints at the screen resolution (usually, 72 dpi); Rough means that the pictures don't print at all. You use the latter two options when you're focusing on the text and layout, not the images, because Low Resolution and Rough greatly accelerate printing time.

✔ **Data.** Typically, your service bureau tells you which of the three settings to use: Binary (smaller file sizes, faster printing, but not editable), ASCII (larger file sizes, slower printing, but editable), and Clean 8-Bit (a hybrid of binary and ASCII, somewhere between the two in size, that can safely be sent to PC-based output devices).

✔ **OPI.** If you don't use an Open Prepress Interface server, leave this option at the default setting (Include Images). If you use OPI, choose Omit TIFF if your OPI server has only high-resolution TIFF files (the most common type of OPI setup), and choose Omit TIFF & EPS if your OPI server contains both EPS and TIFF files. (An OPI server stores the original high-resolution image files on a server and allows your designers to keep smaller, low-resolution versions of images on their local computers. This makes the layouts load and display faster when they are being designed.)

✔ **Overprint EPS Black.** Normally, QuarkXPress prints black by using the trapping settings set in the Trap Specifications dialog box (accessed via the Edit Trap button in the Colors dialog box, which you open by choosing Edit➪Colors or pressing Shift+F12). But EPS files may have their own trapping settings for black defined in the program that created the EPS file. If you check the Overprint EPS Black option, QuarkXPress forces all black elements in EPS files to overprint other colors. This option does not affect how other black elements in QuarkXPress print. Trapping is an expert feature that we recommend you ignore. Don't enable the Overprint EPS Black option without first checking with your service bureau.

✔ **Full Resolution TIFF Output.** This option overrides the Frequency setting in the Output pane when TIFF images are printed. (Other elements are not affected.) If checked, this option sends the TIFF image to the printer at the highest resolution possible, based on the Resolution setting in the Output pane. You use this option when you want your TIFF images (typically, photos and scans) to be as sharp as possible. Sharpness is more an issue for bitmapped images than for text and vector images, which is why Quark offers this feature.

The Preview pane

You can easily set up your Print dialog box and print your job, only to find out that something was offbase after your pages printed. Use the Preview pane (a new feature in QuarkXPress 4.0) to ensure that margins, crop marks, bleeds, and other element-fitting issues actually fit into your target paper size.

Figure 10-7 shows an example Preview pane in which the bleed on the right side of the page goes past the page boundaries. You need to use a larger paper size or make sure that nothing bleeds on the right side of any page. (The other elements in the pane's preview are the crop marks at the corners and the registration marks along the sides.)

Figure 10-7: The Preview pane allows you to see whether all elements fit on the destination paper size.

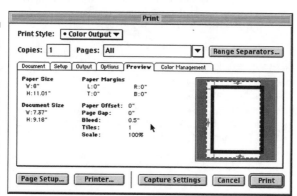

The Color Management pane

If you installed the Quark CMS XTension (by choosing Utilities⇨XTensions Manager) and enabled it (by choosing Edit⇨Preferences⇨Color Management), the Print dialog box includes the Color Management pane. This pane, which is also new in QuarkXPress 4.0, is shown in Figure 10-8.

```
┌─────────────────────────── Print ───────────────────────────┐
│                                                              │
│  Print Style:  • Color Output ▼                              │
│                                                              │
│  Copies: 1      Pages: All              ▼   Range Separators...│
│                                                              │
│  Document  Setup  Output  Options  Preview  Color Management │
│                                                              │
│  Separation Profile:  SWOP Press ▼                           │
│                                                              │
│  Composite Profile:   3M Matchprint ▼                        │
│  ☑ Composite Simulates Separation          ▸                 │
│                                                              │
│                                                              │
│                                                              │
│  Modifications in this dialog will affect preferences.       │
│                                                              │
│  Page Setup...    Printer...    Capture Settings   Cancel   Print │
└──────────────────────────────────────────────────────────────┘
```

Figure 10-8:
The Color Management pane.

Which profile is used (Separation or Composite) depends on whether separations are on. If separations are on, the separations profile is in effect.

If you change the profile for either the separation or composite printer in this pane, QuarkXPress updates the Color Management Preferences dialog box with the new settings. The program also recalibrates every image in your document — a process that could take many minutes — as soon as you exit the Print dialog box (unless you click Cancel).

The options work as follows:

✔ **Separation Profile.** Choose the output device (such as a printing press) for which QuarkXPress should color-correct all images when creating color separations. The default profile is whatever you specified in the Color Management Preferences dialog box.

✔ **Composite Profile.** Choose the output device for which QuarkXPress should color-correct all images when printing colors on a single page (rather than color-separating them). Typically, the output device is an inkjet printer, thermal-wax printer, color laser printer, or dye-sublimation printer, but sometimes, it is a proofing system or a CMYK output device. The default profile is whatever you specified in the Color Management Preferences dialog box.

✔ **Composite Simulates Separation.** If you check this box, QuarkXPress alters the colors on your composite printer to make them match the separations printer as closely as possible. Use this option when you are proofing color on a local composite printer before sending the final document out for color separations.

Because QuarkXPress 4.0 no longer uses the EfiColor color-management system, several options no longer exist in the Print dialog box. Calibrated Output no longer exists, because color calibration now occurs automatically if the color-management system is turned on and a profile is selected. The EfiColor Profile option is gone, replaced by the Separation Profile and Composite Profile options. Finally, the GCR option (gray-component removal, which sharpens blacks and grays in color bitmaps) is also gone — the only substantive functional loss in the switch from EfiColor to Quark CMS.

Establishing Typical Setups

Typically, you set up your printer as follows:

✔ For printing to a laser printer, make sure that Include Blank Pages is unchecked (unless you really want to print blank pages). Also set Orientation to Portrait, Paper Size to US Letter, Printer Description to match your target printer, Print Colors to Grayscale, Halftoning to Printer, Frequency to 60 lpi (for 300-dpi printers) or 80 lpi (for 600-dpi printers), and Data Format to Binary for Mac or Clean 8-Bit for Windows.

✔ For printing to a color printer (such as an inkjet or dye-sublimation printer), make sure that Include Blank Pages is unchecked (unless you really want to print blank pages). Also set Orientation to Portrait, Paper Size to US Letter, Printer Description to match your target printer, Halftoning to Printer, Frequency to 60 lpi (for 300-dpi printers) or 80 lpi (for 600-dpi printers), Profiles to match your target printer or to None, and Data Format to Binary for Mac or Clean 8-Bit for Windows.

✔ For printing to an imagesetter at your site for color separations, make sure that Include Blank Pages is unchecked (unless you really want to print blank pages) and that Separations is checked. Also set Orientation to Portrait, Paper Size to Custom, Page Gap to 3p, Printer Description to match your target imagesetter, Halftoning to Conventional, Resolution to 2540 dpi, Frequency to 133 or 150 lpi, Profiles to match your target printer or to None, and Data Format to Binary for Mac or Clean 8-Bit for Windows.

✔ For printing to an imagesetter for black-and-white or grayscale output, make sure that both Include Blank Pages (unless you really want to print blank pages) and Separations are unchecked. Also set Orientation to Portrait, Paper Size to Custom, Page Gap to 3p, Printer Description to match your target imagesetter, Resolution to 1270 dpi, Halftoning to Printer, Frequency to 120 or 133 lpi, and Data Format Binary for Mac or Clean 8-Bit for Windows.

Working with Spot Colors and Separations

It's very easy to accidentally use spot colors, such as red and Pantone 111 (say, for picture and text-box frames), in a document that contains four-color TIFF and EPS files. The result is that QuarkXPress outputs as many as six plates: one each for the four process colors, plus one for red and one for Pantone 111. You may expect the red to be separated into 100 percent each of yellow and magenta (which is how red is printed in four-color work). And maybe you expect QuarkXPress to separate the Pantone 111 into its four-color equivalent (11.5 percent yellow and 27.5 percent black). So why doesn't QuarkXPress do this? We don't know, but maybe Quark will change this in the next version.

Using the Edit Color dialog box

By default, each color defined in QuarkXPress — including the red, green, and blue that are automatically available in the Colors dialog box (Edit⇨Colors, or Shift+F12) — is set as a spot color. And each spot color gets its own plate, unless you specifically tell QuarkXPress to translate the color into process colors. You do so when defining a new color by unchecking the Spot Color box in the Edit Color dialog box, which is described in Chapter 15.

No matter whether a color was defined as a process or spot color, you can also choose the Convert to Process option (from the Plates pop-up menu in the Output pane of the Print dialog box) when you are printing to convert *all* spot colors to process colors (refer to Figure 10-5). This technique is no good, however, if you want to print a mixture of process colors and spot colors. If you want to color-separate red as 100 percent yellow and 100 percent magenta but print Pantone 111 on its own plate as a spot color, for example, you must use the Edit Color dialog box to set all colors except those that you want to appear on their own plates as process colors.

The advantage of setting the colors to process in the Edit Color dialog box is that the colors are permanently made into process colors. You must choose the Convert to Process option each time you print — a procedure that you can automate via print styles, as described later in this chapter.

If your work is primarily four-color work, either remove the spot colors (such as blue, red, and green) from your Colors dialog box or edit them to make them process colors. If you make these changes with no document open, the settings become the defaults for all new documents.

Transferring duplicate color sets

If you do some spot-color work and some four-color work, duplicate the spot colors and translate the duplicates into process colors. Make sure that you use some clear color-naming convention, such as Blue P for the process-color version of blue (which you create by using 100 percent each of magenta and cyan). The same is true when you use Pantone colors (and Hexachrome, Trumatch, Focoltone, Toyo, DIC, and multiple-ink colors). If you do not check the Process Separation box in the Edit Color dialog box (to display this dialog box, choose Edit⇨Colors and click the New button to create a color or the Edit button to edit an existing color), these colors are output as spot colors. Again, you can define a Pantone color twice, making one of the copies a process color and giving it a name to indicate what it is. Then all you have to do is make sure that you pick the right color for the kind of output you want.

Mixing spot and process colors

You still can mix process and spot colors, if you want. If you want a gold border on your pages, for example. you have to use a Pantone ink, because metallic colors cannot be produced via process colors. So use the appropriate Pantone color, and *don't* check the Process Separation box when you define the color. When you make color separations, you get five negatives: one each for the four process colors and one for gold. That's fine, because you specifically want the five negatives. (Just make sure that any other colors that you create from spot-color models are turned into process colors in the Edit Color dialog box; otherwise, each of these spot colors prints on its own negative, too.)

Creating Print Styles

Quark integrated its former QuarkPrint XTension into QuarkXPress 4.0. This feature adds many new controls and options to the print functions. The most important of these options is the ability to create print styles, which allow you to save settings for specific printers and/or specific types of print jobs. To create or edit a print style, choose Edit⇨Print Styles to display the dialog box shown in Figure 10-9.

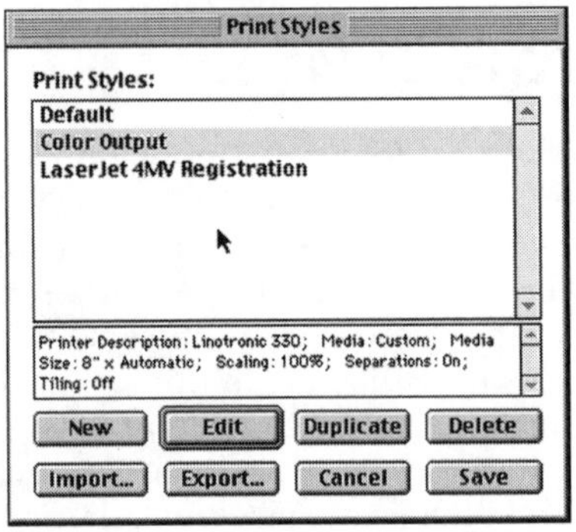

Figure 10-9:
The Print
Styles
dialog box.

> **Print Styles**
>
> Print Styles:
> **Default**
> **Color Output**
> **LaserJet 4MV Registration**
>
> Printer Description: Linotronic 330; Media: Custom; Media Size: 8" x Automatic; Scaling: 100%; Separations: On; Tiling: Off
>
> [New] [Edit] [Duplicate] [Delete]
> [Import...] [Export...] [Cancel] [Save]

When you choose to edit an existing style or create a new style, you get the dialog box shown in Figure 10-10. This dialog box contains four of the Edit⇨Print Style dialog box's panes: Document, Setup, Output, and Options. These panes are the same as those in the Print dialog box, so set them here as you would there. After you set the print style's options, click OK; then click Save in the Print Styles dialog box.

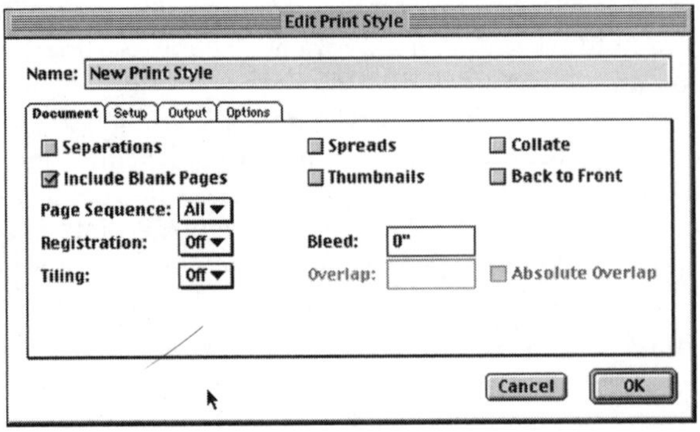

Figure 10-10:
The Edit
Print Style
dialog box.

> **Edit Print Style**
>
> Name: New Print Style
>
> [Document | Setup | Output | Options]
>
> ☐ Separations   ☐ Spreads   ☐ Collate
> ☑ Include Blank Pages ☐ Thumbnails   ☐ Back to Front
> Page Sequence: [All ▼]
> Registration: [Off ▼]   Bleed: [0"]
> Tiling: [Off ▼]   Overlap: [   ]   ☐ Absolute Overlap
>
> [Cancel] [OK]

Unfortunately, QuarkXPress does not allow you to take Print dialog-box settings and create a print style from them. You must recreate the settings in the Print Styles dialog box, so be sure to write them down first.

You may have multiple printers in your office or in your service bureau —
laser printers for basic business use and quick proofing of layouts, color
printers for color proofing, and an imagesetter for final film output. Rather
than specify the various settings for each printer each time you print your
document — an exercise that is subject to mistakes, given the complexity of
QuarkXPress's Print dialog box — use print styles to save all these settings.
Then, in the Print dialog box, just choose the printer setting that you want
to use. Here are a couple of additional tips on using print styles:

- You can share print styles with other users; click the Export button to
  save your styles in a file that your colleagues can import by clicking the
  Import button.

- If you choose a print style in the Print dialog box and make changes in
  the various panes, you see the name of the print style change; a bullet
  (•) precedes the name. This change is meant to remind you that you
  changed the print style's settings for this particular print session. The
  change does not change the print style itself, so the next time you use
  that print style, its original settings will be in effect.

Working with Service Bureaus

Many QuarkXPress users end up sending their work to service bureaus
(including the in-house production departments at a commercial printer) to
print the final copies. After all, QuarkXPress is the publishing tool of choice
for professional publishers, and professional publishers tend to print color
magazines, high-volume newsletters, crisp brochures, and other materials
that need a professional printer, not just a photocopier.

Understanding what a service bureau needs

Working with a service bureau can be a trying experience, particularly if you
don't understand what the service bureau needs. Basically, a service bureau
needs whatever the document has in it or takes advantage of. Here's a
checklist to go over before sending your QuarkXPress files to a service
bureau:

- **Who prints the files?** If you give your QuarkXPress files to the service
  bureau, it can make any adjustments needed for optimal printing or
  solve unexpected problems with, for example, images or colors. But the
  service bureau could make a mistake by changing something that it
  shouldn't. By printing the file yourself, you can prevent this potential
  problem.

When you print the file yourself, you're responsible for the final output; a service bureau can't edit your PostScript print file. In addition to being uneditable, these files can be huge (even larger than the document and associated files on which they're based — in tens of megabytes). In most cases, the service bureau should print from your files, but you should mark on the hard copy all colors, ruling lines, images, and fonts to give the service bureau something to check against.

You also should insist on color-match prints (called by several trade names, such as Matchprints and Fujichromes) for color pages and bluelines for black-and-white or spot-color pages. (*Color-match prints* and *bluelines* are copies of your publication made from the negatives, allowing you to see your publication before the mass printing begins.) Expect to pay about $135 per color-match print page and $20 per blueprint page.

✔ **Does the service bureau use the same version of QuarkXPress that you use?** If you use QuarkXPress Version 4.0 and your service bureau has Version 3.2, the service bureau can't open your files. If you have Version 4.0 and the service bureau has Version 3.3, you can save your files in 3.3 format, but you will lose some 4.0 features, such as Bézier boxes and color profiles. When a version changes, check to ensure that you and your service bureau are in sync. For minor upgrades, such as QuarkXPress 3.31 or 4.01, compatibility problems rarely occur.

✔ **Do you and the service bureau use the same XTensions?** If you use Quark CMS, make sure that your service bureau does, too. Ditto for anything else that affects the printed appearance, such as import filters for unusual graphics formats. You may even want to give your service bureau a copy of all your XTensions to ensure that nothing is missing.

You don't need to worry about XTensions that don't affect the actual content; items that display information on graphics or bypass various warnings don't change the appearance of your document when they're loaded into a system that doesn't have them.

✔ **Does the service bureau use the same fonts that you use?** If you're not sure whether your service bureau has the same fonts that you do, send copies of yours. Most service bureaus can't use TrueType fonts, so check first before sending them. Don't forget to tell the service bureau all the fonts that your document uses.

✔ **Does the service bureau have the right colors?** If you're doing four-color process (CMYK) output, have you made all colors process colors? Do you have some colors that are spot colors, and are they defined as such? Have you deleted any color plates that your document doesn't use? Don't forget to tell the service bureau what colors should print. (Use the Collect for Output feature, described in the "Listing document components" section later in this chapter, to get a list of these items.)

✔ **Does the service bureau have the same color profiles that you have?**
Don't forget to copy the color profiles that are used in your document
as well. Chances are that the service bureau has the basic ones that
came with QuarkXPress, but if you get any color profiles from anywhere
else, make sure that the service bureau gets them, too.

Dealing with platform differences

Most service bureaus are Mac-based; they probably don't know what to do
with your QuarkXPress for Windows files, even though Mac QuarkXPress
can read them. You can probably get the service bureau over the hump of
loading your files, but two gotchas may mean that you need to convert to
Mac QuarkXPress yourself, use the print-to-PostScript-file option, or find a
Windows-savvy service bureau:

✔ First, most XTensions are not available for Windows, and some Windows
XTensions have no Mac equivalents. Therefore, if you depend on such
XTensions, you need to use a Windows-savvy service bureau or forgo
the XTensions.

✔ Second, although PostScript fonts exist for both the Mac and Windows,
you can't give your Windows PostScript fonts to a Mac-based service
bureau. You have to translate the fonts into Mac format by using
a program such as Macromedia Fontographer. (For information
on this program, call 415-252-2000, or check the Web site
`www.macromedia.com`.) Beware of using "almost the same" fonts across
platforms: Even if they look alike, subtle differences in spacing can
cause text to flow differently, perhaps even leading to a story flowing
longer than originally planned and thus having some lines cut off.

Fortunately, this list of questions is manageable. You don't have to worry
about certain things. QuarkXPress keeps all tracking, kerning, and hyphenation information with the document, and your service bureau knows to
click the Keep Document Settings button when it loads your file into its copy
of QuarkXPress and is asked whether to preserve your settings.

Listing document components

QuarkXPress also provides a tool to help you gather all the components of a
document. This tool is called Collect for Output, and you access it by
choosing File⇨Collect for Output. The resulting dialog box is shown in
Figure 10-11. You can collect the document and its components in any folder
or directory, and even create a new folder or directory to store the materials.

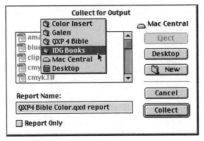

Figure 10-11:
The Collect
for Output
dialog box.

What's in a Collect for Output folder? A copy of the QuarkXPress document itself and all linked graphics are in the folder, as is a text file that has the name of the QuarkXPress document plus the word *report*. (In Windows, the name of the text file is the same as the document's filename, except that the extension is .RPT.) This report contains a treasure trove of information about your QuarkXPress document. We suggest that you send the report to your service bureau or load it into a word processor or QuarkXPress and print a copy for the service bureau to refer to.

Figure 10-12 shows part of a report that includes the following information:

- ✔ A list of all XTensions used, distinguishing between those that are required for opening the document and those that are used in the document.

- ✔ A list of all fonts used, including those used in graphics. Unfortunately, the report lists a graphic each time it is used, not just one time.

- ✔ A list of all styles used.

- ✔ A list of all color profiles used.

- ✔ A list of all H&J (hyphenation and justification) sets used (see Chapter 9 for details on H&J sets).

- ✔ A list of all colors used, including a list of all color plates used.

- ✔ A list of all trapping settings used.

- ✔ Information about the types, sizes, rotations, skews, positions, and scaling of all graphics.

In QuarkXPress 4.0, the Collect for Output dialog box has a new check box: Report Only. This option generates a report about the document's elements without copying all the associated files.

QuarkXPress can tell you which XTensions are required to open a document. But don't assume that an XTension used in a document — but not listed as required in the Collect for Output report — is optional. Take the JPEG filter XTension: you can open a document that has JPEG images even if the filter is not present, but you won't be able to print those JPEG images.

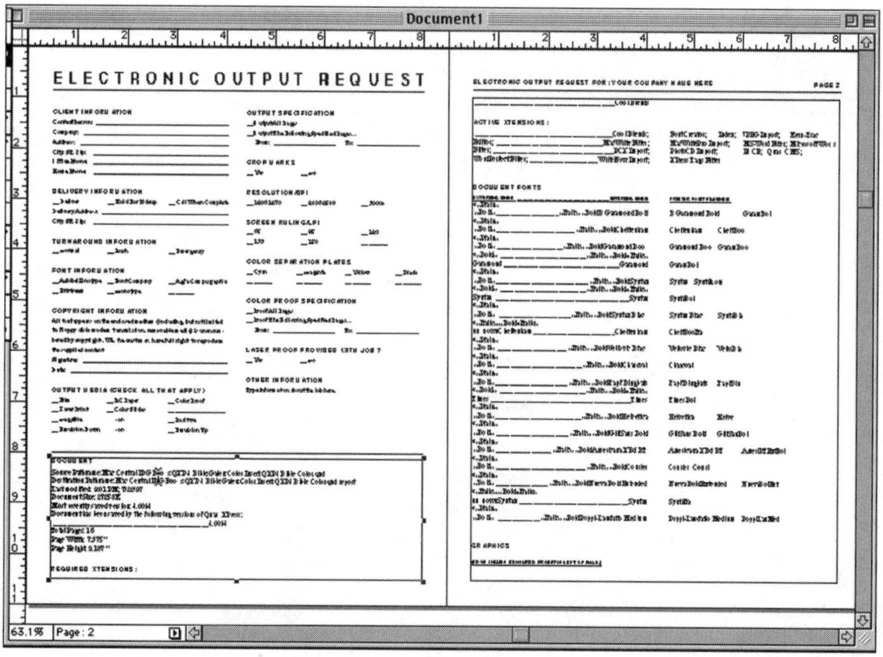

Figure 10-12:
Part of the
report that
QuarkXPress
generates
via the
Collect for
Output
feature.

QuarkXPress also comes with a template called Output Request, which makes a great cover sheet for print jobs sent to a service bureau. (This template is in your QuarkXPress folder; in Windows, it's called COLL4OUT.QXT.) At the bottom of the Output Request form is an empty text box in which you can import the report created by Collect for Output and create a unified cover sheet with all the details that your service bureau — and you — would ever want to know about your document. Remember that you can modify this QuarkXPress document's layout to match your or your service bureau's preferences. When you import the Collect for Output report into the Output Request template to generate a cover sheet for your current document, remember to check the Include Style Sheets box when you choose File⇨Get Text.

Technically speaking, it's illegal for you to copy programs (including XTensions), fonts, and images that you don't own or license and then give them to other people. Practically speaking, though, you have no choice. To ensure compatibility, you and your service bureau need to have the same tools and sources. To stay within the spirit of the law (if not the letter), make sure that your service bureau understands that the programs, fonts, and images that you copy for it are to be used only in connection with printing your documents.

The best advice for working with a service bureau is to ensure a high degree of communication. Talk with your service bureau to see what it needs from you, and make clear to the service bureau what you need. Your service bureau's job is to create the best possible output for you while still make a living wage. Your job is to minimize your headaches and the service bureau's headaches to ensure affordable, cheerful, professional, and timely service.

Part III
The Picasso Factor

The 5th Wave   By Rich Tennant

"Your Elvis should appear bald and slightly hunched-nice Big Foot, Brad-Keep your two-headed animals in the shadows and your alien spacecrafts crisp and defined."

In this part . . .

We named this part of the book after the famous artist because it tells not only how to use QuarkXPress as an illustration tool, but how to take normal-looking text and graphics and distort them. Why would you want to do this? Good question. The answer could be that, like Picasso, you want to present ideas in a visually interesting way. QuarkXPress enables you to manipulate text and art in interesting ways, and we show you how. We also give you a brief primer on color. Put these all together to create documents that dazzle.

Chapter 11

Using QuarkXPress as an Illustration Tool

*B*efore version 4.0, QuarkXPress was generally thought of as only a page layout program. The ability to draw polygon picture boxes and to change the shape of picture boxes and text boxes gave previous versions of QuarkXPress limited drawing capabilities, but if you needed to draw a curved line or curved shape, you were forced to use a dedicated drawing program. Not anymore. QuarkXPress 4.0 adds several nifty drawing-related features, including the ability to draw Bézier lines and shapes, to turn text characters into picture boxes or text boxes, and to flow text along a line or around the contour of a box. (Flowing text along a path is covered in Chapter 16.)

Using Lines

In Figure 11-1, eight tools are highlighted in the Tool palette. You use the top four tools to create straight and curved lines; the bottom four tools are identical to the top four, except that you use them to run text along the lines you create with these tools (see Chapter 16). If you create a line with one of the top four tools and later decide that you want to run text along that line, don't worry; you can do that, too.

Figure 11-1:
The top four
of the
highlighted
tools are for
creating
lines; the
bottom four
are for
creating
text paths.

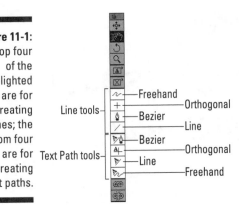

Each of the line-creation tools works a bit differently than the others. In addition to the basic Line tool at the bottom, you have these three, from top down:

✔ **The Freehand Line tool** lets you create Bézier lines using the mouse as a freehand drawing tool. To create a freehand line, click and hold down the mouse button as you drag the mouse in any direction. When you release the mouse button, QuarkXPress creates a line that follows the path of the mouse from where you first clicked to the point where you released the button.

✔ **The Orthogonal Line tool** limits you to horizontal and vertical lines. Click and hold down the mouse button, drag, and then release the mouse to create a line with this tool.

✔ **The Bézier Line tool** lets you create straight-edged zigzag lines, curvy lines, and lines that contain both straight and curved segments:

• To create a zigzag line, click and release the mouse button to establish the first endpoint and then continue clicking and releasing the mouse to add corner points with straight segments between points. Double-click to create the second endpoint or choose a different tool.

• To create a curvy line, click the mouse button to establish the first point, drag the mouse a short distance in the direction of the next point, and then release the mouse button. As you drag, a line segment is drawn through the point where you first clicked. When you release the mouse button, the first endpoint (a symmetrical point) plus two control handles are created. Create additional symmetrical points by clicking and dragging the mouse and then releasing. Don't worry too much about making the line perfectly the first time. You can always go back and tweak if necessary.

• To create a line with both straight and curvy segments, combine the two previous techniques.

Creating text paths with the four text path tools is the same as creating lines with the line tools. Modifying lines and text paths are also the same. Read on.

If you decide to use QuarkXPress to handle illustration tasks, you can use boxes as well as lines to create the pieces of your drawings. See Chapter 16 for information about creating boxes.

Modifying lines

You can modify Bézier lines by clicking and dragging points, control handles, and segments. You can also choose among three types of points and two types of segments.

Figure 11-2 shows a Bézier line with three points selected.

The text that follows describes how these points work:

- ✔ The point on the left is a corner point, indicated by a small triangle. As with smooth and symmetrical points, a corner point can have control handles (the one in the example doesn't). But unlike the other kinds of points, when you move a handle attached to a corner point, the other handle doesn't move. You can delete a handle attached to a corner point by Option+clicking or Alt+clicking it. You can add handles to a corner point that doesn't have them by Control+clicking or by Ctrl+Shift+clicking.

- ✔ The point in the middle is a smooth point, indicated by a small square intersected by a short line with handles at both ends. The two segments that make up the line are unequal in length. You can control the length of the two segments independently by dragging either handle; however, the segments remain at opposite ends of a straight line (unlike the behavior of corner point handles).

- ✔ The point on the right is a symmetrical point, which is much like a smooth point. However, the line segment that passes through it is made up of two equal-length segments. If you change the length of a segment by dragging a handle, the other segment is also resized. A symmetrical point produces slightly smoother curve than a amooth point.

The pointer displayed when you move the mouse over a Bézier line is different depending on whether the pointer is over a point (a small, black square is displayed), a segment (a short, angled line is displayed), or a handle (a small, open diamond is displayed). To move a point, segment, or control handle, click it and then drag the mouse. Shift+click to select multiple points. You can use either the Item tool or the Content tool to select and move points, handles, and segments. Hold down the ⌘ or Ctrl key when dragging to move the whole line.

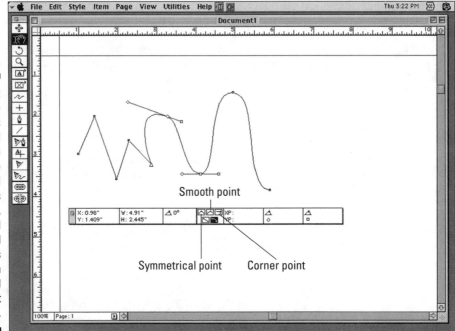

Figure 11-2:
The line
was
created
with the
Bézier line
tool and
contains
corner,
smooth, and
symmetrical
points, as
well as both
curved and
straight
segments.

Five icons in the Measurements palette, shown later in Figure 11-4, let you change points and segments. The top three icons relate to points:

✔ The leftmost icon indicates a symmetrical point. Click a nonsymmetrical point and then click this icon or press Option+F3 or Ctrl+F3 to change it to a symmetrical point.

✔ The center icon indicates a smooth point. Click a point that's not a smooth point and then click this icon or press Option+F2 or Ctrl+F2 to change it to a smooth point.

✔ The rightmost icon indicates a corner point. Click a point that's not a corner point and then click this icon or press Option+F1 or Ctrl+F1 to change it to a corner point.

The bottom two icons relate to lines:

✔ The left icon represents a straight segment. Click it or press Shift+Option+F1 or Ctrl+Shift+F1 to change a curved segment into a straight segment. (A straight segment has corner points at each end.)

✔ The right icon represents a curved segment. Click it or press Shift+ Option+F2 or Ctrl+Shift+F2 to change a straight segment. (A curved segment can end in smooth, symmetrical, or corner points. In all cases, control handles let you control the curve of the segment at both ends.)

In addition to the point/segment controls in the Measurements palette and their keyboard equivalents, the Point/Segment Type command in the Item menu also lets you change the type of points and segments.

You can add a point to a Bézier line by Option+clicking or Alt+clicking on the line. The kind of point that's added depends on the kind of segment you click on. Corner points are added to straight segments; smooth points are added to curved segments. To remove a point, Option+click or Alt+click on it.

To change a line to a text path, select the line; then choose Item⇨Content⇨ Text. You can also use this command to change a text path to a line. If you do, the text is removed from the path (see Chapter 16 for more on text paths).

If you've never worked with Bézier lines before, don't worry. Getting the hang of dragging points, handles, and segments takes some time, but like anything else, the more you practice, the better you get. If you have a chance, spend time practicing with the Bézier line and box tools and try to create a variety of shapes.

Changing the appearance of a line

When you create a line, the line is automatically given the default properties of the tool you used to create it. Unless you change your tool defaults, the lines you create will be black and 1-point in width. You can change the appearance of a line using any of several methods.

Figure 11-3 shows the Line pane of the Modify dialog box (Item⇨Modify or press ⌘+M or Ctrl+M).

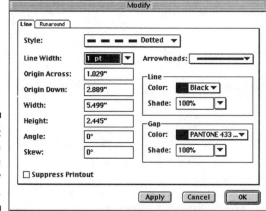

Figure 11-3:
The Line pane of the Modify dialog box.

In the Line pane, you can

✔ Choose a line style — plain, dotted, dashed, or striped — from the Style pop-up menu. (If you've created any line styles through the new Dashes and Stripes feature, covered in Chapter 12, they'll display here.)

✔ Choose a width from the Line Width pop-up or enter a width up to 864 points.

✔ Move the active line by entering new Origin Across and/or Origin Down values.

✔ Change the length of the line by entering a new value in the Width field. If you change line length, all points are repositioned proportionally.

✔ Change the overall height of the line (the distance from the topmost point to the bottommost point) by entering a new value in the height field. Again, all points are repositioned proportionally.

✔ Rotate the line by entering a value between –360° and 360° in the Angle field.

✔ Slant the line by entering a Skew value.

✔ Add an arrowhead and tailfeather by choosing a style from the Arrowheads pop-up menu.

✔ Change the color of the line by choosing a new color from the Color pop-up menu; you can change the shade by choosing a 10 percent increment from the Shade pop-up menu or by entering a percentage value in the field.

✔ If you choose a dotted, dashed, or striped line in the Style menu, you can use the controls in the Gap area to apply a color and shade to the space between dots, dashes, and stripes. If you don't apply color/shade to the gaps, they remain white. (See Chapter 12 for more information about creating custom dashed and striped line styles.)

The Line pane isn't the only place in which you can modify a line. In Figure 11-4, you see some other things you can do:

Figure 11-4 shows the Style menu for lines, the Measurements palette, and the Colors palette.

✔ The style menu displays five commands for modifying the appearance of a line: Line Style, Arrowheads, Width, Color, and Shade.

✔ From left to right, the Measurements palette lets you change the location of a line (X and Y fields), the length and height of a line (W and H fields), the line's angle (Angle field), and the thickness of the line (W field/pop-up). The two pop-up menus on the right side of the palette let you change a line's style and add arrowheads/tailfeathers.

✔ The Colors palette lets you change the color and shade of a line.

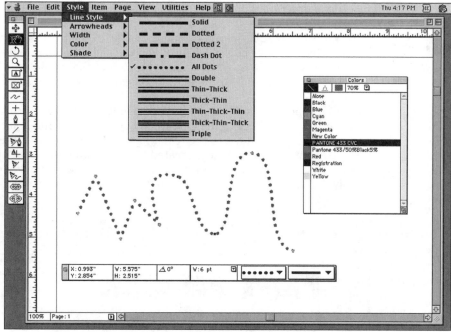

Figure 11-4:
You can
change a
line via the
Style menu,
the
Measure-
ments
palette, or
the Colors
palette.

Converting Text into Boxes

Have you ever had the urge to import a picture into a box that's the shape of a text character? Before QuarkXPress 4.0, you had to use a dedicated drawing program for such tricks. But not anymore. Now you can convert highlighted text into picture boxes or text boxes. Not only is it easy, but the boxes you produce by converting text into boxes behave as a single item. That means you can run a background — a color, blend, or picture — across all of the characters you convert to text as though they were a single box. Features just don't get any cooler than this one.

Here's how you convert text into picture boxes:

1. **Highlight the text you want to convert.**

   You can highlight an individual character or a range of text, but you cannot highlight more than one line of text. You can convert PostScript Type 1 fonts (Adobe Type Manager must be installed) or TrueType fonts. (This feature isn't particularly useful for small font sizes.)

2. **Choose Text to Box from the Style menu.**

   If you hold down the Option or Alt key when you choose Text to Box, QuarkXPress replaces the highlighted text with an individual Bézier picture box for each character and anchors the boxes within the text chain.

If you don't hold down the Option or Alt key, QuarkXPress duplicates the highlighted text using individual picture boxes for each letter. When you click on any of the resulting boxes, all of the boxes are selected, and they behave as a single box. You can put a frame around all of the boxes in a single operation, import a picture that spans all boxes, apply a background color or blend that spans the boxes, and so on.

Figure 11-5 shows a text box with some large text. The text was converted to Bézier picture boxes using the Text to Box command. A one-point frame and a linear blend were added to the resulting collection of boxes (the middle text). The bottom example was created by duplicating the Bézier picture boxes, stretching them by increasing the Height value in the Box pane of the Modify dialog box (Item⇨Modify), and then importing a scanned image.

Figure 11-5:
The text in the text box at the top was converted into picture boxes using the Text to Box command. The resulting boxes were duplicated and stretched to produce the bottom example.

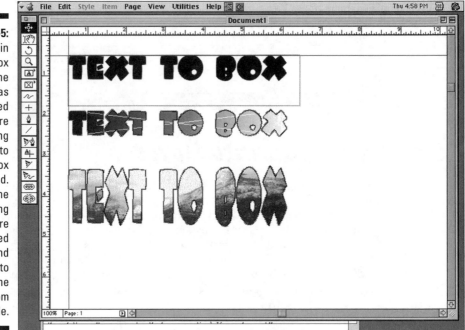

You can split the merged boxes that are produced when you choose Text to Box by choosing the Split command from the Item menu. If you choose Outside Paths, all letters that have holes in them (like Os, Ps, and Bs) remain intact. That is, if you click on one of these letters, all component paths become active. If you choose All Paths, each path that makes up a letter becomes a separate shape that can be individually selected, moved, cut, and so on.

If you want to turn a Bézier picture box created with the Text to Box command into a text box, just click on it and then choose Item⇨Content⇨Text. If you choose None from the submenu, you create a box that can contain neither text nor pictures.

Merging Boxes

The Bézier tools for text boxes, picture boxes, lines, and text paths let you create lines and closed shapes of all kinds. But what if you want to create something like a donut? That is, you want a round box with a round hole in the middle.

The Bézier drawing tools limit you to creating one path at a time; however, the Merge command in the Item menu lets you combine multiple items into complex Bézier shapes that contain multiple paths. For example, check out Figure 11-6. The Merge command was used with the empty picture boxes at the top of the page to produce the three variations below. The Swiss-cheese look of the first variant was created by choosing Difference; the next one is similar but has circular pieces on each end and was created with Exclusive Or; the bottom example was created by choosing Intersection.

Figure 11-6:
You can use the Difference, Exclusive Or, and Intersection options, respectively, to create the three examples from the empty picture boxes at the top.

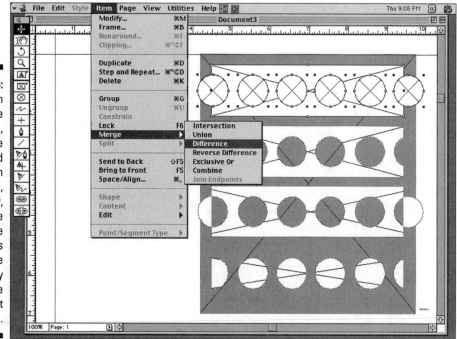

Understanding what each of the Merge options does to selected items takes
some experimentation. The names of the options aren't exactly intuitive,
some circumstances produce cryptic alerts, and some commands require
that selected items overlap. Briefly, here's what each option does:

- ✔ **Intersection** calculates where each of the items (except the backmost
  item) overlaps the backmost item and retains only the overlap areas.

- ✔ **Union** combines all shapes into a single shape. The shapes don't have
  to overlap. If shapes overlap, the overlapped areas are retained along
  with the areas that don't overlap.

- ✔ **Difference** removes all shapes from the backmost shape. This option is
  useful for cutting pieces out of a shape. For example, you can use a
  circular shape to punch a round hole in a box.

- ✔ **Reverse Difference** retains what's left after the background shape and
  all shapes that intersect the background shape are removed.

- ✔ **Exclusive Or** cuts out all areas that overlap, retains areas that don't
  overlap, and creates new shapes for what remains.

- ✔ **Combine** is like Exclusive Or except the paths of the original items are
  retained.

- ✔ **Join Endpoints** is available only when two lines or text paths are active
  and endpoints from each line overlap each other or are within the snap-
  to distance (which is 6 pixels, unless you've changed the default Snap
  Distance setting in the General pane of the document Preferences
  dialog box; Item⇨Modify). Choosing Join Endpoints produces a single
  line or path, with a corner point where the endpoints previously
  overlapped.

Figure 11-7 shows eight pairs of examples. You can create the four on the left
by using the Item⇨Merge⇨Difference option; you create the four on the
right by using Item⇨Merge⇨Union. Each example shows the boxes before
and after they are merged.

You can use the Split command in the Item menu to "deconstruct" any item
that is a single box and contains more than one closed path — including
complex Bézier shapes created with the Merge options — or a path that
crosses itself. When you choose either of the Split options (All Paths or
Outside Paths), multiple Bézier boxes are created. The contents and attributes of the original box are retained in each of the resulting boxes.

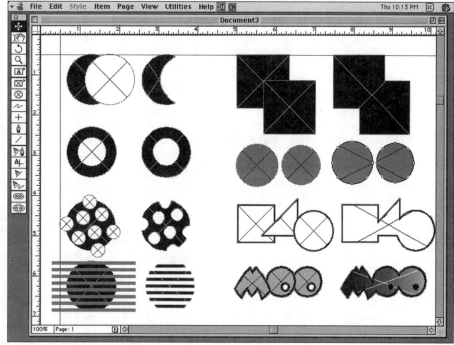

Figure 11-7:
You can
create the
merged
boxes on
the left by
choosing
Difference;
choose
Union to
create the
boxes on
the right.

Grouping Items

If you use multiple items to create, for example, an illustration, the ability to
select all of the items at once so you can do such things as move, copy, and
delete all the items in a single operation is good to have. Repeatedly selecting multiple items soon gets to be a drag. What you really want to do in this
case is to create a group out of the items that make up the illustration. If you
create a group, you can then use the Item tool to select all of the items with
a single click.

QuarkXPress provides several ways to select multiple items in preparation
for creating a group. With either the Item or Content tool, you can hold
down the Shift key as you click several items one by one (in previous
versions of QuarkXPress, you could only select multiple items by using the
Item tool). Each time you Shift+Click on an item, you add that item to the
collection of selected items.

You can also select several items by clicking and dragging a rectangle —
using either the Item or Content tool — that includes any part of the items
you want to select. If you want to select all the items on a page, choose
Select All from the Item menu (the Item tool must be selected) or press ⌘+A
or Ctrl+A. To deselect an item that's among several selected items,
Shift+Click on the item.

To create a group out of multiple-selected items, choose Group from the
Item menu or use ⌘+G or Ctrl-G. At least two items must be selected for this
command to be available. A group can contain as many items as you want,
although the items must be on the same page or facing-page spread. A group
can also contain other groups. Use the Ungroup command to break apart a
group.

When the Item tool is selected, clicking on an item that's part of a group
displays all of the grouped items within a rectangular marquee, called a
bounding box. You can click and drag to move a group with the Item tool;
however, you cannot move an individual item when the Item tool is selected.

When the Content tool is selected, you can select individual items within a
group, move pictures within boxes, enter and edit text, and move lines. If
you want to move an item that's part of a group, hold down the ⌘ or Ctrl
key when the Content tool is selected, then click on the item and drag it to a
new location. When you hold down the ⌘ or Ctrl keys, the Content tool —
and all other tools — temporarily behave like the Item tool.

One very handy new feature in QuarkXPress 4.0 is the ability to scale a
group. To do this, simply click on any of the eight handles on a group's
bounding box and drag. If you want to maintain the proportion of the items
in the group but not the contents of boxes, hold down Shift+Option or
Alt+Shift when you drag a handle. If you hold down Shift+Option+⌘ or
Ctrl+Alt+Shift as you drag, both the items and the contents of boxes are
proportionately resized.

In Figure 11-8, the three boxes in the upper-left corner — a picture box, a
text box, and a framed box with no content (Item⇨Content⇨None) — were
combined via the Group command on the Item menu.

The middle example is a copy of the group that we scaled by clicking and
dragging a handle while holding down Shift+Option+⌘ or Ctrl+Alt+Shift.
Notice that the picture scale and the size of the text are enlarged along with
the boxes that contain them. In the example on the right, a copy of the
original group is scaled down by clicking and dragging a handle while
holding down Shift+Option or Alt+Shift. The boxes are smaller, but the scale
of the picture and the size of text are not affected. Because the text box gets
smaller, but the text size does not, a text overflow results.

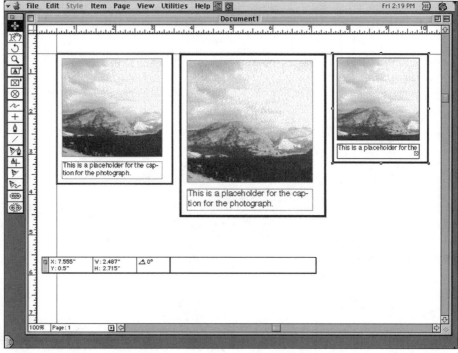

Figure 11-8:
The middle
and right
examples
were
created
by first
duplicating
and then
scaling the
group at
the left.

Changing the Shape of Items

When determining the shape of an item, not only does QuarkXPress provide several different drawing tools for text boxes, picture boxes, lines, and text paths, but after you create an item you can change its shape manually by dragging handles or, in the case of Bézier shapes, by dragging points or segments. You can also have QuarkXPress change the shape of an item for you. The Shape command in the Item menu, shown in Figure 11-9, actually lets you perform a couple of nifty tricks. You can change the shape of an item, and you can change boxes into lines and lines into boxes.

When a single item is active, the nine options displayed in the Shape menu let you change the item into (from top to bottom)

- A rectangular box
- A rounded-corner box
- A beveled-corner box
- A concave-corner box

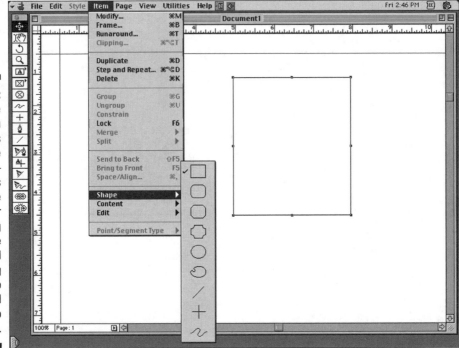

Figure 11-9:
The Shape
submenu
provides
nine
options —
six shapes
and three
lines — for
changing
the shape
of items and
for turning
lines into
boxes and
boxes into
lines.

✔ An oval box

✔ An editable Bézier box (with no change in shape)

✔ A straight line (at any angle)

✔ A straight line that's either vertical or horizontal

✔ An editable Bézier line

As neat as the Shape options are, they can produce some unusual results.
For example:

✔ If you convert a line into a Bézier box, the resulting box is as wide as
the original line. If the original line was thin, opposite edges of the
resulting box will be very close together — so close that the shape may
be difficult to edit.

✔ If you convert a dashed line, striped line, or a line with arrowheads into
a Bézier box, each component is converted into a separate shape, as
shown in Figure 11-10.

✔ If you convert a text box or picture box into a line, any box contents are
deleted. (You are warned in this situation.)

✔ If you change a text path into a shape, a text box is created.

Figure 11-10:
You can
create the
selected
items by
changing a
striped and a
dashed line
into editable
Bézier boxes
via the
Bézier box
option in the
Shape
submenu.

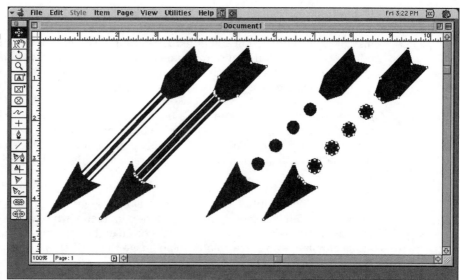

If the active item is a Bézier line, and the endpoints overlap or are close to
each other, holding down the Option or Alt keys when you choose the
Bézier box icon from the Shape submenu (Item⇨Shape) connects the
endpoints (rather than tracing around the width of the line) to create a
closed Bézier box.

If you create a Bézier box via the Shape submenu, you can change the shape
of the box by clicking and dragging points, control handles, or segments
only if the Shape option is selected in the Edit submenu (Item⇨Edit).

If Edit is not checked, you can resize a Bézier box by clicking and dragging
the handles of its bounding box, but you can't move points, handles, or
segments. The Edit submenu also has a Runaround option that lets you
modify runaround paths created via the Runaround pane of the Modify
dialog box (Item⇨Modify or ⌘+M or Ctrl+M, or directly via Item⇨
Runaround or ⌘+T or Ctrl+T) and a Clipping Path option for modifying a
clipping path specified in the Clipping pane of the Modify dialog box (you
can go directly to the Clipping pane via Option+⌘+T or Ctrl+Alt+T).

Creating Masks for Pictures using Clipping Paths

Rectangular picture boxes are like vanilla ice cream. Nice enough, but with
so many other flavors available, why not try something different every once
in a while?

In addition to letting you create Bézier picture boxes, which you can re-shape in any way to crop the image within, QuarkXPress lets you crop an image within a box using an embedded clipping path created in an image-editing or illustration program or a clipping path generated within QuarkXPress. A clipping path is a shape that isolates part of an image; everything outside the isolated area is transparent.

Figure 11-11 shows an image that's been imported into two picture boxes. In the top box, the entire picture is visible because no clipping path was used; in the bottom box, an embedded clipping path created in Adobe Photoshop was used to crop all but a small circular region within the image.

If you look at the Clipping pane of the Modify dialog box (Item➪Modify or Item➪Clipping or Option+⌘+T or Ctrl+Alt+T) in Figure 11-11, you see that Embedded Path is selected in the Type pop-up menu. QuarkXPress lets you crop an image using an embedded path or an embedded alpha channel (an alpha channel is an extra "plate" in an image that's often used as a mask to isolate part of the image). You also have the following options:

- ✔ If you choose *Item,* no clipping path is used; the box border determines what portion of the image is visible.

- ✔ *Picture Bounds* creates a rectangular clipping path around the shape of the picture.

Figure 11-11:
In the top picture box, the entire image is visible because no clipping path was used; in the bottom box, we used an embedded clipping path to crop the image.

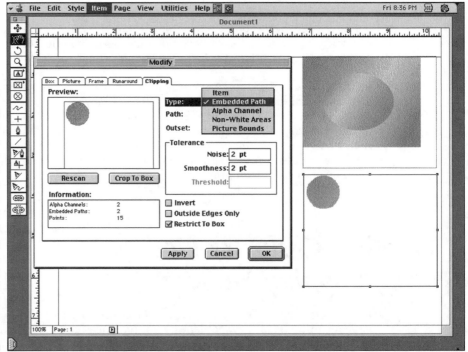

✔ *Non-White areas* creates a clipping path by drawing contours around white areas. You can modify the Threshold value if you want to include light shades as part of the white areas.

The Information area of the Clipping pane provides information about the picture in the active box. If you refer to Figure 11-11, you can see that the picture in the example contains two alpha channels and two embedded paths, any of which could have been used as a clipping path. The Preview area displays what the image and box will look like using the current settings.

The Clipping pane includes a handful of other controls that let you adjust a clipping path. You can fiddle with Tolerance settings to adjust a clipping path and check or uncheck the Invert, Outside Edges Only, and Restrict to Box options to achieve a variety of effects. We can't cover all of the permutations and combinations in this chapter. Suffice it to say that your options are numerous, and using the default settings is a safe way to begin.

The Edit command in the Item menu lets you modify a clipping path in the same way you modify a Bézier box — by clicking and dragging points, control handles, and segments, by adding and deleting points, by changing straight segments to curved segments, and so on. To modify a clipping path, click on a picture box that contains a clipping path, then make sure that Clipping Path is checked in the Edit submenu (Item⇨Edit). You can use the keyboard equivalent Shift+Option+F4 or Ctrl+Shift+F10 to alternately check and uncheck the Clipping Path option in the Edit submenu.

Chapter 12

Other Drawing Tools and Features

In This Chapter

▶ Creating margin, column, and custom guidelines

▶ Saving pages as EPS pictures

▶ Changing the stacking order of items

▶ Grouping items

QuarkXPress users and carpenters have a lot in common. Both use a set of tools to create things. Carpenters build furniture using wood, nails, and glue, while QuarkXPress users build pages out of pictures, text, and lines. And just as every carpenter's tool bag includes a chalk line for creating guidelines, so should every QuarkXPress user's bag of tricks include a hefty supply of guidelines. In this chapter, we show you how to use guidelines in laying out your pages. We also tell you how to save pages as EPS files, how to move layers around, and how to use grouping to save time as you create your graphics.

Using Guidelines for Page Layout

How important are guidelines? Guidelines are so important that QuarkXPress puts guidelines on every page you create unless you tell the program otherwise.

In the New Document dialog box (File⇨New or ⌘+N or Ctrl+N), the values you enter in the Margin Guides and Columns areas determine the position of guidelines that are automatically displayed on your document pages.

> ✔ If you enter 0 (zero) in each field of the Margin Guides area, your pages won't have margin guides.

> ✔ If you also enter 1 in the Columns field, your pages won't have column (vertical) guidelines.

✓ If you later decide that you want to change your default margin and column guidelines, you can do so by displaying Master Page A (Page⇨Display⇨A-master A)and then choosing the Master Guides command from the Page menu. The Master Guides dialog box lets you change the position of the margin and column guides. See Chapter 17 for more information on using master pages.

In addition to margin and column guides, QuarkXPress also automatically creates a grid of horizontal lines, called a *baseline grid,* on your document pages. You can display or hide the baseline grid by choosing Show/Hide Baseline Grid from the View menu or pressing Option+F7 or Ctrl+F7. The Paragraph pane of the Document Preferences dialog box (Edit⇨Preferences⇨ Document or ⌘+Y or Ctrl+Y) includes two fields — Start and Increment — that let you control the placement of baseline grid lines.

Creating Custom Guidelines

Automatic margin, column, and baseline grid guidelines are good to have, but sometimes you want to create custom guidelines. For example, you may want to position several text boxes in such a way that their left edges are aligned, as shown in Figure 12-1.

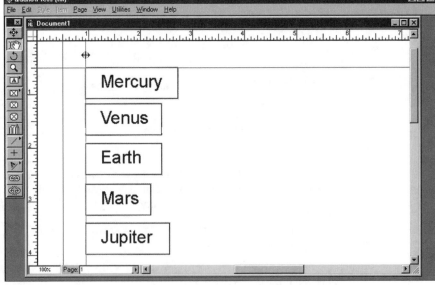

Figure 12-1: The boxes were aligned by dragging their left edges within 6 points of the vertical guideline. You see the pointer above the boxes when you click and drag to create or delete a guideline.

Creating a vertical guideline is a cinch. Here's what you do:

1. **Click on the vertical ruler displayed along the left edge of the document window.**

   If rulers aren't visible along the top and left edges of the document window, choose Show Rulers from the View menu.

2. **Hold down the mouse button and drag until the vertical line that's displayed as you drag is in the position at which you want to place a guideline.**

   As you drag, you see a small pointer with left- and right-pointing arrows.

3. **Release the mouse button.**

   If you release the mouse when the pointer is over a document page, the guideline extends from the top edge of the page to the bottom edge. If you release the mouse when the pointer is over the pasteboard area above or below the page, the guideline extends across both the page and the pasteboard area.

The process for creating a horizontal guideline is the same as for creating a vertical guideline, except that you click on the horizontal ruler along the top of the document window.

To delete a custom guideline, click on it and drag it back to the ruler it came from. You can delete all horizontal guidelines by holding down the Option or Alt key and clicking on the horizontal ruler. All vertical guidelines are removed when you Option+click or Alt+click on the vertical ruler.

If you want to place custom guidelines on all your document pages, add them to your master page(s). We discuss master pages in detail in Chapter 17.

At times, you may not want to display guidelines, such as when you want to see what a page will look like when it prints. The Show/Hide Guides command in the View menu lets you display or hide all guidelines. Pressing F7 alternately displays and hides guidelines, as well.

Be careful! Pages look nice when displayed without guidelines, but don't get in the habit of working this way. You can't see empty boxes!

Snapping items to guidelines

One of the nice things about guidelines of all kinds is that you can have QuarkXPress "snap" an item into alignment with a guideline when you drag the item within several pixels of the guideline. This auto-snapping behavior is controlled by the Snap to Guides command in the View menu. By default, this command is turned on (checked). You can turn off this feature by choosing Snap to Guides when it's checked. (The command toggles between on and off each time you choose it.)

By default, an item snaps to a guideline when it's moved to within 6 pixels of the guideline (regardless of the view percentage). However, you can change this by entering a different value in the Snap Distance field in the General pane of the Document Preferences dialog box (Edit⇪Preferences⇪ Document or ⌘+Y or Ctrl+Y).While you're in the General pane, you may also want to change another guideline-related preference. The Guides pop-up menu offers two choices: In Front and Behind. Choosing In Front draws guidelines in front of items; choosing Behind draws them behind items. Opinions vary about the best option to choose here. One potential problem that's worth noting is this: If you choose Behind and then decide to use a colored or blended background or a large picture as the backdrop for an entire page, you won't be able to see your guidelines. Figure 12-2 shows the two guideline-related preferences in the General pane.

Figure 12-2:
The Guides
and Snap
Distance
preferences
in the
General
pane let you
control the
behavior of
guidelines.

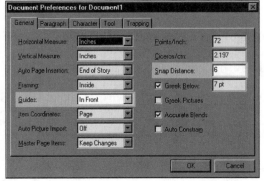

You also have the option to change the appearance of the guidelines in your documents. The Display pane of the Application Preferences dialog box (Shift+Option+⌘+Y or Ctrl+Alt+Shift+Y), shown in Figure 12-3, includes three buttons — Margin, Ruler, and Grid — that let you change the color used for margin/column guides, custom guides created by clicking and dragging on a ruler, and baseline grid lines, respectively. To change the color of a particular kind of guideline, click the appropriate button and then use the color picker that's displayed to choose a new color.

QuarkXPress lets you create only horizontal and vertical guidelines, but you can easily create your own angled guidelines. Just use the Line tool to create a line at any angle; then click Suppress Printout in the Line pane of the Modify dialog box (Item⇪Modify).

Saving QuarkXPress Pages as Pictures

As a rule, you import pictures created via scanners and illustration programs into QuarkXPress picture boxes. But the program also includes a nifty feature that lets you *export* any document page as an EPS graphic. Once you export a page as a picture, you can then import the resulting graphic file into any picture box; crop, scale, skew, and rotate it to your heart's content; and print it as you would print any other imported picture.

What good is such a feature? Suppose that you want to include the cover of last month's magazine in an ad about next month's issue. If you created the cover in QuarkXPress, you're in luck. You can save the cover as a picture, import it into your ad, and then modify as necessary. Or perhaps you created a 5" x 7" ad, and you want to enlarge it to 8.5" x 11" — but you don't want to completely rebuild the ad from scratch. Just save the smaller version as an EPS picture; then import it into a picture box that fills an 8.5" x 11" page and scale it as needed. You're done!

Here's how you save a page as an EPS picture:

1. **Choose Save Page as EPS from the File menu.**

   The Save Page as EPS dialog box, shown in Figure 12-4, appears.

2. **Enter the page number of the page you want to save in the Page field.**

3. **Enter a value in the Scale field if you want to save a scaled-down version of the page.**

   You can enter values between 1 percent and 99 percent. Use the default value of 100 percent if you want to save the page at full size.

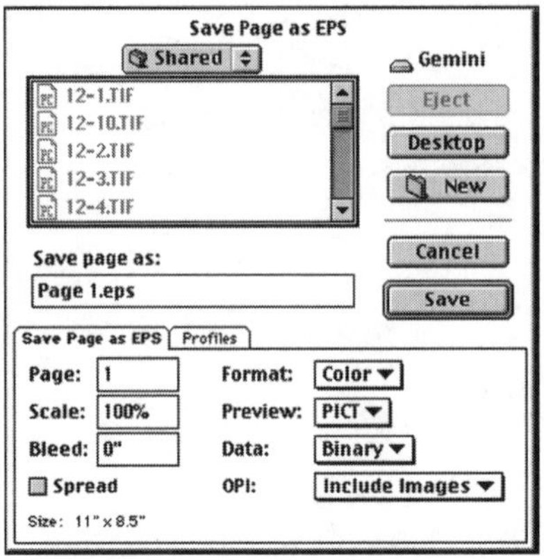

Figure 12-4:
The Save
Page as
EPS dialog
box.

4. **Enter a value in the Bleed field to save a page image that exceeds the page boundaries.**

5. **Choose an option — Color, B&W, DCS, or DCS 2.0 — from the Format pop-up menu.**

   DCS creates a preseparated process color EPS file; DCS 2.0 creates a preseparated EPS with process and spot colors.

6. **From the Preview pop-up list, choose PICT if you'll be using the resulting EPS file on a Mac; choose TIFF if the file will be used in the Windows environment.**

   In QuarkXPress for Windows, you won't get an option to create a PICT preview — just a TIFF preview or no preview.

7. **If the page you're saving has bitmap pictures, choose an option from the Data pop-up menu.**

   Binary data prints more quickly; ASCII data is more widely compatible with printers and print spoolers. (Available in Windows only, the Clean 8-Bit option is similar to ASCII but gets rid of characters that can cause output problems.)

8. **If the page includes TIFF or EPS pictures, choose an option from the OPI pop-up menu.**

   Include Images includes all imported images in the exported EPS file; *Omit TIFF* leaves out imported TIFF files (these files are later replaced with high-resolution printing files by an OPI server); *Omit TIFF and EPS* leaves out TIFF and EPS files (to be replaced by an OPI server).

When you save a page as an EPS picture, the resulting graphic file retains all the text and pictures of the original page. Even better, because the EPS format is vector-based, you can scale the resulting image after you import it into a QuarkXPress picture box —or any other graphic or page layout program that supports the EPS format — and clarity is maintained regardless of how much you enlarge or reduce it.

Changing the Stacking Order of Items

Each time you add an item to a QuarkXPress page, that item occupies one level — the topmost level in the case of new items — in the page's *stacking order*. QuarkXPress treats each item as though it exists on a separate piece of transparent film. The first item you add to a page occupies the backmost level in a page's stacking order; the next item you create is one level above the first item; and so on.

On simple pages that contain only a few items that don't overlap, the stacking order, or layering, of items is not much of an issue. However, as your page layout skills improve, so will the complexity of your designs. Eventually, you'll want to be able to quickly change an item's position in the strata of items on a page in order to accomplish a particular effect. For example, if you want to superimpose text onto an imported picture, the text box must be in front of the picture box. If you create the picture box before you create the text box, you won't have to adjust layers. But if you create the text box before the picture box, you'll have to change its position in the stacking order by moving it in front of the picture box. No problem. You can do it with one hand tied behind your back.

The Item menu contains four commands for changing the layering of items:

✔ **Send Backward (Shift+Option+F5 or Ctrl+Shift+F5)** sends the active item one level backward in the stacking order.

✔ **Send to Back (Shift+F5)** sends the active item to the bottom of the stacking order behind all other items on the page.

✔ **Bring Forward (Option+F5 or Ctrl+F5)** moves the active item one level forward in the stacking order.

✔ **Bring to Front (F5)** moves the active item to the top of the stacking order in front of all other items.

If an item is active and Bring to Front and Bring Forward are not available, the item is at the top of the stacking order; if Send to Back and Send Backward aren't available, it's at the bottom of the stack.

The Windows version of QuarkXPress displays the four commands at once in the Item menu. The Mac version, however, displays only Bring to Front and Send to Back. If you press the Option key before you display the Item menu, Bring Forward replaces Bring to Front, and Send Backward replaces Send to Back.

Figure 12-5 shows the four commands for changing an item's layer and four variations of five layered boxes:

✔ In the upper-left example, you see the middle box selected; the Item menu commands are available for moving the empty box up or down within the stacking order.

✔ In the upper-right example, we moved the middle box to the top of the stack by choosing Bring to Front.

✔ In the lower-left example, we moved the middle box to the bottom of the stack by choosing Send to Back.

✔ In the lower-right example, we moved the middle box one level forward by choosing Bring Forward.

Sometimes an item becomes entirely obscured behind another item or multiple items. If this happens, you don't need to change the stacking order of the items in order to activate the buried item. Select the Item tool or Content tool, hold down Shift+Option+⌘ or Ctrl+Alt+Shift, and then start clicking at the location of the hidden item. Each click selects the next item down in the stacking order. After you reach the bottom of the stack, the next click again activates the topmost item.

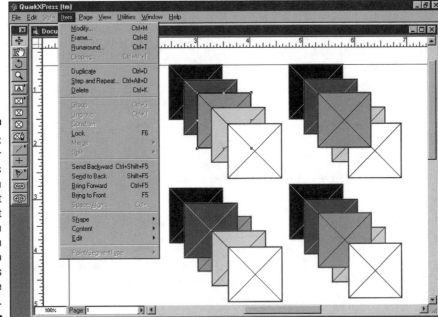

Figure 12-5:
Four commands in the Item menu let you adjust the position of an item relative to other items on the page.

Chapter 13

Frame It!

● ●

● ●

*P*icture this: It's a sultry July day, and you are walking up to the counter at your favorite ice-cream store, money in hand. You ask the clerk to list the flavors that are available today, and he answers, "Vanilla, vanilla, and vanilla." You answer him with a plaintive cry, "Is that all? Don't you have strawberry, or chocolate, or mocha safari delight?" Disappointed when he answers in the negative, you put the dollar back in your pocket and sulk all the way home.

Sometimes, plain old vanilla is just not enough. And sometimes, when you are working on a document, plain old text and picture boxes aren't enough, either. One way to spice up a dull text or picture box is to add a frame — a decorative border placed inside or outside the box. New users like frames because they are easy to understand and easy to use.

Introducing Frames

The capability to frame text and picture boxes is, quite honestly, a minor event when it comes to desktop design. Professional designers usually steer clear of frames or use very simple ones, such as single lines that have the thickness of a hairline (a quarter-point, in publishing measure). But at times, many of us feel that we really need to put a border around a page or box.

When would you want to use a frame? One obvious time is if you are called upon to create a certificate commemorating a special event or a job well done. Figure 13-1 shows a typical certificate that has one of the built-in QuarkXPress frame designs applied to it.

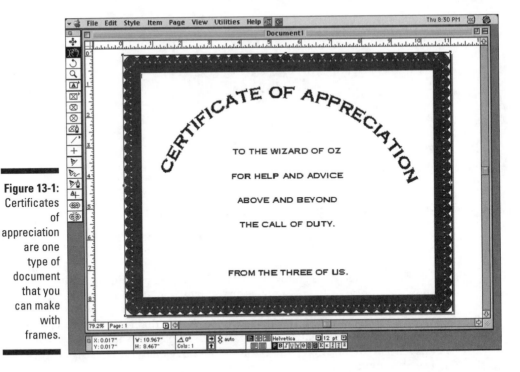

Figure 13-1:
Certificates
of
appreciation
are one
type of
document
that you
can make
with
frames.

You get the picture. Frames go around boxes and make the boxes look fancy. Now we tell you how you can control exactly where around the box the frame should go.

Is it an "innie" or an "outie"?

Innie or outie? No, we're not talking belly buttons here, and we couldn't care less what your belly button looks like. (We like you either way!) What we're referring to is whether the frame that you want to apply to a text or picture box appears inside or outside the border of the box itself.

Look at the frames around the boxes shown in Figure 13-2. The original, unframed picture boxes were identical. A frame was added to the inside of the box on the left and to the outside of the box on the right. The result is that the box on the left maintains its original size and the box on the right gets bigger after the frames are added.

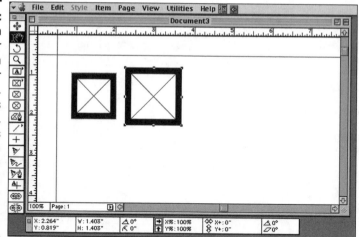

Figure 13-2:
Frames can be inside or outside a text or picture box. In this example, the frame is inside the box on the left and outside the box on the right.

When you come right down to it, does whether the frame is inside or outside the text or picture box really matter? Probably not. Where the frame appears depends on what else is happening on the page. If you are putting a framed box in a page that is already pretty full of text and graphics, you may want to have the frame inside the box so that the frame is less likely to bump into other items on the page.

You control whether frames appear inside or outside boxes by making a selection in the General pane of the Default Document Preferences dialog box. (To display this dialog box, choose Edit⇨Preferences⇨Document, or press ⌘+Y or Ctrl+Y.) As you can see in Figure 13-3, the General pane has a Framing pop-up menu, from which you can specify framing that occurs inside or outside text or picture boxes.

Suppose that you create a document with several framed boxes, all of which have the framing on the outside because — hey, this is logical! — you specified Outside framing (in the General pane of the Document Preferences dialog box). What happens when you set Framing to Inside? Well, all previously created framed boxes keep their frames on the outside, and all newly framed boxes that you create have the frames on the inside. In other words, a changed Framing preference is not retroactive to other frames in the document.

Figure 13-3:
Use the
General
pane to
determine
whether
frames
appear
inside or
outside
boxes.

Document Preferences for Document3	
General	Paragraph	Character	Tool	Trapping

Horizontal Measure: [Inches ▼] Points/Inch: [72]

Vertical Measure: [Inches ▼] Ciceros/cm: [2.197]

Auto Page Insertion: [End of Story ▼] Snap Distance: [6]
[Inside]

Framing: [✓ Outside] ☑ Greek Below: [7 pt]

Guides: [In Front ▼] ☐ Greek Pictures

Item Coordinates: [Page ▼] ☑ Accurate Blends

Auto Picture Import: [Off ▼] ☐ Auto Constrain

Master Page Items: [Keep Changes ▼]

[Cancel] [OK]

How do you specify frames?

When you want to use frames, QuarkXPress lets you have some say in how the frames look. In fact, QuarkXPress lets you specify several characteristics about a frame. To do so, access the Frame pane of the Modify dialog box (choose Item⇨Modify, or press ⌘+M or Ctrl+M) or go directly to that pane (choose Item⇨Frame, or press ⌘+B or Ctrl+B).

Probably the most important fact about the Frame pane of the Modify dialog box (shown in Figure 13-4) is that it allows you to choose among all the default frame styles that come with the program. In addition, this pane allows you to choose among any styles that you have created by using the new Dashes & Stripes feature, which is explained later in this chapter.

How can you tell how the frame will look? Well, it's easy, because the Modify dialog box shows you a sample. As you see in Figure 13-4, the selected frame is Coupon, which is one of several fancy frames in the bottom half of the list box. Notice also that the frame appears in the Preview area of the dialog box. If you decide that you don't care for that particular frame style, simply make a different selection. You get a chance to preview your new selection by watching it appear at the top of the Modify dialog box.

QuarkXPress actually has two kinds of frames: bitmap frames and mathematical (vector) frames. The first 11 of the 20 default frame styles are mathematical frames, as are custom frames created with the Dashes & Stripes command; the last 9 of the default frame styles are bitmap frames. Bitmap frames can go only on rectangular boxes. Mathematically defined frames can be placed on boxes of any shape. In Chapter 4, you see that bitmap graphics can't be stretched too much without getting distorted, whereas vector graphics can be stretched without distortion. For the same reason, you can use the mathematical frames on a box of any shape — the frames can be stretched and bent — but not on the bitmap frames.

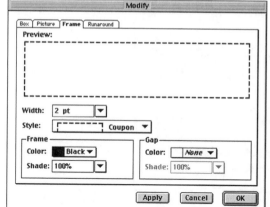

Figure 13-4:
The Frame
pane of the
Modify
dialog box.

To remove a frame that you applied to a box, you must specify a frame width of 0 in the Frame pane of the Modify dialog box.

Using the Frame Editor (For Macs only)

Separate but related. No, we're not talking about your ex, and we're not talking about your in-laws. We're talking about the Frame Editor, which is actually a mini-program that is separate from QuarkXPress and is included only with the Macintosh version of the program. (You have the option of installing the Frame Editor program when you install QuarkXPress. It's placed within your QuarkXPress folder.)

QuarkXPress for Windows and QuarkXPress for Macintosh are, for the most part, only one application that is consistently applied on these different platforms. True, some minor differences exist because of the variations between operating systems, but the vast majority of the program's functions work the same on both platforms. A few features, though, may exist on one platform and not the other. Framing is supported by both platforms, but the Windows version does not include a separate Frame Editor.

To get to the Frame Editor on your Mac, exit QuarkXPress and then open the Frame Editor application. When you open the Frame Editor, the first screen displayed resembles the one shown in Figure 13-5 and contains a scroll list of frame styles.

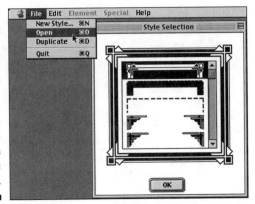

You may decide that you don't want to use one of the frame styles that you see in the Style Selection scroll list. That's okay, because the real purpose of the Frame Editor is to allow you to create your own frame style.

When you have the Frame Editor open and the Style Selection window is displayed, follow these steps to create a new frame style (Don't be confused by the odd interface — these steps will get you through it):

1. **Choose File⇨New Style.**

   The Enter New Size dialog box appears, asking you to enter the width (sometimes called the *weight*) that you want the frame to be.

2. **Enter a width value in the Enter size field and click OK to open the Element Selection window.**

3. **In the Element Selection window (shown in Figure 13-6), click the corner or side that you want to create.**

   When you click a corner or side element, a dialog box is displayed in which you enter height and width values.

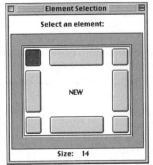

Figure 13-6:
The
Element
Selection
window of
the Frame
Editor.

Notice that by using the Frame Editor, you need to create both the sides and corners of the frames that you are developing. In Figure 13-6, the top-left corner of the frame is selected.

4. **Enter values for the Height and Width of the frame element you are creating; then click OK.**

5. **When you see the Frame Edit window, in the left area of that window, click on the screen to create or delete individual pixels.**

   The Frame Edit window lets you create the frame element one pixel at a time. The element that you are creating appears — magnified to make editing pixels easy — in the scroll window at the left of the Frame Edit window. Figure 13-7 shows a Frame Edit window in which the top-left element of a frame is being edited.

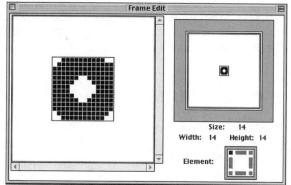

Figure 13-7: In the Frame Edit window, you can design a frame one pixel at a time.

In Figure 13-7, notice that the Element box in the bottom-right corner of the window shows you which frame element you are currently creating. In the figure, a corner element is being created. You do this simply by clicking pixels on and off in the box on the left side of the Frame Edit window. Design your frame element in the same manner. When you're finished designing the element, click the Close box.

6. **Repeat Steps 3, 4, and 5 for each frame element.**

   Notice that you need to create at least one corner element and one side element; then you can copy the elements. (You copy elements by choosing Element⇨Copy Element, clicking the element that you want to copy, and specifying where you are copying the element to.) Also note that you cannot copy a corner to a side element or a side element to a corner. To preview the entire frame, choose Special⇨Display Full Size.

7. **Click the close box to close the Element Selection window (refer to Figure 13-6).**

8. **Save the changes you just made by clicking Yes in the dialog box that appears.**

9. **Close the Size Selection window.**

   The frame that you just created is displayed in the Style Selection menu.

10. **To return to QuarkXPress, quit the Frame Editor and open QuarkXPress.**

Creating Dashes and Stripes

When it comes to putting frames around boxes — and creating lines with the line tools as well — the 11 default mathematical styles are handy, but a serious graphic artist needs more than 11 choices. Fortunately, the Dashes & Stripes feature allows you to create as many custom multiple-line and dashed-line styles as you want.

Creating a dashed line style

Creating a new line style is easy. Here's how you make a dashed line:

1. **Choose Edit⇨Dashes & Stripes.**

   The Dashes & Stripes dialog box appears (see Figure 13-8).

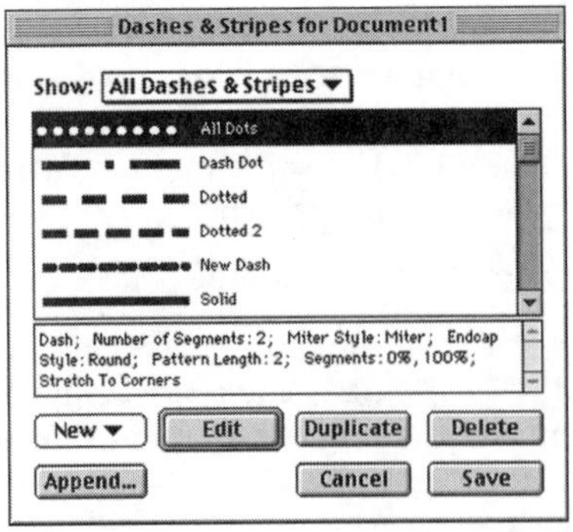

Figure 13-8:
The Dashes & Stripes dialog box lets you create and modify line styles, and append line styles from other documents.

Dashes & Stripes for Document1

Show: All Dashes & Stripes ▼

●●●●●●●● All Dots
━ ■ ━ Dash Dot
━━ ━━ ━━ Dotted
━━ ━━ ━━ Dotted 2
━●━●━●━● New Dash
━━━━━━ Solid

Dash; Number of Segments: 2; Miter Style: Miter; Endcap Style: Round; Pattern Length: 2; Segments: 0%, 100%; Stretch To Corners

New ▼   Edit   Duplicate   Delete
Append...   Cancel   Save

2. Choose Dash from the New pop-up menu.

The Edit Dash dialog box appears, as shown in Figure 13-9. In this dialog box, you specify the attributes of the custom line that you're creating. The Preview area shows what your frame looks like as you create it, and the accompanying slider allows you to preview the frame at various widths.

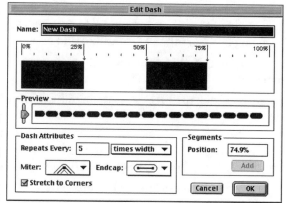

Figure 13-9:
The Edit
Dash dialog
box.

3. Enter a name for your dash in the Name field.

Now you're ready to specify the appearance of your frame by making selections in the Dash Attributes section of the dialog box. The most critical option is Repeats Every. The pop-up menu on the right allows you to choose Times Width or Points. Choosing Times Width is safer. If you choose Points, your frame looks different at varying point sizes. For this example, we stick with the default choice, Times Width.

4. Enter a value in the Repeats Every field.

The value that you enter determines how often the dashed pattern that you create repeats itself relative to the width of the line. The example in the figure uses a value of 5.

5. To create the actual dashes, click the area at the top of the dialog box where percentage values (0, 25, 50, 75, and 100%) are displayed with tick marks between the values.

A small down arrow appears at the point where you click; this point determines the length of the first dashed segment. The area below the percentages starts as a solid black line. When you click it, the portion on the left remains black; the portion to the right becomes white.

6. **To create the next dash, click again in the area where percentage values are displayed (to the right of where you first clicked); then drag the mouse.**

   As you drag, you add another black dash.

7. **Release the mouse button when the dash is the desired length.**

   Two more down arrows appear among the percentage values: one where you first clicked and one where you released the mouse button. You can create as many dashes as you want. If you prefer typing to clicking, you can enter a value in the Position field (in the Segments section of the dialog box) and then click Add to add an arrow.

8. **To modify the width of a dash (or the space between a dash), drag either of the arrows that defines it.**

   Alternatively, you can click the black area defined by a pair of arrows (the hand pointer appears when you click) and drag the mouse left or right.

9. **To delete an arrow, drag it up or down (into the gray area of the dialog box); to delete an entire segment, drag it up or down.**

10. **In the Dash Attributes section of the dialog box, choose a corner style (rounded, beveled, or square) from the Miter pop-up menu.**

11. **Choose a line-ending style (rounded or two flavors of square) from the Endcap pop-up menu.**

12. **We recommend that you check Stretch to Corners so that the empty portion of a dashed line does not wind up in a corner.**

13. **When you're done, click OK in the Edit Dash dialog box.**

   You return to the Dashes & Stripes dialog box.

14. **Click Save in the Dashes & Stripes dialog box.**

Figure 13-10 shows an example of a custom dash style.

Creating a striped line style

If you can become a Dash Master, you can also earn your stripes by creating a new striped line style. Here's how:

1. **Choose Edit⇨Dashes & Stripes.**

   The Dashes & Stripes dialog box appears.

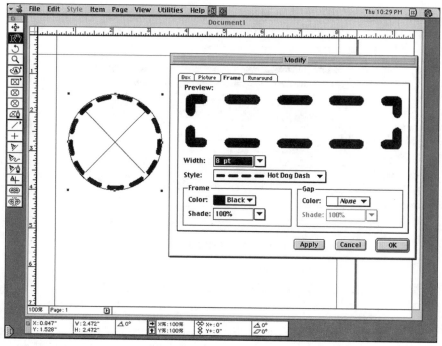

Figure 13-10:
A custom
dash style
was applied
to the empty
picture box.

2. Click the New button and choose Stripe from the pop-up menu that appears.

Figure 13-11 shows the Edit Stripe dialog box. The controls in this dialog box are much the same as those in the Edit Dash dialog box; the Preview area shows you what your striped line looks like as you create it. The only major differences between the Edit Dash and Edit Stripe dialog boxes are that the Edit Stripe dialog box does not include the Repeats Every and Endcap options, and the percentage values are displayed vertically along the left edge of the dialog box. Creating the black-and-white areas of your custom line style is the same as it is for dashed lines.

3. To create the first black area, click within the percentage values.

A small horizontal arrow is displayed where you click.

4. Continue clicking and dragging the mouse to create additional black-and-white areas for your line style.

You can reposition arrows and drag the black areas to modify the appearance of the line.

5. Choose an option from the Miter pop-up menu.

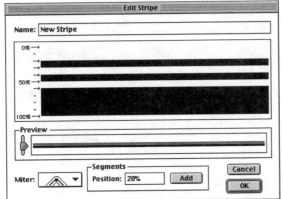

Figure 13-11:
The Edit
Stripe dialog
box.

6. Click OK to close the Edit Dash dialog box.

You return to the Dashes & Stripes dialog box.

7. Click Save in the Dashes & Stripes dialog box.

After you create a new dash or stripe style, you can use it any time you add a frame to a box or modify the appearance of a line. The custom styles that you create are available, along with QuarkXPress's default styles, in the Frame pane of the Modify dialog box (to display this dialog box, choose Item⇨Frame, or press ⌘+B or Ctrl+B), as well as in the Line pane of the Modify dialog box (to display this dialog box, choose Item⇨Modify, or press ⌘+M or Ctrl+M).

Chapter 14

Warped Images

A picture is worth a thousand words. That's a statement of monumental importance. It's a stale saying, but we can all agree that there's some truth in it. Sometimes, words just can't say what pictures can.

And isn't it nice to know that you don't have to settle for reality when it comes to pictures? With QuarkXPress, you can slant, rotate, warp, and tweak pictures to your heart's content. In this chapter, we show you some easy ways to pummel your pictures into shape.

Two Ways to Warp

Although you can warp an image in several ways, the two most common are to use the Picture pane of the Modify dialog box and to use the Measurements palette. Both ways work just fine, and choosing between them is really a matter of finding which works better for you.

The Modify dialog box for pictures

You can make changes in a picture contained in an active picture box by using both the Box pane and the Picture pane of the Modify dialog box, shown in Figure 14-1. To display the dialog box, select the picture box to make it active and then choose Item⇨Modify (or ⌘+M or Ctrl+M).

We don't go into too much detail, but we do give you a general idea about all the things that you can do to a picture by using the Box and Picture panes of the Modify dialog box.

In the Box pane, the Origin Across, Origin Down, Width, and Height fields control the position and size of the picture box. In Figure 14-2, which shows the Box pane, the box origin (the top-left corner of the picture box) is 1 inch from the left edge of the page and 1.25 inches from the top of the page. The picture-box width is 4.125 inches, while the height is 4.375 inches. (We didn't really need to make the width and height three decimal places long; we use these values to illustrate that you can specify measurements in units as small as 0.001 in any measurement system.)

Most of the options in the Box pane of the Modify dialog box determine the appearance of a picture box; only the Angle and Skew fields affect the appearance of the picture within the picture box. Entering a value in the Angle field rotates the picture box — and the picture within — around the center of the box. Box angle values range from –360 to 360 degrees in increments as small as 0.001 degree. The Skew field allows you to slant a box (by offsetting the top and bottom edges) to produce an italic-looking version of the box and its picture.

Entering a value in the Corner Radius field allows you to replace the square corners of a rectangular box with rounded corners. The value that you enter in this field is the radius of the circle used to form the rounded corners. When you first create a rectangular picture box, its corner radius value is 0 (zero). You can enter a radius value from 0 to 2 inches (0 to 24 picas) in 0.001 increments of any measurement system. The radius value also adjusts the bevels on beveled-corner boxes (and so on for the other similar boxes).

If you check Suppress Printout, the active picture box — both picture and frame — does not print when you output the page. This feature is handy for printing text-only page proofs or rough copies of pages. Even better, pages print more quickly when you don't print pictures.

The Color and Shade pop-up menus allow you to add color to the background of a picture box and control the depth (*saturation*) of the color. To add color to the background of an active picture box or to change an existing background color, choose a color from the Color pop-up menu or use the Colors palette (if it's not visible, choose View⇨Show Colors, or press F12, to make it appear). See Chapter 15 for more information on applying colors and creating custom colors.

After you select the background color that you want to apply to the picture box (and you select a color other than None or White), you can specify the saturation level of the color. Choose a predefined shade (0 to 100 percent) from the Shade pop-up menu or enter a custom shade value (in increments as small as 0.1 percent) in the Shade field. You can find a pop-up menu of shade increments in the Colors palette as well (at the top right of the palette), in which you can enter your own values or choose one of the existing values.

The controls in the Blend section of the Box pane allow you to add two-color blends to picture-box backgrounds (you can also use the Colors palette to create blends). To create a blend, choose a blend style from the Style pop-up menu in the Blend section of the dialog box; choose a color from the Color pop-up menu in the Box section and then choose the second color from the Color pop-up menu in the Blend section. The Angle field allows you to rotate a blended background from –360 to 360 degrees in increments as small as 0.001 degree. The Cool Blends XTension must be installed if you want to create blends.

All the controls in the Picture pane of the Modify dialog box affect the appearance of the picture within the active box. Two of our favorite features in the Picture pane of the Modify dialog box are Scale Across and Scale Down.

When you first fill a picture box with a picture (by choosing File⇨Get Picture, or pressing ⌘+E or Ctrl+E), QuarkXPress places the picture in the text box at its full size — that is, at 100 percent scale. But the picture may be larger or smaller than you want. No problem. You can change the picture's size by entering new values in the Scale Across and Scale Down fields. Back in Figure 14-1, we entered a value of 120 percent in each field, which made the picture 20 percent larger than it was when we imported it. You can scale pictures from 10 percent to 400 percent of their original size. Be careful about greatly enlarging TIFF and other bitmap pictures, however; the larger you make them, the fuzzier they look when you print them.

The Offset Across and Offset Down fields allow you to adjust the position of the picture within the box; in Figure 14-1, we set the Offset Across value to .5", which moves the picture box contents to the right by 0.5 inch. (When you import a picture, both the Offset values are 0.)

The Picture Angle field is useful if you want to change the angle of a picture without changing the angle of the picture box itself. Actually, when you enter a value in the Picture Angle field, you cause the picture to rotate around its center within the box.

The Picture Skew field allows you to *skew* (slant) a picture within its box. You can enter values ranging from –75 to 75 degrees, in increments as small as 0.001 degree. If you enter a positive value, the picture leans to the right; if you enter a negative value, the picture leans to the left.

Checking Suppress Picture Printout produces slightly different results from checking Suppress Printout in the Box pane. If you check Suppress Picture Printout, the frame and background of the picture box print, but the contents of the picture box do not. This option is useful if you import low-resolution versions of pictures (for position only) and plan to strip in the actual halftones manually.

The Measurements palette

As you change values in the Picture pane of the Modify dialog box, the Measurements palette also changes to reflect the new values. You can bypass the Modify dialog box for any function displayed in the Measurements palette by entering the appropriate values in the palette itself.

To use the Measurements palette to modify the contents of a picture box, you must first activate the picture box. (If the box is active, its sizing handles are visible around the edge of the box.) You also must display the Measurements palette. (To display the palette, choose View⇨Show

Measurements, or press Option+⌘+M or Ctrl+Alt+M.) The Measurements palette appears in Figure 14-3. You can make several changes in the picture box through the Measurements palette, which is the simplest way to manipulate picture boxes and their contents.

Enter new values in the X and Y fields to change the distance of the picture-box origin (the box's top-left corner) from the page edges.

The W and H fields control the width and height of the picture box. In Figure 14-3, the current dimensions are 3.931 inches by 3.579 inches. Those exacting coordinates indicate that the picture box was drawn by hand; if you size the box via the Measurements palette, you round off the coordinates to something like 4 inches by 3.5 inches.

The Rotation field on the left side of the Measurements palette rotates the picture box. Because the box in Figure 14-3 is not rotated, the Rotation value is 0 (zero) degrees.

The Corner Radius field changes the shape of the picture box's corners.

The Flip Horizontal and Flip Vertical options flip the image along the Y and X axes, respectively. The arrow's direction changes in the icon to tell you whether a picture has been flipped. (You also can choose Style⇨Flip Horizontal and Style⇨Flip Vertical.)

Figure 14-3:
The Measure-ments palette.

The settings in the X% and Y% fields back in Figure 14-3 are percentages. Changing the values in the X% and Y% fields reduces or enlarges the picture in the picture box. To keep the proportions of the picture the same, enter the same values in the X and Y fields.

Clicking either the Horizontal or Vertical Offset arrow moves an image within the picture box. Each click moves the image in 0.1 increments (0.1 inch, 0p1, and so on). To move the image manually, choose the Content tool, move the mouse pointer to the image (the grabber hand appears), and then drag the image. You also can enter values in the Offset fields to move an image within a picture box.

Entering any value except zero in the Rotation field on the right side of the palette rotates the picture *within* the picture box. (The Rotation field on the left side of the palette rotates both the picture box and its picture.) The current value for the picture box in Figure 14-3 is 0, which means that the box is not rotated. Likewise, the value for the image is 0, so it is also not rotated.

Entering any value except 0 in the Skew field slants the contents of the picture box. In Figure 14-3, the picture-box contents are not skewed.

Figure 14-4 shows the effect of rotating the *contents* of the picture box by 30 degrees by entering a value of 30 in the Rotation field on the right side of the Measurements palette.

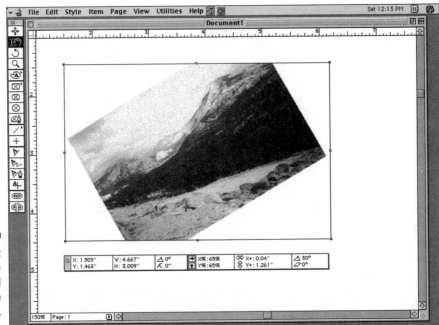

Figure 14-4:
A picture
rotated
within the
picture box.

TIP

Scaling a picture

Sometimes, you want to warp a picture by making it narrower or wider than it was originally, changing its X and Y axes in the process. This process is also known as *changing the picture's aspect ratio*.

Suppose that you have a really neat photo of your favorite climbing rocks. You want to fit the photo into a narrow space, but you don't want to lose any parts of the picture. Also suppose that you don't mind if your picture gets a bit warped (hey, some people would call that *artistic*) in the process.

In the following figure, the picture in the box on the left side is scaled at 100 percent on both its X and Y axes. The picture on the right side is warped in terms of its aspect ratio. The picture on the right is 39.8 percent scale on the X axis and 100 percent on the Y axis. You can achieve this effect by making changes in the Measurements palette or the Picture pane of the Modify dialog box.

Figure 14-5 shows the same picture as Figure 14-4, but this time, the entire box, including its contents, has been rotated by 10 degrees. You can see that we entered a value of 10 in the Rotation field on the left side of the Measurements palette.

Figure 14-5:
A picture box rotated 10 degrees.

After you use the Measurements palette to make changes in the picture box, press Return or Enter, or click the mouse, to apply the changes.

Adjusting the Appearance of Printed Pictures

Most people never worry about line screens (in fact, many desktop publishers don't know what they are), but those screens can have a major effect on how your bitmap images print.

To understand how line screens work, think about a screen door. The spaces between the wires of the screen door allow light to pass through; the wires in the screen keep light out. Line screens split an image into a series of spots and spaces for precisely the same reason — to let some light in and keep some light out.

In traditional printing, a *line screen* is an acetate mask covered with a grid of spots. Printers use line screens to convert a continuous-tone image (such as a photograph) to the series of spots, called a *halftone,* that is required to reproduce such an image on a printing press. Place a magnifying glass over a photo — either color or black and white — in a newspaper or magazine, and you see the spots that the photo is made of. These spots are usually circular, but they can be any of several shapes.

When a halftone is made in the traditional way, a line-screen mask is placed on top of a piece of photographic paper (such as Kodak's RC paper, which has been used for decades in traditional photography). The continuous-tone original is then illuminated in a camera so that the image is projected through the mask onto the photographic paper. The photographic paper is exposed only where the mask is transparent (in the grid holes, or spots), producing the spots that make up the image to be printed. The size of each spot depends on how much light passes through, which in turn depends on how dark or light each area of the original image is. Think about a window screen through which you spray water: the stronger the spray, the bigger the spots behind the screen's holes.

The spots that make up the image are arranged in a series of lines, usually at a 45-degree angle. (This angle helps the eye blend the individual spots to simulate a continuous tone.) The number of lines per inch (the *halftone frequency*) determines the maximum dot size as well as the coarseness (*halftone density*) of the image (thus the term *line screen*).The spots in the mask need not be circular; they can be ellipses, squares, lines, or more esoteric shapes (such as stars). These shapes are called *screen elements*. Circular spots are the most common type, because they result in the least distortion of the image.

Creating effects with line screens

Seeing is believing when it comes to special graphics effects, so you'll want to experiment with the line-screen fields (Frequency, Angle, and Function) in the Picture Halftone Specifications dialog box to see what they can do before you print your document. (To display this dialog box, choose Style⇨Halftone, or press Shift+⌘+H or Ctrl+Shift+H.)

In most cases, rather than deal with Picture Halftone Specifications, you should use the default picture halftone settings, which are specified in the Output pane of the Print dialog box (File⇨Page Setup or File⇨Print). The settings that you make in the Output pane of the Print dialog box are the default settings for all imported images.

But when you want to do something special, you can. As a rule, most people who use line-screen effects prefer coarser halftone frequencies to make the image coarser but bolder; they usually also change the screen element to a line or other shape to alter the image's character. Line screens can be applied only to black-and-white bitmap pictures, or to TIFF line art or grayscale pictures.

Lines and dots by the inch

When you use line screens, you need to know a little bit about lines per inch and dots per inch. Lines per inch (*lpi*) and dots per inch (*dpi*) are not the same. The spots in a line screen are variable-size, whereas dots in a laser printer are fixed-size. *Lines per inch* specifies the grid through which an image is filtered, not the size of the spots that make up the image. *Dots per inch* specifies the number of ink dots per inch produced by the laser printer; typically, these dots are the same size. A 100-lpi image with variable-size dots, therefore, looks finer than a 100-dpi image.

Depending on the size of the line-screen spot, several of a printer's fixed-size dots may be required to simulate one line-screen spot. For this reason, a printer's or imagesetter's lpi number is far less than its dpi number. A 300-dpi laser printer, for example, can achieve about 60-lpi resolution; a 600-dpi laser printer can achieve about 85-lpi resolution; a 1270-dpi image setter can achieve about 120-lpi resolution; a 2540-dpi image setter, about 200-lpi resolution. Resolutions of less than 100 lpi are

considered to be coarse, and resolutions of more than 120 lpi are considered to be fine.

But choosing an lpi setting involves more than just knowing your output device's top resolution. An often-overlooked issue is the type of paper on which the material is printed. Smoother paper (such as *glossy-coated* or *super-calendared*) can handle finer halftone spots, because the paper's coating (its *finish*) minimizes ink bleeding. Standard office paper, such as the kind used in photocopiers and laser printers, is rougher and has some bleed (meaning that ink diffuses easily through the paper), which usually is noticeable only if you write on it with markers. Newsprint is very rough and has a heavy bleed. Typically, newspaper images are printed at 85 to 90 lpi; newsletter images on standard office paper print at 100 to 110 lpi; magazine images are printed at 120 to 150 lpi; calendars and coffee-table art books are printed at 150 to 200 lpi.

Other factors that affect lpi include the type of printing press and the type of ink used. Your printer representative should advise you on preferred settings.

Here's how you specify a custom line screen for a picture:

1. **Click a picture box that contains a black-and-white or grayscale bitmap image; then choose Style⇨Halftone.**

   The Picture Halftone Specifications dialog box appears.

2. **Choose values from the Frequency pop-up menu or enter a value in the text box to change the frequency/lpi of the printed image.**

3. **Choose an option from the Angle pop-up menu or enter a value in the text box to specify a custom screen angle.**

4. **Choose a shape from the Function pop-up menu to specify a custom shape for the screen element.**

5. **Click OK to close the Picture Halftone Specifications dialog box and save your changes.**

In previous versions of QuarkXPress, you had the option of displaying halftoning effects. This option is not available in Version 4.0, however. In Version 4.0, you must print a picture to see the results of the settings that you make in the Picture Halftone Specifications dialog box.

Dithering

Dithering is an effect that replaces gray levels with a varying pattern of black and white. This pattern does not attempt to simulate grays. Instead, dithering merely tries to retain some distinction between shades in an image when the image is output to a printer that does not have fine-enough resolution to reproduce grays. In other words, dithering uses coarse patterns of dots and lines to represent the basic details in a grayscale image.

QuarkXPress uses an equation called *ordered dithering,* which you apply by choosing Ordered Dither from the Function pop-up menu in the Picture Halftone Specifications dialog box. To apply other dithering equations, you must dither the image in a paint or graphics program that supports dithering before importing the image into QuarkXPress.

Chapter 15

Creating Color Publications

● ●

● ●

Color is tricky. It's everywhere, so we take it for granted. We don't usually spend much time thinking about color theory or color physics. (And we don't spend much time on those topics in this chapter, either.)

In the wonderful world of computers, color is becoming more common. You can get good-quality color inkjet printers for less than $500, and they're great for limited-run output (for a few dozen copies or for use in a color copier). You can also buy more expensive color printers (for $5,000 to $20,000) that use technologies with intimidating names such as dye sublimation and thermal wax. These printers are for professional publishers who are doing color proofing of works such as magazines and catalogs, which will be reproduced at a commercial printing plant. Or you can have your work printed by a commercial printer that does color work, in which case, your "lowly" grayscale laser printer is merely a proofing device for your text and image placement.

QuarkXPress's color tools are really aimed at professional color publishers. (IDG Books Worldwide's *Macworld QuarkXPress 4.0 Bible* delves into professional color in detail.) But that fact doesn't mean that you can't benefit from color as well. After all, who can resist using color, especially if you have one of those inexpensive color inkjet printers? But before you can make the best use of color, you need to understand a bit about how color happens — and that process is a lot more complicated than you may think.

Heading off to Color Class

Prepare to see all sorts of acronyms when you explore color. Color theory is like the military — capital letters and confusion everywhere.

RGB vs. CMYK

As far as desktop publishing is concerned, color comes in two basic types: RGB and CMYK. Computer displays use RGB, whereas printers use CMYK. Because the color types differ, you never receive an exact match between what you see on-screen and what your printed output looks like. In fact, sometimes you don't even receive a close match.

These types of color schemes — RGB, CMYK, and others — are called *color models;* the model is the physics behind the colors. *RGB,* for example, stands for *red, green, blue,* which are the three colors of light that a monitor or TV set uses to create all colors. As a kid, you probably played with prisms, which split white light into its constituent colors. White light goes in one side of the prism, and a rainbow comes out the other side. In a monitor or TV set, the opposite occurs red, green, and blue colors go in one side and combine to form white at the other end. Green and red combine to produce yellow. Red and green light have different frequencies, and as they merge, they change to the frequency of yellow light. These colors are known technically as *subtractive colors.* You can think of a monitor as being a prism in reverse. Figure 15-1 shows how subtractive colors combine.

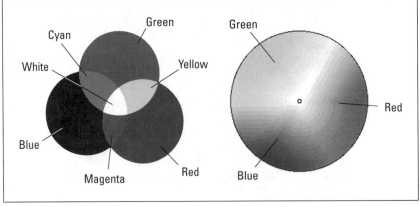

Figure 15-1:
Even in gray, you can see that in the RGB color model, colored light combines differently from. . .

Keep in mind that the colors shown in the figure are the basic ones. Where green and red combine to make yellow, for example, the actual color could be yellow–green (more mustardy) or orange (more flamelike), depending on the proportion of each light. You can get a better feel for this process by looking at the color wheel to the right of the drawing in Figure 15-1 that shows the intersections of the three colors of light.

CMYK stands for *cyan, magenta, yellow, and black*. (The *K* in *CMYK* represents the *k* in black. Publishers don't use *B* because it usually indicates blue.) Cyan is like an electric sky-blue, the color of some mints, mouthwashes, and sapphires. Magenta is a darker hot pink, the one favored in punk haircuts, cycling shorts, and highlighter markers. By mixing the colors in the CMYK combination, you can simulate most colors that the human eye can discern.

Unlike RGB, CMYK does not combine colored light to create colors; instead, it reflects light off ink and combines the reflections to form colors. A yellow ink, for example, actually absorbs all other colors, so only yellow is reflected to your eye. As a kid, when you played with finger paints or crayons, mixing colors together probably gave you dark grays and browns. As with crayons, adding the CMYK colors together on paper causes the colors to become darker (because more colors of light are absorbed), so adding all four makes a supersolid black. These colors are known as *additive colors*.

Figure 15-2 shows how additive colors combine. At right is a cube that represents how the cyan, magenta, and yellow colors combine; black is added through a slider and has the effect of lightening or darkening the colors in the cube.

Figure 15-2:
... the reflections of light of inks in the CMYK color model.

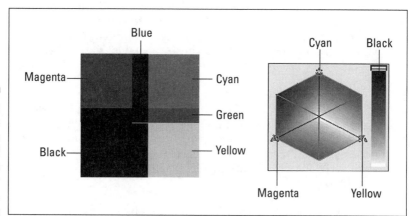

A variant of CMYK is called CMY (no black). Cheaper printers (such as the inkjet printers that sell for less than $400) often use CMY, creating black with a combination of cyan, magenta, and yellow. The problem is that this black is actually a muddy dark gray and doesn't look good, especially in fine details and shadows. Therefore, commercial printers use CMYK.

Because the color that you see on the printed page is based on how light is filtered through and reflects off ink, the type and quality of ink determines the color that you see. For that reason, a flesh tone in a magazine looks better than a flesh tone in a newspaper, and a green printed on an expensive dye-sublimation printer looks better than a green printed on an inexpensive inkjet printer.

Although Quark lets you create colors in the RGB, HSB (hue, saturation, and brightness — a variant of RGB), or LAB (luminosity, *a* axis, *b* axis; an international color standard) models, few printers can accurately reproduce them, so why bother? You should use these models only when you are creating colors for a computer-generated slide show.

Spot colors versus process colors

Commercial color printing presses, as well as most office color printers (such as inkjet printers), use CMYK; RGB just isn't a factor. In publishing lingo, CMYK colors are known as *process colors*. But other special inks are available to create colors that are impossible to make by mixing various amounts of cyan, magenta, yellow, and black. Pastel, metallic, neon, and frosted colors, for example, can't be accurately produced in CMYK. In a photo, you may not mind using CMYK because a photo has so much color that the human eye adjusts to the few that are off. But if you're creating a drawing or using a tint, you'll either have to settle for the closest color that you can get (such as a mustardy orange for gold or a light gray for silver), or you'll have to use special inks. These special inks are called *spot colors* because they are usually used on just part of a page (a spot).

If you've worked with artists or publishers, you've probably heard the word Pantone or the acronym PMS, both of which are shorthand for the Pantone Matching System, the most popular set of spot-color inks. Pantone color sets include one for uncoated (rough) paper and another for coated (glossy) paper. QuarkXPress can work with these colors, along with other colors such as Trumatch, Focoltone, DIC (Dainippon Ink & Chemical), Hexachrome, and Toyo.

You can use both process and spot colors in a document. But — and it's an important but — if you use a spot color and print it on a printer that supports only CMYK, the spot color is translated to the nearest CMYK combination. The process is automatic; you can't do anything about it. Therefore, you really can use spot colors only if you're printing on a commercial printing press, supplying a separate negative for each color used (one for each of the CMYK process colors and one for each spot color). Talk with your printer first about any project you plan to have printed in color.

Of course, if you're using only black and one or two spot colors (maybe for just a logo and some tints behind text boxes) and no other color (no color photos or drawings), you don't have to have the CMYK negatives created. (If you are using both process and spot colors, keep in mind that most commercial printers can't handle more than six colors on a page, and even having six may not be possible on small-run jobs or at small printing plants. Again, talk with you printer first.)

Just to make things a little weirder, the Trumatch spot-color system is based on CMYK, so any Trumatch color can be faithfully converted (*color-separated*, in publishing lingo) into process colors. (That's why the system is called Trumatch.) With Trumatch, you can use a premixed CMYK color for spot colors (cheaper than CMYK if you print fewer than four colors total, including black). And if you end up using more than three colors, you can just have QuarkXPress convert all the Trumatch spot colors to CMYK combinations during output and know that you'll get an accurate rendition. The folks at Pantone realized that they had to respond, so they created a color model called Pantone Process, which basically is just the Pantone colors that have faithful CMYK equivalents. QuarkXPress includes the Pantone Process model as well.

To see an example of colors that don't match their equivalent CMYK combinations, look at Figure 15-3. You see the standard green that QuarkXPress includes as a default in all documents. (Don't worry yet about where this dialog box is or what it does; we get to it soon in the section called "Creating Color.") In the figure, the color model has been changed from the RGB model that QuarkXPress uses to the CMYK color model. You can see the two color swatches next to the words New and Original. New is the green converted to CMYK; Original is the original green. (QuarkXPress shows you the effects of a conversion so that you can cancel, adjust the color yourself, or pick a different color.)

See that even in grayscale reproduction, these colors don't match? The slider bar at the far right is like a dimmer switch; the brighter an RGB color, the less chance that CMYK can print it correctly. If no boundary exists, any color displayed will print accurately.

Below the arrow pointer in Figure 15-3, you see a small black square in the color wheel, which is the green color's position in the color model. If you click the small square and drag it through the color wheel, you see the New swatch's color change. Release the mouse button, and the black square indicates the new color's location in the color wheel.

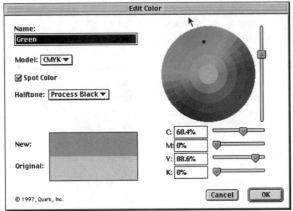

© 1997, Quark, Inc.

Figure 15-3:
The same
green is
different in
the RGB
and CMYK
color
models.

Creating Color

Okay, okay, enough with the theory — on to actually using colors. First, you
have to create the color that you want to use. You can create colors in three
ways:

✔ Define the colors within QuarkXPress itself.

✔ Import the colors defined in another QuarkXPress document.

✔ Import the colors defined in an EPS file.

No matter how you define them, the available colors display in the Colors
palette and in all dialog boxes that let you apply color. If the Colors palette
is not visible, you can display it by choosing View⇨Show Colors, or by
pressing F12. Figure 15-4 shows the default Colors palette.

Figure 15-4:
The Colors
palette
shows
available
colors.

Defining colors in QuarkXPress

To define, alter, or remove colors, use the Colors dialog box (see Figure 15-5). To display this dialog box, choose Edit⇨Colors. The options relevant to basic color use are New (to create a new color), Edit (to change an existing color), Duplicate (to copy an existing color, such as to have one color as both a process color and a spot color), Delete (to remove unwanted colors), and Append (to import colors from other QuarkXPress documents). Don't worry about understanding the Edit⇨Trap command, which changes how colors print when they are side by side. Only the most skilled and knowledgeable color publishers may need to fiddle with it. The QuarkXPress defaults are fine for the work most people do.

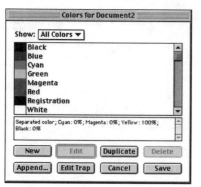

Figure 15-5:
The Colors dialog box allows you to add new colors and modify existing colors.

You may notice that the Edit and Delete buttons are sometimes grayed out. That's because some basic colors cannot be altered: cyan, magenta, yellow, black, and white.

A color called Registration, which looks like black but isn't, can be altered but not deleted. Registration can serve two purposes. One purpose is for elements that you want to appear on all your negatives, such as crop marks and filenames. If you define Registration to be 100 percent of cyan, magenta, yellow, and black, anything in the Registration color prints on all those negatives. Alternatively, you can use Registration to create a rich black — something that looks like outer space or licorice, not flat like a marker. To create a rich black (also known as *superblack*), use 100 percent black and either 100 percent magenta or 100 percent yellow. The combination of black and either of these colors makes the black richer and more appealing when printed.

Creating new process color

Whether you click New or Edit, the dialog box shown in Figure 15-6 appears. If this dialog box looks familiar, that's because it's the one that appears in Figure 15-3 earlier in this chapter. You can use this dialog box to create or modify process and spot colors. We show you how to work with both kinds of colors.

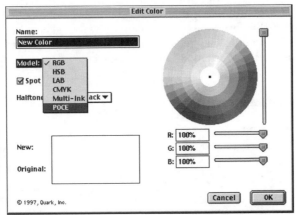

Figure 15-6:
The Edit
Color
dialog box.

First, here's how to create a process color:

1. **Click the Edit button in the Colors dialog box to display the Edit Color dialog box; then choose CMYK from the model pop-up menu.**

2. **Uncheck the Spot Color check box (if it's already checked) if you are using a commercial printer and will be producing CMYK negatives.**

3. **Change the color to the one you want — either by using the CMYK color wheel or the Pantone swatches (see Figure 15-7), or by changing the value in the Cyan, Magenta, Yellow, and black boxes (or by using their sliders).**

4. **Give the color a name in the Name field.**

5. **Click OK to add the CMYK color to your palette and return to the Colors dialog box.**

6. **While the Colors dialog box is displayed, you can create additional colors by clicking the New button, or you can modify any existing color by clicking on the color's name and then clicking the Edit button.**

7. **Click Save in the Colors dialog box when you're done creating or modifying colors.**

   Your Colors palette reflects the new colors.

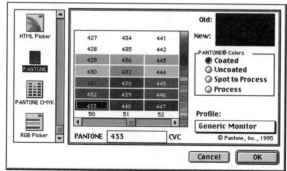

Figure 15-7:
Pantone
spot colors
are
shown in
swatches,
not in a
color
wheel.

Creating a new spot color

Creating a spot color is much like creating a process color, with some
important differences. Here's how you add a new spot color:

1. **Click the Edit button in the Colors dialog box to display the Edit
   Color dialog box; then choose a spot color model, such as Pantone
   Coated or Pantone Uncoated, from the Model pop-up menu.**

   When you choose a spot color model, a corresponding picker is displayed in the right side of the Edit Color dialog box.

   You can also choose POCE from the Model pop-up menu if you want to
   use the Pantone Open Color Environment to specify Pantone color, as
   well as colors from several other color models. If you choose POCE, a
   Select button is displayed in the Edit Color dialog box. Click this button
   to display a dialog box that lets you choose among several color
   models, including Pantone colors. (The POCE option in the Models
   pop-up menu is available only if you've installed the required POCE-
   related system files. Check your QuarkXPress documentation for
   information about these files.)

2. **If it's not already checked, check the Spot Color box.**

   If you check this box, the color you create will be printed on a single
   color plate when you print color separations. If you don't check this
   box, the color will be converted into CMYK components and printed on
   multiple plates when you print separations.

3. **Click a color swatch in the color picker or enter a number in the field
   below the swatches.**

   It's always a good idea to refer to a swatchbook before you create a
   spot color, so at this point, you really should be working with a
   swatchbook. If you are, it's easy to enter the color's number in the text
   field.

4. **Click OK in the Edit Color dialog box; then click Save in the Colors
   dialog box to save your spot color.**

To change the default colors for all future new documents, launch QuarkXPress, but don't open any documents. Then change colors as described in the preceding steps. This process changes the default settings. If a document is open, the color changes affect that document only.

If you have the same color in different color models (such as Pantone 145 as a process color and as a spot color), make sure that the color names reflect this difference. You may have colors named Pantone 145 Spot and Pantone 145 Process, for example. Therefore, you have to choose the right color for accurate reproduction based on whether you plan to print the color as a CMYK color separation or with a special ink.

Although QuarkXPress's Color Management System helps ensure consistency between the colors displayed on-screen and the final printed colors, the differences between color monitors and colored printing inks results in noticeable differences. If you compare the colors of a Pantone color swatchbook with their on-screen counterparts, you can see the differences — more with some colors, less with others. If you're using Pantone colors or colors from any other color-matching system, you should use a swatchbook when choosing colors. Don't rely on the colors displayed in the Edit Color dialog box and the Pantone color picker. See "Using Quark's Color Management System to correct color" later in this chapter for more information.

Mixing colors

Ever since Version 3.0, QuarkXPress has allowed you to mix your own CMYK colors by specifying a percentage for each process color component. But if you wanted to mix, say, a Pantone color with black or with another process color, you had to resort to cumbersome workarounds. QuarkXPress 4.0's new Multi-Ink color model allows you to mix flat (nonseparated) spot colors, such as Pantone colors, with any of the color components of the CMYK or Hexachrome color models. (*Hexachrome* uses six inks — cyan, magenta, yellow, black, orange, and green — to produce full color, a wider range of color than is obtainable with only CMYK inks.) If you're working on a two-color publication and plan to use black plus a single Pantone color, you can also create and apply colors that combine any percentage of black plus your Pantone color.

Adding a multi-ink color is easy. Here's what you do:

1. **Choose Edit⇨Colors and click New to open the Edit Color dialog box (see Figure 15-8), where you create process, spot, and multiple-ink colors.**

Figure 15-8:
In this
example, a
multi-ink
color was
created by
mixing 50
percent of
Pantone 433
with 5
percent
black.

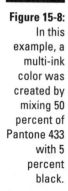

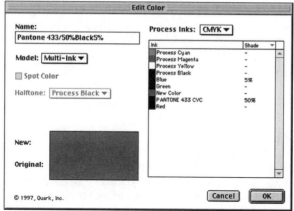

Figure 15-8: In this example, a multi-ink color was created by mixing 50 percent of Pantone 433 with 5 percent black.

If you want to add a color to a particular document, make sure that the document is active when you choose Edit⇨Colors. If no documents are open, any multiple-ink colors that you create are added to the default color palette in QuarkXPress and are included in all new documents.

2. **Choose Multi-Ink from the Model pop-up menu.**

   When you choose Multi-Ink, the Spot Color check box and Halftone pop-up menu are unavailable. That's because a mixed color cannot be separated as a single spot color; the halftone settings of the component colors are automatically used when separations are printed.

3. **Choose CMYK or Hexachrome from the Process Inks pop-up menu.**

   Choose CMYK unless you will be printing with Hexachrome inks.

4. **In the Inks list box, select the spot color that you want to include in your mixed color.**

5. **Choose a percentage from the Shade pop-up menu.**

   You can specify any percentage of a mixed color, from 1 to 100. Choose Other to specify a custom percentage, or choose any of the 10-percent increments displayed in the list.

6. **Select the process color (or other spot color, if you're using more than one spot color) that you want to include in your mixed color.**

7. **Choose a percentage value from the Shade pop-up menu.**

   In Figure 15-8, the multiple-ink color is a two-color mix of 50 percent Pantone 433 and 5 percent black. If your publication uses black and a single spot color, you can create as many two-ink colors as you want by specifying various shade percentages of black plus your spot color. If you're using process colors plus a spot color, you can mix the spot color with any or all of the process colors. The possibilities are endless.

8. Type a name for the color in the Name box.

In the example shown in Figure 15-8, we chose a name for the multi-ink color (433/50%Black5%) that reveals its component colors. You can use whatever naming system you want, but including color information doesn't hurt.

9. Click OK.

You return to the Colors dialog box.

10. Click Save to save your changes.

Be careful if you decide to mix black with a spot color. Even a little bit of black can cause the brightest spot color to look . . . well, black. If you can, print some test swatches to see the results of using various percentages of the component colors in a multi-ink color.

Importing colors

You can import colors defined in other QuarkXPress documents or in an EPS file. Doing so saves work and could save errors in defining a color differently in QuarkXPress than in, say, Adobe Illustrator.

To import a color from a QuarkXPress document, click the Append button in the Colors dialog box. (To display this dialog box, choose Edit⇨Colors.) The Append Colors dialog box appears, as shown in Figure 15-9. Use this dialog box to locate and select the QuarkXPress document from which you want to import colors; then click OK.

Figure 15-9:
In this box choose the document containing the colors that you want to append.

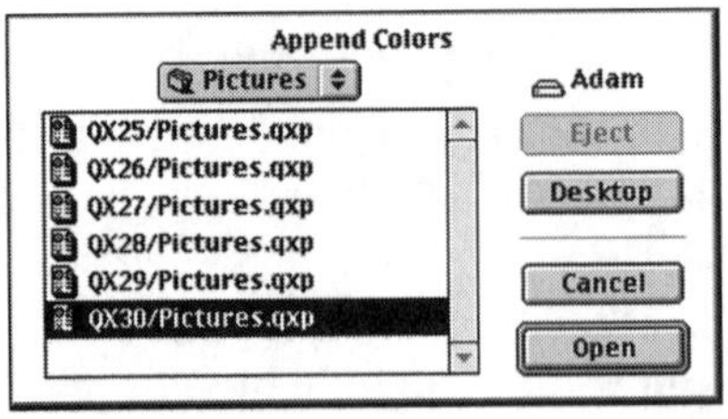

> **Append Colors**
> Pictures ⬍   ⬛ Adam
>
> 🔲 QX25/Pictures.qxp   [Eject]
> 🔲 QX26/Pictures.qxp
> 🔲 QX27/Pictures.qxp   [Desktop]
> 🔲 QX28/Pictures.qxp
> 🔲 QX29/Pictures.qxp   [Cancel]
> 🔲 QX30/Pictures.qxp   [Open]

When you click OK, the Append Colors dialog box shown in Figure 15-10 appears. (You can also display this dialog box by choosing Edit⇨Append and then clicking the Colors tab.) Click the color in the scroll list that you want to append, ⌘+click or Ctrl+click to select multiple colors, or click Include All to append all colors. When you click a color, the Description section displays color-separation information about the color.

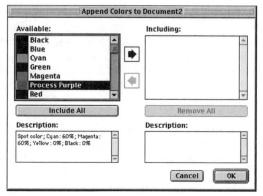

Figure 15-10:
This variation
of the
Append
Colors dialog
box allows
you to
choose the
colors that
you want to
append.

If you try to append a color whose name is already in use by a color in the open document, QuarkXPress displays the Append Conflict dialog box, shown in Figure 15-11. In this dialog box, you have the option to rename the appended color (click Rename), to automatically name the appended color by adding an asterisk in front of its name (click Auto-Rename), to replace the existing color with the appended color (click Use New), or to ignore the appended color and retain the existing color (click Use Existing).

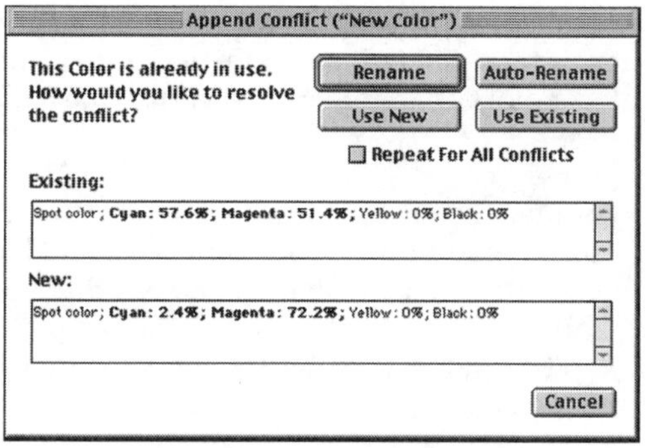

Figure 15-11:
The Append
Conflict
dialog box
allows you to
import colors
from other
QuarkXPress
documents
and solve
conflicts
when
differences
arise.

It's clear why you may need to import a color defined in another QuarkXPress document, but would you need to import a color defined in an EPS file? Yes, for two reasons: You may have a color for a logo or other image that you want to use in your QuarkXPress document, or perhaps the color in the EPS file is defined as a spot color but you want to print it as a process color. By importing the color definition into QuarkXPress, you can edit that color in QuarkXPress to be a process color. Importing the color definition is automatic when you import the EPS file by choosing File⇨Get Picture (or pressing ⌘+E or Ctrl+E). Your Colors dialog box is updated to reflect the imported colors as soon as the image has been imported. Pretty easy, huh?

Actually, there's a third reason for importing a color defined in an EPS file: If EPS colors didn't import into QuarkXPress, QuarkXPress wouldn't be able to color-separate them easily. You can color-separate an EPS file's unimported colors; you have to know which colors are in your EPS file and define colors with the same names in QuarkXPress. That procedure is a great deal of work, however, and you may miss one or two colors. In versions of QuarkXPress earlier than 3.3, you had to go through this torturous process to color-separate colors in EPS files, and most artists converted all colors in their EPS files to CMYK before importing into QuarkXPress — QuarkXPress automatically defines those four colors.

Using Quark's Color Management System to correct color

No matter how carefully you calibrate the hardware required for color publishing, the range of colors produced by scanning devices, computer monitors, color printers, and color printing presses varies from device to device. QuarkXPress offers a tool that helps ensure accurate printing of the colors in your document — colors that you create within QuarkXPress and colors in imported pictures.

The new Quark CMS (Color Management System) XTension replaces the EFIColor XTension that was included with QuarkXPress 3.2 and later. Quark CMS tracks the colors in imported picture files, the colors that your monitor is capable of displaying, and the colors that your printer can produce. If your monitor or printer can't produce a particular color, Quark CMS substitutes the closest reproducible color.

Don't get the Quark CMS XTension confused with a color-matching system. Because the physics of producing color with the red, green, and blue screen phosphors of a computer monitor and with cyan, magenta, yellow, and black printing inks are entirely different, matching colors throughout the production process is impossible. With Quark CMS, however, you can keep the differences to a minimum.

Getting the most from CMS

Quark CMS manages colors via the use of profiles that contain information about the color models and range of colors supported by a particular creator (a scanner or illustration program, for example), display device, and printer. Quark CMS checks the colors that you create and colors in imported pictures, compares them with the colors that your monitor and printer can produce, and adjusts the colors for the closest possible display and output. QuarkXPress 4.0 includes several device profiles, along with system extensions, startup items, and control panels. Make sure you install these files if you want to take full advantage of the Color Management System. (The files are located in the Color Management System folder, which is in the Items for System Folder. These folders are placed in your program folder when you install QuarkXPress.)

To enable Quark CMS, make sure the that XTension is active. You can choose Utilities➪XTensions Manager to see whether it's active and, if not, to activate it the next time you launch QuarkXPress. After you activate the XTension, turn on color management by choosing Edit➪Preferences➪Color Management.

Configuring QuarkXPress

To configure Quark CMS, choose Edit➪Preferences➪Color Management (this command is available only if the Quark CMS XTension is running). The Color Management Preferences dialog box appears (see Figure 15-12). If you want to set program-wide color-management preferences, make sure that no documents are open. At the top of the Color Management Preferences dialog box, three pop-up menus let you choose a default Monitor, Composite Printer, and Separation Printer.

If you want to correct the display of colors, first choose a monitor from the Monitor pop-up menu. The monitor that you choose determines how QuarkCMS adjusts the display of imported colors and colors created within QuarkXPress. To correct color display, you must also turn on Display Correction by choosing On from the pop-up menu at the bottom of the dialog box. You can then choose the color models — RGB, CMYK, or Hexachrome — for which you want to correct display.

For color correction to work, your monitor must be displaying thousands of colors (16-bit) or more (24-bit, for example). Mac users can change the monitor's bit depth via the Monitors & Sound control panel; Windows users use the Display control panel. (If you want truly accurate color display, you should be using a calibrated monitor, which usually includes calibration hardware that measures the color output on-screen.)

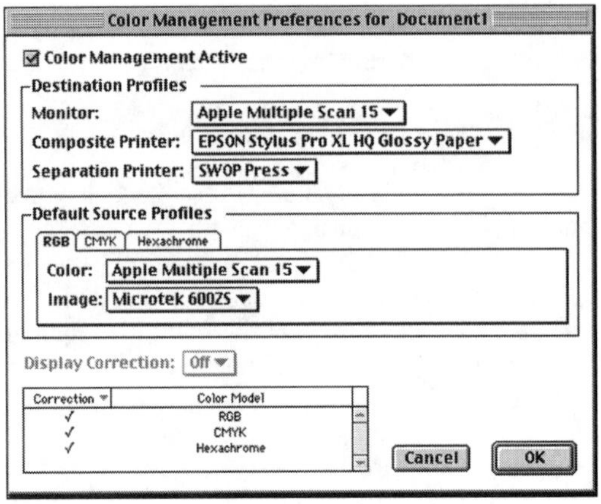

Figure 15-12:
The Color
Management
Preferences
dialog box.

The Composite Printer and Separation Printer pop-up menus let you correct the colors in your printed output. A *composite printer* is often a proofing printer, such as a color inkjet printer; a dye-sublimation printer; or 3M's Matchprint service, which simulates the colors of a printing press by using a series of laminated pages. A *separation printer* is a printing press, such as a Web offset press, that produces color by using multiple color printing plates. (Some composite printers also produce CMYK output.)

You must choose an output device from the Composite Printer and/or Separation Printer pop-up menus for the Display Correction option at the bottom of the dialog box to work because QuarkXPress tries to match the target output device when correcting color display.

Two pop-up menus — Color and Image — let you select default source profiles for the RGB, CMYK, and Hexachrome color models. You can choose a source profile for each color model that you use.

From the Color pop-up menu, choose the device that you will use to define the majority of your colors. If you're producing CMYK colors, you typically choose a printer (the printer that you intend to use); if you're producing RGB colors, choose a monitor.

From the Image pop-up menu, choose the device that you use to create most of your imported pictures. For RGB colors, this device usually is a scanner or a printer. If you use QuarkXPress or other computer graphics programs to generate original drawings, however, you may choose a monitor. For CMYK images, you want to choose your printer.

Changing a profile

When you import a picture into a QuarkXPress document, Quark CMS uses the settings that you specified in the Color Management Preferences dialog box (Edit➪Preferences➪Color Management) unless you choose to override those settings. The Profile pop-up menu at the bottom of the Get Picture dialog box (⌘+E or Ctrl+E; see Figure 15-13) lets you change the profile used for a particular image. If you check the Color Correction check box, you can have an image color corrected.

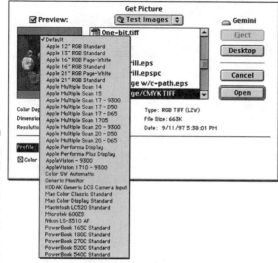

Figure 15-13: The Get Picture dialog box with the Profile list displayed.

When you choose a profile for an imported CMYK image, Quark CMS lets you apply only target printer profiles, because Quark figures that a CMYK image will ultimately be printed. For RGB files, Quark CMS lets you apply monitor profiles and RGB printer profiles, such as the Epson Color Stylus.

After you import a picture, you can display information about the picture and its color profile by displaying the Profile Information Palette (see Figure 15-14). Choose View➪Show Profile Information to display this palette, which identifies the Picture Type, File Type, and Color Space of the picture in the active box. The Profile pop-up menu displays the name of the currently selected color profile. You can change the selected profile by choosing a different one from the list. You also have the option to enable or disable Color Correction.

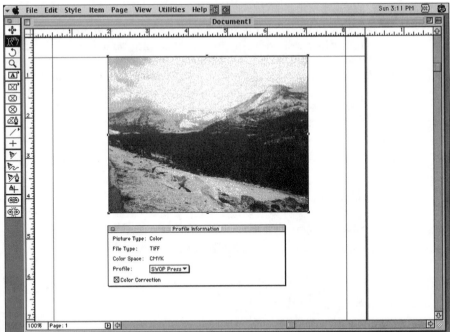

Figure 15 -14:
Profile
Information
palette.

Applying Color

Here comes the fun part. You have your colors; now use them!

You can apply colors to any of the following:

- ✔ A box's background or frame
- ✔ Text in a text box or on a path
- ✔ A grayscale TIFF image
- ✔ A black-and-white TIFF, PICT, PCX, BMP, or other image
- ✔ A line

The easiest way to apply colors is to use the Colors palette. Figure 15-15 shows the palette being used to apply color to a frame.

Notice the three icons at the top of the Colors palette in Figure 15-15. From left to right, these icons are Frame, Contents, and Background. You click the icon that's appropriate for what you want to color (use the Content icon for text or for grayscale and black-and-white images, for example) and then click the color that you want to apply. Simple! The palette changes when a line or a text path is selected, as shown in Figure 15-16.

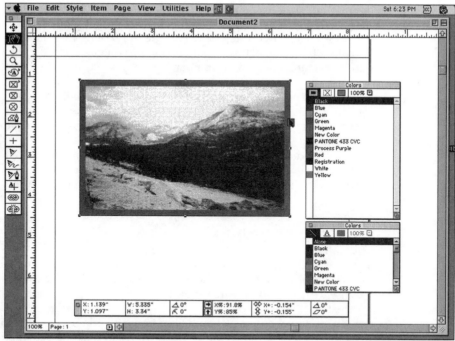

Figure 15-15:
You can change color for any element by using the Colors palette. The icons and lists give you access to all color controls.

Figure 15-16:
When a line or text path is active, the Colors palette lets you change the color of the line or the text.

If you want to apply a shade of a color, first apply the color and then enter a new shade value where you see the percentage in the top-right corner of the Colors palette. You can click the triangle to the left of the current percentage (usually, 100) to display a pop-up menu, or you can highlight the current percentage and type a new number.

If you click a color square in the Colors palette and hold down the mouse button, you can drag a color swatch to a box frame or background, but you cannot drag a color swatch to a picture image. To change the color applied to a picture, you must click the middle of the three icons at the top of the Colors palette and then click a color name. Refer to Figure 15-15 to see this drag-and-drop color feature (look for the mouse pointer "holding" the color square over the box frame).

Creating blends

The most interesting effect is the use of a blend — a gradation of color from one side to the other — for a text box or picture box's background color. QuarkXPress lets you create several types of blends, as Figure 15-17 shows. To create a blend, select a box, click the background icon in the Colors palette, and then choose a blend type from the pop-up list that appears beneath the top-left icons. Notice the two radio buttons — #1 and #2 — as well as a text box for entering the blend's angle in degrees. First click the #1 button; then select a color. Next, click the #2 button and then select a different color. QuarkXPress blends from color #1 to color #2. Change the angle to change the direction of the blend.

You can use white as a the second color when you create a blend. The resulting fadeaway effect is particularly useful for one-color (black) publications.

About the only things that you can't do in the Colors palette are . . . well, actually, you can do everything that you need to do. You can choose Style⇨Color or Style⇨Shade options to change the color of a line or selected text (the Content tool must be selected to change the color of text). You can also use the Box pane of the Modify dialog box to change a box's background. (To display this dialog box, choose Item⇨Modify, or press ⌘+M or Ctrl+M.) Use the Frame pane of the Modify dialog box to change a box's frame color. (To display this pane, choose Item⇨Modify or Item⇨Frame, or press ⌘+B or Ctrl+B.) But these procedures are not as straightforward as using the Colors palette. In fact, the only reason not to use the Colors palette is that you happen to be using these other menus or dialog boxes when you need to change color.

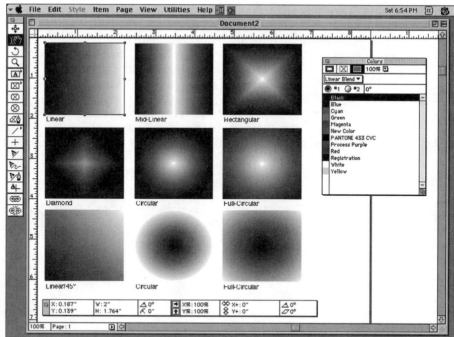

Figure 15-17:
Types of
blends.

Editing colors

Not obvious to most users, another thing you can do from the Colors palette is access the Colors dialog box. How do you do that? Hold down the ⌘ or Ctrl key when you click a color, and you jump directly to the Colors dialog box; the color that you clicked is highlighted. Then click Edit, Delete, Duplicate, and so on, depending on what you want to do with the selected color. What a time-saver!

When you edit a color, you can rename it. But if you want to replace all, say, blues with reds, no specific find-and-replace function exists. But have no fear; you have a makeshift way to find and replace colors in QuarkXPress.

Choose Edit⇔Colors to get a list of current colors in your QuarkXPress document, select the color that you want to change, and then click the Delete button. You're asked what color you want to use to replace the deleted color in objects that use the deleted color, and you choose a re-placement color from the Replace with pop-up menu.

Of course, using this makeshift procedure deletes the original color from the document. If you want to keep that color definition but still replace it in your document with a different color, use the Duplicate button first to make a copy of the color that you want to change. Then go ahead and delete the original color so that you can replace it with a different one. The duplicate color is kept with the other colors in your document.

Hey! Now that you're a color expert and you're ready to add color to your document, just make sure that you don't overdo it and put color everywhere or use clashing colors. Remember: A good effect is one that is used sparingly so that it's noticed, not obnoxious.

Chapter 16

Text as Art

● ●

In This Chapter

▶ Running text along a path

▶ Skewing, rotating, and flipping text

▶ Creating shadows and outlines

▶ Embossing text

▶ Expanding and compressing text

● ●

*T*hanks to the miracle of computer science, the once-mighty barriers between text and art have fallen. Today, you can stretch, squash, and otherwise distort text as though it were taffy. These capabilities open the way for innovative, creative use of text as art, as well as some really hellish-looking materials. But no one reading this book would ever create something like that!

One of the whiz-bangiest new features of QuarkXPress 4.0 is the capability to run text along lines of all kinds (curved, zigzag, and so on), as well as along the contours of closed shapes (rectangles, ovals, Bézier boxes, and the like). Add this capability to the powerful type-formatting options of QuarkXPress, and the possibilities are endless.

You have to know, of course, when to use artistic effects; knowing only how to create the effects is just not enough. You get to the "how to use" part after the "how to create" part.

Special Type Effects in QuarkXPress

Figures 16-1 and 16-2 show what you can do in QuarkXPress. All the variants of the standard Times text were accomplished with QuarkXPress's features. Some of the examples were created with the formatting options in the Style menu; others were created by modifying the box and the text within via the Box and Text panes of the Modify dialog box. (To display this dialog box, choose Item⇨Modify, or press ⌘+M or Ctrl+M.) In some cases, frames are placed around text boxes to show you how the text relates to the box that contains it.

Figure 16-1:
Various
type effects
created
with text
paths.

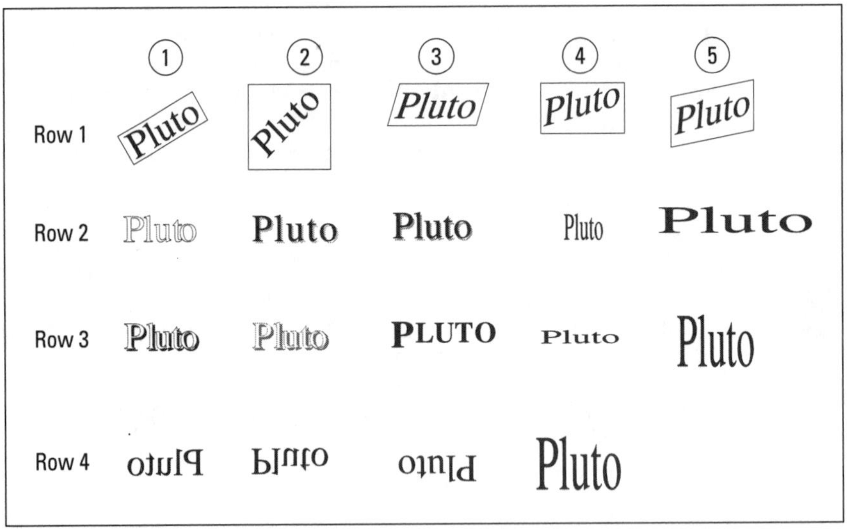

Figure 16-2:
Various
type effects
created by
modifying
text and text
boxes.

Creating text paths

Before we tell you how to create the examples in Figures 16-1 and 16-2, we show you how to create a text path using the Text Path tools shown in Figure 16-3. The procedure is basically the same as that for creating a line, which we discuss in Chapter 11.

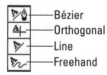

Figure 16-3:
The four
Text Path
tools are on
the bottom
of the Tool
palette.

—Bézier
—Orthogonal
—Line
—Freehand

To create a text path, simply follow these steps:

1. Select one of the four Text Path tools.

The bottom of the Tool palette includes four tools for creating text paths: the Line, Bézier, Orthogonal, and Freehand Text-Path tools. Each of these tools is identified with an *A* next to the type of line that it creates.

2. Create a text path the same way that you create a line (refer to Chapter 11).

The mouse technique that you use depends on the tool that you choose and the kind of line that you want to create. The Line and Orthogonal Text-Path tools allow you to create straight-line paths, the Bézier Text-Path tools allows you to create straight-edged or curvy lines, and the Freehand Text-Path tool allows you to create freehand shapes by using the mouse as a drawing tool. (Refer to Chapter 11 for details about creating and reshaping lines.)

After you create a text path, the Item or Content tool is automatically selected (QuarkXPress reverts to whichever of these tools was selected before you created the path). If you want to place text along the path, make sure that the Content tool is selected, and start typing. A text path behaves much like a text box. If you enter more text than the path can hold, a text-overflow box is displayed at the end of the path. Also like a text box, you can choose File⇨Get Text (or press ⌘+E or Ctrl+E) to import text into a text path.

When the Content tool is selected, you can highlight text along a path and use the commands in the Style menu to modify its appearance, just as you modify text in a box.

If you choose the Item tool before you click a text path, the Style menu displays the same set of commands that it displays when a line is active: Line Style, Arrowheads, Width, Color, and Shape. You can use these commands to add a line along text path and control its appearance. You can also modify the appearance of the line associated with a text path in the Line pane of the Modify dialog box, which offers additional controls for controlling the placement and angle of the line. (To display this dialog box, choose Item⇨Modify, or press ⌘+M or Ctrl+M.)

Things really get fun when you start fiddling in the Text Path pane of the Modify dialog box. (To display this pane, choose Item⇨Modify.) Figure 16-4 shows the Text Path pane.

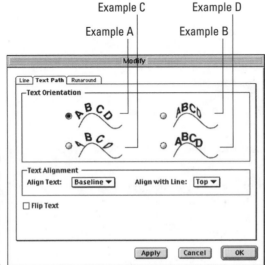

Figure 16-4:
The Text Path pane in the Modify dialog box.

The four options in the Text Orientation area produce four very different visual effects:

- The top-left button rotates each character so that it sits flat on the path (example A in Figure 16-4).

- The top-right button produces a ribbonlike effect. Characters are vertical and are skewed, rotated, and sometimes flipped to give the text a 3-D appearance (example B in Figure 16-4).

- The bottom-left button produces a wild, skewed appearance that's impossible to describe (example C in Figure 16-4).

- The bottom- right button produces a stairstepped effect with vertical, full-size characters (example D in Figure 16-4).

The two pop-up menus in the Text Alignment section of the dialog box allow you to control how the text along a path is placed relative to the path. The Align Text list offers four options: Ascent, Center, Baseline, and Descent.

- ✔ Ascent causes the text to hang from the path, sort of like clothes on a clothesline.
- ✔ Center causes the text to straddle the path.
- ✔ Baseline runs the baseline of the text along the path.
- ✔ Descent is like Baseline, except that the text is lifted slightly so that descenders (*j, p, g,* and so on) are completely above the path.

If you added a wide line to a text path, the three options in the Align with Line pop-up menu — Top, Center, and Bottom — allow you to control what part of the line the text aligns to.

Recreating Figure 16-1

The following sections describe how we created the examples in Figure 16-1.

Example A

We created a zigzag line with the Bézier Text-Path tool, entered the text and then chose Style⇨Horizontal/Vertical Scale to vertically stretch the text to 200 percent of its original height. (All the text in Figure 16-1 was horizontally scaled.)

Example B

We created a curvy line with the Bézier Text-Path tool, added one of QuarkXPress's default stripe line styles, and made the line 12 points wide. We aligned the text with the bottom of the line by using the Align with Text pop-up menu in the Text Path pane of the Modify dialog box. Finally, we applied a Baseline Shift value of –5 to the text (Style⇨Baseline Shift).

Example C

We created a circular shape with the Bézier Text-Path tool and then clicked the top-left radio button in the Text Orientation section of the Text Path pane of the Modify dialog box. The text is aligned with the baseline of the text path.

Example D

We created this example by copying example C and then clicking the top-right radio button in the Text Orientation section of the Text Path pane.

Example E

We created this example by copying example C and clicking the bottom-left radio button in the Text Orientation section of the Text Path pane.

Example F

We created this example by combining examples C and D and then adding a 40 percent shade to the "flattened" text by choosing Style⇨Shade.

Recreating Figure 16-2

The following sections describe how we created the examples in Figure 16-2.

Row 1

We created the images in Row 1 of Figure 16-2 as follows:

(1) We rotated the text box 30 degrees, via the Measurements palette or via the Box pane of the Modify dialog box. The text in all boxes of this row has been centered horizontally (Style⇨Alignment⇨Centered) and vertically (choosing Centered from the Alignment pop-up menu in the Text pane of the Modify dialog box).

(2) We rotated the text within the box 20 degrees via the Text pane of the Modify dialog box.

(3) We skewed the text box 20 degrees via the Box pane of the Modify dialog box.

(4) We rotated the text 16 degrees and skewed the text 20 degrees via the Text pane of the Modify dialog box.

(5) We rotated the text box 16 degrees and skewed the box 20 degrees via the Box pane of the Modify dialog box.

Row 2

We created the images in Row 2 of Figure 16-2 as follows:

①
Pluto

We used the outline type style in the Measurements palette. You can choose Style⇨Type Style instead.

②
Pluto

We used the shadow type style, also in the Measurements palette (accessed via Style⇨Type Style).

③
Pluto

We used two text boxes to create the shadow effect. The frontmost box has a runaround of None (Item⇨Runaround and a background color of none. The text in the shadow box has a 40 shade (Style⇨Shade).

④
Pluto

We compressed the text horizontally to 50 percent by choosing Style⇨Horizontal/Vertical Scale.

⑤
Pluto

We expanded the text horizontally to 200 percent.

An easy way to change the scaling of text is to hold down the ⌘ or Ctrl key when you resize a text box. This action makes the text resize the same way as the box. Click a text-box handle and hold down the mouse button until the item in the box flashes; then drag the text-box handle in the direction in which you want to scale the text. This method allows you to see the effects of the resizing as they happen, so you can see when the new scale is what you want it to be.

Row 3

We created the images in Row 3 of Figure 16-2 as follows:

①
Pluto

We used both the shadow and outline type styles.

②
Pluto

We used the shadow style and changed the text's shade to 60 percent by choosing Style⇨Shade.

⒜ You can also change color by choosing Style⇨Color or by using the Colors palette with the palette's Color content tool selected.

③
PLUTO

We applied the small-caps type style and then applied a baseline shift value of 5 points by choosing Style⇨Baseline Shift.

④

We compressed the text vertically to 50 percent.

Pluto

⑤

Pluto

We expanded the text vertically to 200 percent.

Horizontal and vertical scaling work basically the same way. Because it seems to be human nature to start at the vertical size desired and then scale to make the text skinnier or fatter, most people scale text horizontally. Therefore, the default in the dialog box is Horizontal. That may be because for years, even in the old days before desktop publishing, that's just how the tools worked.

Row 4

We created the images in Row 4 of Figure 16-2 as follows:

①

oʇnlꟼ

We flipped the text horizontally by using the Measurements palette or by choosing Style⇨Flip Horizontal.

Flipping affects the entire contents of the text box, so you may expect that you need to use the Item tool. Well, actually, you're supposed to use the Content tool for this one. Even though you could argue that flipping affects the entire box (in which case, you would use the Item tool), QuarkXPress thinks that flipping affects only the contents of the box, not the box itself. So the Content tool it is. You don't need to highlight text before you flip it. All text in a box is flipped, whether text is highlighted or not.

②

ᴘlnʇo

We flipped the text vertically by using the Measurements palette or by choosing Style⇨Flip Vertical.

③

oʇnlᴘ

We flipped the text both horizontally and vertically.

④

Pluto

We resized the text box while holding down the ⌘ or Ctrl key. The text was enlarged and vertically scaled as we dragged a box handle.

If you fancy yourself to be a typesetter, you can see from Figure 16-1 and Figure 16-2 that QuarkXPress allows you to do almost anything you can imagine to text. Combining the effects in the examples allows you to create some interesting variations.

Creating custom drop caps

Several examples in Figure 16-5 show an example of rotated drop caps (large letters inset into a paragraph; refer to Chapter 6 for more details on QuarkXPress's drop-cap feature). The drop cap is in its own text box; you can't rotate drop caps that were created by means of QuarkXPress's standard drop-cap feature.

Previous versions of QuarkXPress did not allow you to anchor rotated boxes, polygons, or lines within text. But QuarkXPress 4.0 allows you to anchor any kind of item (not groups, however) within text, including drop caps that you place in rotated boxes.

Here's how we created the drop caps:

✔ We rotated the drop cap in the bottom-left corner 30 degrees. The font is different from the one used for the body copy and expanded 200 percent, so that the letter covers the full diagonal of the text that it cuts across.

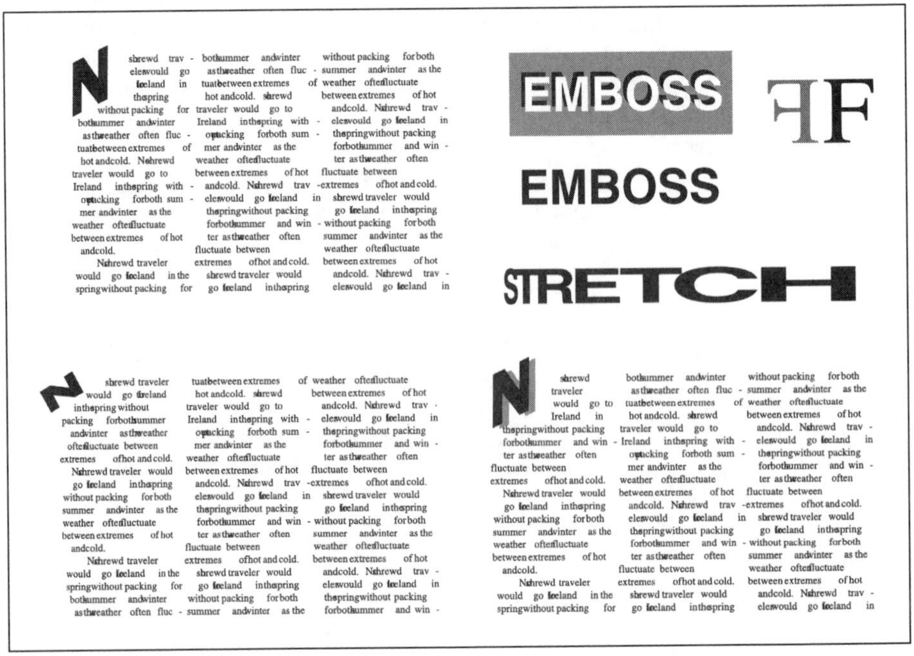

Figure 16-5:
An example
of the type-
distortion
effects that
you can
create in
QuarkXPress.

✔ The drop cap in the top-left corner is a little trickier; it uses a combination of box skewing (15 degrees) and box rotation (25 degrees). The result of this combination has the slanted strokes of the *N* actually run almost vertically.

✔ The drop cap in the bottom-right corner, is a modified version of the other shadowed drop cap in the top-left corner. For the shadow, we didn't use the shadow type style. Instead, we duplicated the text box that contained the initial cap, offset the copy slightly from the original, and sent it behind the original by choosing Item⇨Send Backward. (Mac users must press the Option key to change the Send to Back command to Send Backward.)

We applied a 50 shade to the shadow text and set the runaround for both initial cap text boxes to None. Figure 16-6 shows the runaround turned off (choose Item⇨Runaround).

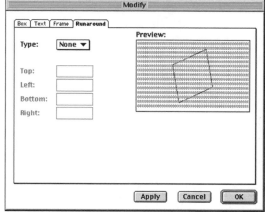

Figure 16-6:
The Runaround pane of the Modify dialog box.

✔ Finally, we added an empty text box and moved it below the two text boxes containing the initial cap and its shadow. The empty box is in front of the three-column box that contains the body text and has an Item runaround that causes the text in the three-column box to run around.

Although this multiple-text-box approach to building drop shadows for text can take some effort, it allows you to create exactly the type of shadow you want, down to the color, shade, and the amount of offset. The QuarkXPress shadow type style cannot be customized; you receive just what QuarkXPress is preprogrammed to do.

When you're done creating a shadow, don't forget to group the text boxes that form it, so one of them doesn't get moved later accidentally. To group the text boxes, choose Item⇨Group (or press ⌘+G or Ctrl+G).

Creating embossed text

Back in Figure 16-5, you see two examples of text that appear to be embossed (top right). Both examples were created with two text boxes. In Figure 16-7, you can see the text boxes that were used to create these effects. In one example of embossed text, the text box contains white text and a runaround of None; the box above it contains black text and a box background of 40 percent black. The two examples are the same, except that the 40 percent black background was replaced by white.

Figure 16-7: Creating embossed text (top) and drop shadows (bottom) by super-imposing text boxes.

Creating other effects

The other two effects shown back in Figure 16-5 are fairly simple to create. The Stretch! text uses the horizontal scaling feature to make each subsequent letter scaled more. The following scale values were used for successive letters, from left to right: 50, 100, 125, 175, 225, 275, and 350.

The reverse F is in a separate text box from the regular F next to it. The idea was to make the F a symbol, almost like in a coat of arms. We also made the flipped F gray to help make the regular F more readable. You can use this effect as a drop cap or as a logo.

Tips for Using Text as Art

It may seem to be obvious, but it's not to many people: Use special effects sparingly:

- ✔ Don't mix dissimilar effects, such as putting skewed text, compressed text that is not skewed, and embossed text on the same page. Unless you're creating a sheet of examples, all you'll do is make the reader notice the dissimilarities and wonder just what you were thinking.

- ✔ For the best appearance, design special text effects to work with other graphical elements. If several items are slanted, for example, have them slant the same amount, whether they're text or lines.

- ✔ Pay attention to spacing. If text looks like a graphic, give it more space than you would if it looked like just a weird part of the text. A good rule of thumb is to put minimal space around warped text if that text is meant to be read with other text. Drop caps, for example, should not be so removed from the rest of the paragraph that the reader doesn't realize that they *are* drop caps.

  Conversely, don't position a graphic that happens to be made of a symbol (such as in a logo) so close to similar text that people try to read it as part of the text. The more different the warped text looks from the regular text, the easier it will be for the reader to know that the text is different, and you won't have to worry so much about spacing.

That's it! You've come to the end of the special effects. Congratulations — this is the most difficult stuff, because it requires an active imagination, an understanding of the tools in QuarkXPress (so that you can to turn that imagination into reality), and patience in applying these tools. Have fun experimenting!

Part IV
Going Long and Linking

The 5th Wave — By Rich Tennant

"WELL, SHOOT! THIS EGGPLANT CHART IS JUST AS CONFUSING AS THE BUTTERNUT SQUASH CHART AND THE GOURD CHART. CAN'T YOU JUST MAKE A PIE CHART LIKE EVERYONE ELSE?"

In this part . . .

1t wasn't so very long ago that you really couldn't create a book using QuarkXPress. Sure, you could make a newsletter or a flyer, but if your document had more than a dozen or so pages, you'd find yourself feeling antsy as you tried to keep track of figure numbers, table numbers, index entries — well, you get the idea. But now, with version 4, crafting long documents is a piece of cake. In this part, we show you how to handle long documents of all flavors, including those that link together several smaller documents into a whole. We also tell you how to make lists and indexes.

Chapter 17

Building Books

. . . .

. . . .

*I*t's been said that everyone has a book in them. Some of you may have several books — stories that are sometimes funny, sometimes serious — waiting to be told. Others of you may want to write fiction or document your family history, skeletons in the closet and all. Still others may need to create books for a living.

Whatever the book you have inside you, QuarkXPress is a good tool to use when you're ready to bring your book from inside to out. This chapter describes new features in QuarkXPress 4 that are designed to help ease the process of getting books and other long documents to look their best.

Planning Your Book

Whatever your dreams of writing the Great American Novel, a book is basically a collection of chapters. Each chapter is a separate document, and you knit the chapters together into a whole book — mentally and physically.

In QuarkXPress 4, a book is also something more: It's a palette. To be precise, it's the Book palette. Like other palettes in QuarkXPress 4, the Book palette is a list of information displaying the chapters that make up the book.

Building a book isn't difficult, especially if you take it one step at a time. The following sections show you how it's done. But before exploring the Book palette and how to use it, you need to do some up-front planning. Here are some pointers to consider before you begin building a book in QuarkXPress 4:

✔ Organize your chapters beforehand. Start by outlining the book, either the old-fashioned way, with pencil and paper, or the modern way, on your computer.

✔ Try using style sheets to format the chapters uniformly (see Chapter 6 for more about style sheets) as you write the book.

✔ Decide on the number, names, and order of the chapters. You can make changes to a chapter's number, name, and order at any time, but figuring out these basics in advance can save you time in the long run.

✔ Make decisions about the format of the book (style sheets, typeface, pagination style, and so on) at the chapter level, beginning with the first chapter. Deciding on the format is important because the first chapter that you add to the Book palette becomes the master chapter (see the section "Working with master chapters" later in this chapter), and attributes of that document form the basis for the other chapters you add to the book.

After you write the chapters and are ready to assemble them, you use the Book palette described in the following sections to combine the separate chapters into a book. After you assemble the chapters, you can update the page numbers, create a table of contents, and create an index for the book (see Chapter 18).

Creating and Opening Books

To open the Book palette and create a new book, choose File⇨New⇨Book (see Figure 17-1).

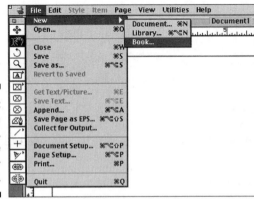

Figure 17-1:
To create a new book, choose File⇨New⇨ Book.

In Figure 17-2, you see a new, open book palette that we named "Cooking Made Easy." The upper part of Figure 17-2 also shows the controls that you use in the Add New Chapter dialog box to locate the chapters that you want to place in the book. To open an existing Book palette, choose File⇨Open, the same as you would to to open a document or a library. To display the Add New Chapter dialog box, click on the Book icon at the upper-left of the Book palette.

Working with master pages

When you're building a book, you're likely to want some elements repeated on multiple pages. For example, you may want to have a running head at the top, outer edge of every page to identify the book. Or you may want a page number to appear at the bottom of every page. Whenever you have elements that repeat on more than one page, you want to use master pages. A master page is a non-printing page that automatically formats pages in a document. A master page may contain items such as page numbers, headers, footers, and other elements that repeat on multiple pages throughout a document.

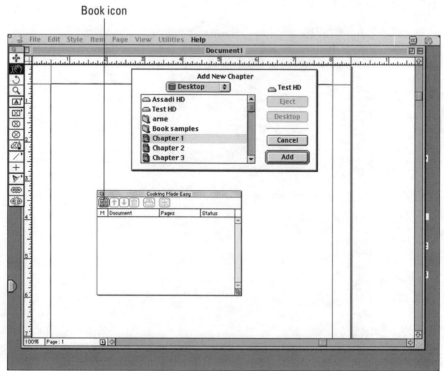

Figure 17-2:
The Book palette and the Add New Chapter dialog box.

You open a master page by choosing Page⇔Display⇔A-Master A (see Figure 17-3). To return to the document page, choose Page⇔ Display⇔Document. You can tell that the master page is displayed if you see the picture of a chain link in the upper-left corner of the page.

On the master page in Figure 17-3, we created a text box and typed the running head "Cooking Made Easy." Now, whenever we use a new document page that is based on the A-Master A master page, the running head appears. Of course, you can always decide to delete any master page item while you have the document open.

Working with master chapters

After you open a new Book palette and list the book's first chapter, QuarkXPress treats that chapter as the master chapter. The master chapter contains attributes that are used in all chapters of the book. For example, we decide to establish a spot color for the "Cooking Made Easy" running head in our cookbook; if this spot color is in the master chapter, it will

Chain link icon

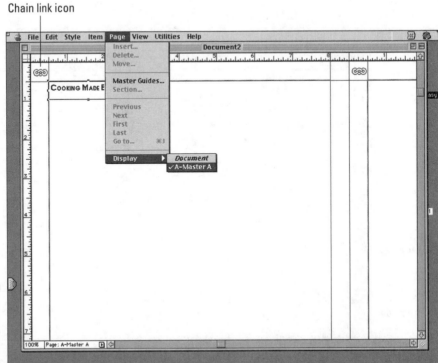

Figure 17-3:
Displaying a
master
page.

appear in all subsequent chapters of the book after you click the Synchronize button on the Book palette. If you add the spot color to a chapter other than the master chapter, the color will appear only in that chapter, not throughout the book. You can tell which chapter is the master chapter by looking for an *M* next to the chapter name in the Book palette. In Figure 17-4, you can see an *M* next to Chapter 1, indicating Chapter 1 was the first chapter we added and is therefore the master chapter. Note that QuarkXPress creates a master chapter even if you choose not to use master pages.

Figure 17-4:
Adding
chapters to
a book; the
first chapter
created
becomes
the master
chapter.

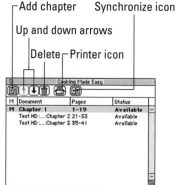

Adding, deleting, and moving document pages

While building the chapters in a book, you may need to insert, delete, or move pages. To do any of these operations, you use the Page menu:

✔ To insert pages, choose Page⇨Insert to display the Insert Pages dialog box.

✔ Deleting pages is a similar function; choose Page⇨Delete, which displays a dialog box that lets you choose the pages to delete.

✔ To move pages, choose Page⇨Move to display a dialog box where you can specify which pages to move and the locations to move them to.

Navigating through a document

As long documents get longer, QuarkXpress offers a couple of quick and easy ways to navigate through their pages:

✔ One way is to enter the number of the page to which you want to go in the Page Number field on the left side of the bar below the document page. QuarkXpress takes you directly to that page.

✔ Another option is to choose Page⇨Go to (⌘+J or Ctrl +J), which displays the Go to Page dialog box.

If you simply want to get from the top to the bottom of a page, use the scroll bar at the right side of the document window.

Using the Book Palette

The Book palette indicates the number of pages in each chapter and tells you the status of the chapters that you've added (see Figure 17-5).

Figure 17-5:
The Book palette, showing the status of individual chapters.

You see one of the following in the status column for each chapter:

✔ **Available:** You can open, edit, or print this chapter.

✔ **Open:** This chapter is currently open, and you can edit or print it. In Figure 17-5, Chapter 1 is open.

✔ **Modified:** This chapter has been changed since the last time the Book palette was open on this computer.

✔ **Missing:** This chapter is unavailable to the Book palette or cannot be located at this time.

Multiple users can open copies of the same book if the book is stored in a shared location on a server. Then, book users can either "check out" chapters of the book and edit the chapters over the network, or they can drag a copy of the chapter to their hard drive to edit it. In this case, if you're in a workgroup and want to prevent other people in your group from editing an original chapter while you're editing a copy of it, move the original chapter to a separate folder. If someone tries to edit the chapter, QuarkXpress lists it with a status of Missing.

Book palette control icons

The icons across the top of the Book palette control the chapters in the book. In order from left to right, here's how the icons work:

 ✔ **To add chapters:** The first icon is the Add Chapter icon. After you click this icon, an Add New Chapter dialog box appears (refer to the upper dialog box in Figure 17-2), allowing you to locate a chapter that you want to add to the Book palette.

 ✔ **To rearrange chapters:** Use the icons with up and down arrows to rearrange chapters within the Book palette. (For example, to move Chapter 1 so that it follows Chapter 3, click Chapter 1 to select it and then click the down arrow three times to move it down three chapters.)

To speed things up, you can also move a chapter in the list by pressing the Option key and clicking and dragging the chapter up or down.

 ✔ **To delete chapters:** The icon of a small trash can (in Windows, the icon is a big "X") is the Delete button. By highlighting one or more chapters and then clicking this icon, the chapters are deleted from the book. Note that the file itself is not deleted, just the link that lists the file as a chapter in the Book palette.

 ✔ **To print a chapter:** The icon that looks like a printer is the Print button.

 ✔ **To synchronize chapter formatting:** The icon with a left- and a right-pointing arrow is the Synchronize button. It allows you to format the other chapters in the book so they are consistent with the master chapter (see the following section for more information).

Synchronizing Chapters

Synchronizing chapters is a great idea if you have a long, involved book that you've worked on over several months (in which case you can easily make a paragraph style change in one chapter and forget to make the change in all other chapters).

Synchronizing is also a good idea if the document has several authors, any of whom may have made local changes without informing the entire group.

Suppose that you already specified Chapter 1 as the master chapter, but you really want to make the whole book look like Chapter 3. The Book palette should first show an *M* to the left of the name of Chapter 1. Click to highlight Chapter 3 and then click the blank area to the left of the chapter name. Chapter 3 then becomes the new master chapter, and the *M* is now to the left of Chapter 3's name.

Synchronizing chapter formatting

Although QuarkXPress lets you make local changes (changes that affect only the chapter you're working on) to chapters at any time, odds are that you'll want to have all the chapters in a book formatted consistently. You do this by using the Synchronize button on the Book palette (the icon on the far right of the palette with a left- and a right-pointing arrow, shown back in Figure 17-5). When you synchronize chapters, QuarkXPress compares each chapter with the master chapter and then modifies the chapters as necessary so that they conform to the master chapter's style sheets, hyphenation and justification (H&J) sets, lists, and so on.

Don't worry about losing any chapter-specific styles, colors, H&J sets, or other things. Synchronize only adds new styles or modifies existing styles that have the same name (but with no guarantee of consistent formatting).

Printing chapters and books

In the Book palette, the icon of a printer is the Print button. You click this icon to print either the entire book or selected chapters listed in the Book palette. Chapters with a status of Missing or Modified won't print, and an error message notifies you of this situation.

✔ To print selected chapters, highlight the chapters that you want to print and click the Print icon (Shift+click to select a range of chapters and Command+click or Ctrl+click to select discontinuous chapters). The Print dialog box appears, as shown in Figure 17-6. (To print the entire book, make sure that no individual chapter is highlighted when you click the Print icon.)

✔ To print all the pages in the selected chapters (or to print the entire book if no chapters are selected), choose All in the Pages pop-up menu of the Print dialog box.

✔ To print a range of pages from selected chapters, choose Selected in the Pages pop-up menu and enter the page numbers.

✔ After entering your printing selections in the Print dialog box, click the Print button at the lower right (or press the Return key) to print the book or the selected chapters.

Working with sections

In long documents, dividing chapters into sections is not uncommon. For example, you may have a Chapter 2 with Sections 1, 2, and 3. QuarkXPress

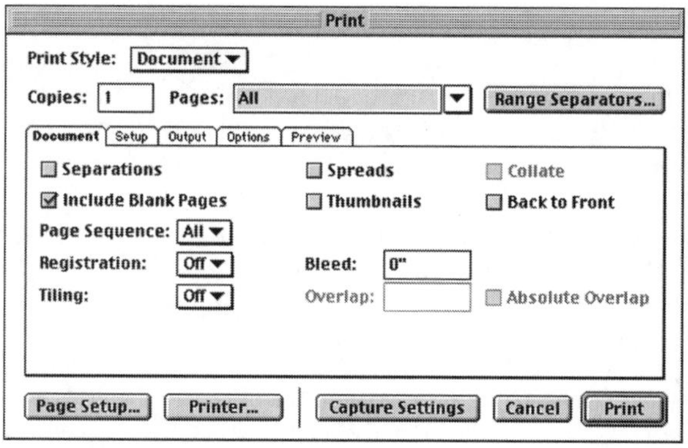

Figure 17-6:
The Print
dialog box.

can help you paginate chapters that have sections. For example, you may want the pages in Section 2 of Chapter 2 to be numbered 2-2.1, 2-2.2, and so on. The following sections show you how this is done.

Creating a section

If you want to create a section in a chapter, open the chapter and then choose Page⇨Section to display the Section dialog box (see Figure 17-7).

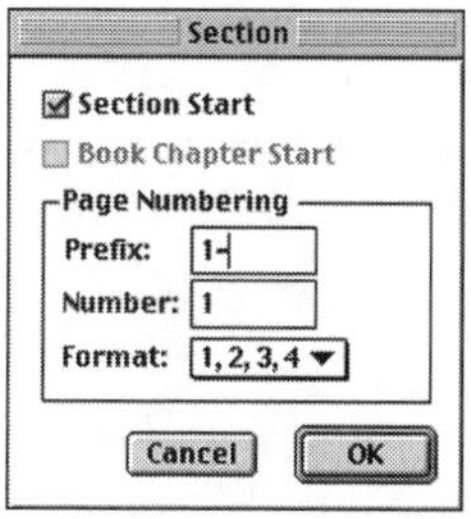

Figure 17-7:
The Section
dialog box.

To paginate the pages in a section, do the following:

1. **In the Section dialog box, check Section Start to disable (uncheck) the Book Chapter Start option we describe in the next section.** After you add, delete, or rearrange pages or chapters, QuarkXPress paginates subsequent chapters according to the settings in the Section dialog box.

2. **If you wish, in the Page Numbering area of the Section dialog box, you can enter a page prefix up to four characters in length in the Prefix box.** (For example, you may want to number the pages in an attachment as *Att-1, Att-2;* in this case, *Att* would be the prefix.)

3. **In the Number box, enter the page number that you want to assign to the first page of a new section.** The Number field requires Arabic numbers, regardless of the Format of the section numbers; for example, if you're using lowercase Roman numerals for the front matter of a book and want the first page of the section to be page iii, enter **3** in the Number field.

4. **Use the Format pop-up menu to select a style for page numbers in a section.** Choices include numeric (1, 2, 3, 4), uppercase Roman (I, II, III, IV), lowercase Roman (i, ii, iii, iv), uppercase alphabetic (A, B, C, D), and lowercase alphabetic (a, b, c, d).

In the Book palette, chapters that contain section starts are indicated by an asterisk next to the numbers in the Pages field.

Using the Book Chapter Start feature

If a chapter doesn't have any sections, QuarkXPress considers it as having a *Book Chapter Start,* which is also the default setting. After you check the Book Chapter Start box in the Section dialog box, QuarkXPress starts numbering the pages of a chapter after the last page of the previous chapter; for example, if the last page in a book's first chapter is page 15, the first page in the second chapter is page 16.

Here's the lowdown on the Book Chapter Start feature:

✔ Whenever you add a chapter without any sections to a book, QuarkXPress numbers pages sequentially throughout the book.

✔ As you add and delete pages from chapters, QuarkXPress also updates the page numbers.

The Book Chapter Start check box is available only if you open a chapter independently of its book by opening it without using the Book palette.

Chapter 18

Making Lists and Indexes

• •

In This Chapter

▶ Building a list of figures or tables

▶ Choosing list styles

▶ Updating a list

▶ Creating an index

• •

Chances are, you know someone who is a listmaker; you know, the person who writes a list of everything to do today, tomorrow, and next week. Listmakers know that lists can help them keep information organized.

Lists, such as a table of contents, work well in publishing, too. In QuarkXPress, a list is actually nothing more than a compilation of paragraphs that are formatted with the same style sheet. Lists are very handy for long documents, but keep in mind that in QuarkXpress, a list cannot contain more than 32 style sheets, and a paragraph in a list is limited to 256 characters. (Your paragraphs can be longer than 256 characters, but when you build a list, only the first 256 characters of each listed paragraph are used.)

After you create a book (or even a single document), QuarkXPress can build a list by scanning the chapters for the style sheets that you specify. For example, if you create a book and have a style sheet that you apply to the figures in the document, you can generate a list of those figures by asking QuarkXpress to list all the paragraphs that use the style sheet named "Figure."

The process described in this chapter works for any kind of list you want to build in QuarkXPress 4.

Building and Maintaining a List

To see how list-building works, suppose that you want to create a list of figures in our example book, *Cooking Made Easy.*

1. **First, create individual documents, or chapters, for the book.**

2. **As you create the chapters, create and apply paragraph style sheets that define chapter heads, figures, and tables.** (See Chapter 16 for more information on creating style sheets.)

3. **Assemble the book using the Book palette.**

Now you're ready to create a list of figures.

Using the Edit List dialog box

Suppose that you elect to list the figures in Chapter 2 of the book. With Chapter 2 open, choose Edit⇨Lists and then click New to display the Edit List dialog box (see Figure 18-1):

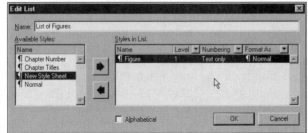

Figure 18-1:
The Edit List
dialog box.

1. **In the Name box of the Edit List dialog box, enter the name of the list that you want to create.**

   In Figure 18-1, we entered the name List of Figures.

2. **Choose a style for the list by highlighting the style name in the Available Styles box; then click the right arrow to transfer the style to the Styles in List box.**

   The Styles in List box includes the following options:

   • **Level:** This pop-up menu includes levels from 1 (highest) to 8 (lowest). The number that you choose represents a level in a hierarchy and is useful for creating complex lists.

- **Numbering:** This pop-up menu defines a page-numbering style for each item in the list; this numbering style determines how page numbers appear in the list. Choosing Page# Text causes items to be preceded by their page number. Other options are Text only, which suppresses page numbers, or Text# Page, which causes an item to appear before its page number.

- **Format As:** This pop-up menu lets you select a style sheet to determine how the text appears in the list. For example, if you're using the list to create a table of contents, you may want all 18-point bold text styled with your Chapter Title style sheet to be reformatted in the list using your 12-point TOC Chapter style sheet.

3. After making your selections, click OK.

QuarkXPress scans the chapter, locates all the paragraphs that are marked with the Figure style, and then uses these items to create a list.

After you create a list, you can use it to navigate through a document. To jump to the place in your document where a listed paragraph occurs, just double-click that entry in the Lists palette. Lists also enable you to view your documents in an outline fashion; paragraphs specified as Level One begin at the left edge of the Lists palette, but lower-level paragraphs are indented.

Placing a list in a book

To put your list into a text box so that you can make the list part of the book, make sure the text box that you want to use is active and then click the Build button in the Lists palette (View➪Show Lists). The Build button is available only when a text box is active. See Chapter 3 for more about text boxes.

Lost your list?

The first time you use the Lists palette's (View➪Show Lists) Build button in a document, QuarkXPress inserts the list into the active text box, wherever the cursor happens to be sitting at that moment. If you click Build while you still have the cursor in the body of your text, QuarkXPress inserts the list right into your manuscript. You can easily forget this fact, because you don't have to worry about it with the Index feature (covered later in this chapter). Fortunately, after you build a list in a document (hopefully in the right place), every time that you click Build, you see a dialog box asking you if you would rather replace the existing list or insert the new version of the list into the active text box.

Updating and rebuilding a list

If you edit a document after you build a list, be sure to update the list by clicking the Update button in the Lists palette. If you previously used the Build button, you need to use it again to replace the old list with the new, updated list. Note that when you create or update a list, QuarkXPress automatically alphabetizes the entries in the list.

Creating an Index

If you've ever had trouble finding information in a book, you can appreciate how important a good index can be. Short, simple documents can get by fine without indexes. But long books almost always need indexes to help the reader locate specific information. Indexing used to be a laborious process, involving lots of index cards. Now, QuarkXPress makes indexing much easier, while still relying on you to make key decisions about formatting. The following sections show you how to do your part in creating an index.

Choosing an indexing style

Before you develop an index, you need to decide on the indexing style that you want to use. Large publishers usually have their own house style guides for indexes. If you don't have a style guide for indexes, we recommend that you read through the indexing guidelines in *The Chicago Manual of Style* (University of Chicago Press). Another option is to use an index you like as a model and then take the steps necessary in QuarkXPress to achieve that index style. Before you begin indexing your document, ask yourself the following questions:

- Do you want to capitalize all levels of all entries, or do you just want to use initial caps?

- Should headings appear in boldface?

- Do you want to capitalize secondary entries in the index?

- Should the index be nested or run-in style? For examples of these indexes, check out the sidebar "Nested or run-in index?" later in this chapter.

Using the Index Preferences dialog box

To index words in QuarkXPress, you *mark* the words that you want to use as index entries in the chapters of your book. These markers appear as colored brackets around the entry. You can choose the color of index markings (in addition to the index separation characters you want to use) by displaying the Index Preferences dialog box (Edit⇨Preferences⇨Index), shown in Figure 18-2. The following sections explain the dialog box options.

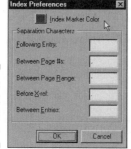

Figure 18-2:
The Index
Preferences
dialog box.

Changing the index marker color

To change the color of the index markers, click the Index Marker Color button in the Index Preferences dialog box; this action displays a color picker. Use the controls in the color picker to define the new color for index markers. Click OK to close the color picker and then click OK in the Index Preferences dialog box to complete the process.

Choosing separation characters

The Index Preferences dialog box also lets you choose the characters and spaces that separate entries in the index. The options in the Separation Characters section of the dialog box work as follows:

- **Following Entry:** Defines the punctuation that immediately follows each index entry. This punctuation is usually a colon (:). For example, the index item `Appetizers: vi, 14, 21-23` uses a colon and space following the index entry "`Appetizers.`"

- **Between Page #s:** Defines the characters or punctuation that separates a list of page numbers. This punctuation is usually a comma (,) or semicolon (;). For example, the index item `Appetizers: vi, 14, 21-23` uses a comma and a space between page numbers.

- **Between Page Range:** Defines the characters or punctuation that indicates a range of pages. This option is usually the word "to" or a dash. For example, the index item `Appetizers: vi, 14, 21 to 23` uses the word "to" between the numbers, indicating a range of pages.

- ✔ **Before X-ref:** Defines the characters or punctuation that appears before a cross reference. This option is usually a period and space, or a semicolon. For example, the index item `Appetizers: vi, 14, 21-23. See also Hors d'oeuvres` uses a period and space before the cross reference.

- ✔ **Between Entries:** Defines the characters or punctuation between entry levels in a run-in index. This option is usually a period or a semicolon. For example, the index item `Appetizers: vi, 14, 21-23; Breads: 25-36; Chicken dishes: 37-45` uses a semicolon between entry levels.

Using the Index palette

When your document is ready to index, open the Index palette (View⇨Show Index or ⌘+Option+I or Ctrl+Alt+I). You use this palette to add words to the index in up to four indent levels, to edit or delete index entries, or to create cross-references. The Index palette appears in Figure 18-3.

Figure 18-3:
The Index
palette.

The controls in the Index palette include the following:

- ✔ **Text:** The Text field in the Entry section of the Index palette is where you type in an index entry or where the text appears that you tagged with index markers. If you highlight text in an open document when the Index palette is open, the first 255 characters of the highlighted text appear automatically in the Text field and are ready to be captured as an index entry.

✔ **Sort As:** Entries in the Sort As field override the default, alphabetical sorting of the index entry. For example, you may want `16-ounce package` to be indexed as if the entry appeared as "`Sixteen-ounce package`"; you can accomplish this task by entering the spelling **Sixteen-ounce package** into the Sort As field.

✔ **Level:** This pop-up menu lets you control the order and structure of index entries. A nested index can have up to four levels, and a run-in index can have only two levels. (Technically a run-in index can have four levels, too, but it doesn't make any sense to use more than two.)

✔ **Style:** The Style pop-up menu (within the Reference section of the dialog box) lets you apply a character style to the page numbers for the current index entry or cross-reference. One example of how you may want to use this option is with a cross-reference like "`See also Kitchen utensils`" where you want to use an italicized character type for the words *Kitchen utensils*.

✔ **Scope:** This pop-up menu in the Reference section lets you control the scope, or range, of the index. For example, you can use it to make an entry a cross-reference, or list an entry as covering a specific number of paragraphs, or suppress the printing of the entry's page number.

✔ **Add button:** This button lets you add an entry to the index.

✔ **Find Next button:** This button finds the next occurrence of an index entry in the active document. The Find Next button does not, unfortunately, find words in the document so that you can index them.

✔ **Pencil icon:** You can edit an active index entry by clicking the pencil icon or by double-clicking the entry name.

✔ **Trashcan icon:** You can delete the selected entry by clicking the trashcan icon on the Mac or the big X in Windows.

Creating an index entry

To create an index entry, highlight the text in your document that you want to use for the index entry. (Don't highlight the whole area that you want the index entry to reference; just highlight the word that you want to appear in the index.) Then click the Add button in the Index palette to add the index entry to the list using the currently selected values in the Entry and Reference areas. When you add index entries, make sure that the capitalization of the words in the Text field matches the style of your index. QuarkXPress does not automatically capitalize (or lowercase) words in your index.

Editing an index entry

Editing an existing index entry is a bit more complicated. To edit an index entry, you must first select it in the Index palette and then go into editing mode; you can either double-click the index entry, or click the index entry and then click the Pencil icon. You can select an entry and make changes to the Entry and Reference areas, but unless you go into editing mode first, you're only changing the settings that will be used when you create the next index entry.

Creating page-number references

Each index entry includes a reference. A reference usually consists of the page number(s) to which the entry refers, but it may also be a cross-reference (see the following section on creating cross-references). To see the page number reference (or cross-reference) for an index entry, click the icon to the left of the entry in the lower section of the Index palette.

Creating cross-references

Cross references enhance an index because they give the reader another way to find pertinent information. The following steps show you how to add a cross-reference to an indexed entry:

1. **Display the Index palette by selecting View⇨Show Index.**

2. **Click Add to create a new entry, or select an existing entry.**

3. **Click the triangle next to the entry name to make its reference available and then double-click that reference to edit it.**

4. **Click the Scope pop-up menu and select X-Ref.**

   This action highlights a field in the palette into which you can enter the cross-referenced term (see Figure 10-4).

5. **From the See pop-up menu choose an option (See, See Also, or See Herein) to govern how the cross-reference appears under the index entry.**

   In Figure 18-4, for the index entry `Cheese Soup`, we have a cross-reference to `Swiss Cheese`. (Note that although Index Preferences controls the punctuation preceding a cross-reference, you still need to insert punctuation following a cross-reference in this field.)

Using index levels

QuarkXPress 4 supports four levels of indexing. The most important thing to remember about creating a level-two, level-three, or level-four index entry is that you must tell QuarkXPress where to put it (that is, you must indicate a higher-level index entry for the subentry to fall under). You provide a higher-level index entry by using the arrow column at the left edge of the index entry list at the bottom of the Index Palette. Suppose that you want to create a level-two entry to an existing level-one entry. First, select the text that you want to add. Next, in the arrow column, click next to the level-one entry under which you want the new entry listed. Then choose Second Level from the Level pop-up menu in the Entry area. Finally, click the Add button to add the new entry.

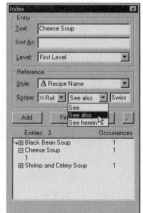

Figure 18-4:
Adding a
cross-
reference
(Swiss
cheese) to
an index
entry
(Cheese
Soup).

If you want to create a third-level entry, but the Third Level option in the Level pop-up menu is dimmed, you probably haven't moved the arrow to a second-level index entry. (You can easily identify second-, third-, and fourth-level entries in the Index palette by their indents.)

Using the Build Index dialog box

To build an index from a list that you generate in the Index palette, choose Utilities⇨Build Index to display the Build Index dialog box, shown in Figure 18-5.

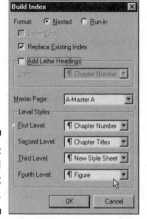

Figure 18-5:
The Build
Index
dialog box.

Nested or run-in index?

There is no right way to index, but common sense should be your guide. The index's hierarchy should determine which index format to use. If your index has only two levels, a run-in format works well, but an index with three or more levels requires a nested format for the sake of clarity.

Nested indexes look like this:

```
Soups
       Black bean, 191
       Cauliflower, 242
       Equipment needed, 92-94,
       96, 99-101
```

```
Hot tomato, 275
Indonesian rice, 180
Sizzling rice, 91
Tortilla and corn, 24
Vegetarian vegetable, 199
```

Run-in indexes look like this:

```
Soups: Black bean, 191;
       Cauliflower, 242; Equipment
       needed, 92-94, 96, 99-101;
       Hot tomato, 275; Indonesian
       rice, 180; Sizzling rice, 91;
       Tortilla and corn, 24;
       Vegetarian vegetable, 199
```

The options in this dialog box work as follows:

- ✔ **Choosing a nested or run-in index:** Your first decision is whether the index is nested or run-in. (See the sidebar "Nested or run-in index?" to help you make a decision.)

- ✔ **Building an index for an entire book:** The Build Index dialog box allows you to build an index for the entire book, rather than for just the open chapter. You select this option by clicking the Entire Book box.

- ✔ **Replacing an existing index:** Indexing is an iterative process, and you'll probably want to build an index a few times through the course of a book project. When you click Replace Existing Index in the Build Index dialog box, QuarkXPress overwrites the existing index with the most current version.

To compare a newer version of an index with its predecessor, uncheck the Replace Existing Index box (Utilities⇨Build Index). Then, when you build the index, QuarkXPress won't replace the previous version.

- ✔ **Adding letter headings:** In long indexes, you may want to divide the index alphabetically so all the index entries that begin with *A* are in a category with the heading *A,* for example. Check Add Letter Headings to use this feature. You can select a paragraph style sheet for the letter headings from the Style pop-up menu.

✔ **Basing an index on a master page:** A Master Page pop-up menu lets you select a master page on which to base the index page. For long indexes, you should consider developing a master page just for that purpose. See Chapter 17 for more about master pages.

✔ **Choosing level styles:** The Level Styles pop-up menus let you choose the paragraph style sheet(s) you want to apply to the various index levels. If you select the Run-in format, all the index levels flow into one paragraph so that only the First Level pop-up menu is available. If you select the nested format, make sure that you specify indentation values for the index level styles that you choose. QuarkXPress does not automatically indent the levels, so if you don't specify indentation values, you won't be able to differentiate between the four index levels.

After you make your choices in the Build Index dialog box, create the index by clicking OK or pressing the Return key.

Part V
Guru in Training

WANDA HAD THE DISTINCT FEELING HER HUSBAND'S NEW SOFTWARE PROGRAM WAS ABOUT TO BECOME INTERACTIVE.

In this part . . .

After you master the basics, why not pick up some of the tricks the pros use? In this part we show you how to customize QuarkXPress so that it works the way you want it to. We also explain how QuarkXPress works on PCs that use Windows and on Macs.

Chapter 19

Customizing QuarkXPress

- -

- -

*P*eople who publish documents come in all shapes and sizes, and they approach their work from different directions. Fortunately, QuarkXPress offers many controls that enable you to customize the program to the way that *you* work. The Application Preferences dialog box lets you control how your copy of QuarkXPress works with all documents. The Document Preferences dialog box lets you set defaults for a single document — if the document is open when you change settings — or for all subsequent documents if you change settings without an open document.

The Preferences option of the Edit menu contains the most important settings. These settings affect both your everyday work and QuarkXPress itself. The Preferences settings are also the least-used settings, because after you set them, you rarely change them.

In this chapter, we cover how to set application and document defaults. Notice that you can also control preferences that affect indexing by choosing Edit⇨Preferences⇨Index (see Chapter 18 for a discussion of Index preferences).

Setting Application Preferences (defaults)

The Application Preferences dialog box contains four panes: Display, Interactive, Save, and XTensions. You tell QuarkXPress your preferences for these settings through the options that are available when you choose Edit⇨Preferences⇨Application (⌘+Option+Shift+Y or Ctrl+Alt+Shift+Y).

Monitor display options

The Display pane, shown in Figure 19-1, lets you set the colors that indicate margin, ruler, and grid lines. Guides and rulers are important tools. They help you position elements on a page, so you need to be able to find them easily. The default settings for these colors work fine for most people, but feel free to change them if, for example, you have a particular fondness for a certain color and want to use it as your margin indicator. These colored lines do not print.

Figure 19-1:
The Display pane of the Application Preferences dialog box.

These guides help you to align items:

- ✓ **Margin (normally blue).** Shows the default column and gutter positions for text boxes.

- ✓ **Ruler (normally green).** Lines that you drag from the horizontal and vertical rulers so that you can tell whether a box lines up to a desired point.

- ✓ **Grid (normally magenta).** The baseline grid shows the position of text baselines.

You probably will use margin guides routinely and ruler guides occasionally. It's a good idea to use the box coordinates (the X and Y positions in the Measurements palette) to make sure that boxes or their margins are placed exactly where you want them.

Other options in the Display pane control how QuarkXPress documents relate to the monitor's screen area. The default view, which appears each time you start the application or open a new document, is Actual Size (100 percent). The following list describes each option:

✔ **Tile to Multiple Monitors.** If you have multiple monitors attached to your Mac, this option tells QuarkXPress to automatically put some document windows on your secondary monitor(s) when you choose Tile Documents (or, in Windows, when you choose Tile Horizontally/ Tile Vertically). Use the Monitors control panel that comes with your System disks to set up multiple monitors.

Because Windows does not support multiple monitors, QuarkXPress for Windows does not support this option.

✔ **Full-Screen Documents.** If you check this box on the Mac, the document window appears on the far-left side of the screen, below the default position of the Tool palette. We recommend that you avoid this option — it can make it difficult to see the close box as it can become obscured by the Tool palette. One advantage of using this option is that it can give your document window enough width to fully display a document. Make sure, however, that you move your Tool palette so that you can click the close box.

This option is not available in QuarkXPress Windows.

✔ **Off-Screen Draw.** This option controls how QuarkXPress displays elements on-screen as you scroll through a document. If checked, this option redraws each element displayed in order of display. If unchecked, the option draws elements in memory first and then displays them all simultaneously. Both options take the same amount of time to redraw the screen, so you have no advantage in either setting.

Two pop-up menus let you specify how pictures appear on-screen:

- **Color TIFFs.** This option lets you specify the color depth of screen previews created for imported color TIFF files. (We discuss TIFF files in Chapter 4.) The default setting is 8-bit, and this setting creates screen previews with 256 possible colors. The other choices are 16-bit and 32-bit on the Mac and 24-bit in Windows. The higher the bit depth, the truer the colors on-screen but the larger your QuarkXPress files and the slower the screen-redraw time.

- **Gray TIFFs.** This option controls the resolution of screen previews for imported grayscale TIFFs. The default is 16 levels.

Notice that the Color TIFFs and Gray TIFFs settings apply only to screen previews and do not affect the resolution of the printed picture.

✔ In Windows only, there is the Display DPI Value option, which is set at 96 by default. A higher number acts like a universal zoom, making everything larger on-screen; a smaller number makes everything smaller. There's rarely a reason to change this setting from the default of 96.

After you make changes in the Display pane, click OK to save them.

Interactive options

The Interactive pane (see Figure 19-2) controls scrolling, smart quotes, the display of dragged items, and pasteboard width. (The pasteboard is the area outside the edges of the document, and you can use the pasteboard as a place to temporarily store layout elements until you are ready to position them on the page.)

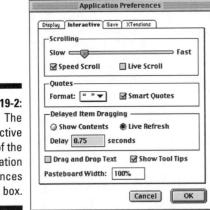

Figure 19-2:
The
Interactive
pane of the
Application
Preferences
dialog box.

The controls in the Interactive pane include the following:

- ✔ **Scrolling.** Use the Scrolling slider to control how fast the page scrolls when you click the arrows in the scroll bars.

  Most people prefer a Scrolling setting somewhere in the middle range. You may have to adjust the setting a few times until it feels right to you. Generally, the setting should be slightly closer to Fast than to Slow so that you don't have to wait for the screen to redraw when you are using the scroll bar to move through a document.

  The other options in the Scrolling section of the dialog box work as follows:

  - **Live Scroll.** If you check this option, QuarkXPress redraws pages while you are dragging the box in the scroll bar. Generally, you should check this option unless you're working on a slower computer.

  - **Speed Scroll.** This option speeds scrolling in graphics-intensive documents by masking out the graphics and blends as you scroll. When you stop scrolling, the graphics and blends are redrawn. Generally, you should check this option.

✔ **Quotes.** Use the pop-up menu in the Quotes section to pick the type of quotation marks to use when you type inside QuarkXPress. The default option is for English quotation marks, but the pop-up menu includes quotation marks from other languages. To have smart (curly) quotation marks automatically substituted when you type them within text boxes, check the Smart Quotes box.

Notice that checking the Smart Quotes option also translates the single-quote character to the smart (curly) style when you type it. This option does not control how straight quotes are translated when you import a text file; to convert keyboard (straight) quotes to curly quotes during import, choose File⇨Get Text (⌘+E or Ctrl+E) and check the Convert Quotes box. To use the standard (straight) keyboard quotes on the Mac, hold down the Control key when you type them. In Windows, press Ctrl+' for foot marks and Ctrl+Alt+' for inch marks.

✔ **Delayed Item Dragging.** The Delayed Item Dragging controls in the Interactive pane determine how QuarkXPress displays items on-screen. If Show Contents is selected, when you hold down the mouse button as you begin dragging an item, the contents of the item are visible as you drag it. If Live Refresh is selected when you hold down the mouse button as you begin dragging an item, the contents of the item are visible as you drag it, *and* the screen refreshes to show item layers and text flow. You can enter a delay time in the Delay seconds box to control the time (in seconds ranging from 0.1 to 5) that you must hold down the mouse button before Show Contents or Live Refresh is activated.

✔ **Drag and Drop Text.** When the Drag and Drop Text option is checked, you can highlight a piece of text and then drag it to a new location (as you can in most word processors), rather than cut it from the old location and paste it in the new one.

✔ **Show Tool Tips.** Checking Show Tool Tips displays the names of the palette or tool icons when the mouse pointer is positioned on them; the default setting is unchecked.

Application preferences control how QuarkXPress works with all documents, so any changes that you make in the Application Preferences dialog box apply to all documents that you create or edit with QuarkXPress.

After you make changes in the Interactive pane, click OK to save them.

File-saving options

The Save pane of the Application Preferences dialog box allows you to control how that QuarkXPress saves and makes backup copies of your documents. The Save pane is shown in Figure 19-3. Here are the options that you can select:

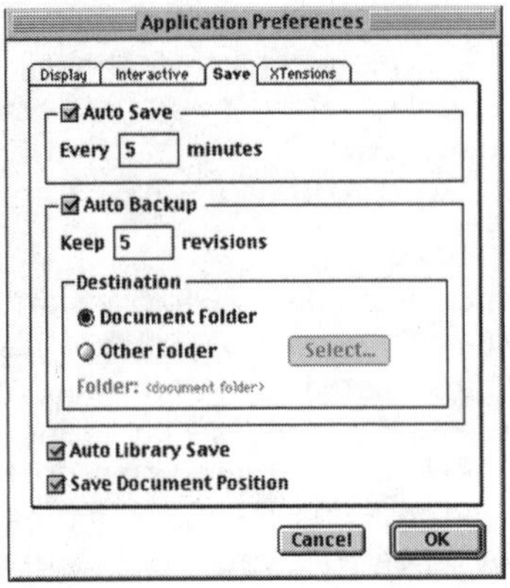

Application Preferences

| Display | Interactive | **Save** | XTensions |

☑ **Auto Save**

Every ⬚5 minutes

☑ **Auto Backup**

Keep ⬚5 revisions

Destination

⦿ **Document Folder**

○ **Other Folder** [Select...]

Folder: ‹document folder›

☑ **Auto Library Save**
☑ **Save Document Position**

[Cancel] [OK]

Figure 19-3:
The Save
pane of the
Application
Preferences
dialog box.

✔ **Auto Save.** When this option is checked, QuarkXPress saves opened documents at regular intervals. You determine that interval through the value that you enter in the Every *X* Minutes box. When an auto save occurs, QuarkXPress creates an auto-save document (with a filename that ends in .AutoSave on the Mac and .asv in Windows). If your computer crashes, you can revert your file to its last auto-saved condition by opening the auto-save document.

✔ **Auto Backup.** You can also have QuarkXPress keep backup copies of your document by checking the Auto Backup box. When this option is checked, QuarkXPress creates a backup copy of your document every time you manually save it. You determine how many previous versions are retained by making an entry in the Keep *X* Revisions box.

✔ **Destination.** You determine where backups are stored by choosing one of the two destination buttons. The default location is the same folder that stores the current document, but you can click the Other Folder button and use the Backup Folder dialog box to select a different folder. (The Backup Folder dialog box works like a standard Open dialog box.)

The backup and auto-save options are independent. If both backup and auto save are enabled, backups are created only when you explicitly save by choosing File➪Save (⌘+S or Ctrl+S).

✔ **Auto Library Save.** The QuarkXPress library feature lets you add items to a library so that the items are available for use in other documents. When the Auto Library Save box is checked, it saves the library whenever something is added to or deleted from it. Otherwise, when the box is unchecked, the library is saved only when you close it (including when you quit QuarkXPress).

✔ **Save Document Position.** When Save Document Position is checked, QuarkXPress saves the size and position of the document window along with the document itself.

After you make changes in the Save pane, click OK to save them.

XTensions options

The new XTensions pane of the Application Preferences dialog box has options that control the built-in XTensions Manager, a utility that lets you turn on and off XTensions (add-on software that gives QuarkXPress new features). Specifically, this pane (see Figure 19-4) lets you choose whether the XTensions Manager displays when you turn on QuarkXPress and, if so, how it displays. We talk more about XTensions in Chapter 9.

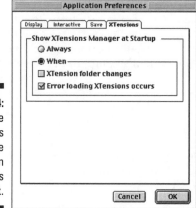

Figure 19-4:
The XTensions pane of the Application Preferences dialog box.

The options you can choose include:

- ✔ **Always.** This option makes the XTensions Manager display each time you launch QuarkXPress.

- ✔ **When XTensions Folder Changes.** When this option is checked, the XTensions Manager dialog box appears when you launch QuarkXPress, but only if you have added or removed XTensions from the XTensions folder.

- ✔ **When Error Loading XTensions Occurs.** When this option is checked, the XTensions Manager dialog box appears when you launch QuarkXPress, but only if you had a problem loading an XTension.

After you make changes in the XTensions pane, click OK to save them.

Setting Document Defaults

The Document Preferences dialog box sets controls for default measurement units, placement and use of layout aids, layout controls, and display of text and pictures.

You can use document preferences either for the current document or for all new documents. If you change the settings while no document is open, all documents that you subsequently create use the new settings. If a document is open when you change the settings, only that document is affected. You can tell whether the settings are global or local because the dialog box's title is Document Preferences for *document name* if the settings are local to that document. To open the Document Preferences dialog box, choose Edit⇨Preferences⇨Document (⌘+Y or Ctrl+Y).

Several dialog boxes in QuarkXPress let you set things that affect all future documents (if no document is open when you set them) or just the currently open document. When you make a default setting for future documents, QuarkXPress displays "Default" at the beginning of the relevant dialog boxes; when your settings are just for the current document, QuarkXPress displays "for *xx*" (where *xx* is the document's name) in the relevant dialog boxes.

General pane options

The General pane in the Document Preferences dialog box lets you specify the defaults for page layout. The following sections describe in detail how you can use the options in the General pane.

Horizontal Measure and Vertical Measure

QuarkXPress lets you select a measurement system for both the horizontal and vertical rulers that you use to lay out a document. You select a measurement system in the General pane of the Document Preferences dialog box, shown in Figure 19-5.

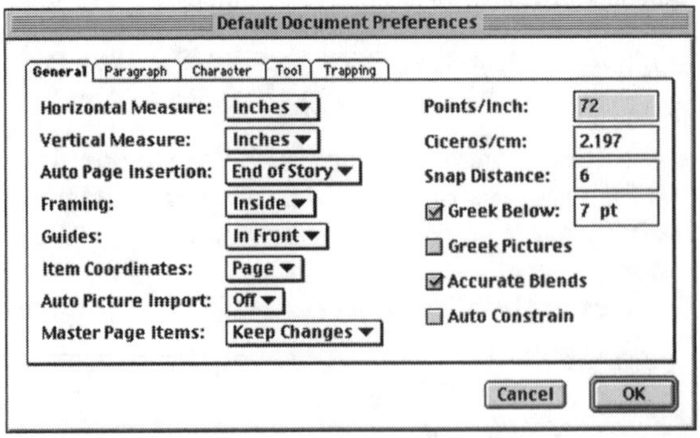

Figure 19-5:
The General pane of the Document Preferences dialog box.

> **Default Document Preferences**
>
> General | Paragraph | Character | Tool | Trapping
>
> Horizontal Measure: [Inches ▼] Points/Inch: [72]
> Vertical Measure: [Inches ▼] Ciceros/cm: [2.197]
> Auto Page Insertion: [End of Story ▼] Snap Distance: [6]
> Framing: [Inside ▼] ☑ Greek Below: [7 pt]
> Guides: [In Front ▼] ☐ Greek Pictures
> Item Coordinates: [Page ▼] ☑ Accurate Blends
> Auto Picture Import: [Off ▼] ☐ Auto Constrain
> Master Page Items: [Keep Changes ▼]
>
> [Cancel] [OK]

You can use any measurement in any dialog box by just entering the code (shown in parentheses in the following list) that tells QuarkXPress what the system is. The measurement system choices, which can be different for the horizontal and vertical rulers, are as follows:

✔ **Inches.** Inches (") are displayed on the ruler divided into eighths, in typical inch format ($^1/_4$ inch, $^1/_2$ inch, and so on).

✔ **Inches Decimal.** Inches (") are displayed on the ruler in decimal format, divided into tenths.

✔ **Picas.** One pica (p) is about 0.166 inch. An inch contains 6 picas.

✔ **Points.** One point (pt) is approximately $^1/_{72nd}$ (.01388) of an inch, or .351 millimeters.

✔ **Millimeters.** A millimeter is a metric measurement unit — 25.4 millimeters (mm) equals 1 inch; 1 mm equals 0.03937 inch.

✔ **Centimeters.** A centimeter is a metric measurement unit — 2.54 centimeters (cm) is 1 inch; 1 cm equals 0.3937 inch.

✔ **Ciceros.** This measurement unit is used in most of Europe; 1 cicero (c) is approximately 0.1792 inch. A cicero is close in size to a pica, which is 0.166 inch.

✔ **Agates.** One agate (ag) is 0.071 inch. (The agate system is new to Version 4 of QuarkXPress.)

Auto Page Insertion

Auto Page Insertion tells QuarkXPress where to add new pages when all your text does not fit into an automatic text box. You must define the text box containing the overflow text as an automatic text box in the page's master page. (A *master page* is indicated by an unbroken chain icon in the top-left corner of the master page; we discuss master pages in more detail in Chapter 17.) In the Auto Page Insertion menu, your options are:

✔ **End of Section.** Places new pages at the end of the current section. (You define sections by choosing Page⇨Section.) If no sections are defined, End of Section works the same as the End of Document option.

✔ **End of Story.** Places new pages immediately following the last page of the text chain.

✔ **End of Document.** Places new pages at the end of the document.

✔ **Off.** Adds no new pages automatically, leaving you to add pages and text boxes for overflow text wherever you want. The existence of overflow text is indicated by a checked box at the end of the text in the text box.

Framing

The Framing option in the General pane of the Document Preferences dialog box tells QuarkXPress how to draw the ruling lines (frames) around text and picture boxes via the Item⇨Frame option (⌘+B or Ctrl+B). You have the following choices:

✔ **Outside.** Places the frame on the outside of the box.

✔ **Inside.** Places the frame inside the box.

Guides

The Guides menu in the General pane of the Document Preferences dialog box specifies whether guides (non-printing lines that help you see where margins are and help you position items on the page) appear in front of boxes (the default setting) or behind them. When guides are behind boxes, you can more easily see what's in the boxes, but you may find it harder to tell whether elements within the boxes line up with margins, gutters, or baselines.

Item Coordinates

Whichever system of measurement you use, you can control how the coordinates for layout elements are calculated. The Item Coordinates setting tells QuarkXPress whether to base your ruler and box coordinates on a page or on a spread (a spread is usually two side-by-side pages, such as the left and right pages that appear together when a bound document is open). If you treat each page as a separate element, keep the option set to Page, which is the default. If you work on a spread as a single unit, change the setting to Spread.

Auto Picture Import

Auto Picture Import lets you update links to your source images automatically. This option is handy if your picture may change frequently and you don't want to forget to update your layout to accommodate the changes. You can choose among the following Auto Picture Import settings:

✔ **On (Verify).** QuarkXPress checks the date and time stamp of the graphics files to see whether they have been modified. The program then displays a list of all the graphics files in your document so that you can decide whether to update the layout with the newest version.

✔ **On.** This setting tells QuarkXPress to automatically import the latest version of changed graphics files.

✔ **Off.** QuarkXPress does not check to see whether the source graphic files have been modified.

You should use On (Verify) or On, even if you don't expect graphic files to change much; that way, if the graphic files do happen to change, your document will contain the most recent versions of the files.

This option works only with graphics that you imported by choosing the QuarkXPress File⇨Get Picture command (⌘+E or Ctrl+E). Graphics that you pasted into QuarkXPress via the Clipboard are not affected, because the pasted file is copied into your document.

Master Page Items

The Master Page Items option controls what happens to text and picture boxes that are defined on a master page when you apply a different master page to your document pages. Your options are Keep Changes (the default) and Delete Changes. We recommend that you leave this setting on Keep Changes. Then, after applying a new master page, you can manually remove any unwanted elements that are left behind. Chapter 17 talks more about master pages.

Points/Inch and Ciceros/Cm

In the General pane of the Document Preferences dialog box, you can set the number of points per inch and the number of ciceros per centimeter through the Points/Inch and Ciceros/Cm options, respectively. QuarkXPress uses a default setting of 72 points per inch and 2.1967 ciceros per centimeter. You may want to change these settings because the actual number of points per inch is 72.271742, although most people now round that figure off to 72.

Snap Distance

To set the threshold for when objects snap to guides (assuming that Snap to Guides is selected in the View menu), enter a value in the Snap Distance text box. The Snap to Guides feature helps you to quickly align items with the non-printing ruler guides and page guides. The default setting for Snap Distance is 6 pixels (this means that when an item is within the threshold of 6 pixels from a guide, the item will "snap" into alignment with that guide); you can specify any value for the Snap Distance from 1 to 216 pixels. The larger the number, the farther away you can place an object from a guide and still have it automatically snap to the guide.

Greek Below and Greek Pictures

One option that is closely related to views is *greeking*. When you use greeking, QuarkXPress displays a gray area to represent text or pictures on the page; this makes the page display more quickly on your monitor. Turning on greeking speeds the display of your QuarkXPress document. When you print, images and text are unaffected by greeking (in other words, they print). The greeking options include:

- **Greek Below.** Tells QuarkXPress to greek the text display when text is below a certain point size. The default value is 7 points, but you can enter a value ranging from 2 to 720 points. To disable greeking, uncheck the Greek Below box.

- **Greek Pictures.** Tells QuarkXPress to display all unselected graphics as gray shapes, which speeds the display considerably. This feature is useful after you position and size your images and no longer need to see them in your layout. You can still look at a greeked picture by clicking it.

Accurate Blends

If you check the Accurate Blends option in the General pane of the Document Preferences dialog box, blends between two colors that you place in a box background (created via the Colors palette or the Box pane of the Modify dialog box) appear more accurately on monitors in 8-bit (256-color) monitor mode. Check this option if you're going to use blends.

Auto Constrain

The Auto Constrain option controls the behavior of boxes that are created within other boxes. If you check Auto Constrain, a box is created within another box — a picture box drawn inside a text box, for example — may not exceed the boundaries of the parent box (in this case, the text box). Neither can you move the box outside the parent box's boundaries. Most people should leave this default option unchecked.

The Item menu offers a toggle for the Constrain/Unconstrain command. This command can override the Auto Constrain setting for any selected box.

After you make changes in the General pane, click the OK button to save them.

Paragraph pane options

The Paragraph pane of the Document Preferences dialog box offers options for horizontal and vertical spacing: leading, baseline grid, and hyphenation (see Figure 19-6).

Figure 19-6: The Paragraph pane of the Document Preferences dialog box.

```
                    Default Document Preferences
  ┌ General │ Paragraph │ Character │ Tool │ Trapping ┐
  ┌─Leading────────────────┐  ┌─Hyphenation──────────────┐
  │ Auto Leading:  20%      │  │ Method: Expanded ▼        │
  │ Mode: Typesetting ▼     │  │                           │
  │ ☑ Maintain Leading      │  └───────────────────────────┘
  └─────────────────────────┘
  ┌─Baseline Grid───────────┐
  │ Start:      0.5"         │
  │ Increment:  12 pt        │
  └─────────────────────────┘
                              [ Cancel ]  [  OK  ]
```

The options are used as described in the following sections.

Leading

The Leading section contains the following options:

✔ **Auto Leading.** Auto Leading specifies the space between lines; the default is 20 percent, which sets leading at 120 percent of the current text size.

A better option is +2, which sets leading at the current text size plus 2 points — a more typical setting among typographers.

✔ **Mode.** Always choose the Typesetting option from the pop-up menu. (Typesetting mode measures leading from baseline to baseline, whereas Word Processing mode measures from top of character to top of character.) Word processing mode is an archaic holdover from pre-desktop publishing days, and there is never any reason to use it.

✔ **Maintain Leading.** This option causes text that falls below an intervening text or picture box to snap to the next baseline grid, rather than fall right after the intervening box's offset. This procedure ensures consistent text alignment across all columns.

Baseline Grid

The Baseline Grid section contains options that specify the default positions for lines of text:

✔ **Start.** The Start option indicates where the grid begins (how far from the top of the page).

✔ **Increment.** This setting determines the grid interval. Generally, the grid should start where the automatic text box starts, and the interval should be the same as body-text leading.

Hyphenation

Set the hyphenation option — Method — to Enhanced or Expanded. Standards exists only to keep the program compatible with earlier versions, which had a less accurate hyphenation algorithm.

After you make changes in the Paragraph pane, click OK to save them.

Character pane options

QuarkXPress lets you define typographic preferences. You specify your preferences in the Character pane of the Document Preferences dialog box (see Figure 19-7).

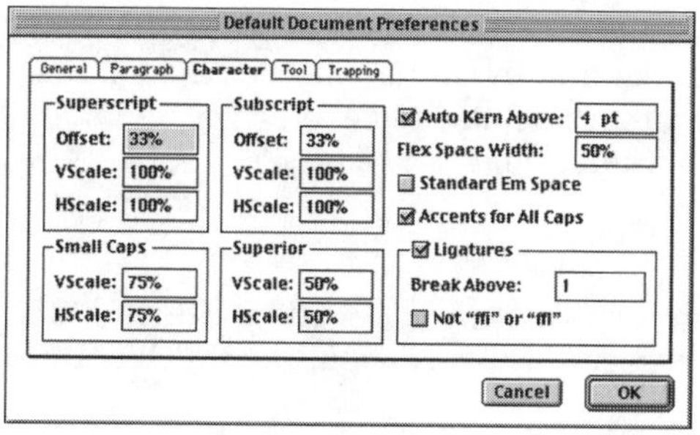

Figure 19-7:
The Character pane of the Document Preferences dialog box.

```
                Default Document Preferences
  General  Paragraph  Character  Tool  Trapping

  ┌Superscript─┐  ┌Subscript──┐   ☑ Auto Kern Above: 4 pt
  Offset:  33%     Offset:  33%    Flex Space Width:  50%
  VScale:  100%    VScale:  100%   ☐ Standard Em Space
  HScale:  100%    HScale:  100%   ☑ Accents for All Caps

  ┌Small Caps─┐   ┌Superior───┐   ┌☑ Ligatures──────┐
  VScale:  75%     VScale:  50%    Break Above:   1
  HScale:  75%     HScale:  50%    ☐ Not "ffi" or "ffl"

                              Cancel      OK
```

Like many changes that you make in the Document Preferences dialog box, any changes of the settings in the Character pane affect only the current document. If no document is open, the changes affect all subsequent new documents.

Several options in the Character pane affect character styles. These options include the four boxes labeled Superscript, Subscript, Small Caps, and Superior.

Superiors are special superscript characters that always align along the *cap line,* which is the height of a capital letter in the current typeface. Superiors typically are used in footnotes.

Superscript and Subscript

The Superscript and Subscript sections share the following options:

- ✔ **Offset.** Dictates how far below or above the baseline QuarkXPress shifts a subscripted or superscripted character. The default settings are 33 percent for both Subscript and Superscript. We prefer 35 percent for superscript and 30 percent for subscript.

- ✔ **VScale** and **HScale.** Determine scaling for the subscript or superscript. Although the default is 100 percent, this setting is useful only for typewritten documents. Typeset documents typically use a smaller size for subscripts and superscripts — usually, between 60 and 80 percent of the text size. The two values should be the same.

Small Caps and Superior

The options in the Small Caps and Superior sections are identical, even though these attributes are very different. VScale and HScale determine the scaling for the small cap or superior. The two values should be the same, because small caps and superiors typically are not distorted along one dimension. Usually, a small cap's scale should be between 65 percent and 80 percent of the normal text, and a superior's scale should be between 50 percent and 65 percent.

Auto Kern Above

Auto Kern Above lets you define the point size at which QuarkXPress automatically kerns letter pairs. Kerning is the process of adjusting the space between two letters so that the letters have a better appearance. For laser-printed documents, 10 points is fine, but typeset documents should be set at a smaller value, such as 8 points.

Flex Space Width

This option lets you define the value for a *flex space,* which is a user-defined space. The default is 50 percent, which is about the width of the letter *t,* called a thin space. A better setting — because you're more likely to use an em space than a thin space — is 200 percent, which is equal to an em space (the width of the letter *M*).

Standard Em Space

This option determines how QuarkXPress calculates the width of an em — a standard measurement in typography upon which most other spacing measurements are based. If you check this box, QuarkXPress uses the typographic measurement (the width of the letter *M*, which is usually equal to the current point size). Unchecked, QuarkXPress uses the width of two zeroes, which is how QuarkXPress has always calculated an em space.

Accents for All Caps

If checked, the option lets accented characters retain their accents if you apply the All Caps attribute to them. In many publications, the style is to drop accents from capitalized letters. This feature lets you control whether this style is implemented automatically.

Ligatures

A ligature is a set of joined characters. The characters are joined because the shapes almost blend together by default, so typographers of yore decided to make them blend together naturally. When you check the ligatures box, QuarkXPress automatically replaces occurrences of *fi, ffi, fl,* and *ffl* with their ligatured equivalents, both when you enter text and when you import it. If you uncheck the Ligatures box, all ligatures in your document are translated to standard character combinations. Not all fonts support ligatures, and many sans-serif typefaces look like their nonligature equivalents. This feature is nice because it means that you don't have to worry about adding ligatures manually; it's also nice because it does not affect spell checking.

> ✔ **Not "ffi" or "ffl":** Some people don't like using ligatures for *ffi* and *ffl*. Check the Not "ffi" or "ffl" box to prevent these ligatures from being used automatically. When you search for text in the Find/Change dialog box, you can enter **ffi**, and QuarkXPress finds the ligature.

> ✔ **Break Above:** The Break Above option for ligatures allows you to set how a ligature is handled in a loosely tracked line. You can enter a value ranging from 0 to 100. That value is the number of units of tracking (each unit is $1/200$th of an em space) at which QuarkXPress breaks apart a ligature to prevent awkward spacing.

Windows does not support ligatures. As a result, Mac files with Ligatures options selected, when moved to QuarkXPress Windows, retain the standard characters.

After you make changes in the Character pane, click OK to save them.

Setting Tool Specifications

QuarkXPress lets you customize how its basic tools work by changing settings in the Tool pane of the Document Preferences dialog box. To set the defaults, first select the tool that you want to modify. Unavailable options are grayed out. After you make changes, click OK to record the changes or Cancel to undo them.

If you access the Tool pane of the Document Preferences dialog box with no document open, all defaults apply to all subsequently created documents. Otherwise, the defaults apply only to subsequently created boxes and lines for the current document.

The tools that you can customize fall into the following groups:

- ✔ **Zoom tool.** At the top of the list is the Zoom tool. You can change the minimum and maximum zoom views to any value between 10 and 800 percent, in increments of 1 percent.

- ✔ **Box tools.** You can set the item settings for all the Text Box and Picture Box tools. You can establish settings for options normally available for the individual boxes via the Item menu's Modify, Frame, and Runaround commands. See Chapter 3 for more information on box settings.

  The ability to customize certain settings comes in handy. You can, for example, give oval picture boxes an offset of 1 pica or set text boxes to have a 3-point frame and a green background.

- ✔ **Drawing tools.** You can establish defaults for new lines that you draw with the Line tools. You can set most regular line options that are normally available through the Item menu. You can also set other line-specification and runaround options, such as line color and weight.

To set the preferences for all text or picture boxes at the same time, click a text or picture box in the scrollable list and then click Select Similar Types before you click Modify. To set the preferences for all boxes of the same shape, click a box that uses that shape and then click Select Similar Shapes before you click Modify.

The Document Preferences dialog box contains another pane, Trapping, which lets you specify defaults for how QuarkXPress traps colors and objects when you separate a document into its color plates. This feature is very advanced, and we recommend that beginners not change the defaults.

Chapter 20

Details for Cross-Platform Users

Face it: The Mac is the platform of choice for desktop publishing. But Windows has been making inroads in the past couple of years, and top programs such as QuarkXPress are now available in Windows versions that have almost all the same features as their Mac counterparts. The few differences between the two QuarkXPress programs are almost always due to differences between the Mac and Windows. Whether you're a cross-platform user who needs to understand the discrepancies between the two versions or a Windows user who is looking for advice that's specific to your needs, read on.

Where the Mac and Windows Differ

Before you get to the differences between the Mac and Windows versions of QuarkXPress itself, knowing about some differences between the Mac and Windows is helpful. Why look at such basic stuff in a book about QuarkXPress? Because the underlying platform differences affect operations everywhere — including QuarkXPress. Table 20-1 lists Mac and Windows equivalents.

Keyboard

PC and Mac keyboards may look alike, but actually, they differ in two major ways.

Table 20-1	**Mac and Windows Equivalents**	
Item	*Windows*	*Macintosh*
Keys		
	Ctrl	⌘ (Command)
	Alt	Option
	Shift	Shift
	no equivalent	Control
	Delete	Delete
	Backspace	Delete
	right mouse button	Control+mouse button*
Close window	Ctrl+F4	⌘+W
Exit program	Alt+F4	⌘+Q
Files		
Document	.QXD	
Template	.QXT	
Library	.QXL	
XTensions	.XNT	

In Mac OS 8 and in some programs in earlier versions of the Mac OS

First, some of the control keys are different, at least in their appearances and names. The Mac has a key that looks like a butterfly (⌘); it's called the Command key, and it's basically the same as a PC's Ctrl key. The Mac also has a key labeled Option, which is basically the same as the PC's Alt. Some Mac keyboards also have a key labeled Control — which is *not* the same as the Command key or the PC's Ctrl key.

The other significant difference is in how you delete. PCs use a key labeled Delete (or Del) to delete text to the right of the insertion point (the thing that Mac folks call the pointer) and a Backspace key to delete text to the left of the cursor. (This key is a holdover from typewriters.) Some Mac keyboards have a Del key, but many don't. On a Mac, the Backspace key is usually called Delete. When a PC user would press Delete, you press Shift+Delete on a Mac. That can feel weird — QuarkXPress for Mac won't allow you to use Del instead of Shift+Delete to delete a range of text, even on keyboards that have the Del key. Instead, you can use Delete for only one character at a time.

You've probably noticed all those underlines in your Windows menus and dialog box options. Those underlines mean that you can access a function by holding down the Alt key and pressing the underlined letter. So even if a shortcut is assigned to a specific function, you always have the option of using the underlined-letter sequence. Ctrl+P, for example, is the shortcut for printing in QuarkXPress — but you also can press Alt+F Alt+P, which opens the File menu and then the Print dialog box.

Files and directories

Almost everyone knows that Windows 95 ended the PC's dumb naming structure: names of eight letters, followed by a period and then by up to three more letters.

Macintosh files follow these rules:

✔ Names are limited to 31 characters.

✔ Any characters can be used except for colons (:), which the Macintosh System software uses internally to separate the folder name (which is not visible on-screen) from the filename.

✔ Case does not matter: FILE, file, and File are all considered to be the same name. If you have a file named FILE and create or copy a file named file, FILE is overwritten.

Windows files follow these rules:

✔ Names are limited to 250 characters.

✔ Names must also have a file extension of up to three characters. Programs almost always add the file extension automatically to identify the file type. A period separates the filename from the extension (FILENAME.EXT). Windows hides these file extensions from view unless you choose View⇨Options in a drive or folder window to make Windows display them.

For QuarkXPress, the extension is .QXD. Similarly, .QXT designates a QuarkXPress template; .QXL, a QuarkXPress library; .QDT, a spelling dictionary; and .XNT, a QuarkXTension add-on program. On a Mac, you just look for the icons.

✔ Names can use any characters except for most punctuation characters. Windows uses pipes (|), colons (:), periods (.), asterisks (*), double quotes ("), less-than symbols (<), greater-than symbols (>), question marks (?), slashes (/), and backslashes (\) to separate parts of paths (file locations, such as drives and folders) or to structure commands. A period is used as the separator between a filename and an extension.

> ✔ Case does not matter: FILE, file, and File are all considered to be the same name. If you have a file named FILE and create or copy a file named file, FILE is overwritten.

The simplest way to ensure that you won't have problems with transferred files looking for incompatible names is to use a naming convention that satisfies both Windows and Mac standards. You should:

✔ Limit filenames to 27 characters or fewer.

✔ Always include the PC file extension (which adds 4 characters to the full name, hitting the Mac limit of 31). Use .QXD for documents, .QXT for templates, .QDT for auxiliary dictionaries, .QPJ for printer styles, and .KRN for kerning tables. Typical extensions for cross-platform graphics are .TIF for TIFF, .EPS for Encapsulated PostScript, .AI for Adobe Illustrator, .PCT for PICT, .PCX for PC Paintbrush, .BMP and .RLE for Microsoft bitmap, .GIF for Graphics Interchange Format, .CGM for Computer Graphics Metafiles, .WMF for Windows metafile, .CDR for CorelDraw, .PLT for HPGL plots, and .SCT or .CT for Scitex.

✔ Don't use the pipe (|), colon (:), period (.), asterisk (*), double quote ("), less-than symbol (<), greater-than symbol (>), question mark (?), slash (/), or backslash (\) characters.

Environment controls

On a Mac, you find a folder called Control Panels (also available via the Apple menu) that contains mini-programs for changing System settings, such as colors, network options, and mouse tracking. In Windows, most of these mini-programs are stored in a program called Control Panel, which you access by choosing Start➪Settings. (The Start button is the Microsoft version of the Apple menu.)

The Control Panel programs and other mini-programs allow you to manage basic operations in Windows. The following sections cover the three that are most important to a QuarkXPress user: printing, multitasking (switching between active programs), and fonts.

Printing

You set up your printers by using the Windows Control Panel's Add Printers icon, but you also can switch printers by using the Printer Setup dialog box in your programs. (Sometimes, this Printer Setup dialog box has its own entry in the File menu; sometimes, it's an option in the Print dialog box. How you access the dialog box depends on the design of the program that you're using. In QuarkXPress, the Printer Setup dialog box is available both ways.) On a Mac, you have to use a program called the Chooser to switch printers — a real pain — or you can use the new Desktop Printer icon.

Multitasking

If you're using QuarkXPress, you probably have a relatively good system — a Power PC-based Mac or a Pentium-based PC. After all, publishing demands solid resources. And you probably have more than one program loaded in memory at a time. The fancy name for this situation is *multitasking* (back in the System 6 days, the Mac called multitasking MultiFinder).

On the Mac, you can switch to and from all active programs via the pull-down menu at the far-right end of the menu bar — the Application menu, although practically no one knows its name. The currently active program's icon appears in the top-right corner of the window; if you select that icon, a menu of all active programs appears.

In Windows, all active programs are available through the taskbar, which is always visible, usually at the bottom of the screen. If you minimize a program — that is, if you click the bar icon in the top-right corner of the program's menu — its icon appears in the taskbar. You can double-click that icon to make it active.

In Windows, you can cycle among open programs by pressing Alt+Tab.

Fonts

Both Macs and Windows PCs support TrueType and PostScript Type 1 fonts (usually through Adobe Type Manager), but fonts are slightly different on the two platforms. In some cases the names differ only slightly, such as Helvetica Compressed on the Mac and HelveticaCompressed in Windows — the Windows names don't have spaces within them. In most cases, Windows fonts have some characters (such as $1/4$ and š) that Mac fonts usually don't. At the same time, though, Mac fonts have some characters — such as Σ, ∂, , and _Δ — that Windows fonts usually don't (even if they do have the same name).

Fonts that have the same name may have different spacing and even character widths. This situation usually occurs with fonts created when an Iron Wall stood between the Mac and the PC — back in the olden days of the '80s, when developers didn't worry about cross-platform users.

You can translate fonts from Mac format to Windows format, or vice versa, with programs such as Macromedia's Fontographer, which is available for both Windows and the Mac. (For more information on this program, call 415-252-2000 or visit the Web site www.macromedia.com.) We recommend that you do your translation on the Mac. Because the Mac's internal file format is weird compared with the PC's, Mac font files created on a PC don't always survive the translation process. Font files are more susceptible to this problem than are data files (such as QuarkXPress, graphics, or text files), because on the Mac, a font is a bit like a program; therefore, it has resource information that can easily get corrupted when it's stored on a PC. We're not saying that you *can't* create Mac fonts on Windows, just that we've had better luck creating them on the Mac. You also can use this program to translate PostScript to TrueType or vice versa.

Not Quite Clones

Even considering the differences between Windows and the Mac, QuarkXPress has some other differences that have less to do with platform differences than with . . . well, just differences in what Quark decided to do in each version. The list is not huge, but it may look bigger than it is because of the illustrations that show the differences.

View controls

To change your view percentage on a Mac, you press Control+V — remember, Control is not the Mac's ⌘ key or the PC's Ctrl key — to quickly highlight the view-percentage box (in the bottom-left corner of the QuarkXPress screen) so that you can enter a new zoom amount. In Windows, press Ctrl+Alt+V.

Quark's Mac and Windows versions also have differences in their Application Preferences dialog box's Display pane, as Figure 20-1 shows. (To display this dialog box, choose Edit⇨Preferences⇨Application, or press Shift+Option+⌘+Y or Ctrl+Alt+Shift+Y.)

Figure 20-1:
Differences in Mac (left) and Windows (right) video support result in a few different options in the Applications Preferences dialog box.

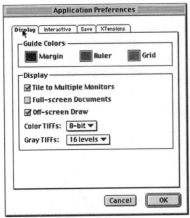

One difference is that Windows QuarkXPress offers a Display DPI Value option. This option is, in essence, a zoom control that stays in place for all QuarkXPress documents until you change it again; if you make the number larger, QuarkXPress shows a more magnified image.

Another difference is that Windows video supports multiple resolutions. You probably know that you can change your desktop from, say, 640 by 480 pixels to 800 by 600 or 1,024 by 768. Such a change makes everything smaller but increases the size of the working area. Until 1994, Macs couldn't work this trick easily, and today, switching resolutions on a Mac still requires a PC-style monitor, although the Mac's Monitors & Sounds control panel now includes the ability to change resolution if you're using a PC-style monitor. The Mac offers several controls that handle the display of documents across multiple monitors. Because Windows doesn't support tiled monitors, Windows QuarkXPress has no equivalent.

The most obvious difference between Windows and the Mac is the View menu. The commands that determine how document windows display are in different places, as Figure 20-2 shows.

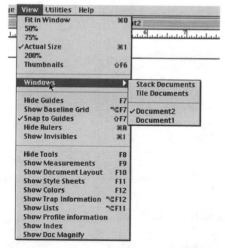

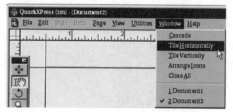

Figure 20-2:
Document windows controls differ in the two versions of QuarkXPress (Mac at top, Windows at bottom).

In Mac QuarkXPress, the View menu has a Windows option with a submenu, whereas in Windows, those options are in their own menu, called Window. Both versions of QuarkXPress support tiled views, which are the automatic arrangement of multiple open QuarkXPress layouts. But the Windows version supports several arrangements — tile horizontally (left to right), tile vertically (top to bottom), cascade (overlapping stacks), and iconized — whereas the Mac version supports only vertical tiling and cascading (stacking). Finally, Windows QuarkXPress has a menu command that closes all the document windows; on the Mac, you use the keyboard shortcut Option+⌘+W (for which no Windows equivalent exists).

Typography

Because Windows doesn't support ligatures — letters that are merged, such as fi and fl — Windows QuarkXPress doesn't offer ligature controls in the Character pane of the Document Preferences dialog box, as the Mac version does. (To display this dialog box, choose Edit⇨Preferences⇨Document, or press ⌘+Y or Ctrl+Y.) Figure 20-3 shows the different dialog boxes.

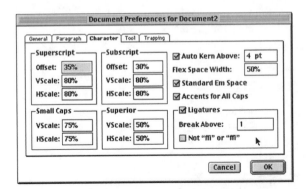

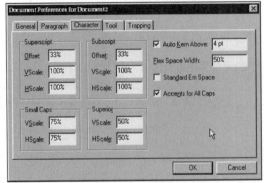

Figure 20-3: Macintosh QuarkXPress (top) supports ligatures, but Windows QuarkXPress (bottom) does not.

If you want to use ligatures in Windows, you need to use a typeface that has them as symbols. Notice that if you use ligatures on the Mac and bring the QuarkXPress document into Windows QuarkXPress, the ligatures are replaced by the standard letter combinations, and they translate back into ligatures when they're loaded into Mac QuarkXPress again. It's unlikely — but possible, in some rare circumstances — that this ligature replacement could affect the text flow as the file is transferred back and forth.

Mac QuarkXPress comes with an XTension called Font Creator, which (if you install it) allows you to create variants of typefaces — as long as they are PostScript Type 1 Multiple Master typefaces. Windows QuarkXPress has no such utility, but you can use Adobe Type Manager 3.0 and later (a must-have font-scaler for anyone who does publishing) to get the same result. Figure 20-4 shows the Mac QuarkXPress Multiple Master editing facility and the corresponding feature of Windows Adobe Type Manager 4.0.

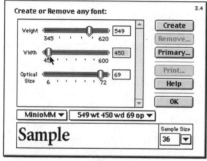

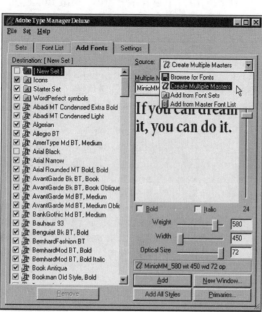

Figure 20-4: Mac QuarkXPress comes with a utility that allows you to create variants of Multiple Master fonts in QuarkXPress (top). In Windows, you need to use a separate program, such as Adobe Type Manager 4.0 (bottom).

Font names on the Mac and Windows can differ, so even if you have the same fonts installed on both systems, you may get a message saying that a font is missing when you open a document. If you click the List Fonts button when you get that message, you can tell QuarkXPress immediately which font to use instead. Alternatively, you can choose Utilities⇨Font Usage to open the Font Usage dialog box, which allows you to do the same thing at any time.

Linked objects

Both versions of QuarkXPress support hot links to objects in other programs. On the Mac, the method is called Publish and Subscribe; in Windows, it's called Object Linking and Embedding (OLE, for short). In both cases, the theory is that you can have your layout retrieve the latest version of a chart or other graphic as soon as the graphic is changed in the original program.

In practice, using hot links requires significant trade-offs:

- ✔ You can't link text this way unless you want it to be converted to an image.
- ✔ If both programs aren't loaded, the object doesn't get updated automatically when changed in its originating program.
- ✔ You need a great deal of memory to use this feature.
- ✔ You can't use most of the QuarkXPress image controls on these images.

We recommend that you not worry too much about hot links, but if you do use them, look at Figures 20-5 and 20-6.

Figure 20-5 shows the differences in menu options. In Windows, you get two sets of choices. The first set is Paste Special and Paste Link, which you can use if you created an OLE object in another program by copying it to the Windows Clipboard (press Ctrl+C or Ctrl+X to do that). Whether the object is embedded (Paste Special) or linked (Paste Link) depends on the application that created it.

The second set of choices is just Insert Object. You use Insert Object to launch a program in which you want to create the OLE object in. (Figure 20-6 shows the Paste Special and Insert Object dialog boxes.)

Then you have the Links and Object options, which allow you to update and edit an OLE object, respectively, whether the object was brought into QuarkXPress via Paste Link, Paste Special, or Insert Object. On the Mac, you have the Subscribe To and Subscriber options to import and update a hot-linked object respectively. The Mac's Subscriber options are basically the same as the Windows Links and Object options.

Figure 20-5:
Because of
different
hot-link
technologies,
the Mac
(left) and
Windows
(right)
versions of
QuarkXPress
have
different
menu
options for
linked-file
import.

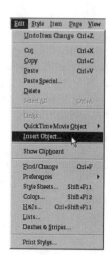

Figure 20-6:
Two options
for creating
hot links in
Windows:
by pasting
in a link
created in
the
Windows
Clipboard
by another
program
(bottom) or
by deciding
what kind of
object you
want to be
linked in
and then
launching a
program
that can
create it
(top).

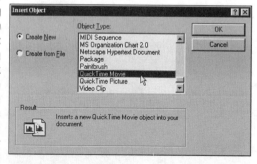

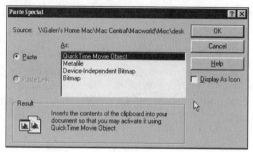

Item manipulation

When you create objects — lines, picture boxes, and text boxes — in QuarkXPress, they are automatically layered so that the most recently created or pasted object is on top of the preceding one. Sometimes, you want to change the stacking order so that a particular box overprints another. Both versions of QuarkXPress offer controls for moving objects, but Windows QuarkXPress makes it easier to use all the controls. In both versions, you can send an object to the front or the back via commands in the Item menu (see Figure 20-7). But in Windows QuarkXPress, you also can move an object one layer at a time by choosing Item⇨Bring Forward or Item⇨Send Backward. (To get these options in the Mac version of QuarkXPress, you have to hold down the Option key before opening the Item menu — and then the Send to Back and Bring to Front options are removed from the menu.)

Figure 20-7:
Windows
QuarkXPress
(right) gives
you finer
control of
the stacking
order for
objects
than Mac
QuarkXPress
does by
letting you
move
objects one
layer at a
time.

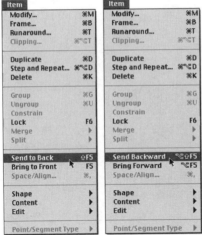

Mac QuarkXPress comes with a utility called Frame Editor, which allows you to create custom frames for use with your text and picture boxes. Figure 20-8 shows this utility's opening dialog box. Windows QuarkXPress can use these frames — it imports them directly from the QuarkXPress document, so don't worry about transferring a special file over — but it can't create its own, because no Windows version of Frame Editor exists.

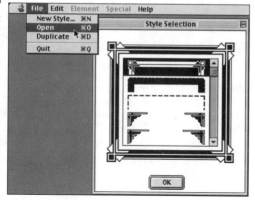

Figure 20-8:
The Mac utility Frame Editor lets you create custom frames for QuarkXPress. Windows QuarkXPress has no equivalent.

EPS pages

Through the Save Page As EPS dialog box, you can export a page of your layout as an EPS file. (To display this dialog box, choose File⊅Save Page As EPS, or press Shift+Option+⌘+S or Ctrl+Alt+Shift+S.) A slight difference exists in the dialog box in the Mac and Windows versions. The Mac version allows you to save the EPS preview image in PICT or TIFF format (or to have no preview), whereas the Windows version gives you a choice of just TIFF and no preview.

Shortcuts

QuarkXPress uses the same shortcuts on both platforms, translating ⌘ to Ctrl and Option to Alt, in almost every case. See Chapter 21 for a complete listing.

Windows 95, Windows NT 4, and Mac OS 8 all use a technique called contextual menus to save you time. By right-clicking an item in Windows or Control+clicking the Mac, you get a menu of options just for that item. This feature saves you time going through menus, dialog boxes, and palettes. QuarkXPress 4.0, unfortunately, really skimps on contextual menus. The feature isn't supported in the Mac version, and the Windows version supports just three contextual menus.

How to Transfer Files

Although the file format for QuarkXPress documents and templates is the same on the two platforms, the Windows version may not recognize a Mac-generated file as a QuarkXPress file unless you do one of the following two things:

✔ Add the file extension .QXD to the Mac-generated file's name.

✔ Choose Display All Files from the File Type pop-up menu in the Open dialog box. (To display this dialog box, choose File⇨Open or press Ctrl+O.)

On the Mac, you may not be able to double-click a Windows QuarkXPress file to get QuarkXPress to launch. Instead, you have to launch QuarkXPress separately and then open the file from within QuarkXPress.

QuarkXPress for Macintosh Version 4.0 can read Windows Version 3.1, 3.3, and 4.0 files. QuarkXPress for Windows Version 4.0 can read Macintosh 3.0, 3.1, 3.2, 3.3, and 4.0 files. (QuarkXPress had no Windows Version 3.2.)

Which elements transfer

The following elements can be transferred across platforms, with the noted limitations:

✔ **Graphics.** Any graphics that are not supported by the platform version are replaced during printing by their PICT preview images (on the Mac) or Windows Metafile preview images (in Windows). The graphics links are retained, however, so if you move the document back to the originating platform, the original graphics are again available for printing.

✔ **Graphics previews.** Some PICT previews from the Mac and some Windows Metafile previews in Windows do not translate correctly when they are transferred. You must reimport or update the link to the graphic to generate a new preview.

✔ **Colors.** Colors are retained and can be imported across platforms.

✔ **Color profiles.** Although color-profile files cannot be exchanged across the two platforms, Mac and Windows QuarkXPress retain color-profile information from the other platform's files. And if both platforms have color profiles for the same device (monitor, scanner, printer, and so on), QuarkXPress applies the correct color profiles. If a color profile is not available on the new platform, you can apply a new profile or ignore the issue. (If you ignore the issue, the correct profile is in place when you bring the document back to the original platform.) If you print with a missing profile, QuarkXPress substitutes the default profile based on the color model used (RGB, CMYK, or Hexachrome).

✔ **Style sheets.** Style sheets are retained and can be imported across platforms.

✔ **H&J sets.** H&J sets for hyphenation and justification are retained and can be imported across platforms.

✔ **Lists.** Lists are retained and can be imported across platforms.

✔ **Dashes and stripes.** Dashes and stripes are retained and can be imported across platforms.

✔ **Bitmap frames.** Bitmap frames created on the Mac are retained in Windows documents. Windows QuarkXPress cannot create bitmap frames.

✔ **Hyphenation exceptions.** Hyphenation exceptions are retained.

✔ **Document preferences.** Document preferences are retained, but the XPress Preferences file cannot be shared across platforms.

✔ **Print styles.** Print styles are retained. These styles can be exported and imported across platforms.

✔ **Auxiliary spelling dictionaries.** Auxiliary spelling dictionaries can be used on both platforms.

✔ **Kerning data.** Kerning data exported from the Mac can be imported into Windows. We do not recommend doing this kind of transfer, however, because the font characteristics on the two platforms are different enough that you should customize the kerning for each platform separately.

✔ **XTensions.** Cool Blends and other XTensions must be present on both platforms if you are moving documents that use XTensions' features. If you don't have an XTension in, say, Windows and try to load a Mac document that uses that XTension's capabilities, you may get an error message saying that the document cannot be opened.

✔ **Document previews.** Although the Windows version does not save preview images for the Open dialog box, such previews created on the Mac are retained even if the document is moved to Windows and back.

To import elements, click the Append button in the relevant dialog box. To export and import elements, click the Export and Import buttons in the relevant dialog box.

Which elements don't transfer

Quark has removed almost every barrier between Mac and Windows in the latest version of QuarkXPress. In Version 4.0, only libraries cannot be moved across platforms. The database systems underlying the libraries are not compatible, so the libraries cannot be shared.

File-transfer products

Moving files between Macs and Windows PCs is easier now than ever before, thanks to products for both platforms that allow each machine to read the other's disks — floppy disks, removable disks such as Zip disks, and even hard disks. Here is a brief summary of the major products:

- ✔ **Easy Open and PC Exchange.** The combination of Mac OS Easy Open and PC Exchange, both of which are included in the Mac System software, allows you to use Windows disks in a Mac floppy-disk drive or removable drive; the Mac recognizes files immediately and knows which applications are compatible with each type of PC file. PC Exchange also can automatically add the right Mac icon and file-type information to a Windows file that is transferred to the Mac, based on the Windows file's extension. (For more information, call Apple Computer at 408-996-1010 or visit their Web site at www.apple.com.)

- ✔ **DOS Mounter 95.** This Mac utility, from Software Architects, is similar to PC Exchange, except that it allows you to choose between Windows 95 filenames and Windows 3.1 filenames. (For more information, call 206-487-0122 or visit the Web site at www.softarch.com.)

- ✔ **Here & Now.** Software Architects' Here & Now gives Windows PCs the capability to read and write Mac disks.

- ✔ **MacLinkPlus.** This Mac program, from DataViz, includes file translation (DataViz's own translators). The program relies on PC Exchange or DOS Mounter 95 to make PC disks accessible on the Mac. The version called MacLinkPlus/PC Connect includes a serial cable through which you can connect a Mac to a PC, making sort of a two-computer network. (For more information, call 203-268-0030 or visit the Web site at www.dataviz.com.)

- ✔ **MacOpener.** The DataViz MacOpener program allows PCs to read and write Mac disks, although it includes none of the file-translation features of the other DataViz products.

- ✔ **Conversions Plus.** The DataViz Conversions Plus gives Windows PCs the capability to read and write Mac disks, as well as to translate file formats.

- ✔ **MacDrive 95.** Media4 Productions' MacDrive 95 works like the Data Viz MacOpener, but just under Windows 95; the NT 4.0-compatible version, called MacDrive 98, should be ready in mid-1998. (For more information, call 515-225-7409 or visit the Web site at www.media4.com.)

How to use a cross-platform network

Another method of transferring files is using a cross-platform network. Here are some products that can assist you:

- **Timbuktu Pro.** The Netopia Timbuktu Pro allows both Macs and Windows 95 PCs to exchange files via an Ethernet or TCP/IP network. (For more information, call 510-814-5000 or visit www.farallon.com.)

- **PC MacLAN.** Miramar Systems' PC MacLAN allows a Windows PC to be a server to Macs and other PCs via an Ethernet or TCP/IP network; Miramar has one version for Windows 95 and another for Windows NT 4.0. Miramar also has a Windows 95-only version that allows PCs to dial into Mac-based Apple Remote Access (ARA) networks. (For more information, call 805-966-2432 or visit www.miramarsys.com.)

- **NetWare IPX.** For larger networks, you'll likely want to use networks based on the Novell NetWare IPX protocol and on Ethernet wiring. You need a consultant or in-house network manager to set up such large networks.

Part VI
The Part of Tens

The 5th Wave   By Rich Tennant

"It says,' Seth - Please see us about your idea to wrap newsletter text around company logo. Production.'"

In this part . . .

This part of the book gives a quick rundown of tools and techniques that help you get the most out of QuarkXPress with the least amount of muss and fuss: Shortcut keys, Web publishing tools, and some great online resources. In fact, you might even be tempted to start reading here and then go back to Chapter 1, but don't. The concepts in this book will make more sense to you if you read the other parts of the book first.

Chapter 21
More than Ten Shortcuts

In This Chapter

▶ Comprehensive list of QuarkXPress keyboard and mouse shortcuts for both the Mac and Windows

QuarkXPress has tons and tons of shortcuts. You won't memorize most of the shortcuts, but you'll no doubt find yourself using one or two all the time. Following is a complete list, broken down by task.

Opening/Closing/Saving

Action	Macintosh	Windows
New publication	⌘+N	Ctrl+N
New library	Option+⌘+N	Ctrl+Alt+N
Open publication	⌘+O	Ctrl+O
Save publication	⌘+S	Ctrl+S
Save as	Option+⌘+S	Ctrl+Shift+S
Get text or picture	⌘+E	Ctrl+E
Save text	Option+⌘+E	Ctrl+Alt+E
Save page as EPS	Option+Shift+⌘+S	Ctrl+Alt+Shift+S
Append	Option+⌘+A	Ctrl+Alt+A
Close current document	⌘+W	Ctrl+F4
Close all documents	Option+⌘+W	not available
Quit	⌘+Q	Ctrl+Q or Alt+F4

Miscellaneous

Action	Macintosh	Windows
Print	⌘+P	Ctrl+P
Undo	⌘+Z	Ctrl+Z
Revert dialog-box values	Shift+⌘+Z	Ctrl+Shift+Z
Help	Help	F1

Preferences/Setup

Action	Macintosh	Windows
Application preferences	Option+Shift+⌘+Y	Ctrl+Alt+Shift+Y
Document preferences	⌘+Y	Ctrl+Y
Paragraph preferences	Option+⌘+Y	Ctrl+Alt+Y
Trapping preferences	Option+Shift+F12	Ctrl+Shift+F12
Document setup	Option+Shift+⌘+P	Ctrl+Alt+Shift+P
Page setup	Option+⌘+P	Ctrl+Alt+P

View

Action	Macintosh	Windows
100%	⌘+1	Ctrl+1
Fit in windows	⌘+0	Ctrl+0
200%	Option+⌘+click	Ctrl+Alt+click
Thumbnails	Shift+F6	Shift+F6
Change view percentage	Ctrl+V	Ctrl+Alt+V
Force redraw	Option+⌘+period	Shift+Esc
Halt redraw	⌘+period	Esc
Go to page	⌘+J	Ctrl+J
Zoom in	⌘+click	Ctrl+spacebar+click

Action	Macintosh	Windows
Zoom out	Option+⌘+click	Ctrl+Alt+spacebar+ click
Windows submenu (tile, stack)	Shift+click title bar	Alt+W
Show/hide invisibles	⌘+I	Ctrl+I
Show/hide rulers	⌘+R	Ctrl+R
Show/hide guides	F7	F7
Show/hide baseline grid	Option+F7	Ctrl+F7
Snap to guides	Shift+F7	Shift+F7

Palettes

Action	Macintosh	Windows
Show/hide Measurements	F9	F9
Show/hide Tools palette palette	F8	F8
Show/hide Document Layout palette	F10	F4
Show/hide Style Sheets palette	F11	F11
Show/hide Colors palette	F12	F12
Show/hide Trap Information palette	Option+F12	Ctrl+F12
Show/hide Lists palette	Option+F11	Ctrl+F11
Show/hide Index palette	Option+⌘+I	Ctrl+Alt+I
Show font use	F13	not available
Show picture use	Option+F13	not available

Navigation

Action	Macintosh	Windows
Page grabber hand	Option+drag	Alt+drag
Enable/disable live scroll	Option+drag scroll box	not available
Display master page	Shift+F10	Shift+F4
Display following master page	Option+F10	Ctrl+Shift+F4
Display preceding master page	Option+Shift+F10	Ctrl+Shift+F3
Display document page	Shift+F10	Shift+F4
Following page	Shift+PageUp or Ctrl+Shift+L	Shift+PageDown
Preceding page	Shift+PageDown or Ctrl+Shift+K	Shift+PageUp
First page	Shift+Home or Ctrl+Shift+A	Ctrl+PageUp
Last page	Shift+End or Ctrl+Shift+D	Ctrl+PageDown
Beginning of document	Home or Ctrl+A	Ctrl+Home
End of document	End or Ctrl+D	Ctrl+End

Object Selection

Action	Macintosh	Windows
Select all	⌘+A	Ctrl+A
Select hidden item	Option+Shift+⌘+click	Ctrl+Alt+Shift+click
Multiple selection (series)	Shift+click	Shift+click
Multiple selection (noncontiguous)	⌘+click	Ctrl+click

Moving Objects

Action	Macintosh	Windows
Nudge selected object 1 point	arrow keys	arrow keys
Nudge selected object $1/10$ point	Option+arrow keys	Alt+arrow keys
Constrain movement	Shift+drag	Shift+drag
Cut	⌘+X or F2	Ctrl+X
Delete	⌘+K	Ctrl+K
Copy	⌘+C or F3	Ctrl+C
Paste	⌘+V or F4	Ctrl+V

Item Commands

Action	Macintosh	Windows
Modify	⌘+M	Ctrl+M
Edit shape	Shift+F4	F10
Frame	⌘+B	Ctrl+B
Clipping	Option+⌘+T	Ctrl+Alt+T
Edit clipping path	Option+Shift+F4	Ctrl+Shift+F10
Runaround	⌘+T	Ctrl+T
Edit runaround	Option+F4	Ctrl+F10
Duplicate	⌘+D	Ctrl+D
Step and repeat	Option+⌘+D	Ctrl+Alt+D
Space/align	⌘+comma	Ctrl+comma
Send to back	Shift+F5	Shift+F5
Bring to front	F5	F5
Send backward	Option+Shift+F5	Ctrl+Shift+F5
Bring forward	Option+F5	Ctrl+F5
Lock/unlock	F6	F6
Group	⌘+G	Ctrl+G
Ungroup	⌘+U	Ctrl+U

Text Selection

Action	Macintosh	Windows
Word	Double-click	Double-click
Paragraph	Quadruple-click	Quadruple-click
Line	Triple-click	Triple-click
Story	⌘+A or quintuple-click	Ctrl+A or quintuple-click
Character to left	Shift+←	Shift+←
Character to right	Shift+→	Shift+→
Word to left	Shift+⌘+←	Ctrl+Shift+←
Word to right	Shift+⌘+→	Ctrl+Shift+→
Up one line	Shift+↑	Shift+↑
Down one line	Shift+↓	Shift+↓
To start of line	Shift+Option+⌘+←	Ctrl+Alt+Shift+← or Shift+Home
To end of line	Shift+Option+⌘+→	Ctrl+Alt+Shift+→ or Shift+End
Up one paragraph	Shift+⌘+↑	Ctrl+Shift+↑
Down one paragraph	Shift+⌘+↓	Ctrl+Shift+↓
To top of story	Shift+Option+⌘+↑	Ctrl+Alt+Shift+↑ or Ctrl+Shift+Home
To bottom of story	Shift+Option+⌘+↓	Ctrl+Alt+Shift+↓ or Ctrl+Shift+End

Spelling

Action	Macintosh	Windows
Check word	⌘+L	Ctrl+W
Check story	Option+⌘+L	Ctrl+Alt+W
Check document	Option+Shift+⌘+L	Ctrl+Alt+Shift+W
Look up spelling	⌘+L	Alt+L
Skip word	⌘+S	Alt+S

Action	Macintosh	Windows
Add word to dictionary	⌘+A	Alt+A
Add all suspect words to dictionary	Option+Shift+click Done button	Alt+Shift+click Close button
Suggest hyphenation	⌘+H	Ctrl+H

Text/Paragraph Formats

Action	Macintosh	Windows
Edit style sheets	Shift+F11	Shift+F11
Edit H&Js	Option+Shift+F11 or Option+⌘+H	Ctrl+Shift+F11
Character attributes	Shift+⌘+D	Ctrl+Shift+D
Paragraph attributes	Shift+⌘+F	Ctrl+Shift+F
Copy format to selected paragraphs	Option+Shift+click	Alt+Shift+click
Apply No Style and then style-sheet	Option+click style-sheet name	Alt+click style-sheet name
Choose font	Option+Shift+⌘+M	Ctrl+Alt+Shift+M
Symbol font (next character)	Shift+⌘+Q	Ctrl+Shift+Q
Zapf Dingbats font (next character)	Shift+⌘+Z	Ctrl+Shift+Z
Change size	Shift+⌘+\	Ctrl+Shift+\
Change leading	Shift+⌘+E	Ctrl+Shift+E
Define tabs	Shift+⌘+T	Ctrl+Shift+T
Define rules	Shift+⌘+N	Ctrl+Shift+N
Increase to next size in type scale	Shift+⌘+>	Ctrl+Shift+>
Decrease to next size in type scale	Shift+⌘+<	Ctrl+Shift+<
Increase 1 point	Option+Shift+⌘+>	Ctrl+Alt+Shift+>
Decrease 1 point	Option+Shift+⌘+<	Ctrl+Alt+Shift+<
Increase scaling 5%	⌘+]	Ctrl+]

(continued)

Action	Macintosh	Windows
Decrease scaling 5%	⌘+[	Ctrl+[
Increase scaling 1%	Option+⌘+]	Ctrl+Alt+]
Decrease scaling 1%	Option+⌘+[	Ctrl+Alt+[
Resize interactively	⌘+drag text-box handle	Ctrl+drag text-box handle
Resize interactively constrained	Shift+⌘+drag text-box handle	Ctrl+Shift+drag text-box handle
Resize interactively proportional	Option+Shift+⌘+drag text-box handle	Ctrl+Alt+Shift+drag text box handle
Increase kerning/tracking $1/20$ em	Shift+⌘+]	Ctrl+Shift+]
Decrease kerning/tracking $1/20$ em	Shift+⌘+[	Ctrl+Shift+[
Increase kerning/tracking $1/200$ em	Option+Shift+⌘+]	Ctrl+Alt+Shift+]
Decrease kerning/tracking $1/200$ em	Option+Shift+⌘+[	Ctrl+Alt+Shift+[
Raise baseline shift 1 point	Option+Shift+⌘+plus	Ctrl+Alt+Shift+)
Lower baseline shift 1 point	Option+Shift+⌘+−	Ctrl+Alt+Shift+(
Increase leading 1 point	Shift+⌘+"	Ctrl+Shift+"
Decrease leading 1 point	Shift+⌘+semicolon	Ctrl+Shift+ semicolon
Increase leading $1/10$ point	Option+Shift+⌘+"	Ctrl+Alt+Shift+"
Decrease leading $1/10$ point	Option+Shift+⌘+ semicolon	Ctrl+Alt+Shift+ semicolon
Normal	Shift+⌘+P	Ctrl+Shift+P
Bold	Shift+⌘+B	Ctrl+Shift+B
Italic	Shift+⌘+I	Ctrl+Shift+I
Underline	Shift+⌘+U	Ctrl+Shift+U
World underline	Shift+⌘+W	Ctrl+Shift+W
Strikethrough	Shift+⌘+/	Ctrl+Shift+/
All caps	Shift+⌘+K	Ctrl+Shift+K
Subscript	Shift+⌘+−	Ctrl+Shift+9
Superscript	Shift+⌘+plus	Ctrl+Shift+0 (zero)

Action	Macintosh	Windows
Superior	Shift+⌘+V	Ctrl+Shift+V
Outline	Shift+⌘+O	Ctrl+Shift+O
Shadow	Shift+⌘+S	Ctrl+Shift+S
Left-justify	Shift+⌘+L	Ctrl+Shift+L
Right-justify	Shift+⌘+R	Ctrl+Shift+R
Center	Shift+⌘+C	Ctrl+Shift+C
Justify	Shift+⌘+J	Ctrl+Shift+J
Force-justify	Option+Shift+⌘+J	Ctrl+Alt+Shift+J

Find/Change

Action	Macintosh	Windows
Find, find/change	⌘+F	Ctrl+F
Close find, close find/change	Option+⌘+F	Ctrl+Alt+F

Special Characters (in Finds)

Action	Macintosh	Windows
Carriage return	⌘+Enter	Ctrl+Enter
Tab	⌘+Tab	Ctrl+Tab
Line break	Shift+⌘+Enter	Ctrl+Shift+Enter
Column	⌘+keypad Enter	\c
Backslash (\)	⌘+\	Ctrl+\
Wildcard	⌘+?	Ctrl+?
Flex space	Shift+⌘+F	Ctrl+Shift+F
Punctuation space	⌘+period	Ctrl+period
Current box's page number	⌘+3	Ctrl+3
Preceding box's page number	⌘+2	Ctrl+2
Following box's page number	⌘+4	Ctrl+4

Special Characters

Action	Macintosh	Windows
Em dash	Option+Shift+−	Ctrl+Shift+=
Nonbreaking em dash	Option+⌘+=	Ctrl+Alt+Shift+=[
En dash	Option+−	Ctrl+Alt+Shift+−
Nonbreaking hyphen	⌘+=	Ctrl+=
Discretionary hyphen	⌘+−	Ctrl+−
Nonbreaking space	⌘+spacebar	Ctrl+5
En space	Option+spacebar	Ctrl+Shift+6
Nonbreaking en space	Option+⌘+spacebar	Ctrl+Alt+Shift+6
Punctuation space	Shift+spacebar	Shift+spacebar or Ctrl+6
Nonbreaking punctuation space	Shift+⌘+spacebar	Ctrl+Shift+ spacebar or Ctrl+Alt+6
Flex space	Option+Shift+spacebar	Ctrl+Shift+5
Nonbreaking flex space	Option+Shift+⌘+spacebar	Ctrl+Alt+Shift+5
Indent here	⌘+\	Ctrl+\
Current page number	⌘+3	Ctrl+3
Preceding box's page number	⌘+2	Ctrl+2
Following box's page number	⌘+4	Ctrl+4
New line	Shift+Enter	Shift+Enter
Discretionary new line	⌘+Enter	Ctrl+Enter
New column	keypad Enter	keypad Enter
New box	Shift+keypad Enter	Shift+keypad Enter
Right-indent tab	Option+Tab	Shift+Tab

Graphics Handling

Action	Macintosh	Windows
Import picture at 36 dpi	Shift+click Open button button in Get Picture dialog box	Shift+click Open in Get Picture dialog box

Action	Macintosh	Windows
Import color TIFF as grayscale	⌘+click Open in Get Picture dialog box	Ctrl+click Open in Get Picture dialog box
Import grayscale TIFF as black and white	⌘+click Open button in Get Picture dialog box	Ctrl+click Open button in Get Picture dialog box
Import EPS without importing spot colors' definitions	⌘+click Open button in Get Picture dialog box	Ctrl+click Open button in Get Picture dialog box
Reimport all pictures in a document	⌘+click Open button in Open dialog box	Ctrl+click Open button in Open dialog box
Center image within box	Shift+⌘+M	Ctrl+Shift+M
Fit image to box	Shift+⌘+F	Ctrl+Shift+F
Fit image proportionally to box	Option+Shift+⌘+F	Ctrl+Alt+Shift+F
Resize box constrained	Shift+drag	Shift+drag
Resize box at aspect ratio	Option+Shift+drag	Alt+Shift+drag
Resize box and scale picture	⌘+drag	Ctrl+drag
Resize box constrained and scale picture	Shift+⌘+drag	Ctrl+Shift+drag
Resize box at aspect ratio and scale picture	Option+Shift+⌘+drag	Ctrl+Alt+Shift+drag
Increase picture scale 5%	Option+Shift+⌘+>	Ctrl+Alt+Shift+>
Decrease picture scale 5%	Option+Shift+⌘+<	Ctrl+Alt+Shift+<
Negative image	Shift+⌘+−	Ctrl+Shift+−
Picture contrast specifications	Shift+⌘+C	Ctrl+Shift+C
Picture halftone specifications	Shift+⌘+H	Ctrl+Shift+H
Change line width	Shift+⌘+\	Ctrl+Shift+\

(continued)

Action	Macintosh	Windows
Increase line width to next size	Shift+⌘+>	Ctrl+Shift+>
Decrease line width to next size	Shift+⌘+<	Ctrl+Shift+<
Increase line width 1 point	Option+Shift+⌘+>	Ctrl+Alt+Shift+>
Decrease line width 1 point	Option+Shift+⌘+<	Ctrl+Alt+Shift+<
Delete Bézier point	Option+click point	Alt+click point
Add Bézier point	Option+click segment	Alt+click segment
Create corner point	Option+F1	Ctrl+F1
Create smooth point	Option+F2	Ctrl+F2
Create symmetrical point	Option+F3	Ctrl+F3
Create straight segment	Shift+Option+F1	Ctrl+Shift+F1
Create curved segment	Shift+Option+F2	Ctrl+Shift+F2

Chapter 22
The Ten Most Common Mistakes

In This Chapter
▶ Forgetting to register

▶ Using too many fonts

▶ Putting too much on a page

▶ Overdoing the design

▶ Not consulting a designer

▶ Not using master pages

▶ Not using smart quotes and dashes

▶ Forgetting to check spelling

▶ Not talking with your printer

▶ Not giving the service bureau all your files

*L*earning how to use QuarkXPress takes time. Learning how to use it right takes even longer! Knowing that, we thought we'd try to save you some time (and maybe even a few tears) by pointing out some of the most common mistakes that people make when they start dabbling in desktop publishing. Take a few minutes to read this chapter. Why? Because we *like* you, that's why.

Forgetting to register

Suppose that you just bought a brand-spanking-new copy of QuarkXPress. You peel off the shrink wrap, open the box, take a peek at the manuals, peel open the disk envelope, and install the software. Ready to rock and roll, right? Not so fast. Don't make the mistake that too many users make: failing to take a few minutes to fill out the disk-based registration information and mail it back to Quark.

What are the advantages of registering your copy of QuarkXPress? Simply put, registering your product puts you in Quark's user database. Being in the database is required if you want to use the free first-90-days-after-purchase technical-support privileges, purchase an extended service plan, or be eligible for product upgrades. And a word to the wise: Quark focuses on providing service to *registered* users and is less likely to be supportive if your name and serial number are never recorded. Registration takes only a few minutes, and we think that those few minutes are well spent.

Using too many fonts

Avant Garde. Bellevue. Centaur Gothic. Desdemona. Fonts have cool names, don't they? Also, it's fascinating to look at a font list and see all the possibilities for fonts that you can use in your document.

Yes, we know that trying out a great many fonts is tempting. This urge overcomes nearly everybody who's just getting into desktop publishing. (The few who *don't* begin their QuarkXPress careers by liberally sprinkling fonts throughout a page are often those who are traditional designers or who have typesetting backgrounds. In other words, they already know better.) In almost every instance, try keeping the number of fonts that you use on a page to two. When you start having three, four, or five fonts, the document takes on an amateurish appearance, quite frankly. Experts in page design never use several fonts together.

Putting too much on a page

You've probably seen them before: pages that are filled to overflowing with *stuff*. Words, pictures, rules — you name it. The pages are filled to overflowing, to the point that you don't know where your eyes need to go.

One of the best things that you'll ever learn about page design is the value of white space — the places on the page that have no text, no pictures, no lines — just the plain paper showing through. Pages that are crammed full of text and pictures are pages that readers avoid. Keep some space between text columns and headlines, and between items on the page and the edges of the page.

Finding white space on a page is like going to a crowded beach and finding — in the middle of the crowd — a perfectly smooth, empty spot that offers you a gorgeous view from your beach blanket. The space "feels" great to your eyes and makes you more likely to get the message that's being conveyed by the words and pictures on the page.

Overdoing the design

QuarkXPress is powerful stuff that allows you to do all *kinds* of nifty things. But this fact does not mean that you should do all those things just because you *can*.

Nothing looks worse than a complex design created by a publishing novice. Professionals know that less is more. Yes, it's possible to rotate text, skew text and graphics, make cool blends, set type on a curvy line, add multiple colors, stretch and condense type, and bleed artwork off the page. But using all these effects at the same time can overwhelm readers and make them miss the whole point of the message you are trying to convey.

Here's a good rule to remember: Limit special effects to a maximum of three on a two-page spread. Here's an even better rule: If you are in doubt about whether to add an effect to a page, *don't*.

Not consulting a designer

We know that it's not rocket science, but designing a document still can get fairly complicated. Knowing when it makes sense to consult a professional graphic designer is a good idea.

The decision is best made by taking into consideration how the document will be used. Is the document a one- or two-color newspaper for a small club or organization? Then it's probably perfectly fine for a new QuarkXPress user to tackle the job. But if the document is a full-color display ad that will run in a national magazine, leave it to the pros.

When you have a high-end document to design, professional graphic designers are worth their weight in gold. Sure, you may have to spend a few bucks to hire a talented designer, but you may save that much and more by having that person craft your document for you. Designers are trained to know what works visually (and, even more important, what doesn't), how to select the right paper, how many colors are appropriate, and how to have the document printed. In short, a good graphic designer can make your pages sing, and you end up smelling like a rose.

Not using master pages

Before you start working on a document, have an idea about what the document will look like. Will the document have two columns? Will the top half of every page have a graphic? Where will the page numbers appear?

After you figure these things out, you really should set up master pages for all the elements that will repeat in the same spot, page after page (such as page numbers). Master pages make things much easier, and they are easy to create. People who don't use master pages are people who like to do things the hard way. And we know you'd rather use the easy way so you can save time for the really hard stuff.

To begin creating a master page, with a document open, choose Page⇨ Display⇨A-Master. Anything that you create on that page becomes part of the master page and appears on every page in the document that is based on that particular master page. Each document can have up to 127 pairs of master pages. See Chapter 17 for help in mastering master pages.

Not using smart quotes and dashes

Nothing, and we mean nothing, bothers a professional designer or publisher more than seeing inch marks where typesetter's quote marks should appear or skinny little hyphens in place of em dashes. (An em dash is a dash that is the same width as the current font's capital *M*.)

Using the correct quotes and dashes is easy in QuarkXPress. In fact, you can choose among a variety of quote formats, including some that work with foreign languages. The point is that you *want* to use typographically correct quotes and dashes, because they make your document look much more professional.

You can get typographically correct quotes by choosing Smart Quotes in the Interactive pane of the Application Preferences dialog box. (Edit⇨ Preferences⇨Application, or press ⌘+Option+Shift+Y or Ctrl+Alt+Shift+Y). To get the right kinds of quotes and dashes when you import text from a word processing application, just make sure that the Convert Quotes box is checked in the Get Text dialog box.

Forgetting to check spelling

Typos are like ants at a summer picnic — they show up all the time. You can avoid some typos if you always remember that the last thing to do any time you are about to print your document is to check spelling. Checking spelling won't catch every possible error (you still need to proofread thoroughly to catch all errors), but using the built-in spelling checker in QuarkXPress is easy to do, and it can prevent embarrassing typos and misspellings.

Not talking with your commercial printer

If you are creating a document that is to be commercially printed, be sure to have a conversation with your printer early in the game. Hey, you may talk to this Jo(e) only once in a while, but your printer prints documents all day long, every day, and sometimes even on Saturdays.

The idea is simple: These folks know their business. A talk with your printer can help you plan your document, pick the right number of colors to use in it, and produce it cost-effectively. Your printer will appreciate your concern, too, and will likely invest extra effort in doing a great job for you if you show that you care enough to consult the pros early on.

Not giving the service bureau all your files

If you've never worked with a service bureau — the place where you take or send your QuarkXPress documents so that they can be output to an imagesetting device — you may think that the people who work at your service bureau are downright snoopy. They poke and prod, ask millions of questions, and want to know every little thing about your document. They give you the third degree, asking about every file for every graphic on every single page.

These people are not out to pick on you; they truly do need to know about all the fonts and files necessary to output your document.

Why? Because they just do, that's why. Seriously, the equipment that a service bureau uses needs to have everything that you used to create a document. If your document includes an EPS file that contains text, for example, the service bureau needs to have the font that is used in the text. If that font is not available, the EPS file prints incorrectly, and the job has to be output again.

The Collect for Output feature in QuarkXPress (choose File⇨Collect for Output) can help. This feature copies all the text and picture files that are necessary to produce your document in a folder; it also generates a report for your service bureau, listing the fonts used in the document, its dimensions, and trapping information.

But the Collect for Output feature can't replace your brain. You still need to think about your document. Ultimately, you are the person who is responsible for making sure that your service bureau has everything it needs to output your document the right way, the first time.

Chapter 23

Ten Essential Tools for Web Publishing

*T*hough QuarkXPress is a tool for print publishers, most publishing sites these days produce electronic publications as well as printed publications. For owners of QuarkXPress who want to repurpose the content of their QuarkXPress documents in an electronic format so they can distribute them over the Internet or a corporate intranet, several conversion tools and utilities are available.

In the sections that follow, the first three XTensions — BeyondPress, HexWeb, and CyberPress — let you export the contents of QuarkXPress documents in HTML format, the most widely used file format for documents available on the WorldWide Web. The next two — PDF Design XT and Article XT for PDF — are also conversion XTensions. They let you save QuarkXPress documents in Adobe's Portable Document Format (PDF), which retains the page design, images, and text flow of the original document. You can view PDF files on the Internet using Netscape Navigator or Microsoft Internet Explorer in tandem with the free Acrobat Reader application.

Shortly before the release of QuarkXPress 4.0, Quark announced that it would be providing PDF import and export filters for QuarkXPress soon after version 4.0 ships. For this reason, you may want to wait until Quark's PDF filters are available before you purchase either of the commercial PDF export XTensions.

The sixth entry is QuarkImmedia, an XTension from Quark that lets you create electronic publications that have interactivity and multimedia. The QuarkImmedia Viewer is needed in order to view projects that are created with QuarkImmedia. We end with an assortment of tools for Web publishers. Here we go.

BeyondPress (Astrobyte)

Since the release of version 1.0 of BeyondPress in 1995, this hefty XTension to QuarkXPress has evolved through two major upgrades. Today, BeyondPress 3.0 is the most full-featured HTML export tool for QuarkXPress. It has strong image- and text-conversion features that let you control the appearance of the pictures and text you choose to include in the Web page you produce.

BeyondPress lets you specify the default settings applied to the items you export. You also have the option to override the default settings for each text and image component you export.

In addition to letting you convert your existing QuarkXPress documents into Web pages, BeyondPress lets you create Web pages from scratch from within QuarkXPress. This means that you can use your QuarkXPress page-layout skills to create Web pages in a familiar, WYSIWYG environment.

Astrobyte has announced that it's developing a Windows version of BeyondPress; however, it is not available as this book goes to print.

HexWeb (HexMac Software Systems)

If you use QuarkXPress to produce many printed pages and you want to convert them into Web pages, you might find that HexWeb is up to the task. Though it doesn't have as many features as BeyondPress, it's a great tool for high-volume Web sites. HexWeb includes a utility called HexWeb Index Pro, which automatically creates frame-based indexes of the Web pages you produce. HexWeb has gained widespread popularity among newspaper publishers who use it to create Web versions of their papers.

HexWeb is available for both Macintosh and Windows platforms. As this book goes to print, it is the only HTML export XTension available for Windows users.

CyberPress (Extensis Corp., Mac only)

Developed by Astrobyte, creators of BeyondPress, CyberPress is essentially a "lite" version of BeyondPress. Though it doesn't have as many features as its more expensive sibling, it's very easy to use. If you're considering making the move to Web publishing, you might want to begin by using CyberPress to convert some simple documents. If you find yourself wanting more, Extensis and Astrobyte offer an upgrade to BeyondPress.

To create a Web page from a QuarkXPress document, you first add text and pictures to the Content list in the CyberPress palette. When you're done selecting the items you want to export, a mouse-click produces a Web page. The CyberPress Preferences settings determine how text and pictures are converted.

PDF Design XT (Techno Design, Mac only)

This XTension lets you create PostScript files that you can then turn into PDF files with Adobe's Acrobat Distiller. When you generate PostScript files using PDF Design XT, you have the option to add bookmarks and hyperlinks.

Article-XT for PDF (Tobias Boskamp, Mac only)

If the QuarkXPress documents you want to convert to PDF format contain articles that span multiple boxes or pages, you can use Article-XT for PDF to embed article definitions within the PostScript files you generate with the XTension. When the resulting PDF files are viewed with Acrobat Reader, such articles are easier to read. If you don't use Article-XT for PDF, you have to use Acrobat Exchange to define complex articles manually, a difficult and time-consuming process.

QuarkImmedia

All of you print publishers who are thinking about moving into multimedia publishing might want to begin by adding QuarkImmedia to your QuarkXPress toolset. QuarkImmedia is an XTension for QuarkXPress that lets you create interactive electronic publications that contain not only text and pictures, but sound, video, and animation, as well. When QuarkImmedia is running, an additional palette — the QuarkImmedia palette — is added to QuarkXPress. This palette lets you convert any QuarkXPress item into an interactive object. Using the QuarkImmedia Viewer, people viewing your QuarkImmedia projects can click on objects to move through a project or to trigger a variety of events — such as playing a sound, displaying a QuickTime movie in a picture box, or hyperlinking to another QuarkImmedia project. When you create projects, you can embed the QuarkImmedia Viewer application or you can include the freely distributable Viewer as a stand-alone program. The Viewer is available free from Quark's Web site and is also included as part of the QuarkImmedia product.

PrecisionPreview XT

This XTension lets you convert imported bitmap images into either the IVUE or FlashPix picture formats. The advantage of these two hierarchical file formats is that you can enlarge imported images within QuarkXPress — either by scaling them or by zooming in on them — without losing image clarity. (PrecisionPreview lets you specify zoom values up to 1200 percent, which is 400 percent greater than QuarkXPress's 800 percent limit.) If you've ever enlarged a low-resolution screen preview a few hundred percent, you've seen the pixellation that occurs. But with PrecisionPreview, IVUE and FlashPix images remain crystal clear no matter how much you enlarge them. For Web publishers, this means that when you create Web pages (using a Web-export XTension) or QuarkImmedia projects that contain scaled-up pictures, the pictures will be much clearer than they would otherwise be if the low-res preview were used.

Web-Safe Colors (QuarkXPress document)

Web browsers support only 216 RGB colors; QuarkXPress lets you add virtually as many colors as you want using any of several color models. By appending the 216 Web-safe colors from the Web-Safe Colors QuarkXPress document and then applying these colors to your QuarkXPress items, you can make sure that the colors in your exported HTML documents will look the same when viewed with any browser on any platform.

HTML XPort

This shareware XTension for QuarkXPress lets you convert the text in QuarkXPress documents into simple Web pages. It doesn't handle pictures.

Web Browsers and Adobe Acrobat

If you use QuarkXPress to create Web pages in HTML format, you need a Web browser to view them. We won't take sides in the Netscape Navigator/ Microsoft Internet Explorer battle except to say that they both work well. The former is inexpensive; the latter is free. Pick one.

If you convert your QuarkXPress documents into PDF files, you need Acrobat Reader to view them. If you need to customize your PDF files, you probably want to spring for Adobe Acrobat, which includes Acrobat Exchange for adding such things as bookmarks, hyperlinks, and document security to your PDF files, and Acrobat Distiller, which converts PostScript files into PDF files.

Chapter 24
Ten Best Online Resources

QuarkXPress users who have an Internet connection or who subscribe to an online service (such as CompuServe or America Online) have access to an abundance of QuarkXPress-related information and freebies. Cyberspace is, indeed, a friendly place for electronic publishers. The next time you're online, check out some of our top 10 QuarkXPress and desktop-publishing sites.

The XPresso Bar

www.xpressobar.com

This site is a great place to begin a quest for information about QuarkXPress. The home page contains seven main links: Top Sites, Tips+Training, Interaction, XTensions, Publications, Niches, and File Archive. Each of these pages contains several links to related sites. You find links to Quark's home page and to other Internet desktop-publishing Web sites, as well as links to a variety of sites dedicated to QuarkXPress-specific topics: scripting, books, publications, XTensions developers, and so on. The File Archive link takes you to the XPresso Bar FTP site that's discussed in the following section.

The XPresso Bar FTP Site

ftp.xpressobar.com

In the words of its creators, this site is "one of the most complete collections of Quark extensions, updaters, and other information for both Mac and Windows." This site is the successor to the Telalink FTP site (which is renowned among QuarkXPress users for its collection of QuarkXPress freebies) and is replete with FAQs, demo XTensions, scripts, word-processing filters, and other utilities. You can access the XPresso Bar FTP site with an FTP client application or with a Web browser. Figure 24-1 shows a directory of Windows-related files and folders at the XPresso Bar FTP site.

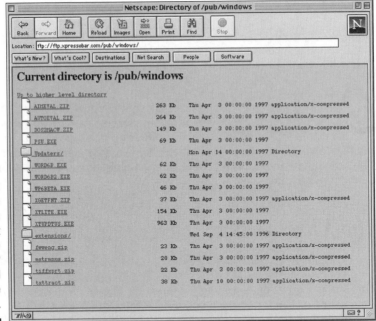

Figure 24-1: The Windows directory at the XPresso Bar's FTP site, viewed in Netscape Navigator.

XTensions Sites

Hundreds of commercial XTensions for QuarkXPress are available for both the Macintosh and Windows; these XTensions handle a wide range of tasks that QuarkXPress cannot. Plenty of information about XTensions is available online, including the Web sites of three XTensions vendors: XT-now (www.xt-now.com), XChange USA (www.xchangeus.com), and The World-Wide Power Company (www.ThePowerCo.com). All these sites provide information about many XTensions. The World-Wide Power Company also has information about plug-ins for other desktop-publishing programs, including Photoshop, Illustrator, PageMaker, and Freehand. Both XT-now and XChange offer downloadable demos, but XT-now is the only site that allows you to purchase XTensions online — and at a discount. In addition to these sites, most XTensions developers have their own sites. To find information about particular developers or XTensions, use your favorite search engine to perform a search for them.

Quark, Inc. Home Page

www.quark.com

In addition to providing information about Quark's entire product line — QuarkXPress, QuarkXPress Passport, QuarkImmedia, Quark Publishing System, and mTropolis — Quark's Web site (see Figure 24-2) offers demo versions of products; technical notes and access to technical support via e-mail; program updaters; and free Quark-developed XTensions, including updated versions of word-processing filters. This site is definitely worth checking regularly, particularly for the import/export filters.

Figure 24-2: For QuarkXPress users, there's no page like home — the Quark, Inc. home page, that is.

Yahoo! — Computers and Internet: Desktop Publishing

`www.yahoo.com/Computers_and_Internet//Desktop_Publishing/`

This site isn't specifically for QuarkXPress users, but it's a great jumping-off point for desktop publishers — both print and Web publishers. Major topics include Fonts, HTML, PostScript, Scanning, and Typography. Clicking any of these topics provides links to several related sites. The site also features links to several online DTP (desktop publishing) publications.

Quark Forums

America Online (keyword: Quark)

CompuServe (Go: Quark)

Subscribers to America Online and CompuServe services can find demos and updaters for commercial XTensions, free XTensions from Quark, free scripts, and message boards for asking and answering questions. CompuServe's QuarkXPress forum has a particularly lively scripting area that offers several useful scripts. If you're looking for general publishing information, both services also have DTP forums. Look for the AOL and CompuServe QuarkXPress forums to change as new XTensions and utilities become available for QuarkXPress 4.0.

Free QuarkXPress Templates for Graphic Design

`desktopPublishing.com/templ_quark.html`

You gotta like anything that's free. At this site, you can find dozens of free QuarkXPress templates for creating brochures, business cards, calendars, envelopes, labels, letterhead, newsletters, postcards — even CD-ROM jewel cases. The documents were created with QuarkXPress 3.32 for Windows, but they can be opened with the Macintosh version of QuarkXPress as well. If you don't have the built-in fonts, you can easily replace them with fonts of your own. The documents even include instructions about how to use them. Free and easy — whatta deal!

QuarkXPress Tips

www.digitrain.com/tips/QX_tips.html

This site has many handy tips for QuarkXPress users, including a list of Top 10 Tips. If you stop at this site, you're guaranteed to learn something new — and useful — about QuarkXPress. The site's top tip: "Use the grabber hand to scroll. Hold the Option (Mac)/Alt (Win) key down, then move the mouse to scroll. Note that if Caps Lock is on, the grabber hand does not work on the Mac." Now, aren't you glad you know that.

Sal's AppleScript Snippets

users.aol.com/nyhthawk/welcome.html

If AppleScript were a cross-platform technology, this site would warrant a higher rating. Alas. Still, this site is a wonderful place to find information about creating AppleScripts for QuarkXPress. Site creator Sal Soghoian is the grand poobah of AppleScript, and the site includes instructional materials for beginning scripters, scripting tools, and free scripts. If the idea of automating QuarkXPress for Macintosh intrigues you, you should definitely check out this site. Be forewarned: Scripting can be addictive.

The QuarkXPress Mailing List

This mailing list (sometimes called the sic list because it was initially called the Quark Express Mailing List) is a mother lode of QuarkXPress expertise. To subscribe, send an e-mail message to listserv@iubvm.ucs.indiana.edu with SUBSCRIBE QUARKXPR (your name) in the body of the message (for example, SUBSCRIBE QUARKXPR PAT SMITH). Because the list is active and diverse, you may want to subscribe only long enough to post a message and gather responses. Be prepared to receive a few dozen messages a day while you're subscribed. (To unsubscribe, send a message to the subscribe address with SIGNOFF QUARKXPR" in the body of the message.)

Index

(continued)

Discover Dummies Online!

The Dummies Web Site is your fun and friendly online resource for the latest information about ...For Dummies® books and your favorite topics. The Web site is the place to communicate with us, exchange ideas with other ...For Dummies readers, chat with authors, and have fun!

Ten Fun and Useful Things You Can Do at www.dummies.com

1. Win free ...For Dummies books and more!
2. Register your book and be entered in a prize drawing.
3. Meet your favorite authors through the IDG Books Author Chat Series.
4. Exchange helpful information with other ...For Dummies readers.
5. Discover other great ...For Dummies books you must have!
6. Purchase Dummieswear™ exclusively from our Web site.
7. Buy ...For Dummies books online.
8. Talk to us. Make comments, ask questions, get answers!
9. Download free software.
10. Find additional useful resources from authors.

Link directly to these ten fun and useful things at
http://www.dummies.com/10useful

For other technology titles from IDG Books Worldwide, go to
www.idgbooks.com

Not on the Web yet? It's easy to get started with *Dummies 101*®: *The Internet For Windows*®*95* or *The Internet For Dummies*®*,* 4th Edition, at local retailers everywhere.

Find other *...For Dummies* books on these topics:

Business • Career • Databases • Food & Beverage • Games • Gardening • Graphics • Hardware
Health & Fitness • Internet and the World Wide Web • Networking • Office Suites
Operating Systems • Personal Finance • Pets • Programming • Recreation • Sports
Spreadsheets • Teacher Resources • Test Prep • Word Processing

IDG BOOKS WORLDWIDE BOOK REGISTRATION

We want to hear from you!

Register This Book and Win!

Visit **http://my2cents.dummies.com** to register this book and tell us how you liked it!

- ✔ Get entered in our monthly prize giveaway.

- ✔ Give us feedback about this book — tell us what you like best, what you like least, or maybe what you'd like to ask the author and us to change!

- ✔ Let us know any other ...*For Dummies*® topics that interest you.

Your feedback helps us determine what books to publish, tells us what coverage to add as we revise our books, and lets us know whether we're meeting your needs as a ...*For Dummies* reader. You're our most valuable resource, and what you have to say is important to us!

Not on the Web yet? It's easy to get started with *Dummies 101*®*: The Internet For Windows*® *95* or *The Internet For Dummies*®, 4th Edition, at local retailers everywhere.

Or let us know what you think by sending us a letter at the following address:

...*For Dummies* Book Registration
Dummies Press
7260 Shadeland Station, Suite 100
Indianapolis, IN 46256-3945
Fax 317-596-5498

BUSINESS AND
GENERAL
REFERENCE
BOOK SERIES
FROM IDG

COMPUTER
BOOK SERIES
FROM IDG